WITHDRAWN

Postmodern
INTERVIEWING

Books are to be returned on or before
the last date below.

7–DAY
LOAN

LIBREX–

Postmodern INTERVIEWING

Jaber F. Gubrium
University of Missouri

Editors James A. Holstein
Marquette University

SAGE Publications
International Educational and Professional Publisher
Thousand Oaks ■ London ■ New Delhi

For information:

 Sage Publications, Inc.
2455 Teller Road
Thousand Oaks, California 91320
E-mail: order@sagepub.com

Sage Publications Ltd.
6 Bonhill Street
London EC2A 4PU
United Kingdom

Sage Publications India Pvt. Ltd.
M-32 Market
Greater Kailash I
New Delhi 110 048 India

Printed in the United States of America

Library of Congress Cataloging-in-Publication Data

Postmodern interviewing / edited by Jaber F. Gubrium, James A. Holstein.
    p. cm.
Includes bibliographical references and indexes.
ISBN 0-7619-2850-2 (Paper)
1. Interviewing. I. Gubrium, Jaber F. II. Holstein, James A.
H61.28.P67 2003
001.4'33—dc21   2003000717

This book is printed on acid-free paper.

05 06 07 08 09 9 8 7 6 5 4 3 2

Acquisition Editor:	C. Deborah Laughton
Editorial Assistant:	Veronica Novak
Production Editor:	Sanford Robinson
Copy Editor:	Judy Selhorst
Typesetter:	Christina Hill
Indexer:	Jean Casalegno
Cover Designer:	Michelle Lee

CONTENTS

INTRODUCTION

1. Postmodern Sensibilities   3
Jaber F. Gubrium and James A. Holstein

PART I. NEW HORIZONS

2. From the Individual Interview to the Interview Society   21
Jaber F. Gubrium and James A. Holstein

3. Postmodern Trends in Interviewing   51
Andrea Fontana

4. Active Interviewing   67
James A. Holstein and Jaber F. Gubrium

5. Internet Interviewing   81
Chris Mann and Fiona Stewart

PART II. REFLEXIVITY

**6. Revisiting the Relationship Between
Participant Observation and Interviewing**   109
Paul Atkinson and Amanda Coffey

7. Personal and Folk Narrative as Cultural Representation   123
   Kirin Narayan and Kenneth M. George

8. The Cinematic Society and the Reflexive Interview   141
   Norman K. Denzin

9. Their Story/My Story/Our Story: Including
   the Researcher's Experience in Interview Research   157
   Carolyn Ellis and Leigh Berger

PART III. POETICS AND POWER

10. Poetic Representation of Interviews   187
    Laurel Richardson

11. Analytic Strategies for Oral History Interviews   203
    Richard Cándida Smith

12. Interviewing at the Border of Fact and Fiction   225
    Paul C. Rosenblatt

13. Interviewing, Power/Knowledge, and Social Inequality   243
    Charles L. Briggs

AUTHOR INDEX   255

SUBJECT INDEX   263

ABOUT THE EDITORS   283

ABOUT THE CONTRIBUTORS   285

INTRODUCTION

1

POSTMODERN SENSIBILITIES

◆ **Jaber F. Gubrium**
James A. Holstein

nterviewing has come a long way since the days of the neutral, face-to-face "conversation with a purpose" between strangers that ostensibly produced facts of experience. For decades, the interview was seen as a conduit for transporting experiential knowledge from the respondent, on the one side, to the interviewer and sponsoring agents, on the other. The two sides hardly met except by way of more or less structured interrogation formats. Problems of interviewing were viewed as technical, reparable when these sides kept their distinct missions in tow and related activities separate from each other. These are the classic contours of the modern interview, with its designated roles, search for objective knowledge, and lack of political consciousness.

The present era of interviewing has taken on board postmodern sensibilities. In this context, the interview conversation is viewed as having diverse purposes, with a communicative format constructed as much within the interview as it stems from predesignated research interests. Interview roles are less clear than they once were; in some cases they are even exchanged to promote new opportunities for understanding the shape and evolution of selves and experience. Standardized representation has given way to representational invention, where the dividing line between fact and fiction is blurred to encourage richer understanding. *Reflexivity, poetics,* and *power* are the watchwords as the interview process is refracted through the lenses of language, knowledge, culture, and difference.

Postmodern Interviewing showcases these developments, presenting cutting-edge discussions of interviewing's new

AUTHORS' NOTE: Parts of this chapter are adapted from Chapter 5, "Postmodernism," in Jaber F. Gubrium and James A. Holstein, *The New Language of Qualitative Method,* New York: Oxford University Press, 1997.

◆ 3

horizons, tellingly distinctive of a new era for this important means of gathering experiential knowledge. Still, as Andrea Fontana notes in his chapter, we would be hard-pressed to discern a distinct structure for the postmodern interview, as hard-pressed as researchers who operated in a modern context were to designate standardized interview formats and good interviewing skills. Postmodern interviewing is more a set of orienting sensibilities that contrast on many fronts with modern interview prescriptions than it is a particular kind of interviewing. As the contributors to this volume show, the interviewing enterprise now properly entertains trenchantly inventive questions and moves in ambitiously new directions, where traditional interviewers with modern sensibilities understandably feared to tread. Hailing from anthropology, family studies, history, and sociology, the contributors present us with the potential of postmodern sensibilities for interviewing, while also alerting us to the now evident shortcomings of an earlier era of ostensibly objective interview practice.

◆ A Crisis of Representation

These developments came of age within the broader context of a crisis of representation in the social sciences. Pauline Rosenau (1992) goes so far as saying that the crisis "haunts" social research. Frequently misunderstood, reviled, or faddishly embraced (Best and Kellner 1991), postmodernism offers an idiom for characterizing lived experience that challenges, if not subverts, traditional forms of empirical description. Of course, postmodernism speaks in diverse voices, so we must be cautious in making blanket assertions about what it is or is not, what it did or did not do to social research. In its more extreme, *skeptical* incarnations, postmodernism questions the very foundations, especially the empirical core, of the social sciences, radically dismissing

it. Its more moderate, *affirmative* formulations set up camp outside of modern paradigms in order to deconstruct them. They encourage re-examination of social scientific goals, assumptions, logic, and methods and promote innovation in how studies, including interview research, might be done and presented (Rosenau 1992).

Paradoxically, the lack of unity within postmodernism reflects one of its most widely shared tenets: the possibility of certainty must be regarded skeptically, if not rejected outright. This reverberates throughout the social sciences as a challenge to comprehensive or veridical descriptions of experience. Postmodernism casts doubt on the possibility of *any* totalizing or exhaustive theories or explanations. Its objective, writes Rosenau, is to

support a refocusing on what has been taken for granted, what has been neglected, regions of resistance, the forgotten, the irrational, the insignificant, the repressed, the borderline, the classical, the sacred, the traditional, the eccentric, the sublimated, the subjugated, the rejected, the nonessential, the marginal, the peripheral, the excluded, the tenuous, the silenced, the accidental, the dispersed, the disqualified, the deferred, the disjointed. . . . Post-modernists, defining everything as a text, seek to "locate" meaning rather than to "discover" it. . . . They offer "readings" not "observations," "interpretations" not "findings" . . . They never test because testing requires "evidence," a meaningless concept within a post-modern frame of reference. . . . They look to the unique rather than to the general, to intertexual relations rather than causality, and to the unrepeatable rather than the re-occurring, the habitual, or the routine. Within a post-modern perspective, social science becomes a more subjective and humble enterprise as truth gives way to tentativeness. Confidence in emotion replaces efforts at impartial observation. Relativism is preferred to objectivity, fragmentation to totalization. (P. 8)

Clearly, with the postmodern turn, social reality in general comes on extraordinarily hard times, as does interviewing in particular. The substantiality of social forms is constantly assaulted. Even the central constructs of sociology—the self as a central presence in experience, for example—may dissolve in the onslaught. While there are certain affinities between the postmodernist impulses that Rosenau lists and long-standing qualitative research approaches such as symbolic interactionism, constructionism, and ethnomethodology, some versions of postmodernism deny the very possibility of qualitative inquiry.

The challenge comes in crisis proportions when it takes social science inquiry away from, and beyond, empirically-grounded questions. The crisis is about representation itself, with radical postmodernism completely displacing reality with representation. Here, questions shift from the substance, process, and indigenous constitution of experience, to the representational devices used by society and researchers to convey the image of objective or subjective reality. Postmodernist inquiry can veer away from how members of society behave to produce their lives and experience, turning more toward the representational practices used by those claiming the authority to offer true representations of those lives and experiences. If the postmodern challenge abides any concern with empirical questions, it is less with the substance of experiential reality than it is with what images of reality are produced and how they are used to signify the real.

◆ Expressions of Postmodernism

Postmodernism is expressed in various ways, across many disciplines. The versions we discuss here is gleaned largely from the influential work of Jean-François Lyotard and Jean Baudrillard. In Lyotard's (1984) expression of the postmodern, master narratives evaporate, as do master vocabularies. The signal terms of classical social theory—self, community, class, society, attitude, sentiment, and reason—no longer apply in the same way. Master narratives, once called "theories," which centered on the relation of "concepts" to "empirical realities," are now viewed as stories, grand tales told about social life and linked with the perspectives and interests of their storytellers. This deprivileges their status as master narratives, or even theory. If these terms are used at all in postmodernism, they are necessarily written within quotation marks, alerting us to postmodernism's nihilistic tendencies.

INCREDULITY

How is the language of inquiry altered in a postmodern context? The introduction to Lyotard's *The Postmodern Condition* (1984) describes postmodernity as a condition of knowledge in highly developed societies that prevents us from simply speaking, writing, or referring to objects and events in the way we did before the late nineteenth century (P. xxiii). Literalism has been lost. We can infer that before this, words in principle referred to things separate from the words themselves. Of course, words could incorrectly represent things, and in that sense transmute knowledge. The "thingness" of things, however, was not so much at issue in description as was their accurate representation. One could, for example, misrepresent situations or incorrectly interpret them, but the discrepancies between representation and reality were taken as a matter categorically distinct from the reality of the situations in its own right.

Lyotard regards the hallmark of postmodernism to be the "breaking up" of the grand narratives, or theories, of the disciplines (Pp. 15 and 31-41). "Simplifying to the extreme," he writes (P. xxiv), "I define *postmodern* as incredulity toward meta-narratives." With respect to social and behavioral research, and to interviewing in particular, we take him to mean that considerations of method can no longer be accepted as principally about the scientific relationship between data and experience. Instead, method—in our case, interview method—is in many ways about itself, about a now ubiquitous way of constructing experience. One might argue, for instance, that the traditional interview researcher's procedural vocabulary not only shapes his or her empirical horizons, but simultaneously constitutes interview subjects. In this vein, a discipline is a set of tacit ontological (or foundational) rules about how to proceed in "doing" or fabricating the reality under consideration. This is postmodern because such disciplinary rules are not just methodological but are viewed as creating what the rules are about, transforming disciplinary realities into empirical language games (cf. Wittgenstein 1958). As will be seen in various chapters of this book, the resulting crisis can turn interview inquiry into the study of its representational practices, leaving one conceptually and methodologically skeptical about the very possibility of empirical footing. Less radically, there is incredulity toward interviews as events distantiated from experience, that interview data can ideally be about experience alone.

According to Lyotard (1984, P. 15), lived experience and the postmodern self do not amount to much; he grants them little substantiality. Still, for postmodernists, the self and experience remain objects of discussion and debate. Two ironies result. First, postmodernists aim to erase essential presence because there is no warrant for it outside its empirical language game, yet they tell us what that lack of presence is like. This, of course, requires presence or at least some semblance of empirical substantiality to communicate what absence resembles. There needs to be something modern—something principally distinct from representation—about the postmodern for the

postmodern to be about anything other than an instantaneous swirl into itself or no-thing.

It is also ironic that, as irascibly reluctant as postmodernists are to be categorized as pre- or post-anything, they do bring intellectual (re)sources to their writing. While they resist the notion of "source," modern theoretical differences—from structuralism to hermeneutics—pervade their descriptions of the postmodern condition as informing narratives. For example, what "postmodernist" Norman Denzin (1988, 1991, 1992) conveys about self and experience reflects his deep involvement in the symbolic interactionist tradition (see, for instance, Lindesmith, Strauss and Denzin 1988). A related naturalism evidently grounds Denzin's evaluation of the reality of cinema images in postmodern or "cinematic" society (Denzin 1991). This contrasts with Baudrillard's (1983b, 1988a) postmodern vision, whose point of departure is critical theory (see Baudrillard 1981).

HYPERREALITY

Because there is no empirical reality to liken to anything in a radically reflexive postmodernism, it is useful to think of these ironies in relation to imagined, empirical sites or metaphorical fields. Baudrillard, for example, locates the postmodern condition in what he terms "hyperreality." He describes the postmodern condition in parallel to electronic media. The print media are linear, "wordy," and relatively slow. They chronicle experience in terms of before, now, and later. A grand theme of the modern thus undergirds the written media: time is ordered sequentially and divided into periods; space is allocated within time so that we engage one event, another, and then another, akin to the empirical impulse animating naturalism.

But, according to Baudrillard, the electronic media, especially television, changes this. Through television, we are taken instantaneously to distant and disparate places. Space in terms of distance doesn't seem to matter. In seconds, contrasting images are juxtaposed, jarring a modern sensibility built on things that are separate and distinct from one another, as Denzin portrays in his chapter on the interplay of cinematic images and interview responses. An advertisement for cotton fabric, sung in nostalgic, melancholy tones, fades into the fantastic glitz and dizzying pastiche of the violent spectacle of professional football, which soon flashes into ads for the coolness and masculinity of light beer and fast cars. This peaks during the Super Bowl and its all-encompassing hype, where the represented and the representational become so intertwined that time, space, and substance—distinguishable order—virtually warp and collapse. And if that is not enough, the viewer can increase the speed of disorder by "channel surfing" via remote control.

Reality, or modern time and space, are "cranked up" to the point where the objects and order normally associated with the real no longer apply. As simulation supplants the actual, substantiality becomes a matter of images. Presence is thrown to the wind in a literally mindless project. Subjects with footing in the world disappear and significances are so flattened that representation ceases to have any particular reference to things. Interview responses become extensions of incitements to speak within predesignated language games. Experiential reality becomes a playful field of signs— signs of other signs and other signs of signs. The hyperreal offers the Gulf War to the American public in the shape of a media simulation or video game—sheer events with no center (Baudrillard 1991a, 1991b). As Douglas Kellner (1992, P. 147) puts it, in this mode, television is a site of "pure noise," "a black hole where all meaning and messages are absorbed into the whirlpool and kaleidoscope of radical semiurgy, of the incessant dissemination of images and information to the point of total saturation."

The stuff of interviews—a field of distinct social events and personal experiences—hardly matters in hyperreality. The self, in particular, is nowhere and everywhere at the same time, totally abstracted and rapidly flitting about in myriad versions of hopelessly leading questions without reference to source or defining circumstance. Writ large, we hear self's authentic, yet fleeting, secrets in gaudily romanticized form on talk shows, as the troubled, tormented, and morally triumphant are incited in interviews to speak of their inner sorrows, deepest fears, and hidden desires. What had once been viewed as profoundly personal becomes unending grist for public display in what has become an interview society (Atkinson and Silverman 1997). Social objects and individual experience are fully visible, commodified for mass consumption.

The hyperreal obviates all attention to the natural, which becomes just one more set of images whose erstwhile metanarrative merely harkens a *rhetoric* for time, being, and authenticity. From a postmodernist perspective, ethnographer William Foote Whyte's (1943) fieldsite called "Cornerville," Elliot Liebow's (1967) fieldsite the New Deal carry-out shop, and the bar and liquor store that social researcher Elijah Anderson (1976) called "Jelly's," are not actual places attracting us on to "be there" in order to know "their participants' worlds" and convey "their stories." Instead, they are rhetorical anchors for images of a particular moral space. The depths of experience, which some social researchers claim ultimately shape what is evident in talk and social interaction, become romanticized representations of the (genuinely) real. What remains is the hyperreal—not social reality, not personal experience, not subjects with agency, not feelings, not members' concrete methods for constructing their social worlds, but a panorama of images and pure representation. In this context, the interview can be likened to an intimate sound stage, with its proper roles and actors, all set to play out scripts of who and what we are.

Hyperreality, of course, has its detractors (see Poster 1988; Best and Kellner 1991; Lash and Friedman 1992; Seidman and Wagner 1992). Mike Featherstone (1988, P. 200), for example, cautions that while Baudrillard describes hyperreality as a representational site epitomized by television, he offers few clues to how the hyperreal relates to practice: "For all the alleged pluralism and sensitivity to the Other talked about by some theorists, one finds little discussion of the actual experience and practice of watching television by different groups in different settings." Referring to the penchant for siting postmodern experience in channel-hopping and multiphrenic imaging, Featherstone also notes that "evidence of the extent of such practices, and how they are integrated into, or influence, the day-to-day encounters between embodied persons is markedly lacking."

In his introduction to Baudrillard's *Selected Writings*, Mark Poster (1988) offers some additional criticisms, even while he later appreciates Baudrillard's contributions to our understanding of the impact of electronic media on society:

> [Baudrillard's] writing style is hyperbolic and declarative, often lacking sustained, systematic analysis when it is appropriate; he totalizes his insights, refusing to qualify or delimit his claims. He writes about particular experiences, television images, as if nothing else in society mattered, extrapolating a bleak view of the world from that limited base. (P. 7)

SOCIAL SCIENCE MANIFESTATIONS

The more skeptical version of the postmodernist idiom is enamored with the nihilistic vision of a world of ungrounded representation. But, as Rosenau suggests, there is a more affirmative variant of the idiom that emphasizes innovative and deconstructive forays into new fields of inquiry, including the social sciences themselves. This version underpins many of the chapters of this book, whose authors cling to the empirical world but approach interviewing in inventive ways. Social researchers adopting and adapting the postmodernist impulse for empirical aims have generally come to terms with reality by examining the constructed content of lives and experiences.

But this notion of content, suggests Rosenau (1992, P. 111), is "'soft,' provisional, and emotional," far from the vision of content held by positivists. Stressing the complex interrelations between texts and phenomena, such postmodern sensibilities allow for the possibility of reflexive patterning in the empirical world and for critical understanding. Explanation is not anathema, as it might be for skeptical postmodernists. Indeed, some affirmatives introduce forms of teleological interpretation, while others reassert the role of unconscious processes in human conduct. Some affirmative versions of postmodernism even remind us of their critical theoretical ancestors, risking epistemological inconsistency in order to resist radical relativism and to offer an authoritative voice of their own (Rosenau 1992).

◆ Confronting the Crisis of Representation

A crisis of representation emanates from some postmodernists' deep skepticism about reality. For Baudrillard, reality yields to the hyperreal. Still others argue that reality is neither the object nor the cause of scientific description but is instead its consequence (Latour and Woolgar 1979). The most radical postmodernists even doubt the need for a *conception* of reality (Rosenau 1992). Lyotard (1984, P. 81) is less extreme and offers a different slant, contending that the aim of postmodernist commentary and description "is not to supply reality, but to invent allusions to the conceivable which cannot be presented."

The radical views clearly imperil the social sciences. For one thing, they turn interviewing into a communicative game ungrounded in experience. If there are "no independently identifiable, real-world referents to which the language of social description is cemented" (Gergen 1986, P. 143), scientific conclusions—like any other account of reality—amounts only and entirely to representation. In the absence of an independent reality, all descriptions refer to other descriptions; none can be authentic (Baudrillard 1981). In skeptical postmodernism, with reality reduced to linguistic convention (Eagleton 1983), representation is relative and arbitrary—linguistically reflexive rather than reality related. Signs "no longer represent anything and no longer have their equivalent in reality" (Baudrillard 1983, P. 19).

There is no substantial basis for distinguishing true from false in this postmodernist scheme of things. There is no content to experience apart from the rhetoric of representation. Rhetoric creates the world that it is supposed to be merely representing; representation produces the truths it supposedly reflects (Ryan 1988). At the same time, however, the modern commonsense belief in an objective world helps conceal the constitutive power of representation. For some postmodernists, modern representation promotes deception, desecration, and domination.

> It signals distortion; it assumes unconscious rules governing relationships. It concretizes, finalizes, and excludes complexity. . . . representation is fraudulent, perverse, artificial, mechanical, deceptive, incomplete, misleading, insufficient, wholly inadequate for the post-modern age. (Rosenau 1992, pp. 94-95.)

If everything is representational rhetoric, where does that leave interviewing and its authoritative texts? Many social researchers are troubled—some even paralyzed—by questions regarding what their empirical material represents. For example, in the context of postmodernism, the constructive questions of qualitative researchers leads them to focus on the researcher's methodological practices as these relate to the production of social reality. Advanced systematically, this has resulted in what might be called the "ethnography of argument" (Woolgar and Pawluch 1985). It has even turned qualitative inquiry toward the "ethnography of ethnography" (Van Maanen 1995a)—representations of others' representations (Marcus 1994).

Of course, the more radical brands of postmodernism have not captivated everyone; adherents remain at the margins of interview research. Other social scientists, such as those represented in this book, provide more inventively affirmative perspectives on the interview process. Many are not convinced of the constitutive hegemony of representation. In their own ways, these social researchers remain committed to objectivist description of one sort or another. According to Dmitri Shalin (1993), undue concern with the crisis of representation risks the loss of reality altogether. It portends the transformation of social experience into a postmodern field of nothing but texts, with the likelihood of that field turning into yet another field of texts, where the real is less grounded in lived experience than inscribed on the written page.

SUSTAINING A REFLEXIVE EMPIRICISM

Many strive to keep the empirical world in place despite the most dire appraisal. In the context of ethnography, for example, George Marcus (1994) points out that studying a field of representations is not necessarily a diversion from fieldwork, but rather an exploration of consummate social facts that might help us better understand the assumptions and practices underpinning what passes for knowledge. Generally agreeing, others, such as Joseph Schneider (1991), are sensitive to the call for reflexively examining the representational practices of the social sciences, but remain concerned about the consequences for empirical description. Clifford Geertz (1988) has observed the effects of postmodern skepticism on ethnographic writing, but has made it a point not to succumb to the anxieties. Each of the authors represented in *Postmodern Interviewing* take postmodern sensibilities to heart while not succumbing to purely textual deconstruction. Rather, they explore and present in new ways empirical texts based on, or related to, interviews, directing us to the many constructive intersections that interviewing has with culture, fiction, history, biography, poetry, and social interaction, contexts that were formerly viewed as principally separate from the interview in its own right.

Commenting on the "nervous present," Geertz contrasts the "scene-setting, task-describing, self-presenting opening pages" of two epistemologically distinct ethnographies, a portrayal which, with the appropriate shift in methodological context, could apply respectively to "authoritative" and postmodern interview studies. One of the ethnographies, Raymond Firth's book *We, the Tikopia*, published in 1936, is written with classic authorial presence. The other, Loring Danforth's book *The Death Rituals of Rural Greece*, which appeared in 1982, is decidedly more self-conscious. Compare the first paragraph of Firth's opening chapter, "In Primitive Polynesia," with the start of Danforth's introduction, called "Self and Other." The difference in tone is remarkable.

We, the Tikopia

In the cool of the early morning, just before sunrise, the bow of the *Southern Cross* headed towards the eastern horizon, on which a tiny dark blue outline was faintly visible. Slowly it grew into a rugged mountain mass, standing up sheer from the ocean; then as we approached within a few miles it revealed around its base a narrow ring of low, flat land, thick with vegetation. The sullen grey day with its lowering clouds strengthened my grim impression of a solitary peak, wild and stormy, upthrust in the waste of waters. (quoted in Geertz 1988, P. 11)

The Death Rituals of Rural Greece

Anthropology inevitably involves an encounter with the Other. All too often, however, the ethnographic distance that separates the reader of anthropological texts and the anthropologist himself from the Other is rigidly maintained and at times even artificially exaggerated. In many cases this distancing leads to an exclusive focus on the Other as primitive, bizarre, and exotic. The gap between a familiar "we" and an exotic "they" is a major obstacle to a meaningful understanding of the Other, an obstacle that can only be overcome through some form of participation in the world of the Other. (Quoted in Geertz 1988, P. 14)

The authorial presence of Firth's writing recalls the naturalism of *Street Corner Society, Tally's Corner,* and *A Place on the Corner.* Firth literally takes us "there," aboard the *Southern Cross.* As the ship nears the beach, we come face-to-face with the native environs and inhabitants. Echoing Whyte, Liebow, and Anderson, Firth is about to open "their world" to view and to tell "their story." Secure in his mission and only musing about the complexities of what he is about to encounter, Firth asks, "I wondered how such turbulent human material could ever be induced to submit to scientific study" (quoted in Geertz 1988, p. 12). In contrast, Danforth echoes the representational questions that, for him, now overshadow anthropology. His concern over how to write the Other lurks at the very heart of the possibility of doing ethnography and writing the real. Such concerns resonate throughout our own book's discussions of new interview horizons, communicative reflexivity, poetics, and power.

Undaunted, Geertz argues that the issue of "being there," as he puts it, is perhaps not so new. It has been a rhetorical problem of ethnography from the start, but we have never been as self-conscious as we are now about it. He compares the rhetorical styles for "being there" of four quite different anthropologists—Claude Levi-Strauss, Edward Evans-Pritchard, Bronislaw Malinowski, and Ruth Benedict—who hail from distinct generations. The crisis of representation that now radicalizes social research questions, it would seem, has been an enduring hurdle of transforming the ethnographer's actual presence in the field into authorial description.

Geertz recognizes that this barrier, while not necessarily insurmountable, makes us more critically aware of the constitutive relation between our methods of procedure and social reality. As Geertz explains, "The advantage of shifting at least part of our attention from the fascinations of field work which have held us so long in thrall, to those of writing is not only that this difficulty will become more clearly understood, but also that we shall learn to read with a more percipient eye" (P. 24). Geertz's sentiments are clear—the need to sustain a reflexive empiricism in the face of the postmodern challenge.

AN APPRECIATION FOR RHETORIC

John Van Maanen, a sociological ethnographer, is equally optimistic. Succinctly stated on the back cover of his book *Tales of the Field* (1988), he writes:

> Once upon a time ethnographers returning from the field simply sat down, shuffled their note cards, and wrote up their descriptions of the exotic and quaint customs they had observed. Today scholars in all disciplines are realizing that *how* their research is presented is at least as important as *what* is presented. Questions of voice, style and audience—the classic issues of rhetoric—have come to the forefront in academic circles. (Emphasis in original)

Van Maanen argues that a growing recognition of the place of rhetoric in representation of all kinds, including that based on interview research, unshackles traditional forms of writing, providing a basis for experimentation in representing worlds of experience. For example, it doesn't trivialize naturalistic accounts of street corner life if we know that naturalists convince us of reality as much by *how* they present their stories as by *what* they convey. Rather, it tells us that "being there" in "their world" in order to convey "their story" is one among many compelling means of writing culture and knowing lives.

Van Maanen focuses on authorial presence in his own writing, distinguishing two primary narrative styles whose "tales" vary in the way the author insinuates him- or herself into the text. The "realist tale" is cool, self-assured, and objective. "Their story" is center stage. When the realist author chooses to take account of the personal trials and tribulations of the ethnographer in the field, details are relegated to a methodological appendix. If naturalist fieldworker William Whyte is present at all in his monograph *Street Corner Society*, it is mostly as a bystander, only occasionally as an active participant in the action. The overall sense of the ethnography is that the reality of corner life is derived from a separate and distinct locale, not from the author's attempts at documentation. Elliot Liebow and Elijah Anderson give us the same feel for the urban scenes surrounding the New Deal carry-out shop and Jelly's bar and liquor store.

In contrast, what Van Maanen calls the "confessional tale" is suffused with concern over how the author has figured in telling "their story." While not necessarily empirically nihilistic, it is nonetheless a self-absorbed account that communicates as much about how the ethnographer contends with his informants and manages his presence in the field as it presents a picture of "their world." Jack Douglas's (1985) account of creative interviewing, for example, shows confessional self-absorption reaching agonizing heights, as does Carolyn Ellis's and Leigh Berger's account in this book of interview research.

Geertz and Van Maanen provide few details of the mechanics by which ethnographic writing constructs reality. Paul Atkinson (1990), however, takes us full tilt into rhetorical territory. His and Amanda Coffey's revisitation in this volume of a famous debate over the relative truth value of participant observation and interviewing offers related insights. In his 1990 book, Atkinson situates his analysis in two ways. First, he points to social researchers' growing awareness of the constitutive relation between the language of analysis and everyday life: "Sociologists have become increasingly sensitive to the cultural significance of spoken and written accounts, texts, and the nature of 'discourse' in the production and reproduction of social forms" (P. 6). While theoretical perspectives have varied, he argues, the reflexivity of texts increasingly preoccupies researchers. They now pay systematic attention to the way texts of all kinds—from media images to methodological writing and ethnographies—construct the realities they otherwise presume to merely present.

Second, as do the authors of the chapters in this book, Atkinson denies that representational matters necessarily cripple social science. He argues instead that all description is rhetorical, including all forms of scientific description.

> The position I adopt . . . will recognize that our methods of reading and writing in ethnography are thoroughly conventional and contrived; it will endorse the view that our social-scientific texts draw on the same conventions as other literary forms, including fictional types; but it will find no reason for anxiety on that score. Many of the cherished parallels and contrasts with "science" are totally misleading. First, the texts of the natural sciences are as rhetorical as any other. . . . Secondly, the recognition that all human inquiry and reportage are essentially the same is not a recipe for nihilism or a loss of scholarly standards. (1992, P. 3)

Atkinson maintains that this provides greater critical consciousness, an awareness of the diverse and complex relation that languages of analysis have with what they are meant to represent, a position that anthropologist Charles Briggs in his chapter of this book takes into the territory of power and cultural domination. Situated as social science is between literature and natural science (Lepenies 1988), its representational practices necessarily straddle the constructive impulses of literature and the objectifying tendencies of natural science. Taking notice of this, Atkinson argues, offers opportunities for enriching experiences and worlds social scientists aim to understand. This is a perspective that family researcher Paul Rosenblatt in his chapter capitalizes on in discussing the uses of fiction in formulating interview topics and writing strategies.

Atkinson (1990) turns to ethnographic texts as a field within which to document rhetorical practices. To illustrate "textual constructions of reality," Atkinson asks us to consider the distancing devices used by ethnographers to separate their own writing from what they write about. The devices are not unique to ethnography, but apply to objectifying practices of various kinds, including those used by interview researchers. As far as ethnography is concerned, the devices deflect the reader from attending to the possibility that ethnographic writing itself "writes" culture, as the title of Clifford and Marcus's (1986) edited volume on the poetics and politics of ethnography implies. Applied to interviewing, it's a viewpoint also broached by sociologists Andrea Fontana, Norman Denzin, Carolyn Ellis and Leigh Berger, and Laurel Richardson; by anthropologists Kirin Narayan and Kenneth George, and Charles Briggs; and by oral historian Richard Cándida Smith, in their chapters of *Postmodern Interviewing.*

One distancing device is the use of exemplary extracts from informants' comments or conversations, a common practice of qualitative researchers in general. While much ethnographic writing is a multifaceted description of events and interactions observed in the field—such as accounts of gang member interactions in Whyte's Cornerville—the ethnographer regularly supplements and rhetorically confirms his or her descriptions with exemplary extracts. In a manner likened to Ricca Edmondson's (1984) characterization of "rhetorical induction," the extracts literally set off and, in effect, separate the ethnographer's commentary from concrete instances of the lived (actual) data that the ethnographer's commentary, and the ethnography as a whole, are taken to be about. Atkinson (1990) explains that "the text [thereby] persuades in so far as the reader concurs or acquiesces in the dialogue between the exemplar and the commentary, and draws on the exemplar so as to find the commentary adequately plausible" (P. 83).

Atkinson describes a related device that capitalizes on a distinction Emile Benveniste (1970) makes in differentiating *histoire* and *discours. Histoire* refers to the story that a text deals with, that is, the actions and events that are commented upon in the text. In the case of qualitative research, the story (*histoire*) ostensibly is what field notes and in-depth interviews are about. On the other hand, *discours,* or narration, presup-

poses a narrator and refers to the narrator's or author's commentary on the story.

While some postmodern sensibilities would question this distinction, it nonetheless can be a persuasive rhetorical device. Atkinson points out that shifts between *histoire* and *discours* in ethnographic writing are commonly marked by changes in tense. What is referred to as the "ethnographic present" often marks *discours,* while *histoire* or the story is told in the past tense. Atkinson uses a passage from *Tally's Corner* to illustrate, which we quote in part. Note the change in tense in the second sentence of the second paragraph extracted below. This serves to persuade the reader that the subjects and their accounts are something separate and distinct from the author's ethnography, providing an analytic distance that underscores the researcher's authority.

> The men had their reasons. Some had separated from their wives and children and did not know their children were hospitalized. Others knew but couldn't or wouldn't make it. Richard had intended going but if something came up, he would probably go tomorrow, and anyway, he never did like being in a hospital, not even to visit someone else.
>
> But whether the fathers were living with their children or not, the result was the same: there were no men visiting the children in Ward E. This absence of the father is one of the chief characteristics of the father-child relationship. The father-child relationship, however, is not the same for all streetcorner fathers, nor does a given relationship necessarily remain constant over time. . . . (Liebow 1967, Pp. 72-73, quoted in Atkinson 1990, P. 98)

Atkinson goes on to discuss and illustrate several other rhetorical devices, such as the use of "characterization" to enhance a text's plausibility. For instance, "memorable characters," such as Whyte's Doc and

Liebow's Tally Jackson, anchor the reader's attention to a story in a way that a flatter characterization would not. Such devices persuade by textually highlighting "their world," keeping it open to view and distinct from what writing otherwise does to separate it from itself.

◆ Postmodern Representation

The notion that representation is more rhetorical than reportorial can lead to both nihilism and guarded optimism. Skeptical postmodernists, for example, suggest that because truth is necessarily relativized, if not impossible, then social scientific reports should enjoy no special privilege over any other set of accounts (see Schneider 1991). Atkinson (1990), in contrast, is more positive. Claiming that social science relies upon the same authorizing devices that support other discourses, he argues that social scientists, especially qualitative researchers, should not be so self-conscious or modest in relation to representational issues that they abandon their work of describing lived experience and social worlds. He doesn't ignore the crisis of representation, but he believes that it shouldn't inhibit social scientific inquiry.

Some have been experimental in addressing representational dilemmas. One response comes in the form of unconventional modes of representation that acknowledge postmodernist concerns while trying to sustain the conventional goal of empirically-based description. Steve Woolgar (1988, 1989a), Schneider (1991), and others (see Woolgar 1989b), for example, have experimented with textual forms in which multiple voices both present and "interrogate" the emerging narrative. These textual experiments suggest that by reflexively examining representational practices at the same time that we rely upon them, we understand better how authoritative texts are constituted. In the process, we might see how textual authority is rendered

"transparent"—its sources made invisible—by practices that are typically cast as "objective" or "neutral" tools for analysis or reporting.

Other encouraging responses to the postmodernist challenge involve applying unconventional textual forms to represent experience, "messy texts" as Marcus (1994) calls them (also see Krieger 1979, 1983; Richardson 1990, 1991; Richardson and Lockridge 1991; Paget 1995). Laurel Richardson (1992; also see Richardson, chapter 10, this volume), for example, self-consciously uses poetry as a means of representing lived experience. In a provocative project, she writes a poem to convey the life story of one of her interview respondents, an unwed mother named Louisa May. Richardson keeps the crisis of representation at bay by making use of, not despairing over, the epistemological reflexivity that a postmodernist perspective entails.

Richardson is concerned that a straightforward transcript of Louisa May's interview might not faithfully represent her story's lived qualities, particularly its "core" tone. She also worries about how a sociological reader, in particular, would relate to the story being told. According to Richardson, a sociologist who reads the transcript of the life story is likely to view it as "data," searching for "background variables" to explain what Louisa May says and does. Such a reading would, inadvertently perhaps, stereotypically construct a sociological subject in the transcripts, taking away from Louisa May's own version of her life.

As a result, and after careful editing, Richardson presents Louisa May's story by reconfiguring the interview transcript into a poem. Richardson explains her motivation for doing so:

> I transcribed the tape [of Louisa May's interview] into 36 pages of text and then fashioned that text into a three-page poem, using only her words, her tone, and her diction. . . . For sociological readers, the poem may seem to omit

"data" that they want to know. But this is Louisa May's narrative, not the sociologist's. She does not choose, for example, to talk about her educational level or her employment. The questions the poem raises for readers about Louisa May thus reflect their own particular subtexts, not universal texts. If they wonder, for example, how Louisa May supports herself, are they tapping into stereotypes about "unwed mothers"? If they feel they cannot understand her unless they know about her schooling, are they telling us something about their own relationship to education, its meaning in their own lives? More generally, have the concepts of sociology been so reified that even interpretivists [among whom Richardson would presumably be counted] cannot believe they "know" about a person's life without refracting it through a sociologically prescribed lens? (Pp. 126-27)

Ultimately, Richardson argues that poetry provides a basis for reading and hearing Louisa May's story that other forms might preclude because the literary form is decidedly interpretive, favoring understandings grounded in the subject's perspective, not the sociologist's.

Richardson wants to be faithful to, or at the very least, be more open to diverse interpretations of Louisa May's life. Regarding the transcript of Louisa May's interview, the initial question for Richardson was, Should the transcribed narrative be turned into substantive sociology? Richardson (1992) describes how she initially resolved the dilemma, leading her to use poetry as a means of conveying what she figured conventional sociological writing could not capture (also see Gubrium 1988):

About this time, a part of me that I had suppressed for more than eight years demanded attention: the part that writes poetry. Writing poetry is emotionally preoccupying; it opens up unexpected, shadow places in my self. As a kind of time-saving/snaring-two-birds-with-one-net strategy, I decided to fashion material from an unmarried mother interview [Louisa May] into a poem. That, I thought, would get me started. . . , acknowledge my need for poetry/play, and maybe—just maybe—provide a new strategy for resolving those horrid postmodernist writing dilemmas. (P. 131)

Richardson goes on to discuss the personal consequences of this decision. As she notes, while the task of presenting Louisa May's story is daunting, it provides an opportunity to respond to both the veridical challenges of positivism and the "horrid" representational hurdles of postmodernism.

Louisa May brings me to different sites and allows me to see familiar sites in new ways. Disillusionment is one of the outcomes. When, for example, a symbolic interactionist conventioneer asks me to "prove" Louisa May exists by showing him the transcript of my interview (as if transcripts were real), or when my feminist postmodernist reading group wants to know about the "validity" of the poem, I experience deeply the hold of positivism on even those I consider my allies, my intellectual companions. In the chasm, I experience isolation, alienation, and freedom, exhilaration. I want to record what they are saying; I want to do fieldwork on them. Science them. My romanticized vision of a postmodernist sociology shaken, I seek alternative sites for sharing sociology. Louisa May's life takes me to poetry bars, literature conventions, women's studies classes, social work spaces, and policy making settings. (Pp. 135-36)

Richardson's writing has elements of Van Maanen's (1988) "confessional tale"; her account is self-revelatory and, for that reason, can be viewed as a kind of "personal sociology" that understandably leads to a professional career of related work (Higgins and Johnson 1988). Her responses also place her among social researchers who self-consciously attempt to plumb the emotional depths of experience (see Ellis and Flaherty 1992; Gubrium and Holstein 1997, chapter 4). But, significantly, Richardson is pointing to something more, bearing directly on the crisis of representation. Her own writing experience is not just a personal field of concern, informing the overall effort but kept scrupulously separate from it in the final analysis. Rather, Richardson actually blends her own writing desires and experience with her respondent's narrative to produce what she believes to be a new, blurred, but more open mode of representation. Further, she believes that a merely accurate transcript would literally misrepresent experience sociologically. Richardson necessarily must write differently, poetically. Her project demands a text that would less stereotypically lead us to read Louisa May's story.

Here again, reflexivity and poetics are evident, and power is certainly implicated in the sociological wings. Every statement of "fact" about Louisa May's story is written in relation both to Richardson's own developing self-understanding and to her understanding of the "Other," who in this case is Louisa May. Richardson affirmatively resolves the crisis of representation by simultaneously and necessarily writing herself along with the Other. Poetry, she argues, permits this, as it quintessentially implicates its subjects, author, and the reader. Good, conventional sociological writing, in this context, unfortunately can only be

about its subject matter. Richardson concludes:

> Representing the sociological as poetry is one way of decentering the unreflexive "self" to create a position for experiencing the self as a sociological knower/constructor—not just talking about it, but doing it. In writing the Other, we can re(write) the Self. That is the moral of this story. (1992, P. 136)

Which also bears on the moral of *Postmodern Interviewing*. As we note in Chapter 2, interviewing is now part-and-part of an interview society. Interview researchers can no longer ignore the cultural, historical, and political environments that both surround and cut through the interview process. Interviewing is as much part of our society as it reflects society to us through respondents. More and more, interviews communicatively re-present who we are; increasingly, its varied formats are the way we know about ourselves, our lives, and about others. Attending to the communicative interplay and the resulting constructed worlds put into place by the interview enterprise points to the broad contours of postmodern interviewing. Whether that is realized against new technical horizons, such as Chris Mann and Fiona Stewart describe in their chapter on internet interviewing, or is conceptualized as the inexorable project that we in our chapter call "active interviewing," postmodern interviewing links the scientific to the moral by showing us how much of what we could be, not just what we are, is conveyed in the interview project.

■ *References*

Anderson, E. 1976. *A Place on the Corner.* Chicago: University of Chicago Press.
Atkinson, P. 1990. *The Ethnographic Imagination.* London: Routledge.

Atkinson, P. and D. Silverman. 1997. "Kundera's *Immortality:* The Interview Society and the Invention of Self." *Qualitative Inquiry* 3: 304-25.

Baudrillard, J. 1981. *For a Critique of the Political Economy of the Sign.* St. Louis, MO: Telos.

Baudrillard, J. 1983. *Simulations.* New York: Semiotext.

Baudrillard, J. 1988. *America.* London: Verso.

Baudrillard, J. 1991a. "La guerre du Golfe n'a pas eu lieu." *Liberation,* March 29.

Baudrillard, J. 1991b. "The Reality Gulf." *The Guardian,* January 11.

Benveniste, E. 1970. *Problems in General Linguistics.* Miami, FL: University of Miami Press.

Best, S. and D. Kellner. 1991. *Postmodern Theory.* New York: Guilford.

Clifford, J. and G. E. Marcus (eds.). 1986. *Writing Culture.* Berkeley: University of California Press.

Danforth, L. 1982. *The Death Rituals of Rural Greece.* Princeton, NJ: Princeton University Press.

Denzin, N. K. 1988. "Blue Velvet: Postmodern Contradictions." *Theory, Culture, and Society* 5:461-73.

Denzin, N. K. 1991. *Images of Postmodern Society.* London: Sage.

Denzin, N. K. 1992. *Symbolic Interactionism and Cultural Studies.* Oxford: Blackwell.

Douglas, J. D. 1985. *Creative Interviewing.* Beverly Hills, CA: Sage.

Edmondson, R. 1984. *Rhetoric in Sociology.* London: Macmillan.

Ellis, C. and M. G. Flaherty (eds.). 1992. *Investigating Subjectivity.* Newbury Park, CA: Sage.

Featherstone, M. 1988. *Postmodernism.* Special issue of *Theory, Culture, and Society,* vol. 5.

Firth, Ra. 1936. *We, the Tikopia.* London: Allen & Unwin.

Geertz, C. 1988. *Works and Lives: The Anthropologist as Author.* Stanford, CA: Stanford University Press.

Gergen, K. J. 1986. "Correspondence versus Autonomy in the Language of Understanding Human Actions." Pp. 136-62 in *Metatheory in Social Science,* edited by D. Fiske and R. Schweder. Chicago: University of Chicago Press.

Gubrium, J. F. 1988. "Incommunicables and Poetic Documentation in the Alzheimer's Disease Experience." *Semiotica* 72:235-53.

Gubrium, J. F. and J. A. Holstein. 1997. *The New Language of Qualitative Method.* New York: Oxford University Press.

Higgens, P. C. and J. M. Johnson (eds.). 1988. *Personal Sociology.* New York: Praeger.

Kellner, D. 1992. "Popular Culture and the Construction of Postmodern Identities." Pp. 141-77 in *Modernity and Identity,* edited by S. Lash and J. Friedman. Oxford: Blackwell.

Krieger, S. 1979. *Hip Capitalism.* Beverly Hills, CA: Sage.

Krieger, S. 1983. *The Mirror Dance.* Philadelphia: Temple University Press.

Lash, S. and J. Friedman (eds.). 1992. *Modernity and Identity.* Oxford: Blackwell.

Latour, B. and S. Woolgar. 1979. *Laboratory Life: The Social Construction of Scientific Facts.* London: Sage.

Lepenies, W. 1988. *Between Science and Literature: The Rise of Sociology.* New York: Cambridge University Press.

Liebow, E. 1967. *Tally's Corner.* Boston: Little, Brown.

Lindesmith, A. R., A. L. Strauss, and N. K. Denzin. 1988. *Social Psychology.* Englewood Cliffs, NJ: Prentice Hall.

Lyotard, J-F. 1984. *The Postmodern Condition.* Minneapolis: University of Minnesota Press.

Marcus, G. E. 1994. "What Comes (Just) After 'Post'? The Case of Ethnography." Pp. 563-74 in *Handbook of Qualitative Research,* edited by N. K. Denzin and Y. Lincoln. Thousand Oaks, CA: Sage.

Paget, M. A. 1995. "Performing the Text." Pp. 222-44 in *Representation in Ethnography,* edited by John Van Maanen. Thousand Oaks, CA: Sage.

Poster, M. 1988. "Introduction." Pp. 1-9 in *Jean Baudrillard: Selected Writings.* Stanford, CA: Stanford University Press.

Richardson, L. 1990. *Writing Strategies.* Newbury Park, CA: Sage.

Richardson, L. 1991. "Postmodern Social Theory: Representational Practices." *Sociological Theory* 9:173-79.

Richardson, La. 1992. "The Consequences of Poetic Representation." Pp. 125-37 in *Investigating Subjectivity*, edited by C. Ellis and M. Flaherty. Thousand Oaks, CA: Sage.

Richardson, La. and E. Lockridge. 1991. "The Sea Monster: An Ethnographic Drama and Comment on Ethnographic Fiction." *Symbolic Interaction* 14:335-40.

Rosenau, P. M. 1992. *Post-modernism and the Social Sciences*. Princeton, NJ: Princeton University Press.

Ryan, M. 1988. "Postmodern Politics." *Theory, Culture, and Society* 5:559-76.

Schneider, J. 1991. "Troubles with Textual Authority in Sociology." *Symbolic Interaction* 14: 296-319.

Seidman, S. and D. G. Wagner (eds.). 1992. *Postmodernism and Social Theory*. Oxford: Blackwell.

Shalin, D. N. 1993. "Modernity, Postmodernism, and Pragmatist Inquiry: An Introduction." *Symbolic Interaction* 16:303-32.

Van Maanen, J. 1988. *Tales of the Field*. Chicago: University of Chicago Press.

Van Maanen, J. 1995. "An End to Innocence: The Ethnography of Ethnography." Pp. 1-35 in *Representation in Ethnography*, edited by J. Van Maanen. Thousand Oaks, CA: Sage.

Whyte, W. F. 1943. *Street Corner Society*. Chicago: University of Chicago Press.

Wittgenstein, L. 1958. *Philosophical Investigations*. New York: Macmillan.

Woolgar, S. 1988. "Reflexivity is the Ethnographer in the Text." Pp. 14-34 in *Knowledge and Reflexivity*, edited by S. Woolgar. London: Sage.

Woolgar, S. 1989a. The Ideology of Representation and the Role of the Agent." Pp. 131-44 in *Dismantling Truth*, edited by H. Lawson and L. Appignanesi. New York: St. Martin's.

Woolgar, S. 1989b. *Knowledge and Reflexivity*. London: Sage.

Woolgar, S. and D. Pawluch. 1985. "Ontological Gerrymandering: The Anatomy of Social Problems Explanations." *Social Problems* 32:214-27.

Part 1

NEW HORIZONS

2

FROM THE INDIVIDUAL INTERVIEW TO THE INTERVIEW SOCIETY

◆ Jaber F. Gubrium
James A. Holstein

At first glance, the interview seems simple and self-evident. The interviewer coordinates a conversation aimed at obtaining desired information. He or she makes the initial contact, schedules the event, designates its location, sets out the ground rules, and then begins to question the interviewee or "respondent." Questions elicit answers in more or less anticipatable format until the interviewer's agenda is completed and the interview ends.

The respondent provides the answers. She or he is usually well aware of the routine and waits until questions are posed before answering. The respondent's obligation is not to manage the encounter or to raise queries, but to offer information from his or her personal cache of experiential knowledge. Respondents are relatively passive in their roles, which are delimited by

the interviewer's coordinating activity and the available repository of answers. Should a respondent ask questions in his or her own right, the interviewer typically treats these questions as requests for clarification. The interviewer's responses are merely a means of keeping the interview and the respondent on track.

This is the familiar asymmetrical relationship that we recognize as interviewing. Except for technical nuances, we are conversant with either role in the encounter. Most educated urbanites, for instance, would know what it means to interview someone and would be able to manage the activity adequately in its broad details, from start to finish, if asked to do so. Likewise, most of us readily respond to demographic questionnaires, product-use surveys, public opinion polls, and health willing and able to provide all sorts of information to strangers about the most intimate aspects of our lives. We carry out such encounters time and again with little hesitation and hardly an afterthought. The individual interview has become a commonplace feature of everyday life.

◆ The Democratization of Opinion

As familiar as it seems today, the interview, as a procedure for securing knowledge, is relatively new historically. Indeed, individuals have not always been viewed as important sources of knowledge about their own experience. Of course, we can imagine that particular forms of questioning and answering have been with us since the beginning of talk. As long as parental authority has existed, for example, fathers and mothers have undoubtedly questioned their children regarding their whereabouts; children have been expected to provide answers, not questions, in response. Similarly, suspects and prisoners have been interrogated for as long as suspicion and incarceration have been a part of human affairs. Healers, priests, employers, journalists, and many others seeking immediate, practical knowledge about everyday life have all undertaken interviewlike activity.

Nevertheless, not so long ago it would have seemed rather peculiar for an individual to approach a complete stranger and ask for permission to discuss personal matters. Daily life was more intimate; everyday business was conducted on a face-to-face basis between persons who were well acquainted with one another. According to Mark Benney and Everett Hughes (1956), there was a time when the interview simply didn't exist as a social form; they noted more than 40 years ago that "the interview [as we now refer to it] is a relatively new kind of encounter in the history of human relations" (p. 139). Benney and Hughes were not saying that the activity of asking and answering questions was new, but rather that information gathering did not always rely upon the interview encounter. Although centuries ago a father might have interrogated his children concerning their whereabouts, this was not interviewing as we have come to know it today. The interview emerged only when specific information-gathering roles were formalized. This encounter would hardly be recognizable in a world of close relationships where the stranger was more likely to signify danger and the unknown than to be understood as a neutral conduit for the transmission of personal knowledge (Benney and Hughes 1956).

The modern interview changed all of this. Especially after World War II, with the emergence of the standardized survey interview, individuals became accustomed to offering information and opinions that had no immediate bearing on their lives and social relations. Individuals could forthrightly add their thoughts and feelings to the mix of "public opinion." Indeed, it became feasible for the first time for individuals to speak with strangers about all manner of thoughts concerning their lives, because these new strangers (that is, interviewers) didn't tell, at least in personally recognizable terms. Individuals—no matter how insignificant they might seem in the everyday scheme of things—came to be viewed as important elements of populations. Each person had a voice and it was imperative that each voice be heard, at least in principle. Seeking everyone's opinions, the interview has increasingly democratized experiential information.

THE MODERN TEMPER

David Riesman and Benney (1956) considered the interview format to be the product of a changing world of relationships, one that developed rapidly following the war years. The new era gradually accepted routine conversational exchanges between strangers; when people encountered interview situations, they were not immediately defensive about being asked for information about their lives, their associates, or their deepest sentiments, even though, in certain quarters, defensiveness was understandable because of perceived linkages between interviewing and oppression. Within this world, we have come to recognize easily two new roles associated with talking about oneself and one's life with strangers: the role of the interviewer and the role of the respondent—the centerpieces of the familiar interview.

This is an outgrowth of what Riesman and Benney called "the modern temper," a term that we take to have both cultural and interpersonal resonances. Culturally, it denotes a shared understanding that the individual has the wherewithal to offer a meaningful description of, or set of opinions about, his or her life. Individuals, in their own right, are accepted as significant commentators on their own experience; it is not just the "chief" community commentator who speaks for one and all, in other words, or the local representative of the commonwealth whose opinions are taken to express the thoughts and feelings of every mind and heart in the vicinity.

This modern temper is also interpersonal, in that it democratizes the interpretation of experience by providing a working space and means for expressing public opinion. Everyone—each individual—is taken to have significant views and feelings about life that are accessible to others who undertake to ask about them. As William James ([1892] 1961) noted at the end of the 19th century, this assumes that each and every individual has a sense of self that is owned and controlled by him- or herself, even if the self is socially formulated and interpersonally responsive. This self makes it possible for everyone to reflect meaning-fully on individual experience and to enter into socially relevant dialogue about it. The modern temper has made it reasonable and acceptable to turn to a world of individuals, most of whom are likely to be strangers, as a way of understanding the social organization of experience.

Just as the interview itself is a recent development, the selection of ordinary individuals as sources of information and opinions is also relatively new (see Kent 1981; Oberschall 1965; Selvin 1985). As Pertti Alasuutari (1998) explains, it was not so long ago that when one wanted to know something important about society or social life, one invariably asked those considered to be "in the know." In contrast to what seems self-evident today—that is, questioning those individuals whose experiences are under consideration—the obvious and efficient choice for very early interviewers was to ask *informed* citizens to provide answers to their questions. Alasuutari provides an example from Anthony Oberschall's work:

> It was natural that the questions were posed to knowledgeable citizens, such as state officials or church ministers. In other words, they were informants in expert interviews. For instance, in a survey of agricultural laborers conducted in 1874-1875 in Germany (Oberschall 1965: 19-20), question No. 25 read: "Is there a tendency among laborers to save money in order to be able to buy their own plot of land later on? Does this tendency appear already among the unmarried workers or only after marriage?" . . . The modern survey would of course approach such questions quite differently. Instead of asking an informed person whether married or unmarried workers have a tendency to save money to buy their own plot of land, a sample of workers would be asked about their marital sta-

tus, savings, and plans about how to use them. (Pp. 135-36)

Those considered to be knowledgeable in the subject matter under consideration, Alasuutari notes, were viewed as informants, not respondents, the latter being superfluous under the circumstances.

AN INDIVIDUALIZING DISCOURSE

The research consequence of the subsequent democratization of opinion was part of a trend toward increased surveillance in everyday life. The growing discourse of individuality combined with an increasingly widespread and efficient apparatus for information processing. Although interviewing and the resulting production of public opinion developed rapidly after World War II, the widespread surveillance of daily life and the deployment of the category of the individual had begun centuries earlier.

Michel Foucault's (1973, 1975, 1977, 1978) iconoclastic studies of the discursive organization of subjectivity shed fascinating light on the development of the concepts of the personal self and individuality. Time and again, in institutional contexts ranging from the medical clinic and the asylum to the prison, Foucault shows us how what he calls "technologies of the self" have transformed the way we view the sources and structure of our subjectivity (see Dreyfus and Rabinow 1982; Foucault 1988).

We use the term *subjectivity* here to indicate the type(s) of subject(s) that individuals and cultures might comprehend and embody. With respect to the interview, we are referring to the putative agent who stands behind the "facades" of interview participants, so to speak, the agent who is held practically and morally responsible for the participants' words and actions. Most of us are so familiar with the contemporary Western image of the individualized self as this agent that we find it difficult to comprehend alternative subjectivities. Clifford Geertz (1984), however, points out that this is "a rather peculiar idea within the context of the world's cultures" (p. 126). In other societies and historical periods, agency and responsibility have been articulated in relation to a variety of other social structures, such as the tribe, the clan, the lineage, the family, the community, and the monarch. The notion of the bounded, unique self, more or less integrated as the center of awareness, emotion, judgment, and action, is a very recent version of the subject.

Foucault offers us new insights into how this sense of subjectivity evolved. Technologies of the self, in Foucault's terms, are the concrete, socially and historically located institutional practices through which a relatively new sense of who and what we are as human beings was constructed. These practices advanced the notion that each and every one of us has an ordinary self—the idea being that each one could acceptably reflect on his or her individual experience, personally describe it, and communicate opinions about it and its surrounding world in his or her own terms. This transformed our sense of human beings as subjects. The now self-evident view that each of us has opinions of public significance became intelligible only within a discourse of individuality.

Foucault argues that the newly formed technologies of surveillance of the 18th and 19th centuries, the quintessential manifestation of which was Jeremy Bentham's all-seeing panopticon, did not just incorporate and accommodate the experiences of individual subjects who populated the contemporary social landscape, but, instead, entered into the construction of individual subjects in their own right. Foucault poignantly exemplifies this transformation in the opening pages of *Discipline and Punish* (1977), a book that is as much about the individuation of society as it is about "the birth of the prison" (its subtitle). In the opening pages, we cringe at a vivid account of the torture of a man condemned to death for attempting to assassinate King Louis

XV of France. We despair as the man's body is flayed, burned, and drawn and quartered in public view. From contemporary commentary, Foucault (1977) describes the events:

> On 2 March 1757 Damiens the regicide was condemned "to make the *amende honorable* before the main door of the Church of Paris," where he was to be "taken and conveyed in a cart wearing nothing but a shirt, holding a torch of burning wax weighing two pounds"; then, "in the said cart, to the Place de Grève, where, on a scaffold that will be erected there, the flesh will be torn from his breasts, arms, thighs and calves with red-hot pincers, his right hand, holding the knife with which he committed the said parricide, burnt with sulphur, and, on those places where the flesh will be torn away, poured molten lead, boiling oil, burning resin, wax and sulphur melted together and then his body drawn and quartered by four horses and his limbs and body consumed by fire, reduced to ashes and his ashes thrown to the winds." (P. 3)

Foucault asks why criminals were subjected to such horrible bodily torture. Why were they made to beg for forgiveness in public spectacles? His answer is that the spectacle of torture was an event whose political culture was informed by a sense of the seamless relations among the body of the king (the crown), social control, and subjectivity. As all people were, Damiens was conceived literally and legally as a subject of the king; his body and soul were inseparable extensions of the crown. An assault on the body of the king had to be attacked in turn, as a red-hot iron might be used to cauterize a festering wound. The spectacle of torture did not revolve around an autonomous agent who was regarded as an independent subject with a self, feelings, opinions, and experiential reality uniquely his own. This might have caused others

sympathetically to consider Damiens's treatment to be cruel and unusual punishment, to put it in today's terms.

The disposition of the times, however, offered no sympathy for what Damiens might have been "going through." In the eyes of others, Damiens's feelings and opinions had no standing apart from the man's station in relation to the sovereign. The spectacle of punishment rested on a discourse of knowledge and power that lodged all experiential truth in the sovereign's shared embodiment. As Hubert Dreyfus and Paul Rabinow (1982) explain: "The figure of torture brings together a complex of power, truth, and bodies. The atrocity of torture was an enactment of power that also revealed truth. Its application on the body of the criminal was an act of revenge and an art" (p. 146). The idea that a thinking, feeling, consequential subject occupied the body of the criminal was simply beyond the pale of contemporary understanding. Individuality, as we know it today, did not exist as a recognizable social form.

A few pages later in *Discipline and Punish,* Foucault presents the new subject who comes into being as part of a discourse that is more in tune with "the modern temper." Discussing the evolution of penal reform, he describes the emergence of the "house of young prisoners" in Paris a mere 80 years after Damiens's death. Torture as a public spectacle has gradually disappeared. The "gloomy festival of punishment" is dying out, along with the accused's agonizing plea for pardon. It has been replaced by a humanizing regimen, informed by a discourse of the independent, thinking subject whose criminality is correctable. Rehabilitation is replacing retribution. Scientific methods of scrutiny and courses of instruction are viewed as the means for returning the criminal to right reason and back to the proper fold of society. The subject is no longer a selfless appendage of a larger entity; this is a new agent, one with a mind and sentiments of his or her own. With the proper regimen, this new agent is incited to individual self-scrutiny and responds to corrective action.

In time, this same subject would duly offer his or her opinions and sentiments within the self-scrutinizing regimens of what Foucault calls "governmentality," the archipelago of surveillance practices suffusing modern life. As James Miller (1993: 299) points out, governmentality extends well beyond the political and penal to include pedagogical, spiritual, and religious dimensions (see also Garland 1997). If Bentham's original panopticon was an efficient form of prison observation, panopticism in the modern temper becomes the widespread self-scrutiny that "governs" all aspects of everyday life in the very commonplace questions and answers posed about ourselves in both our inner thoughts and our public expressions. These are seemingly daily inquiries about what we personally think and feel about every conceivable topic, including our deepest sentiments and most secret actions.

We can readily view the individual interview as part of modern governmentality, impressed upon us by myriad inquiries into our lives. Indeed, the interview may be seen as one of the 20th century's most distinctive technologies of the self. In particular, it gives an "objective," "scientific" cast to the notion of the individual self, terms of reference that resolutely echo modern times. As Nikolas Rose (1990, 1997) has shown in the context of the psychological sciences, the private self, along with its descriptive data, was invented right along with the technologies we now associate with measurement.

"Scientific surveillance" such as psychological testing, case assessments, and, of course, individual interviews of all kinds have created the experiencing and informing respondent we now take for granted. The category of "the person" now identifies the self-reflective constituents of society (see Carrithers, Collins, and Lukes 1985; Lidz 1976); if we want to know what the social world is like, we now ask its individual inhabitants. The individual interview on a personal scale and the social survey on the societal level serve as democratizing agents, giving voice to individuals and, in the process, formulating "public" opinion.

LEARNING FROM STRANGERS

The title of Robert Weiss's (1994) book on interviewing, *Learning from Strangers*, points to the shared expectations that surround the face-to-face experience of interviewing, as the book lays out "the art and method of qualitative interview studies." Although qualitative interviews especially are sometimes conducted with acquaintances, much of Weiss's advice on how an interviewer should proceed is based on the premise that the interviewer does not know the respondent. Behind each bit of advice about how to interview effectively is the understanding that each and every stranger-respondent is someone worth listening to. The respondent is someone who can provide detailed descriptions of his or her thoughts, feelings, and activities, if the interviewer asks and listens carefully enough. The trick, in Weiss's judgment, is for the interviewer to present a caring and concerned attitude, expressed within a well-planned and encouraging format. The aim of the interviewer is to derive, as objectively as possible, the respondent's *own* opinions of the subject matter in question, information that the respondent will readily offer and elaborate when the circumstances are conducive to his or her doing so and the proper methods are applied.

The full range of individual experiences is potentially accessible, according to Weiss; the interview is a virtual window on that experience, a kind of universal panopticon. In answering the question of why we interview, Weiss offers a compelling portrayal of the democratization of opinion:

Interviewing gives us access to the observations of others. Through interviewing we can learn about places we have not been and could not go and about settings in which we have not lived. If we have the right informants, we can learn about the quality of neighborhoods or what happens in families or how organizations set their goals. Interviewing can inform us about the nature of social life. We can learn about the work of occupations and how people fashion careers, about cultures and the values they sponsor, and about the challenges people confront as they lead their lives.

We can learn also, through interviewing, about people's interior experiences. We can learn what people perceived and how they interpreted their perceptions. We can learn how events affect their thoughts and feelings. We can learn the meanings to them of their relationships, their families, their work, and their selves. We can learn about all the experiences, from joy through grief, that together constitute the human condition. (P. 1)

The opportunities for knowing even strangers by way of their opinions are now ubiquitous. We find interviews virtually everywhere. We have come a very long way from the days when individuals' experiences and voices simply didn't matter, a long way from Damiens's "unheard" cries. The interview itself has created, as well as tapped into, the vast world of individual experience that now constitutes the substance of everyday life.

◆ The Interview Society

If the interview has helped to constitute the modern individual, has it simultaneously transformed society? It certainly has transported the myriad details of the most personal experience into the public domain. Indeed, it has established these realms as important sites for securing answers to what it means to be part of everyday life.

Our social world now comprises viable and consequential individual opinions, assembled and offered up by actively agentic subjects, whose responses convey the individual particulars of modern society. With the spread of the discourse of individualized subjectivity, we now are prepared as both questioners and answerers to produce readily the society of which we are a part. The modern temper gives us the interview as a significant means for realizing that subjectivity and the social contexts that bring it about.

THE MEDIATION OF CONTEMPORARY LIFE

Interviewing of all kinds mediates contemporary life. Think of how much we learn about today's world by way of interviews conducted across a broad spectrum of venues, well beyond research practice. Interviews, for example, are a source of popular celebrity and notoriety. Television interview host Larry King introduces us to politicians and power brokers who not only share their thoughts, feelings, and opinions with a mass audience but cultivate their celebrity status in the process. This combines with programming devoted to exposing the deepest personal, not just political or social, sentiments of high-profile figures. Celebrity news commentators/interviewers like Barbara Walters plumb the emotional depths of stars and pundits from across the media spectrum. To this, add the likes of talk-show hosts Oprah Winfrey, Montel Williams, ,Jenny Jones, and Jerry Springer, who daily invite ordinary men and women, the emotionally tortured, and the behaviorally bizarre to "spill their guts" in front of millions of television viewers. Referring to all of these, the interview is becoming the experiential conduit par excellence of the electronic age. And this is only the tip of the iceberg, as questions and answers fly back and forth on the Internet, where chat rooms are now as intimate as back porches and bedrooms.

Interviews extend to professional practice as well. Myriad institutions employ interviewing to generate useful and often crucial information. Physicians conduct medical interviews with their patients in order to formulate diagnoses and monitor treatment and progress. Employers interview job applicants. Psychotherapy has always been a largely interview-based enterprise. Its varied psychological and psychiatric perspectives have perhaps diversified the interview more than any other professional practice. This ranges from traditional forms of in-depth interviewing to more contemporary solution-focused encounters that center on "restorying" experience. Even forensic investigation has come a long way from the interview practices of the Inquisition, where giving the "third degree" was a common feature of interrogation.

As interviewing has become more pervasive in the mass media and in professional practice, the interviewing industry itself has developed by leaps and bounds. Survey research, public opinion polling, and marketing research lead the way. Survey research has always been conducted for academic purposes, but today it is increasingly employed in service to commercial interests as well. The interviewing industry now extends from individual product-use inquiries to group interviewing services, where focus group discussions quickly establish consumer product preferences. Movie studios even use focus groups to decide which versions of motion picture finales will be most popularly received. Indeed, the group interview is among the most rapidly growing information-gathering techniques on the contemporary scene.

The ubiquity and significance of the interview in our daily lives has prompted David Silverman (1997) to suggest that "perhaps we all live in what might be called an 'interview society,' in which interviews seem central to making sense of our lives" (p. 248; see also Silverman 1993). Silverman's reasoning underscores the democratization of opinion that interviewing

has enhanced. Silverman (1997) identifies three conditions required by an interview society. First, an interview society requires a particular informing subjectivity, "the emergence of the self as a proper object of narration." Societies with forms of collective or cosmic subjectivity, for example, do not provide the practical basis for learning from strangers. This is possible only in societies where there is a prevalent and shared sense that any individual has the potential to be a respondent and, as such, has something meaningful to offer when asked to do so.

Second, Silverman points to the need for an information-gathering apparatus he calls the "technology of the confessional." In other words, an interview society needs a practical means for securing the communicative by-product of "confession." This, Silverman (1997) points out, should commonly extend to friendship not only "with the policeman, but with the priest, the teacher, and the 'psy' professional" (p. 248).

Third, and perhaps most important, an interview society requires that a mass technology be readily available. An interview society is not the product of the age-old medical interview, or of the long-standing practice of police interrogation; rather, it requires that an interviewing establishment be recognizably in place throughout society. Virtually everyone should be familiar with the goals of interviewing as well as what it takes to conduct an interview.

Silverman argues that many contemporary societies have met these conditions, some more than others. Not only do media and human service professionals utilize interviews, but it has been estimated that fully 90 percent of all social science investigations exploit interview data (Briggs 1986). Internet surveys now provide instant questions and answers about every imaginable subject; we are asked to state our inclinations and opinions regarding everything from presidential candidates to which characters on TV serials should be retained or ousted. The interview society, it seems, has firmly arrived, is well, and is flourishing as a leading context for addressing the subjective contours of daily living.

THE ROMANTIC IMPULSE

Paul Atkinson and Silverman (1997) point out that the confessional properties of the interview not only construct individual subjectivity but, more and more, deepen and broaden the subjects' experiential truths. We no longer readily turn to the cosmos, the gods, the written word, the high priest, or local authorities for authentic knowledge; rather, we commonly search for authenticity through the indepth interview. The interview society not only reflexively constructs a compatible subject, but fully rounds this out ontologically by taking us to the proverbial heart of the subject in question.

This reveals the romantic impulse behind the interview and the interview society. If we desire to "really know" the individual subject, then somehow we must provide a means to hear his or her genuine voice. Superficial discussion does not seem to be adequate. Many interviewers explore the emotional enclaves of the self by way of "open-ended" or "in-depth" interviewing. Although, technically, "open-endedness" is merely a way to structure the interview process, Atkinson and Silverman suggest that the term also flags a particular social understanding, namely, that the true, internal voice of the subject comes through only when it is not externally screened or otherwise communicatively constrained.

But, as Atkinson and Silverman advise, authenticity in practice is not an ultimate experiential truth. It is itself a methodically constructed social product that emerges from its reflexive communicative practices. In other words, authenticity, too, has its constructive technology. Recognizable signs of emotional expression and scenic practices such as direct eye contact and intimate gestures are widely understood to reveal deep truths about individual selves (see also Gubrium and Holstein 1997; Holstein and Gubrium 2000). In in-depth interviews, we "do" deep, authentic experiences as much as we "do" opinion offering in the course of the survey interview. It is not simply a matter of procedure or the richness of data that turns researchers, the interview society, and its truth-seeing audiences to indepth and open-ended interviewing. It is also a matter of collaboratively making audible and visible the phenomenal depths of the individual subject at the center of our shared concerns.

THE LEADING THEME

It would therefore be a mistake to treat the interview—or any information-gathering technique—as simply a research procedure. The interview is part and parcel of our society and culture. It is not just a way of obtaining information about who and what we are; it is now an integral, constitutive feature of our everyday lives. Indeed, as the romantic impulses of interviewing imply, it is at the very heart of what we have become and could possibly be as individuals.

Whereas some would view the interview primarily as a research technique, we would do well also to consider its broader social, institutional, and representational contours. At the same time, we must be cautious lest the latter overshadow the interview's information-gathering contributions, which have been brilliantly and extensively developed by interview researchers for decades. To recognize, elaborate, and deconstruct the broad contours of the interview is not at all to suggest that we pay less attention to its technology in the conventional sense of the term. Rather, it implies just the opposite; we must think carefully about technical matters because they produce the detailed subject as much as they gather information about him or her.

◆ The Subjects Behind Interview Participants

We began this introductory chapter by noting that the interview seems simple and self-evident. In actual practice, this is hardly the case. If the technology of the interview not only produces interview data but also simultaneously constructs individual and public opinion, what are the working contours of the encounter? What does it mean, in terms of communicative practice, to be an interviewer? What is the presumed subjectivity of this participant? Correspondingly, what does it mean to be a respondent? What is the presumed subjectivity of that participant? These, of course, are procedural questions, to a degree. There is nothing technically simple about the contemporary practice of asking and answering interview questions. But the questions also broker discursive and institutional issues related to matters of contemporary subjectivity. This complicates things, and it is to these issues that we turn in the rest of this chapter as a way of providing a more nuanced context for understanding the individual interview and the interview society.

Let's begin to unpack the complications by examining competing visions of the subjects who are imagined to stand behind interview participants. Regardless of the type of interview, there is always a working model of the subject lurking behind the persons assigned the roles of interviewer and respondent (Holstein and Gubrium 1995). By virtue of the kinds of subjects we project, we confer varying senses of epistemological agency upon interviewers and respondents. These, in turn, influence the ways we proceed technically, as well as our understanding of the relative validity of the information that is produced.

As we noted at the outset, interviewing typically has been viewed as an asymmetrical encounter in which an interviewer solicits information from an interviewee, who relatively passively responds to the interviewer's inquiries. This commonsensical, if somewhat oversimplified, view suggests that those who want to find out about another person's feelings, thoughts, or activities merely have to ask the right questions and the other's "reality" will be revealed. Studs Terkel, the legendary journalistic and sociological interviewer, makes the process sound elementary; he claims that he merely turns on his tape recorder and asks people to talk. Using his classic study *Working* (1972) as an example, Terkel claims that his questions merely evoke responses that interviewees are all too ready to share:

> There were questions, of course. But they were casual in nature . . . the kind you would ask while having a drink with someone; the kind he would ask you. . . . In short, it was a conversation. In time, the sluice gates of damned up hurts and dreams were open. (P. xxv)

As unsophisticated and guileless as it sounds, this image is common in interviewing practice. The image is one of "mining" or "prospecting" for the facts and feelings residing within the respondent. Of course, a highly sophisticated technology tells researcher/prospectors how to ask questions, what sorts of questions not to ask, the order in which to ask them, and ways to avoid saying things that might spoil, contaminate, or bias the data. The basic model, however, locates valued information inside the respondent and assigns the interviewer the task of somehow extracting it.

THE PASSIVE SUBJECT BEHIND THE RESPONDENT

In this rather conventional view, the subjects behind respondents are basically conceived as passive *vessels of answers* for experiential questions put to them by interviewers. Subjects are repositories of facts, feelings, and the related particulars of experience. They hold the answers to demographic questions, such as age, gender, race, occupation, and socioeconomic status. They contain information about social networks, including household composition, friendship groups, circles of care, and other relationships. These repositories also hold a treasure trove of experiential data pertinent to beliefs, feelings, and activities.

The vessel-like subject behind the respondent passively possesses information the interviewer wants to know; the respondent merely conveys, for better or worse, what the subject already possesses. Occasionally, such as with sensitive interview topics or with recalcitrant respondents, interviewers acknowledge that the task may be especially difficult. Nonetheless, the information is viewed, in principle, as the uncontaminated contents of the subject's vessel of answers. The knack is to formulate questions and provide an atmosphere conducive to open and undistorted communication between interviewer and respondent.

Much of the methodological literature on interviewing deals with the facets of these intricate matters. The vessel-of-answers view leads interviewers to be careful in how they ask questions, lest their method of inquiry bias what lies within the subject. This perspective has prompted the development of myriad procedures for obtaining unadulterated facts and details, most of which rely upon interviewer and question neutrality. Successful implementation of disinterested practices elicits objective truths from the vessel of answers. Validity results from the successful application of these techniques.

In the vessel-of-answers model, the image of the subject is not of an agent engaged in the production of knowledge. If the interviewing process goes "by the book" and is nondirectional and unbiased, respondents can validly proffer information that subjects presumably merely store within. Contamination emanates from the interview setting, its participants, and their interaction, not from the subject, who, under ideal conditions, is capable of providing accurate, authentic reports.

THE PASSIVE SUBJECT BEHIND THE INTERVIEWER

This evokes a complementary model of the subject behind the interviewer. Although not totally passive, the interviewer/subject nonetheless stands apart from the actual "data" of the field; he or she merely collects what is already there. To be sure, the collection process can be arduous, but the objective typically is to tap into information without unduly disturbing—and, therefore, biasing or contaminating—the respondent's vessel of answers. If it is not quite like Terkel's "sluice gates" metaphor, it still resembles turning on a spigot; the interviewer's role is limited to releasing what is already in place.

The interviewer, for example, is expected to keep the respondent's vessel of answers in plain view but to avoid shaping the information that is extracted. Put simply, this involves the interviewer's controlling him- or herself so as not to influence what the passive interview subject will communicate. The interviewer must discard serious self-consciousness; the interviewer must avoid any action that would imprint his or her presence onto the respondent's reported experience. The interviewer must resist supplying particular frames of reference for the respondent's answers. To the extent such frameworks appropriately exist, they are viewed as embedded in the subject's world behind the respondent, not behind the researcher. If the interviewer is to be at all self-conscious, this is technically limited to his or her being alert to the possibility that he or she may be contaminating or otherwise unduly influencing the research process.

Interviewers are generally expected to keep their "selves" out of the interview process. *Neutrality* is the byword. Ideally, the interviewer uses his or her interpersonal skills merely to encourage the expression of, but not to help construct, the attitudes, sentiments, and information in question. In effect, the image of the passive subject behind the interviewer is one of a facilitator. As skilled as the interviewer might be in practice, all that he or she appropriately does in principle is to promote the expression of the actual attitudes and information that lie in waiting in the respondent's vessel of answers.

In exerting control in this way, the interviewer limits his or her involvement in the interview to a specific preordained role—which can be quite scripted—that is constant from one interview to another. Should the interviewer go out of control, so to speak, and introduce anything but variations on specified questions into the interview, the passive subject behind the interviewer is methodologically violated and neutrality is compromised. It is not this passive subject who is the problem, but rather the interviewer who has not adequately regulated his or her conduct so as to facilitate the expression of respondent information.

ACTIVATING INTERVIEW SUBJECTS

As researchers have become more aware of the interview as a site for the production of meaning, they have increasingly come to appreciate the activity of the subjects projected behind both the respondent and the interviewer. The interview is being reconceptualized as an occasion for purposefully animated participants to *construct* versions of reality interactionally rather than merely purvey data (see Holstein and Gubrium 1995). This trend reflects an increasingly pervasive appreciation for the constitutive character of social interaction and of the constructive role played by active subjects in authoring their experiences.

Sentiments along these lines have been building for some time across diverse disciplines. Nearly a half century ago, for example, Ithiel de Sola Pool (1957), a prominent

critic of public opinion polling, argued presciently that the dynamic, communicative contingencies of the interview literally activated respondents' opinions. Every interview, Pool suggested, is an "interpersonal drama with a developing plot" (p. 193). The metaphor conveys a far more active sense of interview participation than the "prospector for meaning" suggests. As Pool indicated:

> The social milieu in which communication takes place [during interviews] modifies not only what a person dares to say but even what he thinks he chooses to say. And these variations in expression cannot be viewed as mere deviations from some underlying "true" opinion, for there is no neutral, non-social, uninfluenced situation to provide that baseline. (P. 192)

Conceiving of the interview in this fashion casts interview participants as virtual *practitioners* of everyday life who work constantly to discern and designate the recognizable and orderly features of the experience under consideration. It transforms the subject behind the respondent from a repository of information and opinions or a wellspring of emotions into a productive source of knowledge. From the time a researcher identifies a research topic, through respondent selection, questioning and answering, and, finally, the interpretation of responses, interviewing is a concerted interactional project. Indeed, the subject behind the respondent now, more or less, becomes an imagined product of the project. Working within the interview itself, subjects are fleshed out, rationally and emotionally, in relation to the give-and-take of the interview process, the interview's research purposes, and its surrounding social contexts.

Construed as active, the subject behind the respondent not only holds the details of a life's experience but, in the very process of offering them up to the interviewer, constructively shapes the information. The active respondent can hardly "spoil" what he or she is, in effect, subjectively constructing in the interview process. Rather, the activated subject pieces experiences together before, during, and after occupying the respondent role. This subject is always making meaning, regardless of whether he or she is actually being interviewed.

An active subject behind the interviewer is also implicated in the production of knowledge. His or her participation in the process is not viewed in terms of standardization or constraint; neutrality is not figured to be necessary or achievable. One cannot very well taint knowledge if that knowledge is not conceived as existing in some pure form apart from the circumstances of its production. The active subject behind the interviewer thus becomes a necessary, practical counterpart to the active subject behind the respondent. Interviewer and, ultimately, researcher contributions to the information produced in interviews are not viewed as incidental or immaterial. Nor is interviewer participation considered in terms of contamination. Rather, the subject behind the interviewer is seen as actively and unavoidably engaged in the interactional co-construction of the interview's content.

Interactional contingencies influence the construction of the active subjectivities of the interview. Especially important here are the varied subject positions articulated in the interview process, which need to be taken into account in the interpretation of interview material. For example, an interview project might center on the quality of care and quality of life of nursing home residents (see Gubrium 1993). This might be part of a study relating to the national debate about the organization and value of home versus institutional care. Careful attention to the way participants link substantive matters with biographical ones can vividly reveal a highly active subject. For instance, a nursing home resident might speak animatedly during an interview about the quality of care in her facility, asserting that, "for a woman, it ultimately gets down to feelings," invoking an emotional subject. Another resident might coolly and methodically list specifics about her facility's quality of care, never once mentioning her gender or her feelings about the care she receives. Offering her own take on the matter, this respondent might state that "getting emotional" over "these things" clouds clear judgment, implicating a rationalized subject. When researchers take this active subject into account, what is otherwise a contradictory and inconclusive data set is transformed into the meaningful, intentionally crafted responses of quite active respondents.

The standpoint from which information is offered continually unfolds in relation to ongoing interview interaction. In speaking of the quality of care, for example, nursing home residents, as interview respondents, not only offer substantive thoughts and feelings pertinent to the topic under consideration but simultaneously and continuously monitor who they are in relation to themselves and to the person questioning them. For example, prefacing her remarks about the quality of life in her facility with the statement "Speaking as a woman," a nursing home resident actively informs the interviewer that she is to be heard as a woman, not as someone else—not a mere resident, cancer patient, or abandoned mother. If and when she subsequently comments, "If I were a man in this place," the resident frames her thoughts and feelings about the quality of life differently, producing an alternative subject: the point of view of a man as spoken by a female respondent. The respondent is clearly working up experiential identities as the interview progresses.

Because the respondent's subjectivity and related experience are continually being assembled and modified, the "truth" value of interview responses cannot be judged simply in terms of whether those responses match what lies in an ostensibly objective vessel of answers. Rather, the value of interview data lies both in their meanings and in how meanings are constructed.

These *what* and *how* matters go hand in hand, as two components of practical meaning-making action (see Gubrium and Holstein 1997). The entire process is fueled by the reality-constituting contributions of all participants; interviewers, too, are similarly implicated in the co-construction of the subject positions from which they ask the questions at hand (see in this volume Briggs, Chapter 13).

The multiple subjects that could possibly stand behind interview participants add several layers of complication to the interview process as well as to the analysis of interview data. Decidedly different procedural strictures are required to accommodate and account for alternating subjects. Indeed, the very question of what constitutes or serves as data critically relates to these issues of subjectivity. What researchers choose to highlight when they analyze interview responses flows directly from how the issues are addressed (see Gubrium and Holstein 1997).

◆ Empowering Respondents

Reconceptualizing what it means to interview and to analyze interview material has led to far-reaching innovations in research (see the contributions to this volume by Fontana, Chapter 3; Cándida Smith, Chapter 11; Denzin, Chapter 8; Ellis and Berger, Chapter 9; Richardson, Chapter 10; Rosenblatt, Chapter 12). It has also promoted the view that the interview society is not only the by-product of statistically summarized survey data, but is constituted by all manner of alternative interview encounters and information, the diverse agendas of which variably enter into "data" production. In the process, the political dimensions of the interview process have been critically underscored (see Briggs, Chapter 13, this volume).

The respondent's voice has taken on particular urgency, as we can hear in Eliot Mishler's (1986) poignant discussion of the empowerment of interview respondents. Uncomfortable with the evolution of the interview into a highly controlled, asymmetrical conversation dominated by the researcher (see Kahn and Cannell 1957; Maccoby and Maccoby 1954), Mishler challenges the assumptions and implications behind the "standardized" interview. His aim is to bring the respondent more fully and actively into the picture, to make the respondent more of an equal partner in the interview conversation.

Following a critique of standardized interviewing, Mishler (1986) offers a lengthy discussion of his alternative perspective, one that questions the need for strict control of the interview encounter. The approach, in part, echoes our discussion of the activation of interview participants. Mishler suggests that rather than conceiving of the interview as a form of stimulus and response, we might better view it as an interactional accomplishment. Noting that interview participants not only ask and answer questions in interviews but simultaneously engage in other speech activities, Mishler turns our attention to what the participants, in effect, are doing with words when they engage each other. He makes the point this way:

> Defining interviews as speech events or speech activities, as I do, marks the fundamental contrast between the standard antilinguistic, stimulus-response model and an alternative approach to interviewing as discourse between speakers. Different definitions in and of themselves do not constitute different practices. Nonetheless, this new definition alerts us to the features of interviews that hitherto have been neglected. (Pp. 35-36)

The key phrase here is "discourse between speakers." Mishler directs us to the integral and inexorable speech activities in which even survey interview participants engage as they ask and answer questions. Informed by a conversation-analytic perspective (see Sacks 1992; Sacks, Schegloff, and Jefferson 1974), he points to the discursive machinery apparent in interview transcripts. Highlighting evidence of the ways the interviewer and the respondent *mutually* monitor each other's speech exchanges, Mishler shows how the participants ongoingly and jointly construct in words their senses of the developing interview agenda. He notes, for example, that even token responses by the interviewer, such as "Hm hm," can serve as confirmatory markers that the respondent is on the "right" track for interview purposes. But, interestingly enough, not much can be done to eliminate even token responses, given that a fundamental rule of conversational exchange is that turns must be taken in the unfolding interview process. To eliminate even tokens or to refuse to take one's turn, however minimally, is, in effect, to stop the conversation, hence the interview. The dilemma here is striking in that it points to the practical need for interview participants to be linguistically animated, not just standardized and passive, in order to complete the interview conversation.

It goes without saying that this introduces us to a pair of subjects behind the interviewer and the respondent who are more conversationally active than standardization would imply, let alone tolerate. Following a number of conversation-analytic and linguistic arguments (Cicourel 1967, 1982; Gumperz 1982; Hymes 1967; Sacks et al. 1974), Mishler (1986) explains that each and every point in the series of speech exchanges that constitute an interview is, in effect, open to interactional work, activity that constructs communicative sense out of the participants as well as the subject matter under consideration. Thus, in contrast to the modeled asymmetry of the standardized interview, there is considerable communicative equality and interdependence in the speech activities of all interviewing, where participants invariably engage in the "joint construction of meaning," no matter how asymmetrical the informing model might seem:

The discourse of the interview is jointly constructed by interviewer and respondent. . . . Both questions and responses are formulated in, developed through, and shaped by the discourse between interviewers and respondents. . . . An adequate understanding of interviews depends on recognizing how interviewers reformulate questions and how respondents frame answers in terms of their reciprocal understanding as meanings emerge during the course of an interview. (P. 52)

THE ISSUE OF "OWNING" NARRATIVE

Mishler's entry into the linguistic and conversation-analytic fray was fundamentally motivated by his desire to valorize the respondent's perspective and experience. This was, to some extent, a product of Mishler's long-standing professional interest in humanizing the doctor-patient encounter. His earlier book *The Discourse of Medicine: Dialectics of Medical Interviews* (1984) is important in that it shows how medical interviews can unwittingly but systematically abrogate the patient's sense of his or her own illness even in the sincerest doctor's search for medical knowledge. As an alternative, Mishler advocates more open-ended questions, minimal interruptions of patient accounts, and the use of patients' own linguistic formulations to encourage their own articulations of illness. Similarly, in the context of the research interview, Mishler urges us to consider ways that interviewing might be designed so that the respondent's voice comes through in greater detail, as a way of paying greater attention to respondent relevancies.

According to Mishler, this turns us forthrightly to respondents' stories. His view is that experience comes to us in the form of narratives. When we communicate our experiences to each other, we do so by storying them. When, in turn, we encourage elaboration, we commonly use such narrative devices as "Go on" and "Then what happened?" to prompt further story-like communication. It would be difficult to imagine how an experience of any kind could be conveyed except in narrative format, in terms that structure events into distinct plots, themes, and forms of characterization. Consequently, according to this view, we must leave our research efforts open to respondents' stories if we are to understand respondents' experiences in, and on, their own terms, leading to less formal control in the interview process.

Applied to the research interview, the "radical transformation of the traditional approach to interviewing" (Mishler 1986: 117) serves to empower respondents. This resonates with a broadening concern with what is increasingly referred to as the respondent's *own* voice or authentic story (see the contributions to this volume by Fontana, Chapter 3; Ellis and Berger, Chapter 9). Although *story, narrative,* and the respondent's *voice* are the leading terms of reference, an equally key, yet unexplicated, usage is the term *own*. It appears throughout Mishler's discussion of empowerment, yet he gives it hardly any attention.

Consider several applications of the term *own* in Mishler's (1986) research interviewing text. In introducing a chapter titled "The Empowerment of Respondents," he writes, "I will be concerned primarily with the impact of different forms of practice on respondents' modes of understanding themselves and the world, on the possibility of their acting in terms of their *own* interests, on social scientists' ways of working and theorizing, and the social functions of scientific knowledge" (pp. 117-18; emphasis added). Further along, Mishler explains, "Various attempts to restructure the interviewee-interviewer relationship so as to empower respondents are designed to encourage them to find and speak in their *own* 'voices' " (p. 118; emphasis added). Finally, in pointing to the political potential of narrative, Mishler boldly flags the ownership in question: "To

be empowered is not only to speak in one's *own* voice and to tell one's *own* story, but to apply the understanding arrived at to action in accord with one's *own* interests" (p. 119; emphasis added).

Mishler is admittedly being persuasive. Just as in his earlier book on medical interviews he encourages what Michael Balint (1964) and others (see Silverman 1987) have come to call *patient-centered medicine,* in his research interview book he advocates what might be called *respondent-centered research.* Mishler constructs a preferred version of the subject behind the respondent, one that allegedly gives voice to the respondent's own story. The image is one of a respondent who owns his or her experience, who, on his or her own, can narrate the story if given the opportunity. It is a story that is uniquely the respondent's in that only his or her own voice can articulate it authentically; any other voice or format would apparently detract from what this subject behind the respondent more genuinely and competently does on his or her own. Procedurally, the point is to provide the narrative opportunity for this ownership to be expressed, to reveal what presumably lies within.

But valorizing the individual's ownership of his or her story is a mere step away from seeing the subject as a vessel of answers. As we discussed earlier, this subject is passive and, wittingly or not, taken to be a mere repository of information, opinion, and sentiment. More subtly, perhaps, the subject behind the respondent who "owns" his or her story is viewed as virtually possessing what we seek to know about. Mishler's advice is that we provide respondents with the opportunity to convey these stories to us on their own terms rather than deploy predesignated categories or other structured formats for doing so. This, Mishler claims, empowers respondents.

Nevertheless, the passive vessel of answers is still there in its essential detail. It is now more deeply embedded in the subject, perhaps, but it is as passively secured in the inner reaches of the respondent as the vessel informing the survey respondent's subjectivity. We might say that the subject behind the standardized interview respondent is a highly rationalized version of the romanticized subject envisioned by Mishler, one who harbors his or her own story. Both visions are rhetorics of subjectivity that have historically been used to account for the "truths" of experience. Indeed, we might say that the standardized interview produces a different narrative of experience than does the empowered interviewing style that Mishler and others advocate. This is not meant to disparage, but only to point out that when the question of subjectivity is raised, the resulting complications of the interview are as epistemological as they are invidious.

It is important to emphasize that the ownership in question results from a preferred subjectivity, not from an experiential subject that is more essential than all other subjects. It is, as Silverman and his associates remind us, a romanticized discourse of its own and, although it has contributed immensely to our understanding of the variety of "others" we can be, it does not empower absolutely (see Silverman 1987, 1993; Atkinson and Silverman 1997). Rather, it empowers in relation to the kinds of stories that one can ostensibly own, that would seem to be genuine, or that are otherwise accountably recognized as fitting or authentic to oneself in the particular times and places they are conveyed.

A DISCOURSE OF EMPOWERMENT

Invoking a discourse of empowerment is a way of giving both rhetorical and practical spin to how we conduct interviews. Like all discourses, the discourse of individual empowerment deploys preferred terms of reference. For example, in the discourse of the standardized survey interview, the interview encounter is asymmetrical and the operating principle is control. Participants have different functions: One side asks

questions and records information, and the other side provides answers to the questions asked. Procedurally, the matter of control is centered on keeping these functions and their roles separate. Accordingly, an important operating rule is that the interviewer does not provide answers or offer opinions. Conversely, the respondent is encouraged to answer questions, not ask them. Above all, the language of the enterprise locates knowledge within the respondent, but control rests with the interviewer.

The terms of reference change significantly when the interview is more symmetrical or, as Mishler puts it, when the respondent is empowered. The interviewer and respondent are referred to jointly as interview *participants,* highlighting their collective contribution to the enterprise. This works against asymmetry, emphasizing a more fundamental sense of the shared task at hand, which now becomes a form of "collaboration" in the production of meaning. One procedure for setting this tone is to make it clear that all participants in the interview can effectively raise questions related to the topics under consideration. Equally important, everyone should understand that answers are not meant to be conclusive but instead serve to further the agenda for discussion. The result, then, is more of a team effort, rather than a division of labor, even though the discourse of empowerment still aims to put the narrative ball in the respondent's court, so to speak.

Assiduously concerned with the need to "redistribute power" in the interview encounter, Mishler (1986) argues compellingly for the more equalized relationship he envisions. Seeking a redefinition of roles, he describes what he has in mind:

These types of role redefinitions may be characterized briefly by the following terms referring respectively to the relationship between interviewee and interviewer as informant and reporter, as research collaborators, and as learner/ actor and advocate. Taking on the roles of each successive pair in this series involves a more comprehensive and more radical transformation of the power relationship inherent in traditional roles, and each succeeding pair of roles relies on and absorbs the earlier one. (Pp. 122-23)

The use of the prefix *co-* is commonplace in such discussions, further signaling symmetry. Participants often become "coparticipants" and, of course, the word *collaboration* speaks for itself in this context. Some authors even refer to the interview encounter as a "conversational partnership" (Rubin and Rubin 1995).

Mishler's discourse of collaboration and empowerment extends to the representation of interview material, taking *co-* into new territory. In discussing the role of the advocate, for instance, Mishler describes Kai Erikson's (1976) activity as a researcher hired by attorneys representing the residents affected by the 1972 dam collapse in the Buffalo Creek valley of West Virginia. Erikson was advocating for the surviving residents, several of whom he interviewed, but not the local coal company from which they were seeking damages. The researcher and the sponsor clearly collaborated with each other in representing interview materials.

Others are not as forthrightly political in their corepresentations. Laurel Richardson (see Chapter 10, this volume), for example, discusses alternative textual choices in relation to the presentation of the respondent's "own" story. Research interviews, she reminds us, are usually conducted for research audiences. Whether they are closed- or open-ended, the questions and answers are formulated with the analytic interests of researchers in mind. Sociologists, for example, may wish to consider how gender, race, or class background shapes respondents' opinions, so they will tailor questions and interpret answers in these terms. Ultimately, researchers will represent interview material in the frameworks and languages of their research concerns and in disciplinary terms. But, as Richardson

points out, respondents might not figure that their experiences or opinions are best understood that way. Additionally, Richardson asks us whether the process of coding interview responses for research purposes itself disenfranchises respondents, transforming their narratives into terms foreign to what their original sensibilities might have been (see also Briggs, Chapter 13, this volume).

Richardson suggests that a radically different textual form can help us to represent the respondent's experience more inventively, and authentically. Using poetry rather than prose, for example, capitalizes on poetry's culturally understood role of evoking and making meaning, not just conveying it. This extends to poetry's alleged capacity to communicate meaning where prose is said to be inadequate, in the way that folk poetry is used in some quarters to represent the ineffable (see Gubrium 1988). It is not uncommon, for instance, for individuals to say that plain words can't convey what they mean or that they simply cannot put certain experiences into words, something that, ironically, poetry might accomplish in poetic terms.

How, then, are such experiences and their opinions to be communicated in interviews? Must some respondents literally sing the blues, for example, as folks traditionally have done in the rural South of the United States? Should some experiences be "performed," rather than simply translated into text? Do mere retellings of others' experiences compromise the ability of those who experience them to convey the "scenic presence" of the actual experiences in their lives? A number of researchers take such issues to heart and have been experimenting, for several years now, with alternative representational forms that they believe can convey respondents' experience more on, if not in, their own terms (see Clifford and Marcus 1986; Ellis and Flaherty 1992; Ellis and Bochner 1996; Reed-Danahay 1997; see also in this volume Fontana, Chapter 3; Ellis and Berger, Chapter 9). The border between fact and fiction itself is being explored for its empowering capacity, taking empowerment's informing discourse firmly into the realm of literature (see Rosenblatt, Chapter 12, this volume).

◆ Voice and Ownership

When we empower the respondent (or the informing coparticipant) in the interview encounter, we establish a space for the respondent's *own* story to be heard—at least this is the reasoning behind Mishler's and others' aims in this regard. But questions do arise in relation to the voices we listen to when we provide respondents the opportunity to convey their own stories. Whose voices do we hear? From where do respondents obtain the material they communicate to us in interviews? Is there always only one story for a given respondent to tell, or can there be several to choose from? If the latter, the question can become, Which among these is most tellable under the circumstances? And, as if these questions weren't challenging enough, do the queries themselves presume that they are answerable in straightforward terms, or do answers to them turn in different directions and get worked out in the very course of the interview in narrative practice?

SUBJECT POSITIONS
AND RELATED VOICES

An anecdote from Jaber Gubrium's doctoral supervision duties speaks to the heart of these issues. Gubrium was serving on the dissertation committee of a graduate student who was researching substance abuse among pharmacists. The student was especially keen to allow the pharmacists being interviewed to convey in their own words their experiences of illicitly using drugs, seeking help for their habits, and going through rehabilitation. He hoped to understand how those who "should know better" would account for what happened to them.

When the interviews were completed, the student analyzed the interview data thematically and presented the themes in the dissertation along with individual accounts of experience. Interestingly, several of the themes identified in the pharmacists' stories closely paralleled the familiar recovery rubrics of self-help groups such as Alcoholics Anonymous (A.A.) and Narcotics Anonymous (N.A.). Gubrium noted this, and it turned out that many, if not all, of the pharmacists had participated in these recovery groups and evidently had incorporated the groups' ways of narrating the substance abuse experience into their "own" stories. For example, respondents spoke of the experience of "hitting bottom" and organized the trajectory of the recovery process in relation to that very important low point in their lives. Gubrium raised the issue of the extent to which the interview material could be analyzed as the pharmacists' "own" stories as opposed to the stories of these recovery programs. At a doctoral committee meeting, he asked, "Whose voice do we hear when these pharmacists tell their stories? Their own or N.A.'s?" He asked, in effect, whether the stories belonged to these individuals or to the organizations that promulgated their discourse.

The issue of voice is important because it points to the subject who is assumed to be responding in interviews (Gubrium 1993; Holstein and Gubrium 2000). Voice references the subject position that is taken for granted behind speech. Voice works at the level of everyday life, whereas subject positions are what we imagine to be their operating standpoints. This is the working side of our earlier discussion of the subjects behind interview participants. The possibility of alternative voicings and varied subject positions turned researchers' attention to concerns such as how interview participants collaborate to construct the interview's shifting subjectivities in relation to the topics under consideration.

Empirically, the concept of voice leads us to the question of who—or what subject

—speaks over the course of an interview and from what standpoint. For example, does a 50-year-old man offer the opinions of a "professional" at the apex of his successful career, or might his voice be that of a husband and father reflecting on what he has missed as a result in the way of family life? Or will he speak as a church elder, a novice airplane pilot, or the "enabling" brother of an alcoholic as the interview unfolds? All of these are possible, given the range of contemporary experiences that he could call upon to account for his opinions. At the same time, it is important to entertain the possibility that the respondent's subjectivity and variable voices emerge out of the immediate interview's interaction and are not necessarily preformed in the respondent's ostensible vessel of answers. Indeed, topics raised in the interview may incite respondents to voice subjectivities never contemplated before.

As noted earlier, at times one can actually hear interview participants indicate subject positions. Verbal prefaces, for example, can provide clues to subject position and voice, but they are often ignored in interview research. Phrases such as "to put myself in someone else's shoes" and "to put on a different hat" are signals that respondents employ to voice shifts in position. Acknowledging this, in an interview study of nurses on the qualities of good infant care, we probably would not be surprised to hear a respondent say something like, "That's when I have my RN cap on, but as a mother, I might tell you a different story." Sometimes respondents are quite forthright in giving voice to alternative points of view in precisely those terms, as when a respondent prefaces remarks with, say, "Well, from the point of view of a . . . ." Such phrases are not interview debris; they convey the important and persistent subjective work of the interview encounter.

In the actual practice of asking interview questions and giving answers, things are seldom so straightforward, however. An interview, for example, might start under the assumption that a father or a mother is being interviewed, which the interview's introductions might appear to confirm. But there is no guarantee that particular subjectivities will prevail throughout. There's the matter of the *ongoing* construction of subjectivity, which unfolds with the give-and-take of the interview encounter. Something said later in the interview, for example, might prompt the respondent to figure, not necessarily audibly, that he really had, "all along," been responding from a quite different point of view than was evident at the start. Unfortunately, shifts in subjectivity are not always evident in so many words or comments. Indeed, the possibility of an unforeseen change in subjectivity might not be evident until the very end of an interview, if at all, when a respondent remarks for the first time, "Yeah, that's the way all of us who were raised down South do with our children," making it unclear which subject had been providing responses to the interviewer's questions—the voice of this individual parent or her regional membership and its associated experiential sensibilities.

Adding to these complications, subject position and voice must also be considered in relation to the perceived voice of the interviewer. Who, after all, is the interviewer in the eyes of the respondent? How will the interviewer role be positioned into the conversational matrix? For example, respondents in debriefings might comment that an interviewer sounded more like a company man than a human being, or that a particular interviewer made the respondent feel that the interviewer was "just an ordinary person, like myself." Indeed, even issues of social justice might creep in and position the interviewer, say, as a worthless hack, as the respondent takes the interviewer to be "just one more token of the establishment," choosing to silence her own voice in the process. This raises the possibility that the respondent's working subjectivity is constructed out of the unfolding interpersonal reflections of the interview participants' attendant historical experiences. It opens to consideration, for example, an important question: If the interviewee had not been figured to be just an "ordinary" respondent, who (which subject) might the respondent have been in giving voice to his or her opinions?

As if this doesn't muddy the interview waters enough, imagine what the acknowledgment of multiple subjectivities does to the concept of sample size, another dimension figured to be under considerable control in traditional interview research. To decompose the designated respondent into his or her (multiple) working subjects is to raise the possibility that any single element of a sample can expand or contract in size in the course of the interview, increasing or decreasing the sample n accordingly. Treating subject positions and their associated voices seriously, we might find that an ostensibly single interview could actually be, in practice, an interview with several subjects, whose particular identities may be only partially clear. Under the circumstances, to be satisfied that one has completed an interview with a single respondent and to code it as such because it was formally conducted with a single embodied individual is to be rather cavalier about the complications of subjectivity and of the narrative organization of sample size.

As Mishler (1986) has pointed out, such matters have traditionally been treated as technical issues in interview research. Still, they have long been informally recognized, and an astute positivistic version of the complexities entailed has been theorized and researched with great care and insight (see, for example, Fishbein 1967). Jean Converse and Howard Schuman's (1974) delightful book on survey research as interviewers see it, for instance, illuminates this recognition with intriguing case material.

There is ample reason, then, for some researchers to approach the interview as a set of activities that are ongoingly accomplished, not just completed. In standardized interviewing, one would need to settle conclusively on matters of who the subject behind the respondent is, lest it be impossible to know to which population generalizations can be made. Indeed, a respondent who shifts the subject to whom she is giving voice would pose dramatic technical difficulties for survey researchers, such that, for example, varied parts of a single completed interview would have to be coded as the responses of different subjects and be generalizable to different populations. This takes us well beyond the possibility of coding in the traditional sense of the term, a point that, of course, Harold Garfinkel (1967) and Aaron Cicourel (1964), among others, made years ago and that, oddly enough, inspired the approach Mishler advocates.

OWNERSHIP AND EMPOWERMENT

Having raised these vexing issues, can we ever effectively address the question of who owns the opinions and stories expressed in interviews, including both the standardized interview and the more open-ended, narrative form? Whose "own" story do we obtain in the process of interviewing? Can we ever discern ownership in individual terms? And how does this relate to respondent empowerment?

Recall that ownership implies that the respondent has, or has title to, a story and that the interview can be designed to bring this forth. But the concept of voice suggests that this is not as straightforward as it might seem. The very activity of opening the interview to extended discussion among the participants indicates that ownership can be a joint or collaborative matter, if not rather fleeting in designation. In practice, the idea of "own story" is not just a commendable research goal but something participants themselves seek to resolve as they move through the interview conversation. Each participant tentatively engages the interactive problems of ownership as a way of sorting out the assumed subjectivities in question and proceeds on that basis, for the practical communicative purposes of completing the interview.

When a respondent such as a substance-abusing pharmacist responds to a question about the future, "I've learned [from N.A.] that it's best to take it one day at a time; I really believe that," it is clear that the pharmacist's narrative is more than an individual's story. What he owns would seem to have wended its way through the informing voices of other subjectivities: Narcotics Anonymous's recovery ideology, this particular respondent's articulation of that ideology, the communicative twists on both discourses that emerge in the give-and-take of the interview exchange, the project's own framing of the issues and resulting agenda of questions, the interviewer's ongoing articulation of that agenda, and the reflexively collaborative flow of unforeseen voiced and unvoiced subjectivities operating in the unfolding exchange. What's more, all of these together can raise metacommunicative concerns about "what this [the interview] is all about, anyway," which the respondent might ask at any time. Under the circumstances, it would seem that ownership is something rather diffusely spread about the topical and processual landscape of speech activities entailed in the interview.

Respondent empowerment would appear to be a working, rather than definitive, feature of these speech activities. It is not clear in practice how one could distinguish any one respondent's own story from the tellable stories available to this and other respondents, which they might more or less share. Putting it in terms of "tellable stories" further complicates voice, subjectivity, and empowerment. And, at the other end of the spectrum of what is tellable, there are those perplexing responses that, in the respondent's search for help in formulating an answer, can return "power" to the very source that would hold it in the first place. It is not uncommon to hear respondents remark that they are not sure how they feel or what they think, or that they haven't really thought about the question or topic before, or to hear them actually think out loud about what it might mean personally to convey particular sentiments or answer in a specific way—and ask the interviewer for assistance in doing so.

Philosophically, the central issue here is a version of Ludwig Wittgenstein's (1953) "private language" problem. Wittgenstein argues that because language—and, by implication, stories and other interview responses—is a shared "form of life," the idea that one could have available exclusively to oneself an unshared, private language would not make much sense. Given the reflexive duality of self-consciousness, one could not even share an ostensible private language with oneself. In more practical terms, this means that whatever is conveyed by the respondent to the interviewer is always subject to the question of what it means, in which case we're back to square one with shared knowledge and the various "language games" that can be collaboratively engaged by interview participants to assign meaning to these questions and responses. Empowerment in this context is not so much a matter of providing the communicative means for the respondent to tell his or her "own" story as it is a matter of recognizing, first, that responses or stories, as the case might be, are collaborative accomplishments and, second, that there are as many individual responses or stories to tell as there are recognizable forms of response. This, of course, ultimately brings us full circle to the analytically hoary problem of whose interests are being served when the individually "empowered" respondent speaks, implicating power in relation to the broader social horizons of speech and discourse.

Kirin Narayan and Kenneth George (Chapter 7, this volume) inform us further that empowerment is also a cultural prerogative, something that the interviewer does not expressly control and, given the opportunity, cannot simply choose to put into effect. Cultures of storytelling enter into the decision as to whether there is even a story to convey or relevant experiences to highlight. Although the democratization of opinion potentially turns interviewers toward any and all individuals for their accounts, not all individuals believe that their opinions are worthy of communication. The Asian Indian women Narayan interviewed, for example, did not think they had opinions worth telling unless they had done "something different" with their lives. It had to be something "special"; as one woman put it, "You ate, drank, slept, served your husband and brought up your children. What's the story in that?" This powerfully affected the stories that were heard in the area, tying ownership to the local relevance of one's narrative resources.

GOING CONCERNS AND DISCURSIVE ENVIRONMENTS

Where do tellable stories and other forms of response come from if they are not owned by individuals? How do they figure in what is said in interview situations? It was evident in the previous discussion of the pharmacist drug abuse research that respondents were making use of a very common notion of recovery in today's world, one that seems to have percolated through the entire troubles treatment industry (Gubrium and Holstein 2001). Do this industry and other institutions dealing with human experiences offer us a clue to the question of narrative ownership? Do Narayan's respondents proffer agendas of social, not just individual, relevance?

Erving Goffman's (1961) exploration of what he calls "moral careers" provides a point of departure for addressing such questions. Goffman was especially concerned with the moral careers of stigmatized persons such as mental patients, but the social concerns of his approach are broadly suggestive. In his reckoning, each of us has many selves and associated ways of accounting for our thoughts and actions. According to Goffman, individuals obtain senses of who they are as they move through the various moral environments that offer specifications for identity. A mental hospital, for example, provides patients with particular selves, including ways of presenting who one is, one's past, and one's future. The moral environment of the mental hospital also provides others, such as staff members, acquaintances, and even strangers, with parallel sensibilities toward the patient. In other words, moral environments deploy localized universes of choice for constructing subjectivity, relatedly providing a shared format for voicing participants' selves, thoughts, and feelings. Goffman's view is not so much that these environments govern who and what people are as individuals, but that individuals—everyday actors—strategically play out who and what they are as the moral agents of particular circumstances.

Goffman is mainly concerned with the face-to-face situations that constitute daily life; he is less concerned with institutional matters. Still, his analysis of moral careers in relation to what he calls "total institutions" points us in an important direction, toward what Everett Hughes ([1942] 1984) calls the "going concerns" of today's world. This is Hughes's way of emphasizing that institutions are not only concerns in having formal and informal mandates; they are social forms that *ongoingly* provide distinct patterning for our thoughts, words, sentiments, and actions.

From the myriad formal organizations in which we work, study, pray, play, and recover to the countless informal associations and networks to which we belong, to our affiliations with racial, ethnic, and gendered groupings, we engage a panoply of going concerns on a daily basis. Taken together, they set the "conditions of possibility" (Foucault 1988) for identity—for who and what we could possibly be. Many of these going concerns explicitly structure or reconfigure personal identity. All variety of human service agencies, for example, readily delve into the deepest enclaves of the self in order to ameliorate personal ills.

Self-help organizations seem to crop up on every street corner, and self-help literature beckons us from the book spindles of supermarkets and the shelves of every bookstore. "Psychobabble" on radio and TV talk shows constantly prompts us to formulate (or reformulate) who and what we are, urging us to give voice to the selves we live by. The self is increasingly *deprivatized* (even if it never was private in Wittgenstein's terms in the first place), constructed and interpreted under the auspices of these decidedly public going concerns (Gubrium and Holstein 1995, 2000; Holstein and Gubrium 2000).

Since early in the 20th century, social life has come into the purview of countless institutions whose moral function is to assemble, alter, and reformulate our lives and selves (see Gubrium and Holstein 2001). We refer to these as *discursive environments* because they provide choices for how we articulate our lives and selves. Discursive environments are interactional domains characterized by distinctive ways of interpreting and representing everyday life, of speaking about who and what we are. Institutions such as schools, correctional facilities, clinics, family courts, support groups, recreational clubs, fitness centers, and self-improvement programs promote particular ways of speaking of life. They are families of language games, as it were, for formulating our opinions. They furnish discourses of subjectivity that are accountably put into discursive practice as individuals give voice to experience, such as they are now widely asked to do in interviews.

These going concerns pose new challenges to the concept of the individual respondent, to voice, and to the idea of empowerment. They are not especially hostile to the personal; indeed, they are often in the business of reconstructing the personal from the ground up. Rather, today's variegated landscape of discursive environments provides complex options for who we could be, the conditions of possibility we mentioned earlier. This is the world of multiple subjects and of ways to give voice to

them that respondents now increasingly bring with them into interviews, whose discursive resources also figure significantly in marking narrative relevance.

In turn, these environments also provide the source of socially relevant questions that interviewers pose to respondents. Those who conduct surveys, for example, are often sponsored by the very agents who formulate these applicable discourses. The collaborative production of the respondent's own story is therefore shaped, for better or worse, in response to markets and concerns spread well beyond the give-and-take of the individual interview conversation.

This brings us back, full circle, to the interview society. The research context is not the only place in which we are asked interview questions. All the going concerns mentioned above and more are in the interviewing business, all constructing and marshaling the subjects they need to do their work. Each provides a social context for narrative practice, for the collaborative production of the identities and experiences that come to be viewed as the moral equivalents of respondents and interview responses. Medical clinics deploy interviews and, in the process, assemble doctors, patients, and their illnesses. Personnel officers interview job applicants and collect information that forms the basis for employment decisions. Therapists of all stripes conduct counseling interviews, and now increasingly assemble narrative plots of experiences, which are grounds for further rehabilitative interviewing. The same is true for schools, forensic investigation, and journalistic interviewing, among the broad range of institutional contexts that shape our lives through their collaborative speech activities.

The interview society expands the institutional auspices of interviewing well beyond the research context. Indeed, it would be a mistake to limit this to the research interview alone. Social research is only one of the many sites where subjectivities and the voicing of individual experience are undertaken. What's more, these various going concerns cannot be considered to be independent of one another. As our pharmacist anecdote suggests, the discursive environments of therapy and recovery can be brought directly into the research interview, serving to commingle an agglomeration of institutional voices.

Interview formats are themselves going concerns. The group interview, for example, can take us into a veritable swirl of subject formations and opinion construction, as participants share and make use of narrative material from a broader range of discursive environments than any single one of them might muster to account for his or her experience alone. Life story and oral history interviews extend the biographical particulars of the subject and subject matter in time, producing respondents who are incited to trace opinion from early to late life and across eras, something that can be amazingly convoluted when compared to the commonly detemporalized information elicited from cross-sectional survey respondents (see in this volume Cándida Smith, Chapter 11). The in-depth interview extends experience in emotional terms, affectively elaborating the subject.

◆ *Artfulness and*
  Narrative Practice

Lest we socially overdetermine subjectivity, it is important to emphasize that the practice of interviewing does not simply incorporate wholesale the identities proffered by institutionalized concerns and cultural relevancies. Interview participants themselves are actively involved in how these subjectivities are put into play. Although varied institutional auspices provide particular resources for asking and answering questions, prescribe the roles played by interview participants, and privilege certain accounts, interview participants do not behave like robots and adopt and reproduce these resources and roles in their speech activities. If participants are accountable to particular circumstances, such as job interviews, medical diagnostic encounters, or journalistic interviews, they nonetheless borrow from the variety of narrative resources available to them. In this regard, they are more "artful" (Garfinkel 1967) than automatic in realizing their respective roles and voices. This extends to all interview participants, as both interviewers and respondents collaboratively assemble who and what they are in narrative practice.

Our pharmacist anecdote is an important case in point. Although the interviews in question were formal research encounters, it was evident that respondents were not only reporting their "own" experiences, but were interpolating their "own" stories, in part, in N.A. recovery terms. They drew from their experiences in recovery groups to convey to the interviewer what it felt like to be "taken over" by drugs. Several respondents used the familiar metaphor of "hitting bottom" to convey a trajectory for the experience. But these respondents were not simply mouthpieces for Narcotics Anonymous; they gave their own individual spins to the terminology, which, in turn, were selectively applied in their responses. For example, "hitting bottom" meant different things to different respondents, depending on the biographical particulars of their lives. How hitting bottom narratively figured in one respondent's comments was no guarantee of how it might figure in another's.

Interviewers, too, are artful in coordinating the interview process, even in the context of the standardized survey, which employs rather formalized procedures. In some forms of interviewing, such as in-depth interviews, interviewers may use all of the personal narrative resources at their disposal to establish open and trusting relationships with respondents. This may involve extensive self-disclosure, following on the assumption that reciprocal self-disclosure is likely.

Taking this a step farther, a growing postmodern trend in interviewing deliberately blurs the line between the interviewer and the respondent, moving beyond symmetry to a considerable overlap of roles (see Fontana, Chapter 3, this volume). Although this may have been characteristic of in-depth interviewing for years, postmodern sensibilities aim for an associated representational inventiveness as much as deep disclosure. Artfulness extends to the representation of interviewers' and researchers' own reflective collaborations in moving from respondent to respondent as the project develops, as Carolyn Ellis and Leigh Berger show in their contribution to this volume (Chapter 9). Of course, interviewers and their sponsoring researchers have always collaborated on the design of interviews and offered collaborative feedback to one another on the interview process. But there is a distinct difference here: Ellis and Berger choose not to separate this from their interview materials. In layered writing, they provide us with an intriguing account of how interviewers interviewing each other artfully and fruitfully combine the interview "data" with their own related life experiences to broaden and enrich the results. Their reflections collaboratively impel them forward to complete additional interviews and revisit old ones in new and interesting ways. The separation in conventional research reports of interviewers' experiences from those of respondents, they argue, is highly artificial and produces sanitized portrayals of the "data" in question. According to Ellis and Berger, researchers may capture collaborative richness by forthrightly presenting the full round of narrative practices that generate responses. Artfulness derives from the interpretive work that is undertaken in mingling together what interviewers draw upon to make meaning in the interview process and what respondents themselves bring along.

Further blurring boundaries, Narayan and George (Chapter 7, this volume) provide a delightful jaunt through the artful relationship between what they call personal narratives and folk narratives. The former allegedly are the idiosyncratic individual stories that anthropologists regularly encounter in their fieldwork, accounts of experience considered to be peculiar to their storytellers. Folk narratives, in contrast, are ostensibly those shared tales of experience common to a group or culture. They are part of the narrative tradition and, in their telling, are a cultural accounting of the experiences in question. But, as Narayan and George explain, in their respective attempts to obtain life stories from respondents in various parts of the globe, what was personal and what was folk was never clearly demarcated. Individual respondents made use of what was shared to represent themselves as individuals, so that, narratively, who any "one" was, was mediated artfully by various applications of common usage. In turn, the cultural particulars embodied in folktales were constantly being applied in both old and new ways in personal accounts. Biography and culture, in other words, were mutually implicative and alive in their narrative renderings; their interviews both reproduced and invented participants' lives (see also Abu-Lughod 1993; Behar 1993; Degh 1969; Narayan 1997).

In some sense, then, although the aim of empowering respondents is certainly attractive and to be encouraged in principle, interview participants are always already "empowered" to engage artfully in a vast range of discursive practices. Even "asymmetrical" interview conversations require the active involvement of both parties. Although interview preferences and politics move in various directions, interview participants nonetheless actively and artfully engage the auspices of the interview and their own biographies at many levels. As Foucault might put it, power is everywhere in the interview's exploration and explication of experience. Even the standardized survey interview, which seemingly allocates all power to the researcher, deploys it elsewhere in the collaboratively constructive vocalization of "individual" opinion.

◆ Interviewing as Cultural Production

The interview is certainly more than what it seemed to be at the start of this chapter; we have taken it well beyond a simple and self-evident encounter between interviewer and respondent. As we moved from the individual interview to the interview society, we noted that the interview is among our most commonplace means for constructing individualized experience. We recognized, too, that by virtue of our widespread participation in interviews, each and every one of us is implicated in the production of who and what we are as the collection of individual subjects that populate our lives.

Of course, interviewing is found in places where it has been for decades, such as in applying for jobs, in clinical encounters, and in the telephone surveys of public opinion polling. But it has also penetrated formerly hidden spaces, such as the foothills of the Himalayas and the everyday worlds of children and the seriously ill. Interviews are everywhere these days, as researchers pursue respondents to the ends of the earth, as we offer our opinions and preferences to pollsters, in Internet questionnaires, and to marketing researchers, as we bare our souls to therapists and healers in the "privacy" of the clinic as well as in the mass media.

With its penetration and globalization, the interview has become a worldwide form of cultural production. Regardless of social venue or geographic location—characteristics that were once argued to be empirically distinct or interpersonally isolating—the methodical application of interview technology is bringing us into a single world of accounts and accountability. Despite its community borders and national and linguistic boundaries, it is a world that can be described in the common language of sample characteristics and whose subjectivities can be represented in terms of individualized voices. Whereas we once might have refrained from examining Asian village women's stories in relation to the accounts of their urban European counterparts—because the two groups were understood to be culturally and geographically distinct—the women's ability to respond to interviews now makes it possible for us to compare their experiences in the same methodological terms.

The interview is such a common information-gathering procedure that it seems to bring all experience together narratively. Of course, there are technical challenges and local narrative solutions that cannot be overlooked. But technology is only the procedural scaffolding of what is a broad culturally productive enterprise. More and more, the interview society provides both a sense of who we are and the method by which we represent ourselves and our experiences. The interview is part and parcel of society, not simply a mode of inquiry into and about society. If it is part of, not just a conduit to, our personal lives, then we might well entertain the possibility that the interview's ubiquity serves to produce communicatively and ramify the very culture it ostensibly only inquires about.

■ References

Abu-Lughod, L. 1993. *Writing Women's Worlds: Bedouin Stories.* Berkeley: University of California Press.
Alasuutari, P. 1998. *An Invitation to Social Research.* London: Sage.

Atkinson, P. and D. Silverman. 1997. "Kundera's *Immortality*: The Interview Society and the Invention of Self." *Qualitative Inquiry* 3:304-25.

Balint, M. 1964. *The Doctor, His Patient, and the Illness.* London: Pitman.

Behar, R. 1993. *Translated Woman: Crossing the Border with Esperanza's Story.* Boston: Beacon.

Benney, M. and E. C. Hughes. 1956. "Of Sociology and the Interview." *American Journal of Sociology* 62:137-42.

Briggs, C. L. 1986. *Learning How to Ask: A Sociolinguistic Appraisal of the Role of the Interview in Social Science Research.* Cambridge: Cambridge University Press.

Carrithers, M., S. Collins, and S. Lukes, eds. 1985. *The Category of the Person.* Cambridge: Cambridge University Press.

Cicourel, A. V. 1964. *Method and Measurement in Sociology.* New York: Free Press.

———. 1967. "Fertility, Family Planning, and the Social Organization of Family Life: Some Methodological Issues." *Journal of Social Issues* 23:57-81.

———. 1982. "Interviews, Surveys, and the Problem of Ecological Validity." *American Sociologist* 17:11-20.

Clifford, J. and G. E. Marcus, eds. 1986. *Writing Culture: The Poetics and Politics of Ethnography.* Berkeley: University of California Press.

Converse, J. M. and H. Schuman. 1974. *Conversations at Random: Survey Research as Interviewers See It.* New York: John Wiley.

Degh, L. 1969. *Folktales and Society: Story Telling in a Hungarian Peasant Community.* Translated by E. M. Schossberger. Bloomington: Indiana University Press.

Dreyfus, H. L. and P. Rabinow. 1982. *Michel Foucault: Beyond Structuralism and Hermeneutics.* Chicago: University of Chicago Press.

Ellis, C. and A. P. Bochner, eds. 1996. *Composing Ethnography: Alternative Forms of Qualitative Writing.* Walnut Creek, CA: AltaMira.

Ellis, C. and M. G. Flaherty, eds. 1992. *Investigating Subjectivity: Research on Lived Experience.* Newbury Park, CA: Sage.

Erikson, K. T. 1976. *Everything in Its Path: Destruction of Community in the Buffalo Creek Flood.* New York: Simon & Schuster.

Fishbein, M., ed. 1967. *Readings in Attitude Theory and Measurement.* New York: John Wiley.

Foucault, M. 1973. *Madness and Civilization: A History of Insanity in the Age of Reason.* New York: Vintage.

———. 1975. *The Birth of the Clinic: An Archeology of Medical Perception.* New York: Vintage.

———. 1977. *Discipline and Punish: The Birth of the Prison.* Translated by A. M. Sheridan. New York: Vintage.

———. 1978. *The History of Sexuality,* Vol. 1, *An Introduction.* Translated by R. Hurley. New York: Vintage.

———. 1988. *Technologies of the Self.* Edited by L. H. Martin, H. Gutman, and P. H. Hutton. Amherst: University of Massachusetts Press.

Garfinkel, H. 1967. *Studies in Ethnomethodology.* Englewood Cliffs, NJ: Prentice Hall.

Garland, D. 1997. " 'Governmentality' and the Problem of Crime." *Theoretical Criminology* 1:173-214.

Geertz, C. 1984. " 'From the Native's Point of View': On the Nature of Anthropological Understanding." Pp. 123-37 in *Culture Theory,* edited by R. A. Shweder and R. LeVine. Cambridge: Cambridge University Press.

Goffman, E. 1961. *Asylums: Essays on the Social Situation of Mental Patients and Other Inmates.* Garden City, NY: Doubleday.

Gubrium, J. F. 1988. "Incommunicables and Poetic Documentation in the Alzheimer's Disease Experience." *Semiotica* 72:235-53.

———. 1993. "Voice and Context in a New Gerontology." Pp. 46-63 in *Voices and Visions of Aging: Toward a Critical Gerontology,* edited by T. R. Cole, W. A. Achenbaum, P. L. Jakobi, and R. Kastenbaum. New York: Springer.

Gubrium, J. F. and J. A. Holstein. 1995. "Qualitative Inquiry and the Deprivatization of Experience." *Qualitative Inquiry* 1:204-22.

———. 1997. *The New Language of Qualitative Method.* New York: Oxford University Press.

———. 2000. "The Self in a World of Going Concerns." *Symbolic Interaction* 23:95-115.

———, eds. 2001. *Institutional Selves: Troubled Identities in a Postmodern World.* New York: Oxford University Press.

Gumperz, J. J. 1982. *Discourse Strategies.* Cambridge: Cambridge University Press.

Holstein, J. A. and J. F. Gubrium. 1995. *The Active Interview.* Thousand Oaks, CA: Sage.

———. 2000. *The Self We Live By: Narrative Identity in a Postmodern World.* New York: Oxford University Press.

Hughes, E. C. [1942] 1984. *The Sociological Eye: Selected Papers.* Chicago: Aldine.

Hymes, D. 1967. "Models of the Interaction of Language and Social Setting." *Journal of Social Issues* 33:8-28.

James, W. [1892] 1961. *Psychology: The Briefer Course.* New York: Harper & Brothers.

Kahn, R. L. and C. F. Cannell. 1957. *The Dynamics of Interviewing: Theory, Technique, and Cases.* New York: John Wiley.

Kent, R. 1981. *A History of British Empirical Sociology.* Farnborough, England: Gower.

Lidz, T. 1976. *The Person.* New York: Basic.

Maccoby, E. E. and N. Maccoby. 1954. "The Interview: A Tool of Social Science." Pp. 449-87 in *Handbook of Social Psychology,* Vol. 1, edited by G. Lindzey. Reading, MA: Addison-Wesley.

Miller, J. 1993. *The Passion of Michel Foucault.* Garden City, NY: Doubleday.

Mishler, E. G. 1984. *The Discourse of Medicine: Dialectics of Medical Interviews.* Norwood, NJ: Ablex.

———. 1986. *Research Interviewing: Context and Narrative.* Cambridge, MA: Harvard University Press.

Narayan, K., in collaboration with U. D. Sood. 1997. *Mondays on the Dark Night of the Moon: Himalayan Foothill Folktales.* New York: Oxford University Press.

Oberschall, A. 1965. *Empirical Social Research in Germany.* Paris: Mouton.

Pool, I. de S. 1957. "A Critique of the Twentieth Anniversary Issue." *Public Opinion Quarterly* 21:190-98.

Reed-Danahay, D. E., ed. 1997. *Auto/Ethnography: Rewriting the Self and the Social.* New York: Berg.

Riesman, D. and M. Benney. 1956. "Asking and Answering." *Journal of Business of the University of Chicago* 29:225-36.

Rose, N. 1990. *Governing the Soul: The Shaping of the Private Self.* London: Routledge.

———. 1997. *Inventing Ourselves: Psychology, Power, and Personhood.* Cambridge: Cambridge University Press.

Rubin, H. J. and I. S. Rubin. 1995. *Qualitative Interviewing: The Art of Hearing Data.* Thousand Oaks, CA: Sage.

Sacks, H. 1992. *Lectures on Conversation,* Vols. 1-2. Edited by G. Jefferson. Oxford: Blackwell.

Sacks, H., E. A. Schegloff, and G. Jefferson. 1974. "A Simplest Systematics for the Organization of Turn-Taking for Conversation." *Language* 50:696-735.

Selvin, H. C. 1985. "Durkheim, Booth and Yule: The Non-Diffusion of an Intellectual Innovation." Pp. 70-82 in *Essays on the History of British Sociological Research,* edited by M. Bulmer. Cambridge: Cambridge University Press.

Silverman, D. 1987. *Communication and Medical Practice.* London: Sage.

———. 1993. *Interpreting Qualitative Data: Methods for Analysing Talk, Text and Interaction.* London: Sage.

———. 1997. *Qualitative Research: Theory, Method and Practice.* London: Sage.

Terkel, S. 1972. *Working: People Talk about What They Do All Day and How They Feel about It.* New York: Pantheon.

Weiss, R. S. 1994. *Learning from Strangers: The Art and Method of Qualitative Interview Studies.* New York: Free Press.

Wittgenstein, L. 1953. *Philosophical Investigations.* New York: Macmillan.

3

POSTMODERN TRENDS IN INTERVIEWING

◆ **Andrea Fontana**

Postmodernism has changed our society, the way in which we conceive of it, and the way we see ourselves and relate to others. Whether we consider postmodernism a radical break from modernism or merely modernism's continuation, profound changes have occurred (see Best and Kellner 1991; Dickens and Fontana 1994). We are no longer awed by metatheories about the nature of society and the self (Lyotard 1984), theories that we now question and deconstruct. Today, we focus on smaller parcels of knowledge; we study society in its fragments, in its daily details (Silverman 1997). Postmodernism has affected many fields, from architecture to literary criticism, from anthropology to sociology. It has provided few answers but raised more questions, rendering the reality of the world extremely problematic. Postmodernism also has changed the very nature of experience. The everyday world and the world of media have been merged (Baudrillard 1983), and as the boundaries between the two have collapsed, experience is mediated by the "hyperreality" of the likes of Disneyland, *Real TV,* and *The Jerry Springer Show,* where the imaginary becomes real and the real imaginary (see Denzin, Chapter 8, this volume).

Influenced by postmodern epistemologies, interviewing also has changed; ours has become "the interview society" (Silverman 1993; Atkinson and Silverman 1997). Interviewing is no longer reserved for social researchers or investigative reporters, but has become the very stuff of life as members of society spend much of their time asking questions, being asked questions themselves, or watching TV shows about people being asked questions and answering them in turn. They all seem to have routine knowledge of the rules of interviewing, with no need for instruction.

In this chapter, I discuss postmodern trends in interviewing. I begin by outlining some of the postmodern sensibilities that are relevant to interviewing. Although there is no such a thing as postmodern interviewing per se, postmodern epistemologies have profoundly influenced our understanding of the interview process, so that approaches increasingly take on a postmodern cast. Perhaps it is appropriate, then, given that postmodernism advocates the blurring and fragmentation of theories and methods, that I can present only fragments of postmodern-informed interviewing rather than an overarching, modernistic formulation of "the" postmodern interview.[1]

◆ Postmodernism and Its Influence

Postmodernism, which is not a unified system of beliefs, has been presented and interpreted in a diversity of ways. It can be seen as a crisis of representation in a great variety of fields, from the arts to the sciences, and more generally in society at large (Dickens and Fontana 1994). It has been conceptualized both as the continuation of modernism and as a break from it. In some views, postmodernism advocates abandoning overarching paradigms and theoretical and methodological metasystems (Lyotard 1984). Postmodernism questions traditional assumptions and deconstructs them (Derrida 1972); that is, it shows the ambiguity and contextuality of meaning. It proposes that, in the name of grand theorizing, we have suppressed this ambiguity in favor of a single interpretation, which is commonly touted as "the truth," rather than a choice among many possible truths. Postmodernism orients to theorizing and, indeed, to society itself, not as a monolithic structure but as a series of fragments in continuous flux. It persuades us to turn our attention to these fragments, to the minute events of everyday life, seeking to understand them in their own right rather than gloss over differences and patch them together into paradigmatic wholes (Silverman 1997).

POSTMODERN SENSIBILITIES AND INTERVIEWING

Postmodern sensibilities have greatly affected the methodologies used by social scientists. Researchers influenced by a postmodern agenda have come to display a greatly heightened sensitivity to problems and concerns that previously had been glossed over or scantily addressed. These can be briefly described as follows:

◆ The boundaries between, and respective roles, of interviewer and interviewee have become blurred as the traditional relationship between the two is no longer seen as natural (see Ellis and Berger, Chapter 9, this volume).

◆ New forms of communication in interviewing are being used, as interviewer and respondent(s) collaborate together in constructing their narratives.

◆ Interviewers have become more concerned about issues of representation, seriously engaging questions such as, Whose story are we telling and for what purpose?

◆ The authority of the researcher qua interviewer but also qua writer comes under scrutiny (see Briggs, Chapter 13, this volume). Respondents are no longer seen as faceless numbers whose opinions we process completely on our own terms. Consequently, there is increasing concern with the respondent's own understanding as he or she frames and represents an "opinion."

◆ Traditional patriarchal relations in interviewing are being criticized, and ways to make formerly unarticulated voices audible are now center stage.

◆ The forms used to report findings have been hugely expanded. As boundaries separating disciplines collapse, modes of expression from literature, poetry, and drama are being applied (see in this volume Ellis and Berger, Chapter 9;

Richardson, Chapter 10; Rosenblatt, Chapter 12).

◆ The topic of inquiry—interviewing—has expanded to encompass the cinematic and the televisual. Electronic media are increasingly accepted as a resource in interviews, with growing use of e-mail, Internet chat rooms, and other electronic modes of communication (see in this volume Mann and Stewart, Chapter 5; Denzin, Chapter 8).

These sensibilities, some of which are now old and some new, provide a context for methodological exploration. Let us consider, initially, how these have informed and affected traditional interview roles. Note, especially, that some ostensibly postmodern trends have been close to the heart of qualitative inquiry for decades.

◆ From Traditional to Postmodern-Informed Interviewing

Traditional, structured interviewing establishes a priori categories and then asks pre-established questions aimed at capturing precise data that can be categorized, codified, and generalized. The aim is to provide explanations about the social world. The method assumes that there is a set of discreet facts to be apprehended in the social world and that we can garner them through the use of rigorous techniques. The language of science permeates these techniques. The interviewer is not unlike a highly trained instrument and remains substantively detached from the situation and the respondent. Responses are quantifiable and allow generalizations about society. Ideally, respondents can be viewed as "rational beings" in that they understand all possible choices presented to them and answer as comprehensively and truthfully as possible.

CRITIQUES OF THE DETACHED INTERVIEWER

Some critics claim that the method of traditional interviewing is much more like science fiction than science, a perspective that has not been lost on qualitative researchers. Herbert Blumer (1969), for one, prefaces the introduction of his book *Symbolic Interactionism* with an insightful critique of traditional methodologies. The seminal work of Aaron Cicourel also is a milestone in unveiling the myth of "scientific" interviewing. Cicourel (1964) refers to the hidden complexity of the interview situation:

> All social research includes an unknown number of implicit decisions which are not mirrored in the measurement procedures used. The abstraction process required to describe a set of properties, regardless of the measurement system, automatically imposes some amount of reification. (P. 80)

Discussing and quoting the work of Herbert Hyman and other survey researchers, Cicourel adds, "The authors are not aware that too much stress has been placed on asking questions and recording answers, and that the interviewer is overlooking . . . the many judgments *he made* in the process" (p. 91). Cicourel goes on to suggest that the interview is an interactional event based on reciprocal stocks of knowledge, a point I shall take up again in discussing phenomenological influences on postmodern trends.

The response of interactionist sociologists to problems inherent in structured interviewing was to move interviewers center stage as constructive agents and acknowledge their influence on interview outcomes. They also recognized the importance of feelings on the part of both the interviewer and the respondent, as well as the possibility of deceit in the interview situation. Jack Douglas (1985), in his book *Creative Interviewing*, advocates lengthy, unstructured interviews in which the interviewer uses his or her *personal* skills by adapting to the changing interactional situation of the interview. For Douglas, the creativity is cultivated by the interviewer, who attempts inventively to reach a mutual understanding and intimacy of feelings with the interviewee. Still, it has been pointed out that the interviewee remains a rather passive participant even in this context. Jaber Gubrium and James Holstein (1997; Holstein and Gubrium 1995) consider Douglas's interviewing techniques decidedly "romantic." As they explain, "Douglas imagines his subject, like the image implicit in survey research, to be a repository of answers, but in his case, the subject is a well guarded vessel of feelings not simply a collection of attitudes and opinions" (Gubrium and Holstein 1997:65).

EMERGING VOICES OF INTERVIEWEES

In the 1980s, new trends appeared in qualitative sociology, in both ethnography and interviewing, as researchers attempted to secure the constructive voices of research subjects. Some were concerned with the authorial voice of the researcher speaking for his or her subjects (Van Maanen 1988; Geertz 1988); others took a broader epistemological approach (Marcus and Fischer 1986).

George Marcus and Michael Fischer (1986) gave widely appreciated special attention to these issues. Marcus and Fischer were concerned with the authority of traditional ethnographic texts, commonly derived through a combination of ethnographic work and in-depth interviews. They also addressed problems of representation and selectivity generated by the privileged position of the researcher both as a field-worker and as an author. Marcus and Fischer felt that in "modernistic" interviewing, the researcher is in control of the narrative and highlights what best conveys, in his or her judgment, the social worlds of those being studied (see the discussion of "representational rights" in Briggs, Chapter 13, this volume).

Marcus and Fischer present postmodern alternatives in anthropology that allow diverse voices to come through. Some of these alternatives apply to interviewing as well as to ethnography. One is the need to take a "dialogic" approach, in which the focus is "on the dialogue between anthropologist and informant as a way of exposing how ethnographic knowledge develops" (Marcus and Fischer 1986:69). An exemplar of this work is Kevin Dwyer's (1982) *Moroccan Dialogues,* in which the interviews are only minimally edited and show the problematic nature of interviewing for all participants. Another is the use of "polyphony," which is "the registering of different points of views in multiple voices" (Marcus and Fischer 1986:71). The aim here is to reduce the editorial authority of the researcher. Another alternative is found in Vincent Crapanzano's (1980) ethnography *Tuhami: Portrait of a Moroccan,* where the author presents transcripts from interviews and minimizes his interpretation of them, inviting the reader to help in the process of interpretation. This is rendered more difficult by the informant, Tuhami, who uses complex metaphors in his communication with the researcher, mixing real events with fantasy, both of which Crapanzano takes as valid data.

In sociological work we find similar trends. Susan Krieger (1983) focuses on polyphony by presenting the various perspectives of respondents, highlighting discrepancies and problems rather than minimizing them. Allen Shelton (1995), in a study of victimization, social process, and resistance, uses the machine and other powerful metaphors to convey his message. He mixes sociological data with stories from his past, using visual imagery from paintings to underscore his points. In another context, Shelton (1996) even goes back to the vespers to compellingly embellish his sociological findings.

Norman Denzin's work is a major impetus for applying postmodern sensibilities to research methodology (see Denzin, Chapter 8, this volume). Denzin (1989) focuses on "the meanings persons give to themselves and their life projects" (pp. 14-15). Key elements of the approach are the essentially *interpretive* nature of fieldwork and interviewing and the attempt to let the members *speak for themselves*. In particular, Denzin borrows the concept of epiphanies from James Joyce and orients to these as turning points that reshape people's lives, which, in turn, have significant implications for the selection of interview topics. By focusing on these existential moments, Denzin believes, we can gain access to the otherwise hidden feelings experienced by individuals and bring them to the fore for others to appreciate.

Denzin (1997) continues his dialogue with postmodernism in more recent work, but becomes more distinctly partisan. Here, again, he begins with Joyce and the concern for meaning as perceived by the members of society. However, he is no longer happy with just trying to understand and make these meanings visible. He has become more politically involved with his research subjects. He rejects the traditional canons of researcher noninvolvement and objectivity, and instead advocates "partnership" between researcher and subjects. He is especially partial to subjects' "underdog" status: "This model seeks to produce narratives that ennoble human experiences while facilitating civic transformation in the public (and private) spheres" (p. 277).

In summary, one path from traditional to postmodern-informed interviewing is that the so-called detached researcher and interviewer are recast as active agents in the interview process and attempts are made to deprivilege their agency. Another path is that the interviewee's agency is privileged and, in the name of the interviewee, all manner of experimentation is undertaken to make evident his or her own sense of identity and representational practices. I turn now to the influences of various theo-

retical perspectives on this trend; following that, I will consider how this has affected representational practices for interview material.

◆ Phenomenologically Informed Interviews

Phenomenological sociology first appeared in the 1960s, loosely based on the philosophy of Edmund Husserl and the writings of the social philosopher Alfred Schutz. It is in Cicourel's (1964) work that we see the tie between phenomenology and interviewing most clearly, even as in Harold Garfinkel's (1967) own project there is an added phenomenological influence through ethnomethodology.

Cicourel argues forcefully early on that the interview, no matter how technically perfected its execution, is grounded in the world of commonsense thinking. In fact, according to Cicourel, it must be so, for without the participants' ability to share common or overlapping social worlds and their related communicative understanding, the interview would not be possible. Cicourel follows in Schutz's (1962, 1964, 1966) footsteps here. Schutz discusses the way that members of society share a common stock of knowledge that allows them to understand and reciprocate actions. This extends to markedly mundane and shared knowledge, such as speaking in the same language, knowing that the sun will set, that peanut butter will stick to the roof of your mouth, that the Chicago Cubs will never win the World Series, and that Pamela Anderson's beauty is surgically enhanced.

Years later, following postmodern trends, Irving Seidman resurrects Schutz's sentiments in his book *Interviewing as Qualitative Research* (1991). Seidman explains that by establishing an "I-thou" relationship or reciprocity of perspectives, the interviewee (I) and the interviewer (thou) form a personal relationship. The result is that the interviewee is no longer objectified but becomes a comember of a communicative partnership. In fact, in some instances, this may blossom into a full "we" relationship, according to Seidman (for an example, see Denzin's 1997 model of "collaboration").

Robert Dingwall (1997) seems to be rediscovering these sentiments when he states:

> If the interview is a social encounter, then, logically, it must be analyzed in the same way as any other social encounter. The products of an interview are the outcome of a socially situated activity where the responses are passed through the role-playing and impression management of both the interviewer and the respondent. (P. 56)

Dingwall adds elements of Goffman's dramaturgical view to the basic notions, which he attributes to both Mead and Schutz. Both within and outside of the interview, action is mediated by others' responses and their co-contingent dramatic realizations. According to Dingwall, individuals in interviews provide organizing accounts; that is, they turn the helter-skelter, fragmented process of everyday life into coherent explanations, thus cocreating a situationally cohesive sense of reality.

ETHNOMETHODOLOGICAL IMPULSES

Ethnomethodologists put forward similar sentiments. They share a skeptical approach to standardized methodologies. Garfinkel (1967), for one, informs us that we cannot study social interaction except in relation to the interactive methods employed by social actors themselves to create and maintain their sense of reality. As such, the impulse in interview research would be to attend as much to *how* participants assemble their respective communications as

to *what* is asked and answered (Boden and Zimmerman 1991; Maynard et al. 2001).

Recently, Holstein and Gubrium (1995) have directly linked ethnomethodology with these distinctive questions in their discussion of the "active interview." They specifically apply to interviewing the perspective that the interview is a social production between interviewer and respondent. In other words, it entails collaborative construction between two *active* parties. Because the interview is situationally and contextually produced, it is itself a site for knowledge production, rather than simply a neutral conduit for experiential knowledge, as traditionally believed.

Holstein and Gubrium are further inspired by the ethnomethodological distinction between *topics* (substantive elements of inquiry) and *resources* (procedures used to study the topics) (see Zimmerman and Pollner 1970). They point out that, in interviews, researchers focus too much on the *whats,* or substantive foreground, and tend to gloss over the *hows,* which "refer to the interactional, narrative procedures of knowledge production, not merely to interview techniques" (p. 4). Indeed, given the irremediably collaborative and constructed nature of the interview, a postmodern sentiment would behoove us to pay more attention to the *hows,* that is, to try to understand the biographical, contextual, historical, and institutional elements that are brought to the interview and used by both parties. The interview should be understood in light all of these elements, rather than as a discreet, neutral set of questions and ensuing responses, detached from both the interviewer's and the respondent's constructive and culturally informed agency.

Gubrium and Holstein (1998) continue this line of thinking in a discussion of personal narratives. Their point of departure is the argument that life comes to us in the form of stories, and personal narratives are approached as individualized constructions. In conveying life to us, respondents tell us stories about themselves, but they do not do so in a social vacuum. Rather, as Gubrium and Holstein explain, "personal accounts are built up from experience and actively cast in the terms of preferred vocabularies" (p. 164; compare Garfinkel 1967). A postmodern trend emphasizing social construction is evident in their goal: "We want to make visible the way narrative activities play out in everyday practice to both produce coherence and reveal difference" (p. 165).

Others share similar perspectives. The late Madan Sarup (1996), in analyzing the role of narrative in the construction of identity, distinguishes two parts to each narrative: "The story is the 'what' of the narrative, the discourse is the 'how' " (p. 170). And more: "When we talk about our identity and our life-story, we include some things and exclude others, we stress some things and subordinate others" (p. 16). Although Sarup's focus is identity, the message is much the same—the story (and its identities) is constructed in its communicative unfolding.

Dingwall (1997) takes this impulse further. Following Garfinkel, he states that interviews are "an occasion for the elicitation of *accounts*" and that "accounting is how we build a stable order in social encounters and in society" (pp. 56, 57). Applying this to interviews, Dingwall concludes: "An interview is a point at which order is deliberately put under stress. It is a situation in which respondents are required to demonstrate their competence in the role in which the interview casts them" (p. 58). Once more, we are directed to the collaborative production of contextually based accounts.

◆ Feminist Influences

In analyzing the images of a nude man with his arm raised in greeting and a nude woman imprinted on the *Pioneer* spacecraft, Craig Owens (1983) states: "For in this (Lacanian) image, chosen to represent the inhabitants of Earth for the extraterrestrial Other, it is the man who speaks, who represents mankind. The woman is only represented; she is (as always) already spoken for" (p. 61). It has been much the same in the methodological world of interviewing; women have always already been spoken for in the very structure of the traditional interview. This is exemplified in Earl Babbie's (1992) classic text on research, which has nothing to say about gender differences in interviewing. Indeed, as Carol Warren (1988) reports, female researchers in primitive patriarchal societies were, at times, temporarily "promoted" to the role of male in order to be allowed to witness events and ceremonies from which women were traditionally excluded.

Not any longer. One of the significant influences on the postmodern trends in interviewing comes from feminist quarters (see Hertz 1997). An ongoing concern has been the elastic subject position of the respondent. A leading question here, for example, is, Do women always speak as women, or are other important subject positions part of their response repertoires? If feminists have focused on gender differences, they have not ignored other important factors, such as race.[2] For instance, Kim Marie Vaz (1997) has edited an interdisciplinary book about African and African American women to "unearth" their experiences by telling personal portraits, focusing on how both their gender and their race have affected them. Patricia Hill Collins (1990) uses interviews as well as autobiographical accounts, songs, images, and fiction to bring out the viewpoints of black women. Her interviews are hardly "detached," as they are shaped to provide a sympathetic context for making visible the experiences of being both black and women.

Kath Weston (1998) explores another traditionally silenced subjectivity, sexual nonconformity. As she recounts, "Back in graduate school, when I first decided to study lesbians and gay men in the United States, the faculty members who mentored me pronounced the project 'academic suicide' " (p. 190). Weston persevered nevertheless and, in her book *Long Slow Burn* (1998) she rejects the idea that sexuality is merely a sociological specialization; rather, she considers sexuality as being at the often silent heart of the social sciences, deeply implicating the subject. We infer from this that the interview that realizes alternative sexualities can serve to reveal the sexual contours of all subject positions.

Contrary to the traditional belief that the relation between interviewer and interviewee is neutral and the results of the interview can be treated as independent of the interview process as long as the interviewer is methodologically skilled, gender-consciousness changes the nature of interview results (Denzin 1989). Seidman (1991) shares this view:

> All the problems that one can associate with sexist gender relationships can be played out in an interview. Males interviewing females can be overbearing. Women interviewing men can sometimes be reluctant to control the focus of the interview. Male participants can be too easily dismissive of female interviewers. (P. 78)

If we are to overcome these and other potential problems, the traditional relationship between interviewer and interviewee must change, according to many feminists. The two must become equal partners in a negotiated dialogue. The woman/interviewee should be allowed to express herself freely. Rather than saying or implying, "Answer my question, but don't tell me anything else," interviewers should indeed encourage all respondents to express their feelings, their fears, and their doubts. As Kathryn Anderson and Dana Jack (1991) explain, "If we want to know what women feel about their lives, then we have to allow them to talk about their feelings as well as their activities" (p. 15).

Hertz (1997) urges us to blur the distinction between the interviewer and the respondent. As the interviewer comes to realize that she is an active participant in the interview, she must become reflexive, acknowledge who she is in the interview, what she brings it, and how the interview gets negotiated and constructed in the process. Doing so will alleviate an associated reification of methodological problems. But we need to go beyond methodology, as Hertz points out, to face the ethical problems associated with how much we are willing to become partners and disclose about ourselves (also see Behar 1996). As we turn the interviewee from a faceless member of a category to a person, how much should we divulge about her? How do we maintain her anonymity? Ruth Behar (1996) poses the matter succinctly: "Are there limits—of respect, piety, pathos—that should not be crossed, even to leave a record? But if you can't stop the horror, shouldn't you at least document it?" (p. 2).

A related ethical problem stems from researchers' traditional custom of using interviewees to gather material for their own purposes. As Daphne Patai (1987) explains, no matter how well-intentioned researchers are, if they use interview materials exclusively for their own purposes, they are exploiting the women they interview (Oakley 1981; Reinharz 1992; Smith 1987). As a result, some interviewers take the notion of partnership one step further and become advocates for those they interview (Gluck 1991); others turn interview narratives into political acts as they uncover the injustices to which those studies are subjected (Denzin 1999a).

◆ Virtual Interviewing

For traditional interviewing, the transition to the Internet would seem flawless, moving from telephone questionnaires to the use of e-mail, chat rooms, and Web sites. In one way or another, all of these remain "distant" interviewing, with little or no face-to-face contact. If only about 50 percent of American households have personal computers and about half of these have access to the Internet (Fontana and Frey 2000), new software programs facilitate electronic interviewing and provide the ability to obtain returns of almost 100 percent from some specialized groups (Schaefer and Dillman 1998). At the same time, new ethical problems are surfacing, because anonymity is not feasible in e-mail communication, although in chat rooms the use of pseudonyms is possible (see Mann and Stewart, Chapter 5, this volume).

The move to electronic interviewing is perhaps most problematic for in-depth interviewing. Rather than the parties to the interview being face-to-face, interaction centers on "virtual" respondents and "virtual" interviewers, to which we might add the "virtual" researcher, all of whose empirical groundings are unclear. Indeed, the lack of clarity portends a version of Baudrillard's (1983) "hyperreality," the melding together of everyday and media realities, confounding the traditional boundaries of text, identity, and other.

To explore some of these issues on-line, Annette Markham (1998) created an Internet site where she interviewed and conversed with other on-line media users. In particular, she and the others were "trying to make sense of what it means to be there" (p. 18). The participants, including Markham, were experimenting with their sense of self on-line: "By logging onto my computer, I (or part of me) can seem to (or perhaps actually) exist separately from my body in 'places' formed by the exchange of messages" (p. 17).

People exchanging messages on-line apply a text—on-line dialogue—to communicate with each other and create a sense of reality as well as a sense of on-line identity. According to Markham, despite the fact that communication takes place through fiber-optic cables, the interactants actually "feel *a sense of presence*" (p. 17) of the other: "We feel we meet in the flesh. . . . Everywhere we rub shoulders with each other" (Argyle, quoted in Markham 1998: 17).

The identities that interactants create on-line may differ from their other identities, as the lack of visual communication allows one to create a practically new self if one so wishes. The interaction can also be very different from face-to-face communication, because the interactants, visually hidden as they are, can formulate "false nonverbals," claiming feelings and emotions that do not correspond to their demeanor. This type of interviewing takes away from one of the traditional strengths of qualitative research, which is perennially based on the claim, "I saw it, I heard it, I was there."

In a way, using on-line interviews is not very different from Crapanzano's (1980) use of Tuhami's dreams and lies as data, which he presents as just as valid as Tuhami's recounting of real events. Crapanzano found all of these elements to be of equal help in creating Tuhami's biography. Similarly, whatever elements help people communicating on-line to create and sustain a sense of on-line identity in their dialogue are an integral part of their working subjectivity.

Researchers' increased reliance upon computers has faced the criticism of social commentators for some time (see, among others, Dreyfus 1979; Searle 1984). These critics contend that computers are not mere aids that facilitate research; rather, they drastically change our lives and modes of communication. That modern-day "Luddite" Neal Postman (1993) states, "The fundamental metaphoric message of the computer, in short, is that we are machines —thinking machines, to be sure, but machines nonetheless" (p. 111). According to Postman, reliance on machines will increase human belief in scientism, with the result that we will try to scientize and cloak in the language of science the stories we tell. John Murphy (1999) echoes the sentiment. He sees qualitative researchers as being pressured by the ethos of the times and the demands of academia and granting agencies into the use of computers and software programs such as ETHNO, QualPro, and the Ethnograph. Murphy warns that computers will not merely help us to sort out the data, but will lead us to seek precise responses, removing ambiguity from interview material. Rather than created, negotiated, face-to-face narratives, we will be left with artificially derived categories that will reify our results and have little to do with the world of everyday life.

◆ Representational Practices

One of the most controversial areas of postmodern-informed interview research centers on the question of how empirical material should be represented. Traditionally, the writing of social science has mimicked the sparse prose of the natural sciences (see Geertz 1988). John Van Maanen (1988) has analyzed the more recent changes in reporting styles and found that they are moving toward the literary. With postmodern-informed reporting practices, writing engages new, experimental, and highly controversial forms of representation. Mindful of the postmodern collapse of disciplinary barriers, social researchers are using literature, poetry, and even plays to represent interview narratives.

AUTOETHNOGRAPHY

Carolyn Ellis (1995a), Jeffrey Riemer (1977), and others have been employing autoethnography to conflate the traditional distinction between the interviewer and the respondent. Ellis, for example, writes about her past experiences in what becomes a form of retrospective self-interview and narrative reconstruction of life events. The crucial difference between this work and traditional representation is that Ellis aims to recount her own feelings about interview topics that apply to her as a researcher and subject of the experience un-

der consideration, thus combining the roles of interviewer and interviewee. As a result, we are witness to many personally conveyed epiphanic moments in her life, moments that could be our very own. For example, she has written about the agony of facing the death of her brother in an airplane crash (1993), her uneasy encounter with a friend dying of AIDS (1995b), and the slow spiral toward death of her beloved partner, who was stricken with a terminal illness (1995a). In the same vein, Laurel Richardson (1999) has written a personal narrative of her misadventures with paternalistic faculty colleagues after a car accident. Troy McGinnis's (1999) presentation "The Art of Leaving" is about his stumbling upon his wife and a best friend in an intimate situation, and Norman Denzin (1999b, 1999c) has written stories about his hideout in Montana. These are just a few of the many recent autoethnographic (self-interviewing) representations of experience.

POETRY

Laurel Richardson extends this trend to poetic representation (see Richardson, Chapter 10, this volume). After lengthy interview sessions with a southern, middle-aged, single mother, Richardson (1997) transformed the woman's sad and powerful tale into a poem, which she recites masterfully, in a sorrowful southern drawl. A segment follows, which in Richardson's view comes fully to life only in its recitation.

So, the Doctor said, "You're pregnant."

I was 41. John and I
had had a happy kind of relationship,
not a serious one.
But beside himself with fear and anger,
awful, rageful, vengeful, horrid,
Jody May's father said,
"Get an Abortion."

I told him,

"I would never marry you.

I would never marry you.

I would never." (P. 133)

Others have followed Richardson's lead into the realm of sociological poetry. For example, Patricia Clough's (1999) angst-filled poetic presentation "A Child Is Being Killed" took the place of the keynote address at a recent symposium of the Society for the Study of Symbolic Interaction.

STAGED PLAYS AND PERFORMANCES

Scripted performance also has been rallied to enhance the "scenic presence" (Holstein and Gubrium 2000) of interview-based reports of experience. Richardson, for example, not only constructs poetic accounts but uses plays to tell her stories, at times soliciting participation from her audience (see Richardson 1997). Indeed, dramatic realization has become a broadly popular mode of expression. Jim Mienczakowski and Steve Morgan (1998) have dressed as police officers to act out their counseling interviews, which were completed in Queensland, Australia. I personally donned black clothing and a white mask to portray Farinelli, the castrato, in reporting on a study of transsexuals (Fontana and Schmidt 1998, 1999). Robert Schmidt and I enlisted Jennifer O'Brien's help in producing a polyphonic play based on in-depth interviews with a lap dancer (Schmidt and Fontana 1998).

At times, however, performances have moved from the sublime to the studiously ridiculous. For example, I have witnessed sociologist Stephen Pfohl (1995) strip to black bikini bottoms at the culmination of his video-music play, and, more recently, I watched as a graduate student smeared himself with bean dip to convey the ironies of Latino identity. Postmodern trends have taken representation a long way from the guarded prose of research reports.

◆ Conclusion

Clearly, postmodernism has influenced interviewing, loosening it from many of its traditional moorings. Perhaps it has accomplished its goal—imploding traditional interviewing to leave it in fragments, each crying out to be appreciated in its own way. Some see this fragmentation as a healthy sign, because we have many groups with different approaches and methods all presenting their wares (Adler and Adler 1999). Others feel threatened by it and, in various ways, decry the ostensible chaos (Best 1995; Dawson and Prus 1993; Prus 1996; Sanders 1995; Shalin 1993). Yet another response strikes a balance between the modern and postmodern, staking a middle-ground approach to incorporate innovative postmodern ideas with more traditional precepts (Gubrium and Holstein 1998; Holstein and Gubrium 1995). And, finally, there are those who are oblivious to these trends, who continue to be guided by traditional rules of both qualitative and quantitative inquiry (Murphy 1999; Adler and Adler 1999).

Shadowing the differences is the prospect that the interview can no longer be viewed as a discreet event, the straightforward result of asking questions and receiving answers. Indeed, even the traditional "conversation with a purpose," which until recently was a way of conceptualizing the survey interview, has increasingly given way to evidence of the systematic communicative work that produces interview data. Survey researchers themselves are systematically discovering something they have always suspected: that both the interviewer and the respondent negotiate and work together to accomplish the interview, the resulting "data" being as much a product of interview participants' collaborative efforts as of the experiences under consideration. Postmodern trends in the area are seemingly coming full circle, back to where they began. Increasingly, we are learning that what Paul Rabinow (1977) said about informant and researcher in ethnography also applies to the interviewer and the respondent: "The common understanding they construct is fragile and thin, but it is upon this shaky ground that anthropological inquiry proceeds" (p. 39).

■ *Notes*

1. Following Lee Harvey (1987), I see ethnography and in-depth interviewing as much more intertwined than methodologists usually do. Indeed, fieldwork relies on a combination of both methods. Harvey points out that many of the works of the Chicago school, which are commonly referred to as "ethnographic," actually rely on in-depth interviews. As early as Malinowski's fieldwork in New Guinea, the two methods have been combined. In fact, Malinowski did not actually live in the village with the natives, but would go there only occasionally, with an interpreter, to interview them (Malinowski 1989; also see Lofland 1971).

2. Shifting subject positions have traditionally been glossed over in interview research. Seidman (1991) recounts that in his study of community college faculty, he was treated either with deference because of his affiliation with what was perceived to be a higher status institution (the university) or with suspicion because of his affiliation with the "ivory tower." The difference was important in how it mediated the organization of responses. In my study of poor elderly (Fontana 1977), the fact that I was young led to my being treated with extreme suspicion. This was because the elderly people I approached saw my explanation that I was conducting interviews for my dissertation as a cover for some kind of "con game," because some young men who had recently approached them "for similar reasons" were con men and pimps.

■ *References*

Adler, P. A. and P. Adler. 1999. "The Ethnographer's Ball—Revisited." *Journal of Contemporary Ethnography* 28: 442-50.

Anderson, K. and D. C. Jack. 1991. "Learning to Listen: Interview Techniques and Analyses." Pp. 11-26 in *Women's Words: The Feminist Practice of Oral History,* edited by S. B. Gluck and D. Patai. New York: Routledge.

Atkinson, P. and D. Silverman. 1997. "Kundera's *Immortality:* The Interview Society and the Invention of Self." *Qualitative Inquiry* 3:304-25.

Babbie, E. 1992. *The Practice of Social Research.* 6th ed. Belmont, CA: Wadsworth.

Baudrillard, J. 1983. *Simulations.* Translated by Paul Foss, Paul Patton, and John Johnston. New York: Semiotext(e).

Behar, R. 1996. *The Vulnerable Observer: Anthropology That Breaks Your Heart.* Boston: Beacon.

Best, J. 1995. "Lost in the Ozone Again." Pp. 125-30 in *Studies in Symbolic Interaction: A Research Annual,* Vol. 17, edited by N. K. Denzin. Greenwich, CT: JAI.

Best, S. and D. Kellner. 1991. *Postmodern Theory: Critical Interrogations.* New York: Guilford.

Blumer, H. 1969. *Symbolic Interactionism: Perspective and Method.* Englewood Cliffs, NJ: Prentice Hall.

Boden, D. and D. H. Zimmerman, eds. *Talk and Social Structure: Studies in Ethnomethodology and Conversation Analysis.* Berkeley: University of California Press.

Cicourel, A. V. 1964. *Method and Measurement in Sociology.* New York: Free Press.

Clough, P. T. 1999. "A Child Is Being Killed: The Unconscious of Autoethnography." Keynote address presented at the annual symposium of the Couch-Stone Society for the Study of Symbolic Interaction, February 5-7, Las Vegas.

Collins, P. H. 1990. *Black Feminist Thought: Knowledge, Consciousness, and the Politics of Empowerment.* New York: Routledge, Chapman & Hall.

Crapanzano, V. 1980. *Tuhami: Portrait of a Moroccan.* Chicago: University of Chicago Press.

Dawson, L. and R. Prus. 1993. "Interactionist Ethnography and Postmodern Discourse." Pp. 147-77 in *Studies in Symbolic Interaction: A Research Annual,* Vol. 15, edited by N. K. Denzin. Greenwich, CT: JAI.

Denzin, N. K. 1989. *Interpretive Interactionalism.* Newbury Park, CA: Sage.

———. 1997. *Interpretive Ethnography: Ethnographic Practices for the 21st Century.* Thousand Oaks, CA: Sage.

———. 1999a. "An Interpretive Ethnography for the Next Century." *Journal of Contemporary Ethnography* 28:510-19.

———. 1999b. "Performing Montana." Pp. 147-58 in *Qualitative Sociology as Everyday Life,* edited by B. Glassner and R. Hertz. Thousand Oaks, CA: Sage.

———. 1999c. "Performing Montana, Part II." Presented at the annual symposium of the Couch-Stone Society for the Study of Symbolic Interaction, February 5-7, Las Vegas.

Derrida, J. 1972. "Structure, Sign and Play in the Discourse of the Human Sciences." Pp. 247-72 in *The Structuralist Controversy,* edited by R. Macksey and E. Donato. Baltimore: Johns Hopkins University Press.

Dickens, D. R. and A. Fontana, eds. 1994. *Postmodernism and Social Inquiry.* New York: Guilford.

Dingwall, R. 1997. "Accounts, Interviews and Observations." Pp. 51-65 in *Context and Method in Qualitative Research,* edited by G. Miller and R. Dingwall. Thousand Oaks: Sage.

Douglas, J. D. 1985. *Creative Interviewing.* Beverly Hills, CA: Sage.

Dreyfus, H. 1979. *What Computers Can't Do: The Limits of Artificial Intelligence.* New York: Harper & Row.

Dwyer, K. 1982. *Moroccan Dialogues: Anthropology in Question.* Baltimore: Johns Hopkins University Press.

Ellis, C. 1993. " 'There Are Survivors': Telling a Story of Sudden Death." *Sociological Quarterly* 34:711-30.

———. 1995a. *Final Negotiations: A Story of Love, Loss, and Chronic Illness.* Philadelphia: Temple University Press.

———. 1995b. "Speaking of Dying: An Ethnographic Short Story." *Symbolic Interaction* 18:73-81.

Fontana, A. 1977. *The Last Frontier: The Social Meaning of Growing Old.* Beverly Hills, CA: Sage.

Fontana, A. and J. H. Frey. 2000. "The Interview: From Structured Questions to Negotiated Text." Pp. 645-72 in *Handbook of Qualitative Research,* 2d ed., edited by N. K. Denzin and Y. S. Lincoln. Thousand Oaks, CA: Sage.

Fontana, A. and R. Schmidt (with Jennifer O'Brien). 1998. "The Fluid Self." Presented at the annual meeting of the Society for the Study of Symbolic Interaction, August 22-23, San Francisco.

Fontana, A. and R. Schmidt. 1999. "Castrato: Predetermined to Fluid Self or a Dialogue/Performance Script Intended to Inform Garfinkel about the Possibilities of Gendering." In *Studies in Symbolic Interaction: A Research Annual,* Vol. 23, edited by N. K. Denzin. Greenwich, CT: JAI.

Garfinkel, H. 1967. *Studies in Ethnomethodology.* Englewood Cliffs, NJ: Prentice Hall.

Geertz, C. 1988. *Works and Lives: The Anthropologist as Author.* Stanford, CA: Stanford University Press.

Gluck, S. B. 1991. "Advocacy Oral History: Palestinian Women in Resistance." Pp. 205-20 in *Women's Words: The Feminist Practice of Oral History.* Edited by S. B. Gluck and D. Patai. New York: Routledge.

Gubrium, J. F. and J. A. Holstein. 1997. *The New Language of Qualitative Method.* New York: Oxford University Press.

———. 1998. "Narrative Practice and the Coherence of Personal Stories." *Sociological Quarterly* 39:163-87.

Harvey, L. 1987. *Myths of the Chicago School of Sociology.* Aldershot, England: Avebury.

Hertz, R., ed. 1997. *Reflexivity and Voice.* Thousand Oaks, CA: Sage.

Holstein, J. A. and J. F. Gubrium. 1995. *The Active Interview.* Thousand Oaks, CA: Sage.

———. 2000. *The Self We Live By: Narrative Identity in a Postmodern World.* New York: Oxford University Press.

Krieger, S. 1983. *The Mirror's Dance: Identity in a Women's Community.* Philadelphia: Temple University Press.

Lofland, J. 1971. *Analyzing Social Settings.* Belmont, CA: Wadsworth.

Lyotard, J.-F. 1984. *The Postmodern Condition: A Report on Knowledge.* Translated by G. Bennington and B. Massumi. Minneapolis: University of Minnesota Press.

Malinowski, B. 1989. *A Diary in the Strict Sense of the Term.* Stanford, CA: Stanford University Press.

Marcus, G. E. and M. M. J. Fischer. 1986. *Anthropology as Cultural Critique: An Experimental Moment in the Human Sciences.* Chicago: University of Chicago Press.

Markham, A. N. 1998. *Life Online: Researching Real Experience in Virtual Space.* Walnut Creek, CA: AltaMira.

Maynard, D. W., H. Houtkoop-Steenstra, J. van der Zouwen, and N. C. Schaeffer. 2001. *Interaction and Practice in the Survey Interview.* New York: John Wiley.

McGinnis, T. 1999. "The Art of Leaving." Presented at the annual symposium of the Couch-Stone Society for the Study of Symbolic Interaction, February 5-7, Las Vegas.

Mienczakowski, J. and S. Morgan. 1998. "Stop! In the Name of Love!" Presented at the annual symposium of the Couch-Stone Society for the Study of Symbolic Interaction, February 20-22, Houston, TX.

Murphy, J. 1999. "Computerized Ethnography: Fad and Disaster!" Presented at the annual symposium of the Couch-Stone Society for the Study of Symbolic Interaction, February 5-7, Las Vegas.

Oakley, A. 1981. "Interviewing Women: A Contradiction in Terms?" Pp. 30-61 in *Doing Feminist Research,* edited by H. Roberts. London: Routledge & Kegan Paul.

Owens, C. 1983. "The Discourse of Others: Feminists and Postmodernism." Pp. 57-82 in *The Anti-aesthetic: Essays on Postmodern Culture,* edited by H. Foster. Port Townsend, WA: Bay.

Patai, D. 1987. "Ethical Problems of Personal Narrative, or Who Should Eat the Last Piece of Cake?" *International Journal of Oral History* 8(1):5-27.

Pfohl, S. 1995. "Venus in Microsoft." Presented at the Gregory Stone Annual Symposium of the Society for the Study of Symbolic Interaction, May 19-21, Des Moines, IA.

Postman, N. 1993. *Technopoly: The Surrender of Culture to Technology.* New York: Vintage.

Prus, R. 1996. *Symbolic Interaction and Ethnographic Research.* Albany: State University of New York Press.

Rabinow, P. 1977. *Reflections on Fieldwork in Morocco.* Berkeley: University of California Press.

Reinharz, S. 1992. *Feminist Methods in Social Research.* New York: Oxford University Press.

Richardson, L. 1997. *Fields of Play: Constructing an Academic Life.* New Brunswick, NJ: Rutgers University Press.

———. 1999. "Jeopardy." Presented at the Forum Lecture Series, February 4, University of Nevada, Las Vegas.

Riemer, J. 1977. "Varieties of Opportunistic Research." *Urban Life* 5:467-77.

Sanders, C. 1995. "Stranger Than Fiction." Pp. 89-104 in *Studies in Symbolic Interaction: A Research Annual,* Vol. 17, edited by N. K. Denzin. Greenwich, CT: JAI.

Sarup, M. 1996. *Identity, Culture and the Postmodern World.* Athens: University of Georgia Press.

Schaefer, D. R. and D. A. Dillman. 1998. "Development of a Standard E-Mail Methodology." *Public Opinion Quarterly* 62:378-97.

Schmidt, R. and A. Fontana. 1998. "Deconstructing Peggy Sue." Presented at the annual symposium of the Couch-Stone Society for the Study of Symbolic Interaction, February 20-22, Houston, TX.

Schutz, A. 1962. *Collected Papers I: The Problem of Social Reality.* The Hague: Martinus Nijhoff.

———. 1964. *Collected Papers II: Studies in Social Theory.* The Hague: Martinus Nijhoff.

———. 1966. *Collected Papers III: Studies in Phenomenological Philosophy.* The Hague: Martinus Nijhoff.

Searle, J. 1984. *Minds, Brains and Science.* Cambridge, MA: Harvard University Press.

Seidman, I. 1991. *Interviewing as Qualitative Research: A Guide for Researchers in Education and the Social Sciences*. New York: Teachers College Press.

Shalin, D. 1993. "Modernity, Postmodernism and Pragmatist Inquiry." *Symbolic Interaction* 16:303-32.

Shelton, A. 1995. "The Man at the End of the Machine." *Symbolic Interaction* 18: 505-18.

———. 1996. "Vespers." Presented at the Gregory Stone Annual Symposium of the Society for the Study of Symbolic Interaction, May 19-21, Des Moines, IA.

Silverman, D. 1993. *Interpreting Qualitative Data: Methods for Analysing Talk, Text and Interaction*. London: Sage.

———, ed. 1997. *Qualitative Research: Theory, Method and Practice*. London: Sage.

Smith, D. E. 1987. *The Everyday World as Problematic: A Feminist Sociology*. Boston: Northeastern University Press.

Van Maanen, J. 1988. *Tales of the Field: On Writing Ethnography*. Chicago: University of Chicago Press.

Vaz, K. M., ed. 1997. *Oral Narrative Research with Black Women*. Thousand Oaks: Sage.

Warren, C. A. B. 1988. *Gender Issues in Field Research*. Newbury Park, CA: Sage.

Weston, K. 1998. *Long Slow Burn: Sexuality and Social Science*. New York: Routledge.

Zimmerman, D. H. and M. Pollner. 1970. "The Everyday World as a Phenomenon." Pp. 80-104 in *Understanding Everyday Life: Toward a Reconstruction of Social Knowledge*, edited by J. D. Douglas. Chicago: Aldine.

4

ACTIVE INTERVIEWING

◆ James A. Holstein
Jaber F. Gubrium

In our "interview society" (Silverman 1993), the mass media, human service providers, and researchers increasingly generate information by interviewing. The number of television news programs, daytime talk shows, and newspaper articles that provide us with the results of interviews is virtually incalculable. Looking at more methodical forms of information collection, it has been estimated that 90 percent of all social science investigations use interviews in one way or another (Briggs 1986). Interviewing is undoubtedly the most widely used technique for conducting systematic social inquiry, as sociologists, psychologists, anthropologists, psychiatrists, clinicians, administrators, politicians, and pollsters treat interviews as their "windows on the world" (Hyman et al. 1975).

Put most simply, interviewing provides a way of generating empirical data about the social world by asking people to talk about their lives. In this respect, interviews are special forms of conversation. While these conversations may vary from highly structured, standardized, quantitatively oriented survey interviews, to semiformal guided conversations, to free-flowing informational exchanges, all interviews are interactional. The narratives that are produced may be as truncated as forced-choice survey answers or as elaborate as oral life histories, but they are all constructed *in situ*, as a product of the talk between interview participants.

While most researchers acknowledge the interactional character of the interview, the technical literature on interviewing stresses the need to keep that interaction strictly in check. Guides to interviewing—especially those oriented to standardized surveys—are primarily concerned with maximizing the flow of valid, reliable information while minimizing distortions of what the respondent knows (Gorden 1987). The interview conversation is thus framed as a potential source of bias, error, misunderstanding, or misdirection, a persistent set of problems to be minimized. The corrective is simple: if the interviewer asks questions properly, the respondent will give out the desired information.

In this conventional view, the interview conversation is a pipeline for transmitting knowledge. A recently heightened sensitivity to representational matters (see Gubrium and Holstein 1997)—characteristic of poststructuralist, postmodernist, constructionist, and ethnomethodological inquiry—has raised a number of questions about the very possibility of collecting knowledge in the manner the conventional approach presupposes. In varied ways, these alternate perspectives hold that meaning is socially constituted; all knowledge is created from the actions undertaken to obtain it (see, for example, Cicourel 1964, 1974; Garfinkel 1967). Treating interviewing as social encounter in which knowledge is constructed suggests the possibility that the interview is not merely a neutral conduit or source of distortion, but is instead a site of, and occasion for, producing reportable knowledge itself.

Sociolinguist Charles Briggs (1986) argues that the social circumstances of interviews are more than obstacles to respondents' articulation of their particular truths. Briggs notes that, like all other speech events, interviews fundamentally, not incidentally, shape the form and content of what is said. Aaron Cicourel (1974) goes farther, maintaining that interviews virtually impose particular ways of understanding reality upon subjects' responses. The general point is that interviewers are deeply and unavoidably implicated in creating meanings that ostensibly reside within respondents (also see Manning 1967, Mishler 1986, 1991, Silverman 1963). Both parties to the interview are necessarily and unavoidably *active*. Meaning is not merely elicited by apt questioning, nor simply transported through respondent replies; it is actively and communicatively assembled in the interview

encounter. Respondents are not so much repositories of knowledge—treasuries of information awaiting excavation—as they are constructors of knowledge in collaboration with interviewers. Participation in an interview involves meaning-making work (Holstein and Gubrium 1995).

If interviews are interpretively active, meaning-making occasions, interview data are unavoidably collaborative (see Alasuutari 1995; Holstein and Staples 1992). Therefore, any technical attempts to strip interviews of their interactional constituents will be futile. Instead of refining the long list of methodological constraints under which "standardized" interviews should be conducted, we suggest that researchers take a more "active" view of the interview and begin to acknowledge, and capitalize upon, interviewers' and respondents' constitutive contributions to the production of interview data. This means consciously and conscientiously attending to the interview process and product in ways that are more sensitive to the social construction of knowledge.

Conceiving of the interview as *active* means attending more to the ways in which knowledge is assembled than is usually the case in traditional approaches. In other words, understanding *how* the meaning-making process unfolds in the interview is as critical as apprehending *what* is substantively asked and conveyed. The *hows* of interviewing, of course, refer to the interactional, narrative procedures of knowledge production, not merely to interview techniques. The *whats* pertain to the issues guiding the interview, the content of questions, and the substantive information communicated by the respondent. A dual interest in the *hows* and *whats* of meaning production goes hand in hand with an appreciation for the constitutive activeness of the interview process.

This appreciation derives from an ethnomethodologically informed social constructionist approach (cf. Berger and Luckmann 1967; Blumer 1969; Garfinkel

1967, Heritage 1984, Pollner 1987)) that considers the process of meaning production to be as important for social research as the meaning that is produced. In many significant ways, it also resonates with methodological critiques and reformulations offered by an array of feminist scholars (see DeVault 1990; Harding 1987, Reinharz 1992; Smith 1987). In their distinctive ways, ethnomethodology, constructionism, poststructuralism, postmodernism, and some versions of feminism are all interested in issues relating to subjectivity, complexity, perspective, and meaning-construction. But as valuable and insightful as they are, these "linguistically attuned" approaches tend to emphasize the *hows* of social process at the expense of the *whats* of lived experience. We want to strike a balance between these *hows* and *whats* as a way of reappropriating the significance of substance and content to studies of the social construction process. While the emphasis on process has sharpened concern with, and debate over, the epistemological status of interview data, it is important to not lose track of *what* is being asked about in interviews and, in turn, *what* is being conveyed by respondents. A narrow focus on *how* tends to displace the significant *whats*—the meanings—that serve as the relevant grounds for asking and answering questions.

Taking the activity of all interviewing as our point of departure, we will discuss how the interview cultivates meaning-making. We begin by locating the active view in relation to more traditional conceptions of interviewing, examining alternate images of the subject behind the interview respondent.

◆ Traditional Images of Interviewing

Typically, those who want to find out about another person's feelings, thoughts, or ex-

periences believe that they merely have to ask the right questions and the other's "reality" will be theirs. Studs Terkel, the consummate journalistic and sociological interviewer, says he simply turns on his tape recorder and asks people to talk. Writing of the interviews he did for his brilliant study *Working,* Terkel (1972, p. xxv) notes:

> There were questions, of course. But they were casual in nature . . . the kind you would ask while having a drink with someone; the kind he would ask you. . . . In short, it was a conversation. In time, the sluice gates of dammed up hurts and dreams were open.

As unpretentious as it is, Terkel's image of interviewing permeates the social sciences; interviewing is generally likened to "prospecting" for the true facts and feelings residing within the respondent. Of course there is a highly sophisticated technology that tells researchers how to ask questions, what sorts of questions not to ask, the order in which to ask them, and the ways to avoid saying the wrong things that might spoil, contaminate, or bias the data (Hyman et al. 1975; Fowler and Mangione 1990). The basic model, however, remains similar to the one Terkel exploits so adroitly.

The image of the social scientific prospector casts the interview as a search and discovery mission, with the interviewer intent on detecting what is already there inside variably cooperative respondents. The challenge lies in extracting information as directly as possible. Highly refined interview technologies streamline, systematize, and sanitize the process. This can involve varying degrees of standardization (see Maccoby and Maccoby 1954), ranging from interviews ordered by structured, specifically worded questions and an orientation to measurement, to flexibly organized interviews guided by more general questions aimed at uncovering subjective meanings. John Madge (1965) contrasts what he calls "formative" with "mass" interviews, categorizing them according to whether the respondent "is given some sort of freedom to choose the topics to be discussed and the way in which they are discussed" (P. 165). Formative interviews include the nondirective interviews favored in Rogerian counseling (see Rogers 1945), informal interviews, and life histories. Most large-scale surveys fall into the mass interview category. By and large, classification centers on the characteristics and aims of the interview process, with little attention paid to how interviews differ as occasions for knowledge production.

THE SUBJECT BEHIND THE RESPONDENT

Regardless of the type of interview, there is always a model of the research *subject* lurking behind persons placed in the role of interview respondent (Holstein and Gubrium 1995). Projecting a subject behind the respondent confers a sense of epistemological agency upon the respondent, which bears on our understanding of the relative validity of the information that is reported. In conventional approaches, subjects are basically conceived as passive *vessels of answers* for experiential questions put to respondents by interviewers. They are repositories of facts and the related details of experience. Occasionally, such as with especially sensitive interview topics or with recalcitrant respondents, researchers acknowledge that it may be difficult to obtain accurate experiential information. Nonetheless, the information is viewed, in principle, as held uncontaminated by the subject's vessel of answers. The trick is to formulate questions and provide an atmosphere conducive to open and undistorted communication between the interviewer and respondent.

Much of the methodological literature on interviewing deals with the nuances of these intricate matters. The vessel-of-answers view cautions interviewers to be careful in how they ask questions, lest their manner of inquiry bias what lies within the subject. This perspective offers myriad procedures for obtaining unadulterated facts and details, most of which rely upon interviewer and question neutrality. For example, it is assumed that the interviewer who poses questions that acknowledge alternative sides of an issue is being more "neutral" than the interviewer who does not. The successful implementation of neutral practices elicits truths held in the vessel of answers behind the respondent. Validity results from the successful application of the procedures.

In the vessel-of-answers approach, the image of the subject is epistemologically passive, not engaged in the production of knowledge. If the interviewing process goes "by the book" and is nondirectional and unbiased, respondents will validly give out what they are presumed to merely retain within them—the unadulterated facts and details of experience. Contamination emanates from the interview setting, its participants, and their interaction, not the subject, who, under ideal conditions, serves up authentic reports when beckoned to do so.

What happens, however, if we enliven the image of the subject behind the respondent? Construed as active, the subject behind the respondent not only holds facts and details of experience, but, in the very process of offering them up for response, constructively adds to, takes away from, and transforms the facts and details. The respondent can hardly "spoil" what he or she is, in effect, subjectively creating.

This activated subject pieces experiences together, before, during, and after assuming the respondent role. As a member of society, he or she mediates and alters the knowledge that is conveyed to the interviewer; he or she is "always already" an active maker of meaning. Because the respondent's answers are continually being assembled and modified, the answers' truth value cannot be judged simply in terms of whether they match what lies in a vessel of objective answers.

From a more traditional, scientific standpoint, the objectivity or truth of interview responses might be assessed in terms of reliability, the extent to which questioning yields the same answers whenever and wherever it is carried out, and validity, the extent to which inquiry yields the "correct" answers (Kirk and Miller 1986). When the interview is viewed as a dynamic, meaning-making occasion, however, different criteria apply. The focus is on how meaning is constructed, the circumstances of construction, and the meaningful linkages that are assembled for the occasion. While interest in the content of answers persists, it is primarily in how and what the subject/respondent, in collaboration with an equally active interviewer, produces and conveys about the subject/respondent's experience under the interpretive circumstances at hand. One cannot expect answers on one occasion to replicate those on another because they emerge from different circumstances of production. Similarly, the validity of answers derives not from their correspondence to meanings held within the respondent, but from their ability to convey situated experiential realities in terms that are locally comprehensible.

The active image of the interview is best put in perspective by contrasting it with more traditional images. We will focus on two classic exemplars that differ considerably in their orientations to the experiential truths held by the passive subject. The first approach orients to the rational, factual value of what is communicated. It focuses on the substantive statements, explanations, and reasons with which the respondent articulates experience. We use Jean Converse and Howard Schuman's (1974) candid book *Conversations at Random* as an exemplary text. The second approach orients to the purportedly deeper and more authentic value of the subject's feelings. It emphasizes sentiment and emotion, the core of human experience. We use Jack Douglas' book *Creative Interviewing* (1985) to illustrate this perspective.

SURVEY INTERVIEWING

While Converse and Schuman attempt to elaborate the most standardized of interviewing techniques, their book attempts to consider the survey interview "as interviewers see it," richly illustrating how interpretively engaging, and relatedly difficult and exasperating, the survey respondent can be. It describes the interesting and complex personalities and meanings that interviewers encounter while interviewing, depicting them as "the pleasure of persons" and "connoisseurs of the particular." But the authors caution the reader that, even though it will be evident throughout that the respondent can be quite interpretively active, this does not work against objective information. This information, the reader eventually learns, is derived from the repository of knowledge that lies behind the passive respondent. The authors do not believe that the respondent's conduct implicates his or her subject in the construction of meaning. As lively, uninhibited, entertaining, and difficult as the respondent might be at times, his or her passive subject ultimately holds the answers sought in the research.

While Converse and Schuman grant that survey interviewing involves experiencing the "pleasure of persons," the authors hope that interviewers use their roles to effectively access the vessel of answers behind the respondent. Their book is replete with anecdotal reminders of what interviewers must learn in order to keep that vessel of answers in view and the respondent on target. In part, it is a matter of controlling oneself as an interviewer so that one does not interfere with what the passive subject is only too willing to put forth. The interviewer must shake off self-consciousness, suppress personal opinion, and avoid stereotyping the respondent. Learning the interviewer role is also a matter of controlling the interview situation to facilitate the candid expression of opinions and sentiments. Ideally, the interview should be conducted in private. This helps assure that respondents will speak directly from their vessels of answers, not in response to the presence of others. The seasoned interviewer learns that the so-called pull of conversation, which might have an interpretive dynamic of its own fueled by the active subjectivity of both the respondent and the interviewer, must be managed so that the "push of inquiry" (P. 26) is kept in focus. Ideally, the cross-pressures of conducting inquiry that will produce "good hard data" are managed by means of "soft" conversation (P. 22).

Throughout, Converse and Schuman's book provides glimpses of how problematic the image of the passive subject is in practice. The rich illustrations repeatedly tell us that interviews are conversations where meanings are not only conveyed, but cooperatively built up, received, interpreted, and recorded by the interviewer. While the veteran interviewer learns to manage the pressures of conversation for the purposes of inquiry, orienting to an active, meaning-making occasion seems to be a mere epistemological step away.

CREATIVE INTERVIEWING

Converse and Schuman's approach to interviewing is quite different from the view exemplified in Douglas's book *Creative Interviewing*, but we will also see some marked similarities. The word "creative" in Douglas's title refers primarily to the interviewer, not the respondent, and, according to Douglas, derives from the difficulties he encountered attempting to probe respondents' "deep experience." Douglas writes that in his many empirical studies, he repeatedly discovered how shallow the standard recommendations were for conducting research interviews. Canons of rational neutrality, such as those Converse and Schuman espouse, failed to capture what Douglas calls his respondents' "emotional wellsprings" and called for a methodology for deep disclosure.

Douglas's difficulties relate as much to his image of the passive subject as they do to shortcomings of standard interviewing technique. Like the image of the subject behind the survey respondent, Douglas also imagines his subjects to be repositories of answers, but in his case, they are well guarded vessels of *feelings*. The respondent authentically communicates from an emotional wellspring, at the behest of an interviewer who knows that mere words cannot draw out or convey what experience ultimately is all about. Standard survey questions and answers touch only the surface of experience. Douglas aims more deeply by creatively "getting to know" the real subject behind the respondent.

Creative interviewing is a set of techniques for moving past the mere words and sentences exchanged in the interview process. To achieve this, the interviewer must establish a climate for *mutual* disclosure. The interview should be an occasion that displays the interviewer's willingness to share his or her own feelings and deepest thoughts. This is done to assure respondents that they can, in turn, share their own thoughts and feelings. The interviewers' deep disclosure both occasions and legitimizes the respondent's reciprocal revelations. This, Douglas suggests, is thoroughly suppressed by the cultivated neutrality of the standard survey interview. As if to state a cardinal rule, he writes:

> Creative interviewing, as we shall see throughout, involves the use of many strategies and tactics of interaction, largely based on an understanding of friendly feelings and intimacy, to optimize *cooperative, mutual disclosure and a creative search for mutual understanding*. (P. 25, emphasis in the original)

Douglas offers a rather explicit set of guidelines for creative interviewing. One is to figure that, as he puts it, "genius in creative interviewing involves 99 percent perspiration" (P. 27); getting the respondent to deeply disclose requires much more work than obtaining mere opinions. A second admonition for engaging in "deep-deep probes into the human soul" is "researcher, know thyself" (P. 51). Continual self analysis on the part of the interviewer, who usually is also the researcher, is necessary, lest the creative interviewer's own defense mechanisms work against mutual disclosure and understanding. A third guideline is to show a commitment to mutual disclosure by expressing an abiding interest in feelings. Referring to a neophyte creative interviewer who "has done some wonderously revealing life studies," Douglas writes that the creative interviewer is "driven by . . . friendly, caring, and adoring feelings, but adds to those an endearing, wide-eyed sense of wonderment at the mysteries unveiled before her" (P. 29).

The wellsprings tapped by creative interviewing are said to be emotional, in distinct contrast with the preferred rational image that filters through Converse and Schuman's book. As Douglas puts it, knowledge and wisdom are "*partially* the product of creative interactions—of mutual searches for understanding, of soul communions" (P. 55, emphasis in original). While Douglas's imagined subject is basically emotional, this subject, in the role of respondent, actively cooperates with the interviewer to create mutually recognizable meanings, paralleling what interviewers' accounts in Converse and Schuman's book suggest. In this regard, the mutuality of disclosure—the "creative" thrust of creative interviewing—mediates, adds to, and shapes what is said in its own right. What Douglas does not recognize, however, is that this admittedly active subject could constitute the wellsprings of experience in rational or other terms, not necessarily emotional ones. Thus, the subject behind Douglas's respondent remains an essentially passive, if creatively emotional, fount of experience, not unlike the respondent who "opens up" while having a drink with Studs Terkel.

◆ The Active Interview

Ithiel de Sola Pool (1957), a prominent critic of public opinion polling, once argued that the dynamic, communicative contingencies of the interview literally activate respondents opinions. Every interview, he suggests, is an "interpersonal drama with a developing plot" (P. 193). This metaphor conveys a far more active sense of interviewing than is traditionally conceived, an image of the interview as an occasion for constructing, not merely discovering or conveying, information. As Pool indicates,

> . . . the social milieu in which communication takes place [during interviews] modifies not only what a person dares to say but even what he thinks he chooses to say. And these variations in expression cannot be viewed as mere deviations from some underlying "true" opinion, for there is no neutral, nonsocial, uninfluenced situation to provide that baseline. (P. 192)

THE ACTIVE INTERVIEW AND INTERPRETIVE PRACTICE

Conceiving of the interview as an interpersonal drama with a developing plot is part of a broader vision of reality as an ongoing, interpretive accomplishment. From this perspective, interview participants are practitioners of everyday life, constantly working to discern and designate the recognizable and orderly features of experience. But meaning-making is not merely artful (Garfinkel 1967); meaning is not built "from scratch" on each interpretive occasion. Rather, interpretation orients to, and is conditioned by, the substantive resources and contingencies of interaction.

Meaningful reality is constituted at the nexus of the *hows* and the *whats* of experience, by way of *interpretive practice*—the procedures and resources used to apprehend, organize, and represent reality (Holstein 1993; Holstein and Gubrium 1994). Active interviewing is a form of interpretive practice involving respondent and interviewer as they articulate ongoing interpretive structures, resources, and orientations with what Garfinkel (1967) calls "practical reasoning." Linking artfulness to substantive contingencies implies that while reality is continually "under construction," it is assembled using the interpretive resources at hand. Meaning is not constantly formulated anew, but reflects relatively enduring local conditions, such as the research topics of the interviewer, biographical particulars, and local ways of orienting to those topics (Gubrium 1988, 1989; Holstein and Gubrium 1994). Those resources are astutely and adroitly crafted to the demands of the occasion, so that meaning is neither predetermined nor absolutely unique.

AN ACTIVE SUBJECT

The image of the *active interview* transforms the subject behind the respondent from a repository of opinions and reason or a wellspring of emotions into a *productive source of knowledge*. From the time one identifies a research topic, to respondent selection, questioning and answering, and, finally, to the interpretation of responses, interviewing itself is a concerted project for producing meaning. The imagined subject behind the respondent emerges as part of the project, not beforehand. Within the interview itself, the subject is fleshed out—rationally, emotionally, in combination, or otherwise—in relation to the give and take of the interview process and the interview's broader research purposes. The interview *and* its participants are constantly developing.

Two communicative contingencies influence the construction of the active subject behind the respondent. One kind involves the substantive *whats* of the interview enterprise. The focus and emerging data of the research project provide interpretive resources for developing both the subject and his or her responses. For example, a project might center on the quality of care and quality of life of nursing home residents (see Gubrium 1993). This might be part of a study relating to the national debate about the organization of home and institutional care. If interviews are employed, participants draw out the substantiality of these topics, linking the topics to biographical particulars in the interview process, producing a subject who responds to, or is affected by, the matters under discussion. For instance, a nursing home resident might speak animatedly during an interview about the quality of care in her facility, asserting that, "for a woman, it ultimately gets down to feelings," echoing Douglas's emotional subject, articulating a recognizable linkage between affect and gender. Another resident might coolly and methodically list her facility's qualities of care, never once mentioning her feelings about them. Offering her own take on the matter, the respondent might state that "getting emotional" over "these things" clouds clear judgment, implicating a different kind of subject, more like the rational respondent portrayed in Converse and Schuman's text. Particular substantive resources—such as the common cultural link between women and feelings or the traditional cultural opposition of clear thought and emotionality—are used to form the subject.

A second communicative contingency of interviewing directs us to the *hows* of the process. The standpoint from which information is offered is continually developed in relation to ongoing interview interaction. In speaking of the quality of care, for example, nursing home residents, as interview respondents, not only offer substantive thoughts and feelings pertinent to the topic under consideration, but simultaneously and continuously monitor who they are in relation to the person questioning them. For example, prefacing her remarks about the quality of life in her facility with the statement "speaking as a woman," a nursing home resident informs the interviewer that she is to be heard as a woman, not as someone else—not a mere resident, cancer patient, or abandoned mother. If and when she subsequently comments, "If I were a man in this place," the resident frames her thoughts and feelings about the quality of life differently, producing an alternative subject. The respondent is clearly working at how the interview unfolds.

NARRATIVE INCITEMENT, POSITIONAL SHIFTS, AND RESOURCE ACTIVATION

Interviews, of course, hold no monopoly over interpretive practice. Nor are they the only occasions upon which subjects and their opinions, emotions, and reports are interpretively constituted. Why, then, is interviewing an especially useful mode of systematic social inquiry? One answer lies in the interview situation's ability to incite the production of meanings that address issues relating to particular research concerns. In the conventional view of interviewing, the passive subject engages in a "minimalist" version of interpretive practice, perceiving, storing, and reporting experience when properly asked. Our active conception of the interview, however, invests the subject with a substantial repertoire of interpretive methods and stock of experiential materials. The active view eschews the image of the vessel waiting to be tapped in favor of the notion that the subject's interpretive capabilities must be activated, stimulated, and cultivated. The interview is a commonly recognized occasion for formally and systematically doing so.

This is not to say that active interviewers merely coax their respondents into preferred responses to their questions. Rather, they converse with respondents in such a way that alternate considerations are brought into play. They may suggest orientations to, and linkages between, diverse aspects of respondents' experience, adumbrating—even inviting—interpretations that make use of particular resources, connections, and outlooks. Interviewers may explore incompletely articulated aspects of experience, encouraging respondents to develop topics in ways relevant to their own experience (DeVault 1990). The objective is not to dictate interpretation, but to provide an environment conducive to the production of the range and complexity of meanings that address relevant issues, and not be confined by predetermined agendas.

Pool's dramaturgic metaphor is apt because it conveys both the structuring conditions and the artfulness of the interview. As a drama of sorts, its narrative is scripted in that it has a topic or topics, distinguishable roles, and a format for conversation. But it also has a *developing* plot, in which topics, roles, and format are fashioned in the give and take of the interview. This active interview is a kind of limited "improvisational" performance. The production is spontaneous, yet structured—focused within loose parameters provided by the interviewer, who is also an active participant.

While the respondent actively constructs and assembles answers, he or she does not simply "break out" talking. Neither elaborate narratives nor one-word replies emerge without provocation. The active interviewer's role is to incite respondents' answers, virtually *activating narrative production*. Where standardized approaches to interviewing attempt to strip the interview of all but the most neutral, impersonal stimuli (but see Holstein and Gubrium 1995 for a discussion of the inevitable failure of these attempts), the consciously active interviewer intentionally provokes responses by indicating—even suggesting—narrative positions, resources, orientations, and precedents. In the broadest sense, the interviewer attempts to activate the respondent's stock of knowledge (Schutz 1967) and bring it to bear on the discussion at hand in ways that are appropriate to the research agenda.

Consider, for example, the ways in which diverse aspects of a respondent's knowledge, perspectives, roles, and orientations are activated and implicated in an interview involving an adult daughter who is caring for her mother—a victim of senile dementia—at home. The daughter is employed part-time, and shares the household with her employed husband and their two sons, one a part-time college student and the other a full-time security guard. The extract begins when the interviewer (**I**) asks the adult daughter (**R**) to describe her feelings about having to juggle so many needs and schedules. This relates to a discussion of the so-called "sandwich generation," which is said to be caught between having to raise their own children and seeing to the needs of frail elderly parents. Note how, after the interviewer asks the respondent what she means by saying that she has mixed feelings, the respondent makes explicit reference to various ways of thinking about the matter, as if to suggest that more than one narrative resource (with contradictory responses) might be brought to bear on the matter. The respondent displays considerable narrative activity: she not only references possible *whats* of caregiving and family life, but, in the process, informs the interviewer of *how* she could construct her answer.

I: We were talking about, you said you were a member of the, what did you call it?

R: They say that I'm in the sandwich generation. You know, like we're sandwiched between having to care for my mother . . . and my grown kids and my husband. People are living longer now and you've got different generations at home and, I tell ya, it's a mixed blessing.

I: How do you feel about it in your situation?

R: Oh, I don't know. Sometimes I think I'm being a bit selfish because I gripe about having to keep an eye on Mother all the time. If you let down your guard, she wanders off into the back yard or goes out the door and down the street. That's no fun when your hubby wants your attention too. Norm works the second shift and he's home during the day a lot. I manage to get in a few hours of work, but he doesn't like it. I have pretty mixed feelings about it.

I: What do you mean?

R: Well, I'd say that as a daughter, I feel pretty guilty about how I feel sometimes. It can get pretty bad, like wishing that Mother were just gone, you know what I mean? She's been a wonderful mother and I love her very much, but if you ask me how I feel as a wife and mother, that's another matter. I feel like she's [the mother], well, intruding on our lives and just making hell out of raising a family. Sometimes I put myself in my husband's shoes and I just know how he feels. He doesn't say much, but I know that he misses my company, and I miss his of course. [Pause] So how do you answer that?

The interviewer then goes on to explain that the respondent could answer in the way she believes best represents her thoughts and feelings. But as the exchange unfolds, it becomes evident that "best" misrepresents the narrative complexity of the respondent's thoughts and feelings. In the following extract, notice how the respondent struggles to sort her responses to accord with categorically distinct identities. At one point, she explains that she now knows how a wife could and should feel because she gathered from the way her husband and sons acted that "men don't feel things in the same way." This suggests that her own thoughts and feelings are drawn from a fund of gendered knowledge as well. Note, too, how at several points, the interviewer collaborates with the respondent to define her identity as a respondent. At the very end of the extract, the respondent suggests that other respondents' answers might serve to clarify the way she herself organized her responses, indicating that further narrative contextualizing might encourage even more interpretations of her own experience.

R: I try to put myself in their [husband and sons] shoes, try to look at it from their point of view, you know, from a man's way of thinking. I ask myself how it feels to have a part-time wife and mama. I ask myself how I'd feel. Believe me, I know he [husband] feels pretty rotten about it. Men get that way; they want what they want and the rest of the time, well, they're quiet, like nothing's the matter. I used to think I was going crazy with all the stuff on my mind and having to think about everything all at once and not being able to finish with one thing and get on to the other. You know how it gets—doing one thing and feeling bad about how you did something else and wanting to redo what you did or what you said. The way a woman does, I guess. I think I've learned that about myself. I don't know. It's pretty complicated thinking about it. [Pause] Let's see, how do I really feel?

I: Well, I was just wondering, you mentioned being sandwiched earlier and what a woman feels?

R: Yeah, I guess I wasn't all that sure what women like me feel until I figured out how Norm and the boys felt. I figured pretty quick that men are pretty good at sorting things out and that, well, I just couldn't do it, 'cause, well, men don't feel things the same way. I just wouldn't want to do that way anyway. Wouldn't feel right about it as a woman, you know what I mean? So, like they say, live and let live, I guess.

I: But as a daughter?

R: Yeah, that too. So if you ask me how I feel having Mother under foot all the time, I'd say that I remember not so far back that I was under foot a lot when I was a little girl and Mother never complained, and she'd help Dad out in the store, too. So I guess I could tell you that I'm glad I'm healthy and around to take care of her and, honestly, I'd do it all over again if I had to. I don't know. You've talked to other women about it. What do they say?

I: Well, uh

R: Naw, I don't want to put you on the spot. I was just thinking that maybe if I knew how others in my shoes felt, I might be able to sort things out better than I did for ya.

The respondent's comments about both the subject matter under consideration and how one does or should formulate responses show that the respondent, in collaboration with the interviewer, activates diverse narrative resources as an integral part of exchanging questions and answers. Treating the interview as active allows the interviewer to encourage the respondent to shift positions in the interview so as to explore alternate perspectives and stocks of knowledge. Rather than searching for the best or most authentic answer, the aim is to systematically activate applicable ways of knowing—the possible answers—that respondents can reveal, as diverse and contradictory as they might be. The active interviewer sets the general parameters for responses, constraining as well as provoking answers that are germane to the researcher's interest. He or she does not tell respondents what to say, but offers them pertinent ways of conceptualizing issues and making connections—that is, suggests possible horizons of meaning and narrative linkages that coalesce into the emerging responses (Gubrium 1993). The pertinence of what is discussed is partly defined by the research topic and partly by the substantive horizons of ongoing responses. While the active respondent may selectively exploit a vast range of narrative resources, it is the active interviewer's job to direct and harness the respondent's constructive storytelling to the research task at hand.

◆ Implications for Analysis

Compared to more traditional perspectives on interviewing, the active approach seems to invite unacceptable forms of bias. After all, far more is going on than simply retrieving the information from respondents' repositories of knowledge; "contamination" is everywhere. This criticism only holds, however, if one takes a narrow view of interpretive practice and meaning construction. Bias is a meaningful concept only if the subject is seen to possess a preformed, pure informational commodity that the interview process might somehow taint. But if interview responses are seen as products of interpretive practice, they are neither preformed, nor ever pure. Any interview situation—no matter how formalized, restricted, or standardized—relies upon the interaction between participants. Because meaning construction is unavoidably collaborative (Garfinkel 1967, Sacks, Schegloff, and Jefferson 1974), it is virtually impossible to free any interaction from those factors that could be construed as contaminants. All participants in an interview are inevitably implicated in making meaning.

While naturally occurring talk and interaction may appear to be more spontaneous, less "staged" than an interview, this is true only in the sense that such interaction is staged by persons other than an interviewer. Resulting conversations are not necessarily more "realistic" or "authentic." They simply take place in what have been recognized as indigenous settings. With the development of the interview society, and the increasing deprivatization of personal experience (see Gubrium and Holstein 1995; Gubrium, Holstein, and Buckholdt 1994), the interview is becoming more and more commonplace, making it much more of a "naturally occurring" occasion for articulating experience.

Nevertheless, discussion of some topics, while being deeply significant, may nonetheless be relatively rare in the normal course of everyday life, even in the interview society. For example, as seemingly ubiquitous as is talk about family and domestic life, we have found it useful to study "family discourse" in a relatively circumscribed range of settings, most of which intentionally provoke talk about family as an integral part of conducting routine business, such as in a family therapy agency, for example (see Gubrium and Holstein 1990, Gubrium 1992). Active interviews can thus be used to gain purchase on interpretive practice relating to matters that may not be casually topical. By inciting narrative production, the interviewer may provoke interpretive developments that might emerge too rarely to be effectively captured "in their natural habitat," so to speak.

Finally, given the unconventional nature of active interviewing, how does one make sense of its data? Analyzing data concerning interpretive practice is something of an "artful" matter in its own right. This does not mean, however, that analysis is any less rigorous than that applied to conventional interview data; on the contrary, active interview data require disciplined and sensitivity to both process and substance.

Interviews are conventionally analyzed as more or less accurate descriptions of experience, as reports or representations (literally, re-presentations) of reality. Analysis takes the form of systematically grouping and summarizing the descriptions, and providing a coherent organizing framework that encapsulates and explains aspects of the social world that respondents portray. Respondents' interpretive activity is subordinated to the substance of what they report; the *whats* of experience overwhelm the *hows*.

In contrast, active interview data can be analyzed to show the dynamic interrelatedness of the *whats* and the *hows*. Respondents' responses are not viewed as reality reports delivered from a fixed repository. Instead, they are considered for the ways that they construct aspects of reality in collaboration with the interviewer. The focus is as much on the assembly process as on what is assembled. Using sociologically oriented forms of narrative and discourse analysis, conversational records of interpretive practice are examined to reveal reality-constructing practices as well as the subjective meanings that are circumstantially conveyed (see DeVault 1990, Gubrium and Holstein 1994, Holstein and Gubrium 1994, Propp 1968, Riessman 1993, Silverman 1993). The goal is to show how interview responses are produced in the interaction between interviewer and respondent, without losing sight of the meanings produced or the circumstances that condition the meaning-making process.

The analytic objective is not merely to describe the situated production of talk, but to show how what is being said relates to the experiences and lives being studied.

Writing up findings from interview data is itself an analytically active enterprise. Rather than simply letting the data "speak for themselves," the active analyst empirically documents the meaning-making process. With ample illustration and reference to records of talk, the analyst describes the complex discursive activities through which respondents produce meaning. The goal is to explicate how meanings, their linkages and horizons, are actively constituted within the interview environment. The analyst's reports do not summarize and organize what interview participants have said as much as they "de-construct" participants' talk to show the reader both the *hows* and the *whats* of the narrative dramas of lived experience.

■ *References*

Alasuutari, P. 1995. *Qualitative Methods and Analysis.* London: Sage.

Berger, P. L. and T. Luckmann. 1967. *The Social Construction of Reality.* New York: Doubleday.

Blumer, H. 1969. *Symbolic Interactionism.* New York: Prentice Hall.

Briggs, C. 1986. *Learning How to Ask: A Sociolinguistic Appraisal of the Role of the Interviewer in Social Science Research.* Cambridge: Cambridge University Press.

Cicourel, A. V. 1964. *Method and Measurement in Sociology.* New York: Free Press.

Cicourel, A. V. 1974. *Theory and Method in a Study of Argentine Fertility.* New York: Wiley

Converse, J. M. and H. Schuman. 1974. *Conversations at Random: Survey Research as Interviewers See It.* New York: Wiley.

DeVault, M. 1990. "Talking and Listening from Women's Standpoint: Feminist Strategies for Interviewing and Analysis. *Social Problems* 37:96–117.

Douglas, J. D. 1985. *Creative Interviewing.* Beverly Hills, CA: Sage.

Fowler, F. J. and T. W. Mangione. 1990. *Standardized Survey Interviewing.* Newbury Park, CA: Sage.

Garfinkel, H. 1967. *Studies in Ethnomethodology.* Englewood Cliffs, NJ: Prentice Hall.

Gorden, R. L. 1987. *Interviewing: Strategy, Techniques, and Tactics.* Homewood, IL: Dorsey.

Gubrium, J. F. 1988. *Analyzing Field Reality.* Beverly Hills: Sage.

Gubrium, J. F. 1989. "Local Cultures and Service Policy." Pp. 94–112 in *The Politics of Field Research,* edited by J. F. Gubrium and D. Silverman. London: Sage.

Gubrium, J. F. 1992. *Out of Control.* Newbury Park, CA: Sage.

Gubrium, J. F. 1993. *Speaking of Life: Horizons of Meaning for Nursing Home Residents.* Hawthorne, NY: Aldine de Gruyter.

Gubrium, J. F. and J. A. Holstein. 1990. *What is Family?* Mountain View, CA: Mayfield.

Gubrium, J. F. and J. A. Holstein. 1994. "Analyzing Talk and Interaction." Pp. 173–88 in *Qualitative Methods in Aging Research,* edited by J. Gubrium and A. Sankar. Newbury Park, CA: Sage.

Gubrium, J. F. and J. A. Holstein, 1995. "Biographical Work and New Ethnography." Pp. 45–58 in *The Narrative Study of Lives,* vol. 3, edited by R. Josselson and A. Lieblich. Newbury Park, CA: Sage.

Gubrium, J. F., J. A. Holstein and D. R. Buckholdt. *Constructing the Life Course.* Dix Hills, NY: General Hall.

Harding, S. (ed.). 1987. *Feminism and Methodology.* Bloomington: Indiana University Press.

Heritage, J. 1984. *Garfinkel and Ethnomethodology.* Cambridge: Polity.

Holstein, J. A. 1993. *Court-Ordered Insanity: Interpretive Practice and Involuntary Commitment.* Hawthorne, NY: Aldine de Gruyter.

Holstein, J. A. and J. F. Gubrium. 1994. "Phenomenology, Ethnomethodology, and Interpretive Practice." Pp. 262–72 in *Handbook of Qualitative Research,* edited by N. K. Denzin and Y. Lincoln. Newbury Park, CA: Sage.

Holstein, J. A. and W. G. Staples. 1992. "Producing Evaluative Knowledge: The Interactional Bases of Social Science Findings." *Sociological Inquiry* 62:11–35.

Hyman, H. H., W. J. Cobb, J. J. Feldman, C. W. Hart, and C. H. Stember. 1975. *Interviewing in Social Research.* Chicago: University of Chicago Press.

Kirk, J., and M. L. Miller. 1986. *Reliability and Validity in Qualitative Research.* Beverly Hills, CA: Sage.

Maccoby, E. E. and N. Maccoby. 1954. "The Interview: A Tool of Social Science." Pp. 449–87 in *Handbook of Social Psychology,* edited by G. Lindzey. Reading, MA: Addison-Wesley.

Madge, John. 1965. *The Tools of Social Science.* Garden City, NY: Anchor.

Manning, P. L. 1967. "Problems in Interpreting Interview Data." *Sociology and Social Research* 51:301–16.

Mishler, E. G. 1986. *Research Interviewing.* Cambridge: Harvard University Press.

Mishler, E. G. 1991. "Representing Discourse: The Rhetoric of Transcription." *Journal of Narrative and Life History* 1:255–80.

Pollner, M. 1987. *Mundane Reason.* Cambridge: Cambridge University Press.

Pool, I. de Sola. 1957. "A Critique of the Twentieth Anniversary Issue," *Public Opinion Quarterly* 21:190–98.

Propp, V. I. 1968. *The Morphology of the Folktale.* Austin: University of Texas Press.

Reinharz, S. 1992. *Feminist Methods of Social Research.* New York: Oxford University Press.

Riessman, C. Kohler. 1993. *Narrative Analysis.* Newbury Park, CA: Sage.

Rogers, C. R. 1945. "The Non-Directive Method as a Technique for Social Research." *American Journal of Sociology* 50:279–83.

Sacks, H., E. Schegloff, and G. Jefferson. 1994. "A Simplest Systematics for the Organization of Turn-Taking in Conversation." *Language* 50:696–735.

Schutz, A. 1967. *The Phenomenology of the Social World.* Evanston, IL: Northwestern University Press.

Silverman, D. 1993. *Interpreting Qualitative Data.* London: Sage.

Smith, D. E. 1987. *The Everyday World as Problematic: A Feminist Sociology.* Boston: Northeastern University Press.

Terkel, S. 1972. *Working.* New York: Avon.

5

INTERNET INTERVIEWING

◆ **Chris Mann**
Fiona Stewart

Interviews provide ready access to human experience in our everyday world. Now researchers in the 21st century are challenged by the simultaneously familiar yet mysterious worlds that lie "behind the screen" of the computer. They are the three-dimensional worlds of friends, colleagues, and strangers manifested in on-screen text. They are also the virtual worlds of on-line communities with their own images, rules, and interpersonal dynamics created in text. Sitting at a computer, using the Internet, researchers can interview disembodied people from across the earth and also the personae who frequent the imagined environments of cyberspace.

In this chapter we discuss interviewing using widely available Internet technology. First, we describe the key characteristics of computer-mediated communication and identify pioneering studies that have used this medium for interviewing. We then con-

sider some of the more important costs and benefits of conducting interviews on-line. Next, we discuss in detail the different kinds of expertise that researchers might need in order to conduct quantitative and qualitative interviews on-line. Finally, we consider options that might become available to researchers using the Internet as an interviewing medium in the future.

◆ Computer-Mediated Communication

Computer-mediated communication (CMC) allows computer users to interact directly with each other, using text, via keyboards. Text-based CMC is available in two main modes. Asynchronous CMC, the feature of most e-mail messaging systems, allows users to type extended messages that are then electronically transmitted to recipients who can read, reply, print, forward, and file them at any time they choose. Synchronous CMC, or "real-time chat," involves the interchange of messages between two or more users simultaneously logged on at different computers or computer terminals.

CMC systems also divide into semi-private and public arenas. The former include e-mail, one-to-one discussions using "chat" software, and conferences/forums (asynchronous discussion groups). These systems allow the interviewer (and participants) some level of control with regard to the nature and content of interaction. Public areas of CMC, in contrast, are beyond the direct control of the interviewer, and interaction may be extremely volatile (McLaughlin, Osborne, and Smith 1995). The main public arenas using CMC are bulletin board systems (BBSs) and news groups, such as those found in Usenet, the WELL, and ECHO, and undirected real-time chat systems such as those found in most Internet relay chat (IRC) and MU* environments.[1] Whichever modes they adopt for interviewing, researchers are becoming aware that CMC has characteristics that do not fit within more traditional modes of data collection (Mann and Stewart 2000); these characteristics are challenging some standard assumptions about language (Herring 1996), interpersonal relationships (Walther 1996), and group dynamics (Lea 1992; Garton, Haythorn-thwaite, and Wellman 1999).[2]

Although Internet use is still evolving, the potential of CMC as an interviewing medium has already been recognized, and pioneering studies have begun to identify the possibilities and pitfalls of Internet interviewing. Some researchers adopt CMC as an interviewing medium because it seems the "logical" (O'Connor and Madge 2000), indeed "the only authentic and congruent" (Smith-Stoner and Weber 2000) method of investigating Internet usage. Research has focused on the demographics of Internet use (Kehoe and Pitkow 1996) and also many aspects of on-line experience. Some investigations are associated with discussions of Internet culture (Baym 1995; Turkle 1995) and the impact of this culture, or variations of this culture (Shields 1996), on debates around identity (Bruckman 1992; Reid 1991), gender (Matheson 1992; Bannert and Arbinger 1996; Spender 1995), race (Burkhalter 1999), and cross-cultural relations (Hantrais and Sen 1996).

Other interviewers have investigated the experiences of people engaged in such on-line activity areas as distance learning (Salmon 2000; Smith-Stoner and Weber 2000), gay men's chat (Shaw 1997), virtual worlds (Correll 1995), use of Web sites (O'Connor and Madge 2000) and e-mail-mediated help services (Hahn 1998), virtual focus groups (Sweet 1999), on-line versions of a subculture (Hodkinson 2000), rural women's use of interactive communication technology (Daws 1999), and the empowering use of technology for people with disabilities (Seymour, Lupton, and Fahy 1999).

In addition, as Joseph Walther (1999) has pointed out, interviewers may use "computer-based tools and computer-accessible populations to study human behavior in general" (p. 1). Some examples of researchers who have used CMC to interview people about off-line experiences are Fiona Stewart, Elizabeth Eckerman, and Kai Zhou (1998), who collected data on a range of health issues and practices using on-line or "virtual" focus groups involving participants from the Fiji Islands, China, Australia, and Malaysia; Elizabeth Anders (2000), who conducted an international study of issues faced by women with disabilities in higher education; Anne Ryen and David Silverman (2000), who undertook a case study of an Asian entrepreneur in Africa; and Chris Mann, who looked in depth at factors that might relate to differences in academic performance among undergraduates (this research is discussed in Mann and Stewart 2000).

In these studies, the researchers chose CMC because it eliminated constraints that would have made face-to-face (FTF) research impractical. It allowed researchers to interview participants on different continents, to maintain day-by-day contact with many students throughout the course of work on their degrees, and to reach people who would have been unable to participate face-to-face because of disability, financial difficulties, and/or language and communication differences. Yet other interviewers have capitalized on the anonymity of the technology to access the voices of members of socially marginalized communities, such as gay fathers (Dunne 1999) and men who might have avoided discussing emotions if interviewed face-to-face (Bennett 1998). Psychologists are also beginning to explore CMC as a research medium (Senior and Smith 1999). For instance, on-line discussion groups have enabled researchers to access and then interview individuals with specific disorders, such as panic attacks (Stones and Perry 1998).

Clearly, CMC interviewing has a great deal to offer, but is it an interviewing medium suitable for all inquiries and all potential interviewees? This question can be answered only with reference to the methodological choices made in any research study. Research questions may focus on the form/nature or the extent/prevalence of phenomena. Generally, nonstandardized qualitative interviews, conducted with individuals or groups, investigate the former; standardized quantitative interviews map the latter. As other chapters in this book describe, qualitative and quantitative methods have costs and benefits at both practical and methodological levels. A particularly significant factor in this context is that the majority of conventional qualitative interviews are conducted face-to-face, whereas larger-scale quantitative interviews are frequently self-administered. These issues will come into play in the next section, where we discuss whether CMC increases the benefits and/or reduces the costs associated with off-line research.

◆ Some Costs and Benefits of Internet Interviewing

The costs and benefits of Internet interviewing can be assessed along a number of dimensions, some of which parallel traditional interviewing concerns and some of which are unique to the Internet medium. Let us begin by considering the first challenge that faces all interviewers: gaining access to participants.

SAMPLING AND RECRUITMENT

There is no doubt that the unrepresentativeness of current Internet access remains the greatest problem for data collection online. Given that only approximately 0.01 percent of the world's population was online at the start of 2000, it is not surprising that some writers focus on the "cyberspace divide" (Loader 1998) and the ascendancy of the literate and the computer literate in this mode of communication. Microsoft's Bill Gates (1997) has admitted that, in terms of the Internet, the problem of "the haves versus the have-nots has many dimensions: rich versus poor, urban versus rural, young versus old, and perhaps most dramatically, developing countries versus developed countries" (p. 34). Interviewers need to be aware that access to and use of the Internet is a matter not only of economics, but also of one's place in the world in terms of gender, culture, ethnicity, and language (Mann and Stewart 2000).

The patchiness of Internet access has clear implications for interviewing approaches that seek representative sampling. In statistical terms, large samples (which are certainly possible with e-mail-based and, in particular, Web-page-based surveys) do not mean anything unless they are representative of a target population, a goal that currently would clearly be difficult to attain except for specialized populations. With regard to the latter, Georgia Tech University's Graphics, Visualization, and Usability (GVU) Center's series of World Wide Web surveys attempted to identify the demographics of the Internet population itself (Kehoe and Pitkow 1996).[3] E-mail surveys have also been used to study small-scale homogeneous groups of on-line users (Parker 1992; Smith 1997; Tse et al. 1995; Winter and Huff 1996). Resourceful use of the Internet can expand the boundaries of how such interviewees may be identified. A variety of on-line formats, such as chat rooms, mailing lists, BBSs, and conferences, focus on specific topics, drawing together geographically dispersed participants who may share interests, experiences, or expertise. With a growing total of more than 25,000 news groups accessible to more than 40 million users (Kennedy 1998), the Internet is an extremely convenient way of identifying people with similar interests.

These same arenas are also available to qualitative researchers who seek purposive rather than representative samples of participants. The virtuality of the medium offers unprecedented possibilities for extending the range of participants beyond those who are available for FTF interviewing, such as mothers at home with small children, shift workers, and people with disabilities. The Internet also offers researchers a possible means of communicating with people in sites to which access is restricted (such as hospitals, religious communities, prisons, government offices, the military, schools, and cults).

The technology can offer interviewers practical access to sites previously "closed" to researchers with visible attributes that would make them stand out within the population of interest, such as age, gender, ethnicity, or even physical "style" (bikers, surfers, Goths, punks, jet-setters and so on)—although there are ethical considerations surrounding researchers' disguising their identities to become acceptable to insiders. CMC also extends the possibilities of conducting research in politically sensitive or dangerous areas (see Lee 1993).

Physical distance and the possibility of anonymity offer protection to both researchers and participants (see, for instance, Coomber's 1997 study of illicit drug dealers). Political and religious dissidents or human rights advocates might feel able to participate in on-line interviews without excessive risk. Researchers can access censored and/or politically or militarily sensitive data without needing to be physically in the field. They can interview people living or working in war zones, or sites of corruption or criminal activity, or places where diseases are rife, without needing to grapple with the danger—and the bureaucracy—involved in actually visiting the area. The disembodiment of CMC also allows researchers to distance themselves physically from ideological camps, reducing the likelihood of suspicion and innuendo that might alienate some participants. Researchers could communicate, for instance, with both police and criminals without being seen visiting either; or researchers could interview both Israelis and Palestinians, say, without leaving themselves open to charges of spying.

Many interviewers recruit on-line participants using the Internet itself; another option for recruitment is to include a contact e-mail or Web address when advertising the research more conventionally in publicity leaflets and journals. Recruiting individual participants involves acquiring their e-mail addresses, either through earlier interaction (on- or off-line) or by soliciting responses from Internet users. Placing a request for contacts or information when logging onto appropriate Internet sites is one possibility (Kehoe and Pitkow 1996). Some researchers also target individuals by writing to their e-mail addresses, which are generally attached to postings in many public CMC environments. However, this can create problems if the researcher moves directly to sending research materials without first gaining a user's consent. Cooperative participants can also assist with recruitment by "snowballing" messages using the "forwarding" option provided by e-mail software (Hodkinson 2000).

Other options for interviewers are to invite participation passively by posting recruitment messages that set out to attract anyone who happens to "surf" or "lurk" around chat rooms and conference areas linked to particular Web sites, or to set up their own Web sites with "hotlinks" that draw in potential participants (O'Connor and Madge 2000). However, a certain degree of proactivity is needed to attract participants. Interviewers who advertise their research need a "hook" that will gain attention. For instance, Ross Coomber (1997) targeted drug dealers in news groups by using the subject headline "Have You Ever Sold Powdered Drugs? If So, I Would Like Your Help." Coomber also suggests that recruitment messages should be posted on a weekly basis, as news group posts are gradually replaced and sites attract new visitors all the time.

Why should individuals participate in on-line interview research at all? As with conventional research, they may be attracted by material reward or may have altruistic reasons. However, once interviewees are recruited, CMC offers them many bonuses. They can participate at their convenience from their own homes or places of work. Women, older people, and members of socially marginalized groups can communicate from familiar and physically safe environments. CMC is also experienced as relatively trouble-free, eliminating the "hassle" of finding pen and paper, buying stamps, and keeping FTF appointments. It is possible that low technical skills, particularly keyboarding skills, may marginalize some participants. On the other hand, CMC is generally informal and conversational in style and thus accessible to the everyday writer.

Sustaining CMC interaction over time, in view of both Internet "churn" (loss of access to the technology) and the ease with which participants can disappear without a trace into cyberspace, presents researchers with a new challenge. Early evidence suggests that, as in conventional research, the participants' commitment to the research purposes is a paramount factor in ensuring continuity of communication (Mann and Stewart 2000).

EXPENSE AND TIME

The lower cost of Internet research in relation to other modes is one of its most powerful advantages (and one that may increasingly encourage research sponsors to inquire whether conventional fieldwork could not be conducted through CMC). Once the necessary computer equipment has been acquired, the principal expenses for users of standard CMC are Internet service provider fees and telephone costs. In some parts of the world, phone calls for Internet use are already free, and, in a highly competitive and rapidly changing market, free Internet access is becoming increasingly available. For users with institutional access to the Internet, the cost to researchers or projects may be zero.

However, low-cost access to the on-line community has different implications for virtual versions of FTF and self-administered interviews. With conventional FTF interviewing, time and travel expenses can lead to compromises regarding where interviews are held and with whom. These problems are compounded as the research extends further afield. Interstate or interregional comparisons increase time and expense as the researcher and/or participants have to travel to different locations and conduct multiple sessions. In addition, venues for FTF interviews need to be easily accessible to participants in terms of location, timing (before work, in the evening, after children are dropped at day care), lifestyle (some participants may require child-care facilities, others may need on-site venues in businesses, schools, or hospitals), and physical access. Interviewers will also have their own requirements for FTF venues, depending upon the nature of the research (such as on-site if the research concerns a nursing home, or in a neutral location if it concerns abused wives). The requirements of researcher and participants can lead to costs in terms of the time to organize (and frequently reorganize) interview venues as well as the usage costs themselves.

In contrast, CMC is a practical and cost-efficient way of conducting in-depth interviews with individuals or groups who are geographically distant, and it also facilitates collaboration between colleagues who may be at different sites, even on different continents (Cohen 1996). With on-line participation, the venue becomes the sites at which CMC is available. There may still be site-related hire costs (such as usage rates in cybercafés), and there will still be considerations about the impacts of the venue (e.g., is computer access in a public, professional, or home context?). In practical terms, however, many of the difficulties and financial considerations associated with organizing FTF venues disappear. A further consideration is that, with on-line research, interaction results in the immediate production of a text file. Unlike in research using FTF interviews, the researcher has no need to budget for recording equipment, transcribing equipment, or transcription costs, and delays caused by transcription are eliminated.

The Internet also offers researchers the potential for substantial financial savings when their studies involve self-administered interviews (Bachmann, Elfrink, and Vazzana 1996; Mehta and Sivadas 1995). E-mail and Web-page-based surveys eliminate paper, are cheap to send, and, once initial start-up costs have been met, involve minimal costs for implementation and analysis (Sheehan and Hoy 1999). Apart from the benefit to researchers of direct access to large numbers of people, the speed of response in such surveys offers substantial time-cost savings. Comparative studies confirm that e-mail questionnaires are returned faster than their paper equiva-

lents (Schaefer and Dillman 1998; Comley 1996). Web-page-based surveys can speed up responses even further (Comley 1996; Smith, 1997); studies have shown that hundreds of responses may be generated over a single weekend (Sheehan and Hoy 1999), and there are anecdotal accounts of "thousands of responses" being received within a few hours (Gjestland 1996). However, savings are not automatic. E-mail surveys can consume time if the researcher has to search around for addresses, if many addresses turn out to be invalid, and if the form of the survey has to be explained to participants. There are also hidden costs associated with the level of technology involved. As we shall discuss below, researchers may need to set aside a considerable period for coping with the technical challenges and problems that might be involved in implementing on-line surveys (Couper, Blair, and Triplett 1999).

WORKING WITH DIGITAL DATA

Working with digital data offers researchers substantial benefits but also presents them with great challenges. There is no doubt that the technological base of the interviewing medium complements the computerized practices that are becoming so familiar to researchers. Individual interviews and even large databases from CMC surveys can be moved effortlessly into other computer functions. Electronic messages can be recalled on a computer monitor, saved and accessed in word-processing packages, and stored either as hard-copy printouts or on computer diskettes or compact discs.

The analysis of interview data can also benefit from the development and convergence of technologies. For instance, interview data can be moved directly into qualitative or quantitative analysis software packages (Creswell 1997; Fielding and Lee 1998; Tesch 1990) that might themselves interconnect (some qualitative software packages already have SPSS export facilities). There is likely to be a huge increase in such interconnection of digital processes in the future.

On the other hand, working with digital data in a virtual environment, researchers cannot avoid engaging with legal and ethical issues that are still in a state of flux. Research projects may involve interviewers in the processes of

> authentication (checking that someone is who he claims to be, or a website what it seems to be); authorisation (controlling access in a sophisticated ... way); confidentiality (keeping private information private); integrity (ensuring that information has not been tampered with); and non-repudiation (being sure the terms of a transaction are binding and legitimate). ("Future of the Internet," 1999:35)

Many of these areas require further legal definition and link in with other issues of intellectual property, security (including personal security from virtual assault, harassment, and stalking), encryption, digital signatures, and certification (see Kramarae and Kramer 1995; Thomas, Forcht, and Counts 1998). Researchers cannot overlook these issues, as some countries are establishing laws concerning, for instance, data protection and/or encryption that would apply to data generated in academic as well as commercial research.

The confusion about the legal implications of on-line research is matched by a lack of clarity about "good practice" on-line. There is little agreement about how to proceed ethically in a virtual arena, and few research practice conventions are available. Researchers are just beginning to grapple with the implications of the legal and ethical minefield and to discuss issues of confidentiality, participant risk, and informed consent in on-line research (Mann and Stewart 2000). As funding bodies and institutional review boards are adopting mandatory good-practice norms for on-line research, it would be politic for interviewers who intend to work on-line to give time to these issues and to find out at early stages of their research about current discussions that may have impacts on their research designs.[4]

◆ Technical Skills and Standardized Interviews

Dorothy Myers (1987) suggests that there are two kinds of experts on-line: the technically astute and the "relationally" astute (that is, the social experts who nurture and direct on-line relationships and create interpersonal bonds). On-line interviewers certainly need competence in both these areas, but do they need expertise? A great deal depends on the type of interview. As we shall discuss, conducting standardized interviews on-line is technically taxing. In a review of on-line surveys, Christine Smith (1997) concludes that "the lack of standardization among operating systems, servers, and browsers creates a challenging milieu in which a researcher must be technologically savvy as well as methodologically sound." For nonstandardized qualtative interviews, the technology may be more accessible but the acquisition of relational expertise is emphasized. Face-to-face, the human interviewer "can be a marvelously smart, adaptable, flexible instrument who can respond to situations with skill, tact, and understanding" (Seidman 1991:16); the challenge is to transfer these qualities on-line.

The technical challenges faced by researchers who have attempted structured interviews on-line have been documented more extensively than the work of researchers using qualitative approaches. Studies of self-completion surveys conducted on-line began to be published around the end of 1995 (for reviews, see Comley 1996; Couper et al. 1999; Witmer, Colman, and Katzman 1999) and offer considerable practical insights for any researcher who intends to use CMC in this way. We next consider the demands for technical expertise placed on researchers conducting standardized interviews using e-mail and the World Wide Web.

E-MAIL SURVEYS

In an e-mail survey, the questions are usually sent to respondents as the text of a conventional e-mail message. To complete the survey, respondents use the "reply" facility of their e-mail system and add their answers to the text of the returned message. The answers received can then be typed into an analysis program in the same way as for a conventional survey. Alternatively, a program can be written that will interpret the e-mailed responses and read the answers directly into a database; this approach offers significant savings in terms of data entry. Commercial survey-creation programs are available that, as well as assisting in producing the text of a survey, can carry out this interpretation of replies, provided the survey has been completed correctly (see also Smith 1997).[5]

Text-based e-mail surveys are convenient for respondents because they require no facilities or expertise beyond those the respondents use in their day-to-day e-mail communication. However, technical problems still arise. The size of the survey may also be a difficulty. Peter Comley (1996), for instance, had to split his survey into two e-mails. Some organizations use e-mail systems that convert messages over a certain size (such as questionnaires) into attachments. In one study a number of employees reported that they had received attachments but didn't know what to do with them (Couper et al. 1999).

A further drawback is that a text survey can appear dry and uninteresting. E-mail in its simplest form does not allow formatting of text (e.g., use of boldface, italics, different fonts). In addition, the researcher has no control over the format of the responses. There is nothing to prevent a respondent from answering outside the boxes, selecting three choices where only one is required, or deleting or altering questions. In a study conducted by Mick Couper and his associates (1999), 21 percent of all e-mail respondents did not make use of the reply feature as intended, but used a word processor or text editor instead. In such cases, researchers may still be able to interpret what respondents mean, as with badly completed paper questionnaires, but the need to edit responses removes the advantages of automated data entry and can greatly increase per case costs.

If all potential respondents are using relatively modern e-mail systems that can understand HTML, the researcher can alleviate some design problems by using an HTML-based e-mail survey.[6] Because HTML uses only standard text characters, the survey is still sent as the text of an e-mail. But because the e-mail system interprets HTML commands, the message can be laid out in an attractive way. In addition, the researcher has control over participants' responses: Answers can be typed only in text-entry boxes, and if only one choice is required, only one will be accepted. HTML-based e-mail combines these advantages (usually associated with Web-based surveys) with the direct response advantage of e-mail. However, until HTML-enabled e-mail systems become more common, these benefits are possible only if the survey participants are within a defined population where the researcher knows what systems they are using.

A further possibility is for the researcher to present the survey not in the body of the e-mail message itself but as a file (for example, a word processor document or a spreadsheet) attached to the e-mail. The respondent opens the attached file, completes the survey using the relevant program, saves the file, and then attaches the saved file to a return e-mail. This gives the researcher control over the appearance of the survey, but completion and return require that respondents have more technical ability. In addition, respondents must all have access to the program (such as Microsoft Word or Microsoft Excel) in which the attached document was created. As with HTML-based mail, the approach is suitable only for a defined population where the researcher knows the abilities of the respondents or can provide them with training and support. In addition, some organizations may prohibit users from receiving e-mail attachments because of fears about viruses.

Researchers can overcome some of these problems by using survey-creation software to produce self-contained interactive survey programs.[7] The software allows researchers to create elegant, responsive, and efficient surveys, and the survey programs can produce formatted answer files that can be mailed back to interviewers for automated input to a database. However, such programs have a number of limitations. For example, a program created for the Windows operating system will not run on a Macintosh, and vice versa. Even with a single operating system, researchers may run into unexpected technical difficulties when trying to run their programs on the wide range of computers likely to be used by respondents; Couper et al. (1999) found problems with all seven of their pretest subjects. For instance, the program files produced may be large (in the case of Couper et al.'s study, approaching one megabyte), which may result in unacceptable volumes of Internet traffic and may be beyond the size permitted for incoming e-mail attachments. Because of such problems, most of the e-mail surveys reported to date have used the straightforward text-based route. However, Couper et al. (1999) "remain optimistic about the potential for e-mail as an alternative to the traditional mail survey" (p. 54).

WEB-PAGE-BASED SURVEYS

David Schaefer and Don Dillman (1998) note that their experiment with e-mail surveys "revealed the possibility that [these] represent only an interim surveying technology" (p. 392). Many researchers are turning their attention to the World Wide Web as a more suitable medium for administering questionnaires (for further information, see Comley 1996; Kehoe and Pitkow 1996; Coomber 1997; O'Connor and Madge 2000; for a comparison with e-mail surveys, see Patrick, Black, and Whalen 1995). However, the main drawback of the Web approach is the high level of technical expertise that researchers must acquire or have available to them. This includes the knowledge of HTML required to create the Web pages. Survey-creation programs, as discussed previously, can provide "what you see is what you get" editing of pages, removing much of the mystery of HTML, but identifying and learning a suitable program presents another hurdle to be overcome. Once the pages have been created, they must be uploaded to a host Internet server, another technically complex procedure (Mann and Stewart 2000).[8]

Why might researchers grapple with the challenges attendant on using the Web to interview? A Web-page-based survey has the advantage that it appears identical (subject to the browser used) to all respondents. Through the use of text formatting, colors, and graphics, the survey can be given an attractive appearance. Web-page-based surveys are also easy for respondents to complete, typically by selecting responses from predefined lists or entering text in boxes and then simply clicking a "submit" button when finished. The data received by the researcher are in a completely predictable and consistent format, making automated analysis possible without the editing that may be necessary with text-based e-mail surveys.

Despite the technical challenges involved, Christine Smith (1997) has predicted that Web-based survey software will soon become an indispensable research tool, "along with or even instead of analytical tools like SPSS." The significant advantages that Web-page-based surveys offer suggest they will become more and more common, especially for commercial market research. It may not be long before the creation of Web survey pages is routinely taught in social science research methods courses.

◆ Relational Skills and Nonstandardized Interviews

In nonstandardized interviews, the focus moves from the preformulated ideas of the researcher to "the meanings and interpretations that individuals attribute to events and relationships" (May 1993:94). It is this emphasis that leads many practitioners to refer to such interviews as qualitative, and it is to the relational skills required in such interviews that we now turn.

SOFTWARE OPTIONS IN NONSTANDARDIZED INTERVIEWS

Researchers are familiar with the methodological reasons that might inform a decision to interview one-to-one or in groups (Mann and Stewart 2000). However, when interviewing is conducted on-line, the decision to use in-depth interviews or "virtual" focus groups involves further issues relating to temporality—that is, whether interviews should take place synchronously (with delayed response) or in "real" or synchronous time. There are various forms of software available:

Individual Interview
Options Software

◆ *E-mail:* E-mail allows asynchronous interviews one-to-one.

◆ *Real-time one-to-one chat:* Software such as AOL's Instant Messenger and ICQ

(I Seek You; see www.icq.com) allows users to chat in real time one-to-one (or with groups of people).

Group Interview
Options Software

◆ *Real-time many-to-many chat:* This is communication in which messages are written and read at the same time, although in different places. What one person types is visible to everyone else on the same "channel." Chat software can range from "shareware" (software programs that are freely downloadable, such as mIRC; see www.mirc.com) to licensed software packages such as Hotline Client and FirstClass Conferencing, which are ideal for moderated real-time focus groups.[9] Typically, a chat program will have a conversation flow area, where a participant can read all contributions, as well as a separate composition area, where participants can write their own messages.

◆ *Asynchronous many-to-many conferencing:* In this form of communication, as in e-mail, participants can respond to messages from other participants at some time in the future. Unlike e-mail, however, conferencing is conducted at a "conference site" (as opposed to individual e-mail addresses), which can have restricted or public access. A typical conference site may be a type of folder, like the one that appears on both Macintosh and Windows computer screens. Confer- encing provides an effective means of conducting non-real-time on-line focus groups. Conferencing systems include FirstClass (from SoftArc, Inc.) and CoSy (from Softwords Research International). In addition, both Microsoft and Netscape have their own systems and distribute them widely in combination with software and system packages. Conferencing systems are also known as groupware systems, of which Lotus-

Notes (from Lotus) is perhaps the best known.

CMC AND THE DEVELOPMENT OF RAPPORT IN NONSTANDARDIZED INTERVIEWS

Generating textual data using e-mail or chat software is rarely a technical challenge (although group software involves extra complications). However, nonstandardized interviews also require researchers to acquire "relational" expertise. Successful qualitative interviewing depends upon interviewers' developing rapport with participants (Fontana and Frey 1994). Traditionally, this has been associated with a mutual reading of presentation of self. In any social situation, each party makes a swift appraisal of the other's age, gender, and ethnicity; of accent, dress, and personal grooming; of conventionality, eccentricity, and subcultural markers; of confidence levels, physical attractiveness, and friendliness or restraint. In addition, oral dimensions of language (pitch, tone, and so on) might identify whether what is said is spoken from a position of confidence, doubt, irony, and so forth. The sense of the other attained by such means allows each person to assess (a) how others are interpreting what he or she says and (b) the genuineness of intent in queries and responses.

If, as a result of this delicate interaction, participants come to trust in the sincerity and the motivation of the interviewer, they may be prepared to share in-depth insights into their private and social worlds. At the same time, the interviewer will increasingly be able to sense the appropriateness of questions and the meaningfulness of answers. Reading signs of the other is a human characteristic that many FTF qualitative researchers develop to the level of a skill. But is it possible to "connect" at these emotional and mental levels when communicating on-line?[10] Is it possible for an interviewer to develop rapport with participants

whom he or she may never have seen or heard? We posed these questions to two researchers who had conducted qualitative e-mail interviews. They responded differently:

> Generating an atmosphere of rapport online can be a problem, and given the lack of tone or gesture and the length of time between exchanges it can lead to something of a formal, structured interview. This is in contrast to the spontaneous speeding up, slowing down, getting louder, getting quieter, getting excited, laughing together, spontaneous thoughts, irrelevant asides etc. etc. which I have experienced in off-line interviews. The best words I can think of to separate off-line from E-mail interviews then, are FLOW, and DYNAMICS, both of which, in my view are liable to contribute to greater depth and quality of information in an off-line interview than over e-mail. (P. Hodkinson, e-mail communication, March 1999)

> Is rapport online possible? Absolutely!!!! Rapport comes from being very up front with what you are doing and responding as you would with anyone. Laughing, listening and connecting are the key. (M. J. Smith-Stoner, e-mail communication, March 1999)

These perspectives reflect current debates about in-depth communication online. In one view, CMC cannot achieve the highly interactive, rich, and spontaneous communication that can be achieved in FTF interviewing. Communication differences between media are often conceptualized in terms of bandwidth, or the "volume of information per unit time that a computer, person, or transmission medium can handle" (Raymond 1993, cited in Kollock and Smith 1996:15). CMC is said by some to have a narrow or lean bandwidth, in contrast to the "rich" bandwidth of FTF interaction (see Sala 1998). As it allows insufficient transmission of social cues to establish the human "presence" of the other, CMC is seen as impersonal and distancing (Hewson, Laurent, and Vogel 1996; Kiesler, Siegel, and McGuire 1984; Short, Williams, and Christie 1976). Particularly in groups, the psychological distances separating participants and the depersonalization of "the other" that can result may lead to various kinds of unsociable behavior, such as flaming (Dubrovsky, Kiesler, and Sethna 1991). When CMC is seen as an "impoverished" communication environment (Giese 1998), it is not surprising that it is mainly considered appropriate for tasks requiring little social interaction or intimacy (Rice and Case 1983). Walther's (1992) review of this literature sums up the implications for research if CMC is viewed in this way: If investigations seek "information that is ambiguous, emphatic, or emotional . . . a richer medium should be used" (p. 57).

If CMC is indeed a "lean" communication medium that is neither conducive to establishing good interpersonal relationships nor capable of addressing delicate information, then it is clear that the work of the on-line qualitative interviewer will be challenging, if not doomed to failure from the beginning. However, relational development theorists have challenged these findings, pointing out that most assumptions about interpersonal relationships (such as the need for physical proximity) predate CMC and may not be fully applicable to on-line settings (Lea and Spears 1995; Parks and Floyd 1996). In his review of nonexperimental studies of CMC, Walther (1992) found evidence that warm relationships can and do develop on-line. He points out that the same motives that drive people in other contexts drive them in CMC. People want to interact, they seek social reward, they want to be liked. Thus research interactants, like communicators in any context, will "desire to transact per-

sonal, rewarding, complex relationships and . . . they will communicate to do so" (p. 68). We shall now consider factors that might contribute to the successful development of rapport on-line.

USING TECHNOLOGY TO CREATE RAPPORT

Some on-line interviewers use linguistic conventions available in CMC to help convey the mood of the communication and to make social and emotional connections. Electronic paralanguage consists of repetitions, abbreviations, and verbal descriptions of feelings and sounds, such as "hehehe" for laughter, "lol" for "lots of laughs," and "LJATD" for "let's just agree to disagree" (discussion going nowhere).

"Emoticons"—such as :-) for smiling/happy and :-o for surprise/shock—offer interviewers another textual means to show feelings and to soften the potentially distancing abruptness of some CMC messages by adding humor or whimsicality (Murphy and Collins 1997). However, the use of emoticons is not transparent in communicative terms. First, emoticons may reflect the social and communicative practices of a subculture (see Baym 1995). Second, emoticons may not always work cross-nationally. In Japan, where signs of respect are finely graduated and where relationships develop in indirect ways, a highly complex system of emoticons attempts to parallel some of the delicacy of FTF interaction. However, these emoticons are not familiar to most Western interviewers. Such emoticons are read in a traditional horizontal format rather than sideways: (-o-) for "I'm sorry"; (^o^;) for "excuse me!"; (^o^) for happy; (^-^;; for awkward (see Aoki 1994).

Emoticons may also be "read" in different ways by participants in a research project. To some, they may indicate a friendly but rather impersonal approach (Aycock and Buchignani 1995). To others, as with varying responses to such friendship gestures as handshakes and open body language in FTF research, they may seem an inappropriate way of "doing research." They can also be seen as lazy and unimaginative, possibly alienating some members of sophisticated on-line communities. As Stacy Horn (1998) has warned, it is possible that "people will assume that you are without language, or conversation and suggest that you go back to America Online (a place known for its liberal use of emoticons)" (p. 63). It would seem that interviewers should use electronic paralanguage judiciously. Even if they do, in the opinion of one participant in Mann's study of academic performance at the University of Cambridge, CMC will never be subtle enough to compare to FTF interaction:

> You'll see people annotate their mails using smilies, HTML-style tags, capital letters, etc., but even so there is no reliable way of conveying tone. How you say something is often more important than what you say—and e-mail doesn't have this dimension. (Quoted in Mann and Stewart 2000:14)

Clearly, qualitative interviewers who seek to establish rapport on-line need to look beyond electronic paralanguage. In the following sections we discuss factors that have seemed of most importance in interview studies.

IMPORTANCE OF SHARED RESEARCH AGENDA FOR RAPPORT

Participants with a superficial interest in the research topic may be initially intrigued and attracted by the option of interacting on-line, but this might not be enough to sustain their ongoing interest without the impetus of enthusiasm and focus that can be injected in the FTF setting by a skilled interviewer who is "firing on all cylinders." On-line, interviewers may not be able to offer enough verbal "dazzle" to compensate for the charm or charisma that can be so effective face-to-face. If participants have no particular vested interest in a study or a low boredom threshold, there may be a tendency for less involved participants to drop away:

> The longest of my e-mail interviews has been a few weeks . . . usually I found that people lost interest before I am able to get to the same degree of detail as a face to face interview. (P. Hodkinson, e-mail communication, March 1999)

However, a shared research agenda and/ or being given an opportunity to be "heard" in a meaningful way can "lead virtual relationships to become very personal very quickly" (Smith-Stoner and Weber 2000). In these circumstances, interest in the interaction is sustained.

> Respondents often spoke of the value of our dialogues for helping them to make sense of their lives. They remarked on the time they had taken in thinking through their responses (some taking several hours) and messages were usually very long. (Dunne 1999:3)

Marilyn Smith-Stoner and Todd Weber (2000), who report having had excellent rapport with their participants, point out that the women they interviewed were very enthusiastic about the research topic: It did not "require any selling at all." Not only did these women want to tell their stories, they "expressed deep satisfaction with the process and were grateful to be able to do in online." A similar overlap of appreciating methodological and personal factors ensured the effectiveness of O'Connor's real-time focus group discussions with new parents:

> The interviews all provided high levels of self-consciousness, reflexivity and interactivity. Whether it was owing to the nature of the interviewees (self-selected, motivated, frequent on-line users), or owing to the nature of the

subject matter, clearly very close to the hearts of the women involved, it is difficult to judge. (O'Connor and Madge 2000:4)

ESTABLISHING TRUST AS A BASIS FOR RAPPORT

It is generally recognized that mutual trust is the basis for the development of rapport in interviews. One way for researchers to dispel respondents' feelings of caution and to increase trust is to be as open as possible about the purposes and processes of the research. For semistructured interviews, the researcher can do this by making an interview schedule available well before the interview and inviting clarifying questions. Another way for the researcher to display "openness" would be to inform participants fully about the time frame of the interaction. Some researchers may conclude that in-depth research, particularly regarding sensitive topics, would benefit if people met face-to-face before attempting to conduct an on-line relationship.

There are, however, precedents for researchers' conducting deeply personal interviews without ever meeting the respondents in person. One means of establishing trust, and bridging the geographic and perhaps personal distance that may characterize on-line interviews (Moore 1993), is for interviewers and participants to share information about themselves (Murphy and Collins 1997). Richard Cutler (1995) has suggested that the more an individual discloses personal information on-line, the more others are likely to reciprocate, and the more individuals know about each other, the more likely it is that trust, satisfaction, and a sense of being in a safe communication environment will ensue. Caroline Bennett (1998), in her in-depth e-mail interviews, sought to establish relationships that would "nurse" equal degrees of self-disclosure between herself and her coinvestigators. She made initial disclosures about herself to encourage this pattern of discourse, and her participants responded in kind.

Technical ease of contact in CMC gives researchers the option of repeating interview interactions over time. There is evidence that trust and warmth in CMC relationships increases over extended interactions (Walther 1992). As Nancy Baym (1995) notes, "In CMC, as in real life, relationships take time to build" (p. 158). This has been the experience of qualitative researchers who have used sequential one-to-one e-mail interviews (Bennett 1998; Dunne 1999; Mann and Stewart 2000). However, findings from sequential interviews using e-mail suggest that the outcomes in terms of intimacy are not predictable. In part, this reflects differences in research design. In Gill Dunne's (1999) study of gay fathers, it was the participants' strong desire to be "heard" that led spontaneously to interviewer-participant closeness. This continued after the formal closure of the research and, in some cases, led to FTF meetings. In other studies, the development of long-term relationships was a part of the research design (see Mann and Stewart 2000; Ryen and Silverman 2000; Bennett 1998). Both Bennett and Anne Ryen and David Silverman (2000) sought to strengthen relational bonds through online disclosure, phone calls, exchange of photographs, and, in Ryen's case, some FTF meetings. In Chris Mann's research into experiences of higher education, extended relationships were the inevitable result of Mann's contacting students regularly over the course of their work on their degrees. There, the aim was to establish mutual trust rather than intimacy, thus Mann did not initiate talk about herself, nor did she see students face-to-face. This was not a misguided attempt to claim research "neutrality"; rather, Mann accepted that she was a very minor part of the students' lives and preferred to keep the focus of the interaction on the issues and students' perspectives on the issues.

In all these studies, the interviewers may be presumed to have different agendas. It is perhaps unsurprising that this should lead interviewers to different conclusions about whether electronic communication can sustain personal relationships over time. For Bennett and Ryen, the intensity of the relationship with participants seemed to peak and then falter somewhat, leading Bennett to admit that "maintaining long-term relationships is much more difficult than it appears" (e-mail communication, March 1999). In Bennett's study the frequency of on-line interaction over a seven-month period might explain a participant's disengagement due to pressures of time and a (sometimes reluctant) need to prioritize other commitments. Another possibility might have been a sense (from the participant's point of view) that all that could be said had been said. Ryen suggests that, as the novelty of the research project wears off, a participant might use the interaction for more instrumental purposes. In her case study, Ryen's e-mail correspondent seemed to move from commitment to the research process to a general desire to keep in touch because the interviewer might prove a possible useful contact in his business world. In Mann's study, a "slow and steady" approach to developing relationships within a time-limited, albeit extensive (three- to four-year) period was required. The interviewer-student relationships lacked the intensity of the relationships in Bennett's and Ryen's studies, but, perhaps for that very reason, most of the relationships were sustained for the duration of the research.

Considering these differing research patterns, it seems likely that human relationships have the same kind of variability on-line as they do in "real life." Some remain at a constant level of good neighborliness, whereas others reach deeper levels of intimacy that must increase (which would alter the research relationship), change in nature, or diminish. Although the ease and availability of CMC allows for extended communication, it does not follow that the technology can circumvent those life patterns.

INTERACTIVE SKILLS

There are several key areas where on-line interviewers may have to adapt expertise gained in FTF interviews in order to increase rapport in a virtual venue. We discuss these areas briefly below.

Reassurance

Cooperating in research in general, and on-line research in particular, may be a new and challenging experience for many people. Working one-to-one, participants may need regular confirmation that they are communicating in appropriate ways, that their contributions are valued, and that the faceless researcher is trustworthy. In on-line groups, participants may become anxious about how the group is operating or about what is expected of them, and facilitators have to be alert to signs of confusion or withdrawal into silence (Sweet 1999). It seems that in most on-line interviews participants benefit from frequent and explicit verbal assurances from the researcher.

Listening

An attentive pause to listen is a key feature in FTF interviewing skills. However, this may be a luxury in some CMC contexts. For instance, the characteristic rapid fire of chat can preclude pausing, whether it be for thought or for effect. In addition, participants may experience an interviewer's pause to listen not as attentiveness but as indifference, as absence. Cues that an interviewer is listening reassure participants of continuing interest. An interviewer who listens too much (read as being absent from the screen) may cause participants in focus groups to feel "leaderless and uncomfortable" (Gaiser 1997). Similarly, interviewers in turn may be unsure whether "silences" in real-time chat are "owing to the fact that the participant is thinking, is typing in a response and has not yet hit the return button, or has, in fact, declined to answer the questions" (O'Connor and Madge 2000:2).

Nonresponse in a virtual venue can undermine a developing sense of rapport. It is clear that on-line listening needs to be expressed as words, not silence. An interviewer may express listening with interest by "responding promptly to questions, overtly expressing interest in particular points made, asking follow up questions, or perhaps enthusiastically sharing similar experiences to that described by the interviewee" (P. Hodkinson, e-mail communication, March 1999). Meanwhile, the interviewer is also "listening" to the written script created by participants. The researcher needs to be alert to changes in the tone of the conversation, to any fracture in the flow of a response that might point to a reluctance to speak or a failure to understand language or concepts, and to verbal "cues" that might suggest that participants would be happy to talk more about something if asked. Marilyn Smith-Stoner notes ways in which participants flag that they are prepared to talk in more detail:

> Often they put a tag line at the end of the phrase—"let me know if you want to know more"—or they bring the subject up more than once. I think many people need to be invited to expound on a topic, they are courteous about people's time and don't want to abuse it. (E-mail communication, March 1999)

Verbal Expertise

Sustaining rapport depends upon an interviewer's skill in dealing with sensitive issues and/or potentially embarrassing or conflictual interaction. How can researchers negotiate delicate interaction on-line? As with reassurance, language has to be explicit. Nuances in tone of voice, facial expression, and subtlety of gesture are un-available. However, the use of mild imperatives (for example, "You may want to check out") and mitigation ("if you'd like") show how the skillful choice of words can avoid making presumptions about the reader (Galegher, Sproull, and Kiesler 1998:517). In real-time interaction, interviewers have to make rapid choices about how to handle sensitive issues. For Henrietta O'Connor and Clare Madge (2000), who interviewed together, the interaction felt abstracted from real life, and on-line language use often seemed inadequate: "There were occasions when we were 'lost for words,' taking some time to decide on what to send as a message, because we felt like our written comments sounded banal or our questions too direct and leading" (p. 3).

E-mail allows more time for interviewers to choose their words in one-to-one or asynchronous group interactions. For instance, in Wendy Seymour et al.'s (1999) asynchronous long-term conferencing study, in which the participants had disabilities, an exacerbation of a disability could interrupt the process of some interviews:

> These events required gentle and sensitive communication to ensure that participants did not feel pressured to continue, so that they felt valued, and so that they would feel welcome to continue with the project once the episode had passed. (P. 3)

Anne Ryen was afraid that sensitive issues might arise when she was conducting interviews over a long period with someone on another continent (Tanzania/Kenya versus Norway) and from another culture (Asian versus Norwegian). Her approach was to try to clear the ground at an early stage in the interaction, as she did in the following e-mail communication with a research subject:

> Well, I am very happy indeed that you will go on with the interview. If there are questions you find odd, or that you

do not "appreciate," please do not hesitate to tell me. That is the only way to make me learn or to avoid repeating the mistake . . . (e-mail 10.12.98). (Quoted in Ryen, e-mail communication, March 1999)

This direct approach, where the interviewer makes no attempt to disguise the possibility that questions might come across as crass or impertinent, may also be a way to negotiate the questions themselves. This is an approach Mann has used in her own research: "I should like to ask you more about something you said, but if you feel my question is too intrusive please do not bother to reply to this—I shall not bring it up again" (see Mann and Stewart 2000).

Explaining Absences

Finally, absence, in terms of long gaps in communication in asynchronous studies, can be deeply unsettling for both interviewers and participants. Committed participants may take time to explain irregular messages. In Ryen's study, her correspondent's laptop broke down while he was traveling. However, he phoned to inform her of this. In Mann's study, students frequently e-mailed to explain that work had taken over their time. Similarly, Mann alerted students when she would be away at conferences. Interviewers have greater responsibility than participants to explain absences, even though, as Bennett (1998) discovered, this can be a taxing process:

For example, when I was ill in bed I still had to check in with my co-investigators; write replies, explain that I was ill and that my conversations would only be short, but thus maintaining the link between us. Whilst this may seem to make online interaction appear both tenuous and transient, I would argue that it is simply the nature of the environment that makes it so, and not the people who are involved. (P. 39)

However, as Bennett points out, neglecting to explain absences can seriously jeopardize the rapport that has been built up in earlier interactions.

RELATIONAL EXPERTISE IN GROUP DISCUSSIONS

In one-to-one investigations, qualitative researchers who ask questions are usually referred to as interviewers. However, asking questions in groups requires additional skills, as suggested by such titles as *moderator* and *facilitator*. David Morgan (1988) has argued that the key role of the focus group moderator is "to control the assembly and the running of the session" (p. 15). This is a task with multiple strands, and it is clearly a challenge to transfer these skills on-line. In another view, a moderator is a "person who reminds, tracks, clarifies, prompts, reviews, distills, negotiates, mitigates, mediates, arbitrates" (Davis and Brewer 1997:70). In the fast-paced and hectic environment of real-time chat, flexibility and patience (with everyone involved) are definite virtues (Sweet 1999). From a human relations perspective, the task of moderating/facilitating groups has two principal aspects: (a) developing rapport between all interactants and (b) providing a noncontentious atmosphere for all—even at the cost of exerting control over the few. We discuss these issues next.

DEVELOPING RAPPORT AMONG MULTIPLE PARTICIPANTS

Many of the participants who are prepared to join on-line group discussions already have experience in chat rooms, so they are adept at creating on-line relationships quickly. However, as Casey Sweet (1999) reports, the guided group discussion "draws participants out and personalities begin to emerge, thereby creating a dynamic that develops during the group and varies just like in-person groups. . . . The amount of interaction between online participants can vary and may be influenced by the topic and moderator" (p. 3).

The initial moments of an on-line focus group are perhaps the most crucial, as this is when introductions are made and group rapport is first attempted. In the Young People and Health Risk study (Stewart et al. 1998), rapport was encouraged in two ways. First, the facilitator posted a welcome message in a non-real-time conference center ahead of time. This message sought to set the tone and atmosphere for the on-line groups to follow. Second, as the group facilitator, Stewart entered the young women's real-time focus group with the following lines:

Fiona Stewart: Welcome Yellow Beijing—I am fiona the controller, please introduce yourselves and tell the other girls about your hobbies, your subjects at school and then we can proceed. Have you read the welcoming message?

It was anticipated that messages such as this would create a sense of personal connection among the young people participating, who resided in four different countries. Another approach that facilitators can use to encourage group rapport is to ask all participants about their immediate physical environments (Sweet 1999).

CONTROL IN GROUPS

In a face-to-face focus group, a facilitator may choose to be passive, exercising "mild, unobtrusive control over the group" (Krueger 1988:73), but in an on-line focus group this is rarely possible. Certain procedures have been shown to ensure the smooth running of group interviews (Sweet 1999; Mann and Stewart 2000). First, by establishing their expectations, facilitators can minimize participant confusion and enhance adherence to both subject matter and protocol. Second, facilitators need to state some ground rules. In cyberspace, arguments and disagreements "can erupt with little warning" (Horn 1998:56), and facili-

tators do not have the option of ignoring outrageous, patently false, or volatile comments. Rules are one means by which facilitators can manage the potential for conflict, although it can rarely be eliminated. Some listowners, such as Horn (1998), in ECHO, develop "mission statements" as the baseline rule of conduct. This can prove an effective mechanism for facilitating discussion and containing conflict, although its ongoing implementation is not without problems.

Rule setting is important for managing the volatility of real-time groups. It also acts as a means of encouraging effective group self-management, which is particularly important in asynchronous groups. Rules make explicit the ways in which participants may engage in the on-line discussion and can set a positive tone for the interaction. However, there is also a risk that the facilitator may inadvertently create a hostile and unwelcoming environment by seeking to establish behavioral guidelines. The facilitator's challenge is to introduce rules in a way that is positive and acceptable to participants.

Facilitators also rely on text to maintain order in on-line groups. Because a facilitator cannot use body language, such as shuffling papers or turning away (Krueger 1988:84), the style of the textual communication must be clear and precise. Such facilitation can range from subtle to more assertive and formal approaches. Sweet has found that subtle approaches can sometimes be more successful on-line than face-to-face:

> I find in FTF groups that some dominators can push a position over and over and over again even after I, as moderator, have repeated it to them and asked them to indicate if I have heard correctly. Online, I find they can fizzle out, or if I put it in print that, "I understand your point of view to be . . . ," or "you dislike the idea because . . . ," they seem to back off. They don't seem to have

the same impact on the group as FTF. (E-mail communication, March 1999)

Facilitator intervention on-line may seem overbearing when compared with FTF conventions, but it is sometimes the only response to a fast-moving situation. Real-time groups are characterized by high interactivity, and a facilitator may not be able to intervene quickly enough to prevent an outburst of flaming. Even if the facilitator steps in promptly, there is no guarantee that intervention will be successful. The example below is taken from the Young People and Health Risk study (Mann and Stewart 2000:147). In this extract, although flaming did not occur, the young male participants did need to be reprimanded. As facilitator, however, Stewart was not sure that her request for an apology would be honored. She was thankful when it was.

Facilitator: Does anyone know what the health pyramid is?

Red Beijing: We know many good jokes

Facilitator: Red oz why don't you explain what the health pyramid is?

Red Australia: i don't like fiona

Facilitator: I beg your parden red oz

Facilitator: you should apologise for saying that

Red Australia: can you tell me a joke?

Red Australia: sorry

Red Beijing: the health pyramid is the meaning of different food. for example, bread meat milk

As we see, the need to reprimand participants can detract from the quality of the discussion. In the on-line environment there is no such thing as a quiet word in the ear of an individual participant. What is more, in the middle of attempting to obtain a public apology, the facilitator may need to repeat a particular question, even if this means spending more time than anticipated on a particular subject. In the example above, it was only after the facilitator pursued a line of questioning about the health pyramid that the participants contributed meaningfully to the dialogue. This was despite the fact that discussion and the flow of the dialogue had been disrupted for only a moment.

◆ Conclusion

In this chapter we have focused on the costs and benefits of using the Internet to interview and the skills that researchers may require to interview effectively on-line. As we have seen, researchers who consider conducting interviews on-line have many factors to weigh in the balance. The excitement of working with an interviewing medium that is not constrained by boundaries of time and space, and that offers digital data literally at one's fingertips, is matched by the growing realization that the virtual venue makes practical, legal, ethical, and interpersonal demands that move beyond the knowledge and expertise that researchers may have acquired in conducting off-line interview studies.

In addition, as long as CMC remains a text-based interchange, there are factors— such as the nature of language use on-line and the implications of disembodiment for issues of identity and/or power relations in cyberspace—that many researchers would wish to consider in designing their studies (Mann and Stewart 2000). It could be argued that using CMC to conduct interviews calls for such intensification of technical and interpersonal skills that only interviewers with considerable expertise in conventional research could feel confident about moving to a virtual venue. However, although pioneering researchers have alerted prospective on-line interviewers to some of the challenges of the medium, the majority of these pioneers have retained their initial excitement with regard to Internet interviewing. Most seem determined to develop the skills needed to conduct on-line interviewing in current circumstances and also to keep abreast of rapid technological developments that promise to extend interviewing possibilities in terms of both scope and style.

As we have discussed, the main barrier to more widespread participation in on-line interviews lies in the hardware and (in some countries) infrastructure costs associated with the desktop computer/modem/landline technology that currently dominates Internet access. Truly global access will require the development of other technologies, and the shape of these is becoming clear. Already, some mobile phones can be used to send and receive e-mail (Alanko et al. 1999). E-mail will also soon be offered as an offshoot of digital television (in conjunction with a telephone connection). Phones and other mobile devices, such as personal organizers or Palm Pilots, will use wireless application protocol to "gain access to the Internet using a 'microbrowser,' which displays web pages specially formatted for tiny screens" ("Future of the Internet" 1999:30). If such devices follow the pattern of mobile voice telephony, we can expect that hardware costs will drop dramatically after the first couple of years (although usage costs may remain high) and that these devices will prove especially popular in countries (not only developing countries) where conventional telephone services are inadequate or unreliable.

For researchers, these developments offer the exciting prospect of Internet-based communication (and hence research) with a far wider spectrum of socioeconomic groups and nationalities than is currently available. They also hold the promise of new forms of interviewing. Text-based CMC may eventually be seen as one of many ways to interview using the Internet, and as new technologies develop, new interviewing skills will develop to meet them.

■ Notes

1. ECHO and WELL (Whole Earth 'Lectronic Link) are on-line towns emanating from New York and California. MU* environments, which include MUDS and MOOs, are multiuser, text-based, role-playing areas of CMC.

2. See Mann and Stewart (2000) for discussion of these issues.

3. The GVU Center uses repeat participation in Web surveys to map current and changing Internet user characteristics and attitudes (see Kehoe and Pitkow, 1996; see also www.gvu.gatech.edu/user_surveys/). More than 55,000 respondents were involved in the first five surveys, and new versions of the survey are sent out biannually.

4. The Economic and Social Research Council, which is a core funding body for social science research in the United Kingdom, has already responded to European Union data protection legislation with a guidance document relating to copyright and confidentiality. The Scientific Freedom, Responsibility and Law Program within the American Association for the Advancement of Science convened a workshop in 1999 to examine the challenges facing scientists conducting Internet research involving human subjects. The outcomes of the workshop deliberations were used to draft a chapter for the *Guidebook for Institutional Review Boards on Internet Research,* produced by the NIH Office for Protection from Research Risks in 2000. The latest information is available at the AAAS Web site (see www.aaas.org/spp/dspp/sfrl/projects/intres/main.htm).

5. As of March 2000, available survey-creation programs included

MaCATI (www.senecio.com),
Survey Internet (www.aufrance.com),
Survey Said (www.surveysaid.com),
Survey Select (www.surveyselect.com),
SurveySolutions (www.perseus.com),and
SurveyTracker (www.surveytracker.com).

MaCATI's editing program is for the Macintosh only, and it has versions of its data collection program for the Mac, Windows, and Java. All of the other programs listed run under Windows only. Smith (1997) has pointed out that although Web survey development software is increasingly available, packages have huge variations in terms of price, functions, and server compatibility. It remains to be seen which, if any, of these packages will become the standard.

6. HTML stands for HyperText Markup Language, which is the coding system used to create pages that can be displayed by Web browsers. It consists of a series of "tags" that give instructions to the browser about how to display the text. For example, the text "<b>bold words<bsb> and <i>italic words<bsi>" would be displayed by a Web browser (or HTML-enabled e-mail system) as **bold words** and *italic words*. However, if the same text were read using a standard e-mail system, all the characters would be displayed exactly as typed: <b>bold words<bsb> and <i>italic words<bsi>. Originally, authors created HTML documents by typing the tags using a text editor. However, it is increasingly common to create HTML using "what you see is what you get" editing programs, where the author applies the formatting required (such as bold or italic) and the program automatically adds the relevant tags.

7. An example of such software is Perseus SurveySolutions Interviewer (www.perseus.com).

8. In this context, a server is a large computer that forms part of the worldwide network of permanently connected computers that is the Internet. Your pages are held on your host server. When someone requests a page, the request is routed to your host server and the page information is passed back to the requester's computer via the network.

9. FirstClass Conferencing has real chat and asynchronous conferencing options.

10. Patricia Wallace (1999) provides an excellent psychological framework for asking these questions.

■ *References*

Alanko, T., M. Kojo, M. Liljeberg, and K. Raatikainen. 1999. "Mobile Access to the Internet: A Mediator-Based Solution." *Internet Research: Electronic Networking, Applications and Policy* 9:58-65.

Anders, E. 2000. "Women with Disabilities: Higher Education, Feminism and Social Constructions of Difference." Ph.D. thesis, Deakin University, Melbourne.

Aoki, K. 1994. "Virtual Communities in Japan." Presented at the Pacific Telecommunications Council Conference.

Aycock, A. and N. Buchignani. 1995. "The E-Mail Murders: Reflections on 'Dead' Letters." Pp. 184-231 in *CyberSociety: Computer-Mediated Communication and Community,* edited by S. G. Jones. Thousand Oaks, CA: Sage.

Bachmann, D., J. Elfrink, J., and G. Vazzana. 1996. "Tracking the Progress of E-Mail vs. Snail-Mail." *Marketing Research* 8:30-35.

Bannert, M. and P. Arbinger. 1996. "Gender-Related Differences in Exposure to and Use of Computers: Results of a Survey of Secondary School Students." *European Journal of Psychology of Education* 11:269-82.

Baym, N. 1995. "The Emergence of Community in Computer-Mediated Communication." Pp. 139-63 in *CyberSociety: Computer-Mediated Communication and Community,* edited by S. G. Jones. Thousand Oaks, CA: Sage.

Bennett, C. 1998. "Men Online: Discussing Lived Experiences on the Internet." Honors dissertation, James Cook University, Townsville, Queensland, Australia.

Bruckman, A. 1992. "Identity Workshops: Emergent Social and Psychological Phenomena in Text-Based Virtual Reality." MIT Media Laboratory. Unpublished manuscript. Available from author (e-mail): Bruckman@media.mit.edu

Burkhalter, B. 1999. "Reading Race Online: Discovering Racial Identity in Usenet Discussions." Pp. 60-75 in *Communities in Cyberspace,* edited by M. A. Smith and P. Kollock. London: Routledge.

Cohen, J. 1996. "Computer Mediated Communication and Publication Productivity among Faculty." *Internet Research: Electronic Networking, Applications and Policy* 6(2-3):41-63.

Comley, P. 1996. "The Use of the Internet as a Data Collection Method." Presented at the ESOMAR/EMAC Symposium, Edinburgh.

Coomber, R. 1997. "Using the Internet for Survey Research." *Sociological Research Online* 2(2). Available Internet: http://www.socresonline.org.uk/socresonline/2/2/2.html

Correll, S. 1995. "The Ethnography of an Electronic Bar: The Lesbian Cafe." *Journal of Contemporary Ethnography* 24:270-98.

Couper, M. P., J. Blair, and T. Triplett. (1999). "A Comparison of Mail and E-Mail for a Survey of Employees in US Statistical Agencies." *Journal of Official Statistics* 15:39-56.

Creswell, J. W. 1997. *Qualitative Inquiry and Research Design: Choosing among Five Traditions.* Thousand Oaks, CA: Sage.

Cutler, R. H. 1995. "Distributed Presence and Community in Cyberspace." *Interpersonal Communication and Technology: An Electronic Journal for the 21st Century* 3(2):12-32. Available Internet: http://jan.ucc.nau.edu/~ipct-j/1995/n2/cutler.txt

Davis, B. H. and J. P. Brewer. 1997. *Electronic Discourse: Linguistic Individuals in Virtual Space.* Albany: State University of New York Press.

Daws, L. 1999. "Cattle, Special Education, Old Hats and Rain: Investigating Rural Women's Use of Interactive Communication Technologies." Center for Policy and Leadership Studies, Queensland University of Technology, Kelvin Grove. Unpublished manuscript. Available from author (e-mail): l.daws@qut.edu.au

Dubrovsky, V. J., S. Kiesler, and B. N. Sethna. 1991. "The Equalization Phenomenon: Status Effects in Computer-Mediated and Face-to-Face Decision-Making Groups." *Human-Computer Interaction* 6:119-46.

Dunne, G. 1999. "The Different Dimensions of Gay Fatherhood: Exploding the Myths." Report to the Economic and Social Research Council, London School of Economics.

Fielding, N. G. and R. M. Lee. 1998. *Computer Analysis and Qualitative Research.* Thousand Oaks, CA: Sage.

Fontana, A. and J. H. Frey. 1994. "Interviewing: The Art of Science." Pp. 361-76 in *Handbook of Qualitative Research,* edited by N. K. Denzin and Y. S. Lincoln. Thousand Oaks, CA: Sage.

"The Future of the Internet." *Economist,* November 13, 1999.

Gaiser, T. 1997. "Conducting On-Line Focus Groups." *Social Science Computer Review* 15:135-44.

Galegher, J., L. Sproull, and S. Kiesler. 1998. "Legitimacy, Authority, and Community in Electronic Support Groups." *Written Communication* 15:493-530.

Garton, L., C. Haythornthwaite, and B. Wellman. 1999. "Studying On-Line Networks." In *Doing Internet Research: Critical Issues and Methods for Examining the Net,* edited by S. G. Jones. Thousand Oaks, CA: Sage.

Gates, W. 1997. "Keynote Address." In *The Harvard Conference on the Internet and Society.* Cambridge, MA: O'Reilly.

Giese, M. 1998. "Self without Body: Textual Self-Representation in an Electronic Community." *First Monday* 3(4) [On-line]. Available Internet: http://www.firstmonday.dk/issues/issue3_4/giese/

Gjestland, L. 1996. "Net? Not Yet." *Marketing Research* 8:26-29.

Hahn, K. L. 1998. "Qualitative Investigation of an E-Mail Mediated Help Service." *Internet Research: Electronic Networking, Applications and Policy* 8:123-35.

Hantrais, L. and M. Sen. 1996. *Cross-National Research Methods in the Social Sciences.* Guildford, England: Biddles.

Herring, S. C., ed. 1996. *Computer-Mediated Communication: Linguistic, Social and Cross-Cultural Perspectives.* Amsterdam: John Benjamins.

Hewson, C., D. Laurent, and C. Vogel. 1996. "Proper Methodologies for Psychological and Sociological Studies Conducted via the Internet." *Behavior Research Methods, Instruments and Computers* 28:186-91.

Hodkinson, P. 2000. "The Goth Scene as Trans-Local Subculture." Ph.D. dissertation, Center for Urban and Regional Studies, University of Birmingham.

Horn, S. 1998. *Cyberville: Clicks, Culture, and the Creation of an Online Town.* New York: Warner.

Kehoe, C. M. and J. E. Pitkow. 1996. "Surveying the Territory: GVU's Five WWW User Surveys." *World Wide Web Journal* 1(3):77-84.

Kennedy, A. 1998. *The Internet and the World Wide Web: The Rough Guide.* London: Penguin.

Kiesler, S., J. Siegel, and T. McGuire. 1984. "Social Psychological Aspects of Computer-Mediated Communication." *American Psychologist* 39:1123-34.

Kollock, P. and M. Smith. 1996. "Managing the Virtual Commons: Cooperation and Conflict in Computer Communities." Pp. 109-28 in *Computer-Mediated Communication: Linguistic, Social and Cross-Cultural Perspectives,* edited by S. Herring. Amsterdam: John Benjamins.

Kramarae, C. and J. Kramer. (1995). "Legal Snarls for Women in Cyberspace." *Internet Research: Electronic Networking, Applications and Policy* 5(2):14-24.

Krueger, R. A. 1988. *Focus Groups: A Practical Guide for Applied Research.* Newbury Park, CA: Sage.

Lea, M., ed. 1992. *Contexts of Computer-Mediated Communication.* Brighton, England: Harvester-Wheatsheaf.

Lea, M. and R. Spears. 1995. "Love at First Byte? Building Personal Relationships over Computer Networks." In *Under-studied Relationships: Off the Beaten Track,* edited by J. T. Wood and S. Duck. Thousand Oaks, CA: Sage.

Lee, R. M. 1993. *Doing Research on Sensitive Topics.* Newbury Park, CA: Sage.

Loader, B. D., ed. *Cyberspace Divide: Equality, Agency and Policy in the Information Society.* London: Routledge.

Mann, C. and F. Stewart. 2000. *Internet Communication and Qualitative Research: A Handbook for Researching Online.* London: Sage.

Matheson, K. 1992. "Women and Computer Technology: Communicating for Herself." Pp. 66-88 in *Contexts of Computer-Mediated Communication,* edited by M. Lea. Brighton, England: Harvester-Wheatsheaf.

May, T. 1993. *Social Research: Issues, Methods and Processes.* Buckingham: Open University Press.

McLaughlin, M. L., K. Osborne, and C. Smith. 1995. "Standards of Conduct in Usenet." Pp. 90-112 in *CyberSociety: Computer-Mediated Communication and Community,* edited by S. G. Jones. Thousand Oaks, CA: Sage.

Mehta, R. and E. Sivadas. 1995. "Comparing Response Rates and Response Content in Mail versus Electronic Mail Surveys." *Journal of the Market Research Society* 37:429-39.

Moore, M. 1993. "Theory of Transactional Distance." In *Theoretical Principles of Distance Education,* edited by D. Keegan. London: Routledge.

Morgan, D. L. 1988. *Focus Groups as Qualitative Research.* Newbury Park, CA: Sage.

Murphy, K. L. and M. P. Collins. 1997. "Communication Conventions in Instructional Electronic Chats." *First Monday* 2(11) [On-line]. Available Internet: http://www.firstmonday.dk/issues/issue2_11/murphy/

Myers, D. 1987. "Anonymity Is Part of the Magic: Individual Manipulation of Computer-Mediated Communication Context." *Qualitative Sociology* 10:251-66.

O'Connor, H. and C. Madge. 2000. "Cyber-Parents and Cyber-Research: Exploring the Internet as a Medium for Research." Center for Labour Market Studies, University of Leicester. Unpublished manuscript.

Parker, L. 1992. "Collecting Data the E-Mail Way." *Training and Development,* July, pp. 52-54.

Parks, M. and K. Floyd. 1996. "Making Friends in Cyberspace." *Journal of Communication* 46(1):80-97.

Patrick, A. S., A. Black, and T. E. Whalen. 1995. "Rich, Young, Male, Dissatisfied Computer Geeks? Demographics and Satisfaction from the National Capital FreeNet." Pp. 83-107 in *Proceedings of Telecommunities 95: The International Community Networking Conference,* edited by D. Godfrey and M. Levy. Victoria, BC: Telecommunities Canada. Available Internet: http://debra.dgbt.doc.ca/services-research/survey/demographics/vic.html

Raymond, E., ed. *The New Hacker's Dictionary.* 2d ed. Cambridge: MIT Press.

Reid, R. 1991. "Electropolis: Communication and Community on Internet Relay Chat." Honors thesis (electronically distributed version), Department of History, University of Melbourne.

Rice, R. E. and D. Case. 1983. "Electronic Message Systems in the University: A Description of Use and Utility." *Journal of Communication* 33(1):131-52.

Ryen, A. and D. Silverman. 2000. "Marking Boundaries: Culture as Category Work." *Qualitative Inquiry* 6:107-27.

Sala, L. 1998. "The Paradox: Megabandwidth and Micromedia." Presented at the International Sociology Conference. Montreal.

Salmon, G. 2000. *E-Moderating: The Key to Teaching and Learning Online.* London: Kogan Page.

Schaefer, D. and D. A. Dillman. 1998. "Development of a Standard E-Mail Methodology: Results of an Experiment." *Public Opinion Quarterly* 62:378-97.

Seidman, I. 1991. *Interviewing as Qualitative Research: A Guide for Researchers in Education and the Social Sciences.* New York: Teachers College Press.

Senior, C. and M. Smith. 1999. "The Internet . . . A Possible Research Tool?" *Psychologist* 12:442-44.

Seymour, W., D. Lupton, and N. Fahy. 1999. "Negotiating Disability, Technology and Risk: Towards a New Perspective." Report, School of Social Work and Social Policy, University of South Australia, Magill.

Shaw, D. 1997. "Gay Men and Computer Communication: A Discourse of Sex and Identity in Cyberspace." Pp. 133-46 in *Virtual Culture: Identity and Communication in Cybersociety*, edited by S. G. Jones. Thousand Oaks, CA: Sage.

Sheehan, K. B. and M. G. Hoy. 1999. "Using E-Mail to Survey Internet Users in the United States: Methodology and Assessment." *Journal of Computer-Mediated Communication* 4(3) [On-line]. Available Internet: http://www.ascusc.org/jcmc/vol4/issue3/sheehan.html

Shields, R., ed. 1996. *Cultures of Internet: Virtual Spaces, Real Histories, Living Bodies.* London: Sage.

Short, J., E. Williams, and B. Christie. 1976. *The Social Psychology of Telecommunication.* London: John Wiley.

Smith, C. B. 1997. "Casting the Net: Surveying an Internet Population." *Journal of Computer-Mediated Communication* 3(1) [On-line]. Available Internet: http://www.ascusc.org/jcmc/vol3/issue1/ smith.html

Smith-Stoner, M. J. and T. A. Weber. 2000. "Developing Theory Using Emergent Inquiry: A Study of Meaningful Online Learning for Women." Ph.D. dissertation, California Institute of Integral Studies. Available from authors (e-mail): mssrn@aol.com

Spender, D. 1995. *Nattering on the Net: Women, Power and Cyberspace.* Melbourne: Spinifrex.

Stewart, F., E. Eckerman, and K. Zhou. 1998. "Using the Internet in Qualitative Public Health Research: A Comparison of Chinese and Australian Young Women's Perceptions of Tobacco Use." *Internet Journal of Health Promotion*, December 29 [On-line]. Available Internet: http://www.monash.edu.au/health/IJHP/1998/12

Stones, A. and D. Perry. 1998. "Preliminary Evaluation of the World Wide Web as a Tool for Data Collection in the Area of Panic Research." Presented at the Computers in Psychology Conference, April, University of York.

Sweet, C. (1999) "Anatomy of an On-Line Focus Group." *Quirk's Marketing Research Review*, December. Available Internet: http://www.quirks.com/articles

Tesch, R. 1990. *Qualitative Research: Analysis Types and Software Tools.* New York: Falmer.

Thomas, D. S., K. Forcht, and P. Counts. (1998). "Legal Considerations of Internet Use: Issues to Be Addressed." *Internet Research: Electronic Networking, Applications and Policy* 8:70-74.

Tse, A. C. B., K. C. Tse, C. H. Yin, C. B. Ting, K. W. Yi, K. P. Yee, and W. C. Hong. 1995. "Comparing Two Methods of Sending Out Questionnaires: E-Mail versus Mail." *Journal of the Market Research Society* 37:441-46.

Turkle, S. 1995. *Life on the Screen: Identity in the Age of the Internet.* London: Weidenfeld & Nicolson.

Wallace, P. 1999. *The Psychology of the Internet.* New York: Cambridge University Press.

Walther, J. B. 1992. "Interpersonal Effects in Computer-Mediated Interaction: A Relational Perspective." *Communication Research* 19:52-90.

———. 1996. "Computer-Mediated Communication: Impersonal, Interpersonal, and Hyperpersonal Interaction." *Communication Research* 23:3-43.

———. 1999. "Researching Internet Behavior: Methods, Issues and Concerns." Presented at the National Communication Association Summer Conference on Communication and Technology, July, Washington, DC.

Winter, D. and C. Huff. 1996. "Adapting the Internet: Comments from a Women-Only Electronic Forum." *American Sociologist* 27:30-54.

Witmer, D., R. Colman, and S. Katzman. 1999. "From Paper-and-Pencil to Screen-and-Keyboard: Toward a Methodology for Survey Research on the Internet." Pp. 145-63 in *Doing Internet Research: Critical Issues and Methods for Examining the Net,* edited by S. G. Jones. Thousand Oaks, CA: Sage.

Part II

REFLEXIVITY

REVISITING THE RELATIONSHIP
BETWEEN PARTICIPANT OBSERVATION
AND INTERVIEWING

◆ Paul Atkinson
Amanda Coffey

In this chapter we propose a reevaluation of the relationship between participant observation and interviewing in sociological field research. Comparisons between these two methods of data collection have been part of the discourse of qualitative methodologists for more than four decades. The starting point for this reexamination is a paper published by Howard Becker and Blanche Geer in the 1950s in which they outline the relative merits of participant observation and interviewing (Becker and Geer [1957] 1970a). (The paper and its ensuing debate were reprinted in 1970 in a collection edited by William Filstead; page references here are to the version published in that anthology.) That paper was, and has remained, an influential

reference point for scholars engaged in field research. The subject matter and arguments presented in the paper remain valuable in their own right, as well as provide a means of tracing significant changes in how the conduct of field research is conceptualized.

In the first half of this chapter, we reread the paper by Becker and Geer through a contemporary lens, as a step to rethinking relationships between participant observation and interviewing. We consider briefly the use of the notion of triangulation to mediate the relationships between participant observation and interviewing. We then move on to propose a possible approach to ethnographic data that subsumes participant observation and interviewing.

Developing our argument initially through a reconsideration of the classic position exemplified by Becker and Geer, we argue that field researchers must not assume that what is done should enjoy primacy over what is said, and that therefore observation and interviewing stand in opposition to one another. Actions, we argue, are understandable because they can be talked about. Equally, accounts—including those derived from interviewing—are actions. Social life is performed and narrated, and we need to recognize the performative qualities of social life and talk. In doing so, we shall not find it necessary to juxtapose talk and events as if they occupied different spheres of meaning. We thus propose an analytic stance that transcends some of the methodological puzzles that have appeared to confront qualitative methods for several decades.

◆ Rereading Becker and Geer

In the 1960s, sociologists in the interactionist tradition in the United States—and, to a lesser extent, elsewhere—were formulating a view of field research that was to become canonical. The authors who represented the "second Chicago school," as identified by Gary Alan Fine (1995), including Howard Becker, Blanche Geer, Everett Hughes, Anselm Strauss, and Leonard Schatzman, did much to promote empirical field research in a variety of institutional and other settings: hospitals, schools, colleges and universities, and other workplaces. Their interest in research methods was firmly grounded in their shared commitment to practical empirical research. They wrote from a blend of interests that reflected a shared intellectual culture: symbolic interactionism, social psychology, pragmatist epistemology, organizational and occupational sociology. Their starting point was normally the practice of social research rather than abstract epistemology. They blended their personal experience of and commitment to field

research with the desire to promote systematic and coherent research among their students and colleagues. The diaspora from Chicago itself led to the promotion of such methodological perspectives in various centers of excellence in the United States. The publication of various textbooks and edited collections helped to promote and disseminate the new methodological systems in the 1960s and early 1970s (Schatzman and Strauss 1973; Lofland 1971; McCall and Simmons 1969; Filstead 1970). Becker and Geer's paper "Participant Observation and Interviewing: A Comparison" was a key ingredient in this movement. It was anthologized and became part of the codification of research methods, incorporated into the craft knowledge of several generations of graduate students and researchers.

The advice offered by authors such as Becker and Geer, Schatzman, and Strauss was essentially sensible, straightforward, and practical. It bears all the hallmarks of the work of researchers who were thoroughly versed in the practical work of field research and who also appreciated the value of clear and systematic advice for their peers and their advanced students. The development and spread of qualitative research methods owes much to that particular generation of authors. However, with the benefit of hindsight, much of that methodological advice now looks dated, and the common sense of one generation can seem limited to another.

In the original paper, Becker and Geer compare the relative strengths and applications of participant observation and interviewing. The paper deals with both the relationships between these techniques and the possibility of complementarity. Although it would be quite unwarranted to accuse Becker and his colleagues of naïveté, from today's perspectives (and we use the plural here advisedly) one is struck by the extent to which the data collection methods are treated as relatively unproblematic in themselves. A closer reading of Becker and Geer is worthwhile, not merely for historical purposes, but in order to unpack some of the implicit assumptions that informed the original paper and understandings of field research that stemmed from them. It is helpful to reread the paper in conjunction with Martin Trow's ([1957] 1970) reply and the rejoinder by Becker and Geer ([1957] 1970b). We do so not in order to belittle the contributions of Becker and Geer or of their contemporaries. On the contrary, we think that the issues they raised remain worthy of fresh consideration. We would pay them least respect were we merely to treat their ideas as part of a stock of taken-for-granted ideas.

A GOLD STANDARD?

Becker and Geer ([1957] 1970a) claim a specific advantage for participant observation over other kinds of data collection strategy, based in part on their own research on medical students (Becker et al., 1961). They suggest:

> The most complete form of the sociological datum, after all, is the form in which the participant observer gathers it: An observation of some social event, the events which precede and follow it, and explanations of its meaning by participants and spectators, before, during, and after its occurrence. Such a datum gives us more information about the event under study than data gathered by any other sociological method. Participant observation can thus provide us with a yardstick against which to measure the completeness of data gathered in other ways, a model which can serve to let us know what modes of information escape us when we use other methods. (P. 133)

Trow's ([1957] 1970) response challenges this apparent claim for participant observation's status as a gold-standard method for sociological data collection. Trow reiterates the commonplace assumption that the choice of research methods should be dictated by the research problem,

rather than the unchallenged superiority of one kind of strategy:

> It is with this assertion, that a given method of collecting data—any method—has an inherent superiority over others by virtue of its special qualities and divorced from the nature of the problem studied, that I take sharp issue. The authoritative view, and I would have thought this the view most widely accepted by social scientists, is that different kinds of information about man and society are gathered most fully and economically in different ways, and that the problem under investigation properly dictates the methods of investigation. (P. 143)

Here is not the place to divert attention to unpacking the value of this particular topos, except to note that in the world of real research, social scientists do not dream up "problems" to investigate out of thin air, divorced from concerns of theory and methodology, and only then search for precisely the right method. Clearly, problems and methods come as part of packages of ideas—whether or not one chooses to call them "paradigms." The notion that one can simply apply the best method to an independently derived problem is at best unrealistic. However, the rebuttal by Becker and Geer ([1957] 1970b) clarifies their original argument and helps sharpen our own focus. They point out that theirs was not a sweeping claim for the superiority of participant observation over all other methods in all cases. On the contrary, they stress their original emphasis on the observation and understanding of *events:*

> It is possible Trow thought we were arguing the general superiority of participant observation because he misunderstood our use of the word "event." We intended to refer only to specific and limited events which are observable, not to include in the term such large and complex aggregates of spe-

cific events as national political campaigns. (P. 151)

Contrary to some possible, glib readings of their paper, then, Becker and Geer are certainly not advocating the wholesale superiority of participant observation over interviewing, nor are they proposing participant observation as the only valid method for sociological fieldwork.

EVENTS AND COMPLETENESS

Becker and Geer claim that the significance of participant observation and its superiority over interviewing rests on the "completeness" of the data. They propose that observation of events in context yields a more *complete* record and understanding of *events* than reliance on interviewing *about those events* alone. Their comparison between participant observation and interviewing is not wholesale, therefore. Becker and Geer make specific claims. In some ways, the original argument—especially as clarified by Becker and Geer—is unremarkable. Indeed, as formulated it is virtually unassailable. It is hard to quarrel with the assertion that the study of observable events is better accomplished by the observation of those events than by the collection of retrospective and decontextualized descriptions of them. Clearly, Becker and Geer are advocating a holistic approach to data collection and its interpretation. They believe that the sociological understanding of a given social world is optimized by the deployment of participation, observation, and conversation (in the form of field interviews). What is remarkable, however, and what strikes us from a contemporary vantage point, is the extent to which Becker and Geer treat "events" as self-evident and the extent to which they assume that the observation of "events" is a primary goal of participant observation. In turn they also seem to assume that interviews are primarily about events.

Their own illustration of the phenomenon is telling, and it bears reexamination. Their remarks on research methods were informed by their recent fieldwork with medical students at the University of Kansas (Becker et al. 1961). The example they give from their fieldwork is illuminating about the general perspective from which they wrote. Becker and Geer give an extract from their field materials in which they discuss medical students' perceptions of their teachers. Being in a subordinate position, the students, Becker and Geer ([1957] 1970a) argue, are likely to develop a kind of mythology about their teachers, and so to interpret their actions in a particular way: "Any such mythology will distort people's view of events to such a degree that they will report as fact things which have not occurred, but which seem to them to have occurred" (p. 138). In comparing participant observation and interviewing, therefore, Becker and Geer suggest that observation can be a corrective, allowing for adjudication of what "really" happened:

The point is that things can be reported in an interview through such a distorting lens, and the interviewer may have no way of knowing what is fact and what is distortion of this kind; participant observation makes it possible to check such points. (P. 138)

The actual example Becker and Geer use to demonstrate this assertion strikes a false note with the contemporary reader. The medical students had, apparently, formed the view that particular resident physicians on the teaching staff would regularly humiliate the students. The extract of field notes reproduced in the paper shows either Becker or Geer (the author of the data extract is not specified) reflecting on his or her observations of a particular teaching episode and students' reflections on it. Following a particular encounter with one of the residents, a student reported to his fellow students that the resident had "chewed him out." The observer felt able to intervene and say that the resident had actually been "pretty decent." Another student disputed the observer's description and affirmed that such behavior by a resident was always "chewing out," no matter how "God damn nice" the resident might be. In evaluating this episode, Becker and Geer ([1957] 1970a) conclude:

> In short, participant observation makes it possible to check descriptions against fact and, noting discrepancies, become aware of systematic distortions made by the person under study; such distortions are less likely to be discovered by interviewing alone. (P. 139)

They add a caveat to this point, distinguishing between the descriptive content and the process of the interview:

> This point, let us repeat, is only relevant when the interview is used as a source of information about situations and events the researcher himself has not seen. It is not relevant when it is the person's behavior in the interview itself that is under analysis. (P. 139)

Notwithstanding that last proviso—to which we shall return later—Becker and Geer may strike the contemporary reader as naive, schooled as that reader now is in the complexities of accounts, actions, and interpretations, and at home amid the ambiguities of postmodern analysis (Gubrium and Holstein 1997; Silverman 1993; Atkinson 1996). They seem to be operating with a strangely unproblematic view of "events," and thus of the social world. They strongly imply that there are "events" that are amenable to definitive description and evaluation by sociological observers. Consequently, the observer can adjudicate between a true description of events and a distorted one, and can therefore evaluate degrees of "distortion" in such descriptions.

It is, incidentally, instructive to read the data extract used in the paper and to which

we have referred here—a passage from processed field notes in narrative form, incorporating short verbatim quotes. It does not contain a description of the events that are under consideration and that are the subject of the disputed interpretation. The "events" that are described are the students' comments about the resident and the subsequent conversation between the observer and the students. The original interaction between the resident and the student, on which the latter's claim of being "chewed out" is based, is summarized in the most cursory fashion. Strikingly, it is totally impossible to reconstruct the original interaction from the data provided. Any adjudication as to the reasonableness of the student's complaint, the observer's corrective intervention, or the second student's reaffirmation of the students' perspective—their "mythology" as the authors describe it—is not possible.

In principle, this treatment of data is congruent with the general analysis that is enshrined in *Boys in White* (Becker et al. 1961). Becker and his colleagues do not actually base their account on "events" in the sense that they report and analyze much of what medical students or their teachers actually do. Their analysis is concerned with the development of students' perspectives rather than with, say, their embodied skills or their actual encounters with hospital patients. To that extent, Becker and Geer are consistent: The published monograph and their methodological prescriptions are congruent. The problems we raise, by contrast, reflect their treatment of observation, interviewing, accounts, and events as all rather unproblematic.

One might argue in defense of Becker and Geer that they use the data extract only by way of illustration, that the general argument is important rather than the details of a particular example. Yet this is not just an isolated incident or a minor discrepancy. It is thoroughly characteristic of the wider research project from which it is taken, which is in turn representative of a lot of work based on some combination of participant observation and interviewing, of a kind typical among the generation of researchers represented by Becker and Geer. Any reading of *Boys in White* (Becker et al. 1961), other than a most cursory one, will emphasize the problem. Although the Chicago research team spent a considerable amount of time engaged in participant observation with the medical students and their teachers, the book does remarkably little to report what these social actors actually did. We gain few glimpses of, say, the actual work with patients on hospital wards or in clinics. The "data" seem to consist primarily of what the students themselves *said about* their lives and work. The primary data, in practice, therefore seem to be conversations about events and actors' perspectives on events and happenings. At least, it is those data that are reported directly in the monograph.

A reexamination of the original formulation of the problem by Becker and Geer highlights some significant issues and problems. As we have seen, their argument is a very specific one that is extremely plausible. Even within their argument's restricted scope, Becker and Geer seem to establish a strong case for the value of participant observation. On closer inspection, however, the argument seems less straightforward, and raises some potentially intriguing issues that we shall attempt to address afresh in the final section of this chapter. Before that, in the next section we turn to consider another approach to the combination of participant observation and interviewing, through the notion of methodological triangulation.

◆ Triangulation

One of the key areas in which claims have been made for the productive *combination* of participant observation and interviewing is in the methodological discussion of *triangulation*. Although authors such as Norman Denzin (1970) have certainly not in-

tended to promote a naive or vulgar view of research methods and their proper relationships, the rhetoric of between-method triangulation clearly implies for many enthusiasts the possibility of combining participant observation and interviewing so as to capitalize on the respective strengths of these methods, or to counteract the perceived limitations of each.

Denzin's original formulation of methodological triangulation also conveys the impression that researchers could combine methods such as participant observation and interviewing to draw on the methods' complementary strengths and offset their respective weaknesses. Denzin's (1978) own summary of methodological triangulation captures the essence of this approach:

> In organizational studies, for example, it is extremely difficult to launch large-scale participant-observation studies when the participants are widely distributed by time and place. In such extractions participant observation may be adapted only to certain categories of persons, certain events, certain places, or certain times. The interview method can then be employed to study those events that do not directly come under the eyes of the participant observer. (P. 303)

Here interviewing is treated as a potential proxy for direct observation: It is implied that researchers can glean data about events and actors through indirect means in order to supplement the method of direct observation.

It is clear that Denzin's formulation of the relationships between methods is actually addressed to an issue that is slightly different from the one examined by Becker and Geer. But (in his early writings) Denzin too treats the methods themselves as relatively unproblematic. His early views of triangulation assume that research methods should be determined by research problems and that methods can be combined in terms of their respective strengths and weaknesses: "Methodological triangulation involves a complex process of playing each method off against the other so as to maximize the validity of field efforts" (Denzin 1978:304). Denzin emphasizes the degree to which the combination of methods is a matter of strategic decision making, and that research design and choice of methods are emergent features of concrete projects: "Assessment cannot be solely derived from principles given in research manuals—it is an emergent process, contingent on the investigator, the research setting, and the investigator's theoretical perspective" (p. 304).

Subsequent editions of Denzin's text reflect the changing character of methodological thinking and make explicit reference to potential, and actual, criticisms of this approach to triangulation. Denzin acknowledges that his accounts of the relationships between methods such as interviewing and observation were open to the interpretation, and the accusation, that they were unduly positivistic (for critiques of the early Denzin approach, see Silverman 1985, 1993). Indeed, Denzin did seem to imply that research problems are prior to and independent from methods, and that methods can be brought to bear on research problems in unproblematic ways. Although Denzin himself was clearly no naive positivist in intention, the implications of his text certainly seemed to suggest an easy accommodation between methods, and between methods and problems. The rhetoric of research problems driving the choice of methods too readily implied an independent and prior "list" of researchable topics divorced from the theories and methods that constructed those topics.

The simplest view of triangulation treats the relationships between methods as relatively unproblematic, and those methods themselves as even more straightforward in themselves. More sophisticated versions of triangulation may treat the relationships between methods in a less straightforward fashion—stressing the differences between them rather than complementarity—but

can still be predicated on unproblematic views of the methods themselves. Current perspectives on methodology and epistemology incline toward a quite different view. Treatments of participant observation and interviewing would not try to privilege one over the other, or try to seek out ways simply to integrate them or treat their outcomes in an additive way.

REFLEXIVITY

The underlying problem with the simple or "optimistic" version of triangulation is that it treats the nature of social reality as unduly unproblematic and the relationships between the social world and the methods of investigating it as transparent. But we cannot assume a unitary and stable social world that can simply be viewed from different standpoints or from different perspectives. Rather, we have to pay due attention to the principle of reflexivity. *Reflexivity* is a term that is widely used, with a diverse range of connotations (and sometimes with virtually no meaning at all). Here we use it in a specific way: to acknowledge that the methods we use to describe the world are—to some degree—constitutive of the realities they describe (Hammersley and Atkinson 1995; Gubrium and Holstein 1997). In other words, the research methods we use imply or depend on particular kinds of transactions and engagements with the world. Each kind of transaction therefore generates a distinctive set of descriptions, versions, and understandings of the world. These are not arbitrary or whimsical. They are generated out of our systematic and methodical explorations of a given social world; they are not private fantasies. Equally, they are not purely contingent. There are systematic relationships between methods and representations, but they cannot be washed out or eliminated through simpleminded aggregation. Rather, we have to address what methods do construct and what sense we can make of those constructions. Such a realization does not de-prive us of different modes of data collection and analysis. It does, however, require us to address the distinctive and intrinsic attributes of particular methods, to retain some fidelity to those methods and their products.

From this perspective, for instance, the status of interview data is especially problematic. In particular, the precise referential value of interviews is questionable. Interviews are not regarded as intrinsically worthless sources of data. Rather, as Silverman (1993) points out, we cannot approach interview data simply from the point of view of "truth" or "distortion," and we cannot use such data with a view to remedying the incompleteness of observations. By the same token, we cannot rely on our observations to correct presumed inaccuracies in interview accounts. On the contrary, it is argued that interviews generate data that have intrinsic properties of their own. In essence, we need to treat interviews as generating accounts and performances that have their own properties and ought to be analyzed in accordance with such characteristics. We need, therefore, to appreciate that interviews are occasions in which are enacted particular kinds of narratives and in which "informants" construct themselves and others as particular kinds of moral agents. Examples of this kind of approach include Margaret Voysey's (1975) analysis of parents' accounts of life with handicapped children and Nigel Gilbert and Michael Mulkay's (1980) analysis of natural scientists' accounts of scientific discoveries.

These and analyses like them by no means reject the utility of interview data, but they insist on a particular analytic strategy. The data are examined for their properties as accounts. Voysey, for instance, suspended the taken-for-granted view that the presence of a handicapped child disrupts normal family life; she examined, rather, how parents constructed moral accounts of "normal" parenting and family conduct. Likewise, Gilbert and Mulkay document

scientists' often inconsistent and contradictory accounting devices in their descriptions of scientific discovery, which construct science and scientists in distinctive ways. These are coherent and consistent ways of dealing with interview data. They do not, however, lend themselves to aggregation to observational data in order to achieve "triangulation" in any conventional sense.

From such perspectives, then, the analyst does not worry about whether "the informant is telling the truth" (Dean and Whyte 1958), if by that one understands the analyst's task to be that of distinguishing factual accuracy from distortion, bias, or deception. Similarly, ironic contrasts between what people do and what they say they do (see Deutscher 1973) become irrelevant. Rather, attention is paid to the coherence and plausibility of accounts, to their performative qualities, the repertoires of accounts and moral types that they contain, and so on. In the remainder of this chapter we address the implications of this position a little further. In essence, we argue that participant observation and interviewing are themselves distinctive forms of social action, generating distinctive kinds of accounts and giving rise to particular versions of social analysis. Each yields particular sorts of textual representation: There are other kinds of texts and other kinds of representation in and of social fields. If we cannot simply add them together and superimpose them to make a single coherent narrative or picture, what are the proper relations between them?

◆ Talk, Experience, and Action

Radical criticisms of the interview can treat naturally occurring social action as primary and talk about action as but a poor substitute for the observation of action, echoing Becker and Geer's original argument. From that perspective, we cannot take the interview as a proxy for action. Hence we cannot rely on it for information about what people do or what they have done; rather, it serves only as a mechanism for eliciting what people say they do. From this perspective, the interview inhabits a quite different universe from the observation of social action. One can readily move to the position that grants primacy to the recording of naturally occurring social interaction and relegates virtually everything else to the periphery of sociological interest. This particular view is sometimes accompanied by appeals for primary reliance on the analysis of permanent recordings of spoken activity, such as conversation analysis (Atkinson and Heritage 1984; Boden and Zimmerman 1991; Sacks 1992).

This is one possible position, but it is an unnecessary and unhelpful one. It is unduly insensitive to the variety of social action. It is also in danger of endorsing a particular kind of naturalism; the endorsement of one sort of action or activity over another implicitly attributes authenticity to one while denying it to others. It runs the risk of assuming that some sort of actions are "natural" whereas others are "contrived" (Hammersley and Atkinson 1995; Silverman 1985, 1993).

A more productive way of thinking about these relationships is to start from a more symmetrical perspective, rather than trying to privilege one source, or method, over another. This approach is, in one respect at least, more in keeping with contemporary epistemology. It is also antipathetic to the excesses of some recent enthusiasms that have rejected the study of action in situ in favor of an almost exclusive focus on interviews, narratives, and accounts (Atkinson and Silverman 1997). We can fruitfully begin to think of what we observe (and the work of observing) and the contents of interviews (and the work of interviewing) as incorporating social actions of different kinds and yielding data of different forms. We can thus be released from trying to combine them to produce information from them about something else and concentrate more on the performance of the social actions themselves.

Indeed, we know enough about the performance of everyday social action to be thoroughly suspicious of methodological formulations that even appear to attach particular kinds of authenticity to it. All of Erving Goffman's work, for instance, is—with varying degrees of explicitness—concerned with rendering problematic such a naive view. Admittedly, some of Goffman's key insights might seem to suggest the contrary. His famous essay on role distance, for example, seems to imply a dichotomy, not a continuity, between an ironic distance and a wholehearted commitment (Goffman 1961). Likewise, some accounts that are thoroughly or partially indebted to Goffman, such as Arlie Hochschild's *The Managed Heart* (1983)—an account of the self-conscious management of emotional work among workers such as airline flight attendants—seem to imply a contrast between authentic and insincere social actions. Hochschild distances herself from Goffman's vision of the social self, and her analysis depends on the presence of a deep self that preexists and authors authentic and inauthentic performances. But if we take full and serious account of the performativity of social life (the dramaturgical metaphor), then it clearly makes no more sense to assume any action as inherently authentic, and thus to grant it priority.

Part of the reported comparison between participant observation and interviewing has revolved around the ironic contrast between what people do and what people say (they do). This has also fed into the equally hoary question posed to and by field researchers: How do you know if your informant is telling the truth? These related problems equally reflect the position we have characterized as naive: the contrasts between actions and accounts, and between truth and dissimulation.

INTERVIEWING AS ACTION

This approach to interviewing as action can be illustrated with reference to the topic of memory. One way of thinking about interviews and the data they yield is to think about informants producing descriptions of past events. In part, therefore, the interview is aimed at the elicitation of memories. Viewed from a naive perspective, it also follows that one of the main problems of this kind of data collection concerns the accuracy or reliability of such recollections. Such a perspective certainly presents pressing problems if—to return to the preoccupations of Becker and Geer—one is using the interview to gather information about "events." The same is true of the elicitation of "experiences." It is possible to view the interview as a means for the retrieval of informants' personal experiences—a biographically grounded view of memories and past events.

The analytic problems of memory and experience are equivalent from our point of view. It is possible to address memory and experience sociologically, and it is possible to address them through the interview (and through other "documents of life"). But it is appropriate to do so only if one accepts that memory and experience are social actions in themselves. They are both enacted. Seen from this perspective, memory is not (simply) a matter of individual psychology, and is certainly not only a function of internal mental states. Equally, it is not a private issue. (We are not denying the existence of psychological processes in general, or the personal qualities and significance of memories—ours is a methodological argument about the appropriate way of conducting and conceptualizing social research.) Memory is a cultural phenomenon, and is therefore a collective one. What is "memorable" is a function of the cultural categories that shape what is thinkable and what is not, what is counted as appropriate, what is valued, what is noteworthy, and so on. Memory is far from uniquely (auto)biographical. It can reside in material culture, for instance: The deliberate collection or hoarding of memorabilia and souvenirs—photographs, tourist artifacts, family treasures, or other bric-a-brac—is one enactment of memory, for instance. Equally, memory is grounded in what is tellable. In many ways the past is a narrative enactment.

Memory *and* personal experience are narrated. Narrative is a collective, shared cultural resource (see in this volume Cándida Smith, Chapter 11; Narayan and George, Chapter 7). Authors such as Ken Plummer (1995) have reminded us that even the most intimate and personal of experiences are constructed through shared narrative formats. The "private" does not escape the "public" categories of narrativity. Just as C. Wright Mills (1940) demonstrated that "motive" should be seen as cultural and linguistic in character, and not as a feature of internal mental states or predispositions, we must recognize that memories and experiences are constructed through the resources of narrative and discourse. Narratives and the resources of physical traces, places, and things—these are the constituents of biography, memory, and experience. When we conduct an interview, then, we are not simply collecting information about nonobservable or unobserved actions, or past events, or private experiences. Interviews generate accounts and narratives that are forms of social action in their own right.

EVENTS AND ACCOUNTS AS ENACTMENTS

At this point we return to the original formulation offered by Becker and Geer ([1957] 1970a). They refer to the study of "events," arguing that observation provides access to events in a way that interviews cannot. In one sense, that is self-evidently true. We can observe and we can make permanent recordings of events. On the other hand, we need to ask ourselves what constitutes an "event." Clearly an event is not merely a string of unrelated moments of behavior, nor is it devoid of significance. In order to be observable and reportable, events in themselves must have some degree of coherence and internal structure. An "event" in the social world is not something that just happens: It is made to happen. It has a beginning, a middle, and an end. It is differentiated from the surrounding stream of activity. Its structure and the observer's capacity to recognize it are essentially narrative in form. In that sense, therefore, a radical distinction between "events" that are observed and "accounts" that are narrated starts to become less stark, and the boundary maintenance becomes more difficult to sustain.

Does this mean that we still acknowledge the primacy of particular kinds of social actions? Not necessarily. By acknowledging that accounts, recollections, and experiences are enacted, we can start to avoid the strict dualism between "what people do" and "what people say." This is a recurrent topic in the methodological discourse of social science. It rests on the commonplace observation that there may be differences or discrepancies between observed actions and accounts about action. (This may be proposed as a rather vulgar counterargument against vulgar triangulation.) They are different kinds of enactments, certainly, but we would argue that the specific dualism that implicitly asserts an authenticity for what people (observably) do and the fallibility of accounts of action is both unhelpful and "untrue." By treating both the observed and the narrated as kinds of social action, we move beyond such simple articulations and instead reassert the methodological principle of symmetry.

We therefore bracket the assumption of authenticity, or the "natural" character of "naturally occurring" action, and the contrasts that are founded on that implicit dualism. If we recognize that memories, experiences, motives, and so on are themselves forms of action, and equally recognize that they and mundane routine activities are en-

acted, then we can indeed begin to deal with these issues in a symmetrical, but nonreductionist, way. In other words, it is not necessary to assert the primacy of one form of data over another, or to assert the primacy of one form of action over another. Equally, a recognition of the performative action of interview talk removes the temptation to deal with such data as if they give us access to personal or private "experiences." We need, therefore, to divorce the use of the interview from the myth of inferiority: the essentially romantic view of the social actor as a repository of "inner" feelings and intensely personal recollections. Rather, interviews become equally valid ways of capturing shared cultural understandings and enactments of the social world.

THE POSITION OF THE RESEARCHER

We have thus far said very little about the position of the researcher within these different kinds of research "events." One of the distinctions between participant observation and interviewing has pivoted on the relationship of the researcher to the field of study. In the case of observational work, claims have been made that participant observation enables the researcher to participate firsthand in the happenings of the setting; these claims have been countered, of course, by warnings that the researcher may affect (contaminate) the setting or become too much of a participant, and thereby lose the capacity to observe critically. In contrast, the interview has been perceived as an artificial enactment, with unequal relations and potentially less contamination between participants, and more recently as a site for collaboration and the genuine sharing of experiences.

Here we would wish to stress again the symmetry of the two broad approaches. This does not necessary imply complementarity or sameness, but recognizes the complexity of research experiences and relationships. Through both participant observation and interviewing there is the potential for "contamination," although this is a paralyzing and unhelpful way of characterizing the research process (and can actually render all research inadequate). Rather, through active reflexivity we should recognize that we are part of the social events and processes we observe *and* help to narrate. To overemphasize our potential to change things artificially swells our own importance. To deny our being "there" misunderstands the inherent qualities of both methods—in terms of documenting and making sense of social worlds of which we are a part (either through participant observation or as facilitators of shared accounts and narrative strategies).

The (auto)biographical work that is common to both approaches is also worth noting. Again, in digressing from Becker and Geer's assertion of the primary goal of describing events, we should recognize that the process of undertaking research is suffused with biographical and identity work (Coffey 1999). The complex relationships among field settings, significant social actors, the practical accomplishment of the research, and the researcher-self are increasingly recognized as significant to all those who engage in research of a qualitative nature (whether that be participant observation, interviewing, or some combination of the two).

◆ Conclusion

We began this chapter with a retrospective evaluation of Becker and Geer's ([1957] 1970a) original observations concerning the respective merits and weaknesses of participant observation and interviewing. We did so for two reasons. First, Becker and Geer's paper is a locus classicus in the corpus of methodological writing in qualitative sociology. Second, it helps us to identify a particular constellation of as-

sumptions concerning observation and interviewing characteristic of that period, during which many aspects of qualitative fieldwork were being codified. We repeat our acknowledgment that the scholars of that generation were responsible for the demystification of qualitative methods, providing practical advice manuals for the research community as well as acting as methodological advocates. Their contribution should not be underestimated, and it was never our intention to do so. However, we have reached a point that suggests a position very different from that articulated by Becker and Geer. This difference reflects a good deal of methodological change and development over the intervening years, not least in the burgeoning of qualitative methods texts and the increased acceptance and innovative use of the whole variety of qualitative research strategies.

For a long time, ethnographers and other qualitative researchers have relied on the ironic contrast between "what people do" and "what people say they do." That contrast is—as we have suggested—based on some further differences. It assumes that what people do is unproblematic and is amenable to direct observation and description; what people say, on the other hand, is treated as a much more unstable category. The relationship between action and talk is perceived as problematic because accounts can distort: Accounts can be motivated in various ways, and can function as excuses, legitimations, rationalizations, and so on. However, actors may falsify their accounts. Deliberate deception, wishful thinking, recipient design for difficult audiences—these can all affect the accuracy and reliability of actors' accounts (according to a well-established tradition). As a consequence, discussions of interviewing have often sought to address the question, How do you know if your informant is telling the truth? As we have now seen, however, these issues are radically changed if one abandons the initial presumption of difference. If we accept that interview talk is action—is performative—then ironic contrasts between "doing" and "acting" become increasingly redundant. Taken-for-granted distinctions between talk and action are erroneous and irrelevant when one recognizes that talk is action. In a performative view, interviews, and other accounts, need not be seen as poor surrogates or proxies for unobserved activities. They can be interrogated for their own properties—their narrative structures and functions. Accounts are, or are composed of, speech acts and may therefore legitimately be regarded as games or types of action in their own right.

By the same token, actions or events, even observed firsthand, are not inherently endowed with meaning, nor is their meaning unequivocally available for inspection. The kinds of "events" that Becker and Geer ([1957] 1970a) discuss are recognized as such precisely because they are describable and narratable by participants and by onlookers, including ethnographers and other observers. After all, the "data" of participant observation are the events as narrated (written down, often retrospectively) by observers, and hence rely on the same culturally shared categories of memory, account, narrative, and experience. In retrospect, it seems odd that Becker and Geer felt able to legislate for "what really happened" and to discount the tellings of medical students. From our point of view, they could and should have paid much more attention to several things: how the "events" were performed; how the medical students narrated and evaluated the "events"; how certain events or classes of events were endowed with significance through the medical students' own tellings; and how they themselves, as observers, recorded and described the "events." They might thus have found themselves dealing with classes of performance and rhetoric, in different contexts, in different modes, rather than incommensurable kinds of phenomena. And once articulated in this way, their particular distinction between participant observation and interviewing, and the primacy of the former, becomes untenable. This does not deny the different qualities of these methods as data collection strategies. Rather, in emphasizing their commonalities in terms of social action and performance (and extinguishing the false dichotomy), we may actually be in a better, and certainly a more informed, position to "choose."

■ *References*

Atkinson, J. M. and J. Heritage, eds. 1984. *Structures of Social Action: Studies in Analysis.* Cambridge: Cambridge University Press.

Atkinson, P. 1996. *Sociological Readings and Re-readings.* Aldershot, England: Ashgate.

Atkinson, P. and D. Silverman. 1997. "Kundera's *Immortality:* The Interview Society and the Invention of Self." *Qualitative Inquiry* 3:304-25.

Becker, H. S. and B. Geer. 1970a. "Participant Observation and Interviewing: A Comparison." Pp. 133-42 in *Qualitative Methodology: Firsthand Involvement with the Social World,* edited by W. J. Filstead. Chicago: Markham. Reprinted from *Human Organization* 16 (1957):28-32.

———. 1970b. "Participant Observation and Interviewing: A Rejoinder." Pp. 150-52 in *Qualitative Methodology: Firsthand Involvement with the Social World,* edited by W. J. Filstead. Chicago: Markham. Reprinted from *Human Organization* 16 (1957):39-40.

Becker, H. S., B. Geer, E. C. Hughes, and A. L. Strauss. 1961. *Boys in White: Student Culture in Medical School.* Chicago: University of Chicago Press.

Boden, D. and D. H. Zimmerman, eds. 1991. *Talk and Social Structure: Studies in Ethnomethodology and Conversation Analysis.* Berkeley: University of California Press.

Coffey, A. 1999. *The Ethnographic Self: Fieldwork and the Representation of Identity.* London: Sage.

Dean, J. P. and W. F. Whyte. 1958. "How Do You Know If the Informant Is Telling the Truth?" *Human Organization* 17:34-38.

Denzin, N. K. 1970. *The Research Act.* Chicago: Aldine.

———. 1978. *The Research Act.* 2d ed. New York: McGraw-Hill.

Deutscher, E. 1973. *What We Say/What We Do: Sentiments and Acts.* Glenview, IL: Scott, Foresman.

Filstead, W. J., ed. 1970. *Qualitative Methodology: Firsthand Involvement with the Social World.* Chicago: Markham.

Fine, G. A., ed. 1995. *A Second Chicago School? The Development of a Postwar American Sociology.* Chicago: University of Chicago Press.

Gilbert, N. and M. Mulkay. 1980. *Opening Pandora's Box: A Sociological Account of Scientists' Discourse.* Cambridge: Cambridge University Press.

Goffman, E. 1961. *Encounters: Two Studies in the Sociology of Interaction.* Indianapolis: Bobbs-Merrill.

Gubrium, J. F. and J. A. Holstein. 1997. *The New Language of Qualitative Method.* New York: Oxford University Press.

Hammersley, M. and P. Atkinson. 1995. *Ethnography: Principles in Practice.* 2d ed. London: Routledge.

Hochschild, A. R. 1983. *The Managed Heart: Commercialization of Human Feeling.* Berkeley: University of California Press.

Lofland, J. 1971. *Analyzing Social Settings.* Belmont, CA: Wadsworth.

McCall, G. J. and J. L. Simmons, eds. 1969. *Issues in Participant Observation: A Text and Reader.* Reading, MA: Addison-Wesley.

Mills, C. W. 1940. "Situated Actions and Vocabularies of Motive." *American Sociological Review* 5:439-52.

Plummer, K. 1995. *Telling Sexual Stories: Power, Change and Social Worlds.* London: Routledge.

Sacks, H. 1992. *Lectures on Conversation,* Vols. 1-2. Edited by G. Jefferson. Oxford: Blackwell.

Schatzman, L. and A. L. Strauss. 1973. *Field Research: Strategies for a Natural Sociology.* Englewood Cliffs, NJ: Prentice Hall.

Silverman, D. 1985. *Qualitative Methodology and Sociology.* Aldershot, England: Gower.

———. 1993. *Interpreting Qualitative Data: Methods for Analysing Talk, Text and Interaction.* London: Sage.

Trow, M. 1970. "Comment on 'Participant Observation and Interviewing': A Comparison." Pp. 143-49 in *Qualitative Methodology: Firsthand Involvement with the Social World,* edited by W. J. Filstead. Chicago: Markham. Reprinted from *Human Organization* 16 (1957):33-35.

Voysey, M. 1975. *A Constant Burden.* London: Routledge & Kegan Paul.

PERSONAL AND FOLK NARRATIVE AS CULTURAL REPRESENTATION

◆ **Kirin Narayan**
Kenneth M. George

There is a thirst among the Paxtun women for autobiography. There is also a correct way to "seek the person out" with questions. One day, when my daughter's nanny had observed me eliciting a life story from someone, she later tried to correct me on the grounds that I did not know how to interrogate properly. "You foreigners don't know how to search [*latawel*] one another," she reproached me. "When we Pakistanis ask a person's story, we don't let a single detail go by. We dig in all the corners, high and low. We seek the person out. That's how we do things. We are storytellers and story seekers. We know how to draw out a person's heart." (Grima 1991:81-82)

As this outspoken Paxtun woman from Northwest Pakistan reminds us, asking people for and about stories is a widespread practice, even though the ways of asking and the kinds of stories told may vary. Indeed, most of us are already old experts at coaxing, inviting, or outright demanding stories in our everyday lives. From a child's wheedling "Tell me" to a friend's bright-eyed prod "And then what happened?" we regularly make and receive such requests.

In pursuing stories within an interview context, however, we create a frame of analytic reflection around storytelling transactions. The delights of a well-told tale may continue to sweep us along, but as interviewers we usually elicit and evaluate stories from the vantage points of particular

AUTHORS' NOTE: We extend our great thanks to Lila Abu-Lughod and Maria Lepowsky for their helpful critiques of this chapter.

professional agendas. Like Benedicte Grima's (1991) Paxtun critic, the people we seek to interview sometimes already have their own ideas about how a person should go about extracting stories. For them too, stories move about in a range of interpersonal and institutional settings, and the presence of a researcher eagerly seeking stories may provide yet another occasion for retellings. In addition to scholars, there are other specialists with their own purposes and methods for eliciting stories—therapists, shamans, lawyers, doctors, talk-show hosts, priests, immigration officers, police detectives, journalists, human rights workers, and so on. This interactive process of extracting and yielding stories plays an ongoing role in the shaping of social life.

Our task in this chapter is to describe interviewing for two sorts of stories: personal narratives and folk narratives. The distinction between these may seem commonsensical at first: Personal narratives are idiosyncratic, whereas folk narratives are collective. However, we will argue that the distinction is actually less clear. Second, we explore the process of eliciting stories in interviews, emphasizing the need for researchers to be aware of the social life of stories that extends beyond the interview. Third, we argue that it is important for researchers to supplement interviews *for* stories with interviews *about* stories in order to comprehend the interpretive frames that surround storytelling transactions. Finally, we point out the usefulness of critically examining interview transcripts in evolving practice.

Many excellent publications offering insights and guidelines for ethnographic interviewing, or folkloristic interviewing more generally, are already available (Atkinson 1998; Briggs 1986; Holstein and Gubrium 1995; Ives 1995; Jackson 1987; Langness and Frank 1981; Spradley 1979). Rather than rehash insights from these other works, we direct interested readers to them. Here we will draw on a selection of memorable examples of prior interviews

for stories, working from the larger ethnographic record and also from our own fieldwork experiences.

◆ Folk Narrative and Personal Narrative

For the better part of the 20th century, most anthropologists, folklorists, and literary specialists assumed that personal narratives are uniquely individual, shaped more by the vagaries of experience than by the conventions of collective tradition. From this vantage point, experience appears to dictate the content and form of personal narrative, and so the teller is of central importance. In contrast, folk narratives have been seen as highly conventional, widely shared cultural representations mediated by the narrative community at large. As Franz Boas (1916) asserts, folk narratives, like myths, "present in a way an autobiography of the tribe" (p. 393). Yet, time and again, the people with whom anthropologists work have not made the same distinction between "personal" and "folk" in terms of the significance of stories to individuals' lives.

Personal stories are also shaped through the use of culturally recognized—and, sometimes, transculturally negotiated—narrative and linguistic conventions that are themselves differentially put to use by people positioned by gender, age, or class. As life story research in anthropology has shown, such stories are closely tied to cultural conceptions of personhood (Langness and Frank 1981). So, for example, when Renato Rosaldo (1976) asked his Ilongot "brother" Tukbaw to speak about his own life, he found that Tukbaw chose to build stories around the wise words and advice of his father rather than provide introspective vignettes about feelings or events. Or, when Grima (1991) went to Northwest Pakistan in the hope of researching Paxtun women's romance narratives, she soon learned that the stories the women themselves most liked to tell involved tragic tales of personal suffering—the more tragic the better. A woman who had not suffered was assumed not to have a life story. For example, a 30-year-old unmarried schoolteacher told Grima: "I have no story to tell. I have been through no hardships" (p. 84).

Similarly, in Northwest India, Kirin Narayan was also startled when Vidhya Sharma, an educated Kangra village woman, claimed that she had no life story. "Look, it's only when something different has happened that a woman has a story to tell," Vidhya said, speaking Hindi. "If everything just goes on the way it's supposed to, all you can think of is that you ate, drank, slept, served your husband and brought up your children. What's the story in that?" (Narayan n.d.:1). Building on cultural conceptions, individuals may also elaborate their own tastes and convictions about appropriate life stories. Ruth Behar (1993), for example, found that the Mexican peddler—Esperanza—whose life story she recorded followed a narrative structure that moved from suffering to rage to redemption and appeared to expect other women's narratives to follow this pattern too. When Behar proposed to ask other women for their life stories, Esperanza objected to Behar's choice of a respected schoolteacher, declaring, "But she, what has she suffered? I never heard that her husband beat her or that she suffered from rages" (p. 12).

The genre that anthropologists have developed to write about people's lives is labeled *life history,* but we prefer the term *life story* or even *life stories* because it draws attention to the fragmentary and constructed nature of personal narratives (see Peacock and Holland 1991). Sometimes, asking someone to tell a life story may appear altogether too overwhelming or foreign a request, whereas asking about particular eras or incidents may stimulate retellings. For example, Migdim, an old, semiblind Bedouin woman, waved off Lila Abu-Lughod's (1993) request for her life story, stating,

"I've forgotten all of that. I've got no mind to remember with any more." Migdim then proceeded to add some generalities about the past nomadic experiences of the group: "We used to milk the sheep. We used to pack up and leave here and set up camp out west" (p. 46). As Abu-Lughod points out, for this old woman, like others in the community, "the conventional form of 'a life' as a self-centered passage through time was not familiar. Instead there were memorable events, fixed into dramatic stories with fine details" (p. 46). As Abu-Lughod learned, when Migdim reminisced in the company of family members about particular past events, she was indeed a spirited storyteller with a sharp memory for things that had happened to her.

Whether entire life stories or passing anecdotes, personal narratives emerge within what is culturally "storyworthy." By looking at the subjects that people choose to dwell on in narrating their lives, we are in a position to see what most matters to them, from their point of view. Describing the hunting stories that Ilongot men of the Philippines love to tell, Rosaldo (1986) observes, "Narrative can provide a particularly rich source of knowledge about the significance people find in their workaday lives. Such narratives often reveal more about what can make life worth living than about how it is routinely lived" (p. 98).

In addition to being implicitly encoded in cultural practice, conventions for talking about lives can also be actively inculcated by institutional demands of various kinds (see Holstein and Gubrium 2000; Gubrium and Holstein 2001). As Kenneth George (1978) learned in his fieldwork with pastor John Sherfey, the religious doctrines of evangelical Protestant congregations in the United States require adherents to "testify" to their spiritual salvation through stories about their personal conversion experience (see also Harding 1987; Titon 1988; Titon & George 1977, 1978). Or as Carole Cain (1991) has argued, Alcoholics Anonymous teaches newcomers how to tell stories in which they are not just drinkers, but alcoholics who have hit rock bottom and need help. Through pamphlets, the examples of others' storytelling, and feedback from fellow participants at A.A. meetings, people joining the group learn how to shape personal experience along the lines of this key story form.

Ironically, the presence of conventions for telling the right stories about particular kinds of life experience means that people who have not actually lived through these experiences might nonetheless learn how to recount convincing stories of their own. So, for example, Bruce Jackson (1996) writes about meeting Jim, a "perfect informant" who readily told long, detailed tales about his war experiences in Vietnam. Jim kept not only Jackson but other veterans spellbound. It eventually turned out, however, that Jim had never been in Vietnam at all; he had so steeped himself in widespread accounts of being there that he told the stories as his own. Other veterans had sniffed out the inconsistencies and exaggerations even before Jackson became aware of the hoax. Yet when Jackson asked them, "Why didn't you ever blow the whistle on him?" one of the veterans responded in a classic defense of a mesmerizing storyteller, "Wasn't doing me any harm. And he told such great stories. I loved listening to him tell those goddamned stories. I mean, I was *there* and I couldn't tell stories like that guy" (p. 220).

Even as personal narratives are shaped by shared conventions, folk narratives circulating within and across communities are personalized through retellings. After all, people remember and retell shared stories—myths, legends, folktales, parables, jokes, and so on—because these are personally as well as socially meaningful. Yet folk narratives have tended to be so analytically yoked to communities that many collections and analyses have rarely mentioned tellers, or have alluded to them only by name—as though their existence is important only because they serve as conduits of traditional knowledge. Shifting attention from traditional stories to the story-

tellers, it becomes clear that storytellers put their own creative and aesthetic stamp on folk narratives, personalizing them through retellings to fit particular occasions (Azadovskii 1974; Dégh 1969). As Swamiji, a Hindu holy man who delighted in making moral and spiritual points through stories once reflected to Narayan, people tell stories according to their own feelings and the feelings of their audience. As Swamiji said: "When you tell a story, you should look at the situation and tell it. Then it turns out well. If you just tell any story any time, it's not really good. You must consider the time and shape the story so it's right. All stories are told for some purpose" (Narayan 1989:37).

Occasionally, tellers may make explicit links between their folk narratives and their lives. So, for example, Urmilaji, a woman in the Himalayan foothills, once compared hard times she had experienced to the wanderings of an exiled king and queen in one of the folktales she had told Narayan. In making this explicit connection, Urmilaji was shedding light not just on her own life, but on the traditional tale as well. Similarly, when Urmilaji's family priest retold the same story, foregrounding the beleaguered king and downplaying the travails of his loyal wife, it became clear that both tellers were recasting the tale according to their own gendered experiences (Narayan 1997: 121-24; see also Taggart 1990).

Reading life histories, one can occasionally sense the subject straining against an anthropologist's conceptions of appropriate "personal" content in an interview. So, for example, when the energetic !Kung woman Nisa suggested to Marjorie Shostak (1981), "Let's continue our talk about long ago. Let's also talk about the stories that the old people know" (p. 40), it is possible that Nisa was trying to include some of her repertoire of traditional tales within the frame of her life stories. Sometimes, subjects are more emphatic. Julie Cruikshank (1990), for example, found that three Yukon women elders whose life stories she was recording insisted that their myths were *part* of their lives and so should be included along with their more personal reminiscences.

Breaking down the division between personal and folk narratives forces researchers to revise their assumptions about how to conduct interviews and about what they should include in their texts. Rather than suppressing the disjunction between the kinds of stories researchers might seek and the forms of discourse that they receive in interviews, exploring this gap between "analytic categories" and the locally conceived genres that index social power can be a source of creative scholarly insight and creativity (see Ben-Amos [1969] 1976; Bauman and Briggs 1992; Briggs 1986). As Michael Young (1983) admits in his prologue to *Magicians of Manumanua: Living Myth in Kalauna,* the book emerged from his attempt to make sense of the ritual expert Iyahalina's puzzling response to a request for his life history:

> Instead of telling me tales from his childhood, recounting the circumstances of his marriage, or enumerating his mature achievements, he narrated a sequence of myths and legends that described the activities of his ancestors. He concluded with a passionate peroration on the ritual duties they had bequeathed him, the central task of which was to "sit still" in order to anchor the community in prosperity. (Pp. 3-4)

As Young learned, Iyahalina and other hereditary guardians of myths on Goodenough Island identified with the heroes of their myths and drew on mythic themes to construct their own autobiographical narratives. At the same time, possession of these myths was a means of asserting status. Similarly, Maria Lepowsky (1994:126) found that in Vanatinai, New Guinea, women could also own authoritative versions of myths, a fact that she links to women's stature within this more gender-egalitarian society.

Whether folk or personal, narratives are not just a means of cultural representation; they are also potent tools in social interaction, a form of cultural work. By *cultural work,* we mean the ways that narrators and audiences use narrative resources for political and social ends. Although stories of different kinds certainly contain representations of cultural values, concerns, and patterns, we cannot forget that stories are also practices intended to get things done: to entertain, edify, shock, terrorize, intimidate, heal, comfort, persuade, testify, divulge, and so on. Narrative form, then, not only conjures up other worlds, whether imagined or remembered; it is also a way of artfully arranging words for social and political consequences in the immediacies of this world.

◆ Getting Stories

Alert researchers should ideally try to be present when stories are narrated as part of ongoing social life, and so be in a position to overhear spontaneously evoked commentaries, debates, revisions, and retellings. Yet researchers are not always so lucky as to be in the right place at the right time, to participate in the many varied moments when people tell or comment upon stories that circulate in everyday life. When researchers do have a chance to listen in, their very presence cannot help but shape different aspects of the storytelling occasion. Further, being present for a single narrative performance is usually not enough for a researcher to gain insight into the larger ongoing life of stories and storytelling encounters. Interviews, then, are a useful supplement to the ethnographer's taking part in social life in an engaged, observant way (see Atkinson and Coffey, Chapter 6, this volume).

Because all storytelling events are situationally unique, narratives heard or exchanged in interviews should not be carelessly confused with or substituted for narratives that take place outside of the interview context. All stories emerging from an interview will bear the mark of an interviewer's presence and the hierarchical dynamics of the interview situation. Yet we should not dismiss interview narratives as contrived or worthless. Like so many other social encounters, interviews are culturally negotiated events worthy of analysis (see Briggs 1986). Because the interview can be an invitation to narrate, it is a wonderful opportunity for the researcher to grasp—or at least begin to think about—the complexity of stories exchanged elsewhere in a community.

The word *interview* has roots in Old French, and at one time meant something like "to see one another." Although we cannot ignore the social hierarchies of inquiry, we want to underscore how "seeing one another" in interviews requires close attentiveness and an openness to the surprises of dialogue and exchange. How an interview runs its course depends very much on all participants involved. It is important for the interviewer to be flexible and ready to follow unexpected paths that emerge in the course of talking together with interviewees. In fact, in our experience, interviews often end up having less to do with structured questions or answers than with the animated exchange of stories. The interviewer's willingness to reveal his or her own stories can also add to the depth of an interview, inspiring the person being interviewed to open up, knowing that the interviewer is willing to be vulnerable too.

The ethnographic interview is a bid on the part of a researcher to get an interviewee to converse openly about a set of issues of concern to the researcher. The political conditions surrounding the consent and participation of interviewees in ethnographic interviews—and in the negotiated elicitation of stories—have been anticipated in human subjects protocols designed to hold in check the potentially coercive impulses of social scientific and humanistic inquiry. Setting up an interview becomes an invitation to narrate, albeit one that can be refused, subverted, or turned back on the interviewer.

Most basically, when looking for stories in interviews, researchers should keep in mind that all people are not equally skilled storytellers. Some people are energetic raconteurs who will use the interview as a welcome occasion to spin stories. Stories may pour toward the researcher in such dizzying numbers that all he or she need do is show engagement with nods or murmurs while the recording equipment rolls. In the presence of such practiced storytellers, an interviewer may have to struggle to direct the stories toward subjects suited to his or her specific interests. Sometimes, the interviewer may need to clarify details. But mostly, when a storyteller takes charge, an interviewer's work is to listen with attentive care so as to be able to formulate necessary questions when the retelling is over.

In other cases, the interviewer has to work harder. With some respondents, it may take a while for the interviewer to formulate the right questions that will inspire the telling of stories. Questions that can be answered with a simple yes or no are particular hazards, and can give an interviewer a sense of getting nowhere at all. Sometimes, a person is more willing to tell stories outside the formal context of an interview, without recording devices or notebooks at hand. Occasionally, a person being interviewed is willing to tell stories about some things, but not others. Here, for example, is a moment from Narayan's fieldwork in the Northwest Himalayan foothills: Suman Kumari (SK), a woman who had been animatedly telling stories about her grandmother's and mother's difficult lives, comes to a place in her narrative for which there no longer appears to be a clear prior story. Narayan had already been struggling to keep the stories flowing by asking what Suman's mother's brothers had made of Suman's father's not working. Finally, giving up on questions that received brief answers, Narayan (KN) asked as broad a question as possible.

KN: And after that?

SK: After that what can I say? What can I say, Bahenji? [Turns to her half sister, who, along with the mother, is listening in] After that—that's all: sons and all that, and daughters-in-law.

KN: [Seeing that SK is still speaking from the perspective of her mother, tries to turn the interview to SK's own life] And your earliest memories were of this place? What was your childhood like?

SK: [Looking at her sister again] What should I tell her about my childhood, Bahenji?

Sister: That you went to school in your childhood—that's just fine. [Both sisters laugh]

SK: What happened is that we went to school, we ate food. Sometimes there would be mangoes on the trees and we'd eat a lot. In the house, she [indicating her mother] would say, "Go to sleep." But as soon as she was asleep, then all three of us would run out!

In a cursory way, Suman Kumari spoke about collecting mangoes, of going to school, of knitting, yet her own life clearly did not have as much interest to her as did the lives of her mother and grandmother. Although Narayan tried to refuel the narrative with questions, these reminiscences soon sputtered to a halt.

Asking people to be more specific can sometimes be a good way of getting them to expand on stories. For example, if someone says, "Life was hard," the interviewer might ask in what ways life was hard, or if there are any particular moments that stand out as being especially hard; such probes can result in the unpacking of stories. However, the more an interviewer works at extracting a story, the less sure he or she can be that it is a story already present in the person's repertoire rather than one created only by the interview. This is one of the reasons it has been suggested that researchers should include the questions they asked interview respondents in their final published works; this information can be crucial to showing how the materials emerged as part of a dialogic process (Dwyer 1982).

Folklorists make the distinction between "active bearers" and "passive bearers" (von Sydow 1948:12-15). Active bearers are those who are actively engaged in transmitting folk knowledge; passive bearers are those who may know folklore, but who may not think of themselves as competent tellers to pass the folklore on. The distinction is fluid: Sometimes an active bearer may slip into a passive role, for example, with age and failing memory. Equally, a passive bearer might assume a more active role through various circumstances, such as growing seniority, migration, or the death of an active bearer. In some contexts, a perfectly competent active bearer of stories may be forced to defer to the authority of a storyteller who is socially recognized. In Kangra, for example, when Narayan worked with women's ritual tales, she found that many women were passive bearers of ritual tales. Yet it was the senior women in patrilineages, considered "very wise," who were called on to tell stories in the context of ritual worship. In cases where related, less senior women interrupted, telling their own versions, there were enormous tensions around these transgressions, with relatives of the older women sometimes advising Narayan to erase her tapes.

It is important, then, for researchers to ascertain where individual storytellers stand in relation to wider social conventions around narrative practices and how a storyteller might be evaluated within his or her own community. Also, researchers will find it valuable to reflect on the structural relations between interviewers and interviewees, and what motives may be built into the transmission of stories from the interviewees' side. For example, in Barbara Myerhoff's (1978) memorable ethnogra-

phy about elderly American Jews, the re-
tired tailor, Shmuel, seemed to hint at how
vital transmitting his memories to the safe-
keeping of an ethnographer was for his
own peace of mind. After recounting incidents from his childhood in Eastern Europe, he mused:

> For myself, growing old would be alto-
> gether a different thing if that little
> town was there still. . . . But when I
> come back from these stories and re-
> member the way they lived is gone for-
> ever, wiped out like you would erase a
> line of writing, then it means another
> thing altogether for me to accept leav-
> ing this life. If my life goes now, it
> means nothing. But if my life goes, with
> my memories, and all that is lost, that is
> something else to bear. (P. 74)

Shmuel sent Myerhoff home with what he
called "all this package of stories"; a day
later, he died in his sleep. Shmuel's frank
words remind us that sometimes interviews
are of value not just to scholars. Transmitting memories to an eager audience, ensuring the survival of stories beyond a limited lifetime, an interviewee may also have
a stake in the process.

The elicitation of stories in interviews
may be subject to wider constraints around
narrative practice. Examples abound in
many Native American communities,
where storytelling is often intimately
linked to seasons, especially winter. Telling
or eliciting stories at other times can be
complicated. So, for example, if a storyteller among the Anishanaabe (Ojibwa)
wishes to tell myths outside the winter
months, he or she can put on a white weasel
pelt, as though simulating snow. Exploring
indigenous sacred traditions in highland
Sulawesi, George (1996) found he had to
adjust his interview work to take into account taboos that regulated the time and
place for narrative activity. During the long
months that stretched from the time of preparing rice fields to the time of harvest,
communitywide prohibitions against story-

telling and singing were in place and effectively prevented George from gathering
and discussing narrative materials. Once
the postharvest ritual season began, a period that extended for about two months, he
was at liberty to record and discuss traditional songs and stories. Even then, certain
taboos remained in effect, such as those
that allowed *sumengo*—a genre of ritual
song associated with head-hunting narratives—to be performed and discussed for
only one week out of the year in any given
community. As a result, George had to adjust his research, moving from community
to community as sets of taboos came into
effect in one and relaxed in another.

The kinds of stories appropriate to tell
may vary not just with calendrical cycles,
but with social location. Gender and age
are particularly important factors to consider. For example, among Southeast Asia's
Ilongot (Rosaldo 1986), Karo Batak
(Steedly 1993), Meratus Dayak (Tsing
1993), and Pitu Ulunna Salu (George 1996)
communities, personal stories about the experience of going on journeys figure as an
especially prominent genre for adult males
in both everyday and ritual life. Interestingly, many of the mythic and historical
narratives in these regions feature male
"culture heroes" whose journeys led to the
foundation of the communities in question.
Thus men's contemporary tales of personal
journeys resonate well with the foundational narratives of any specific locale.
Women in these same communities have
less to say about personal journeys but com-
paratively more when it comes to talking
about trance experience (George 1996;
Steedly 1993; Tsing 1993). Although both
men and women in these communities go
on journeys and go into trance, in an important sense it is more relevantly male to
make a story of personal travel and more
relevantly female to talk about trance experience. The very familiarity and pervasive-
ness of this pattern makes it all the more
striking when, for example, a woman recounts the dangers of a journey she has
made. Her move into a typically "male"

narrative terrain, then, is an exceptionally revealing and socially salient example of gender play and transgression.

Storytelling forms are not static. Like other genres, kinds of stories evolve within the play of power in ongoing social life and in dialogue with other genres (Bauman and Briggs 1992). This means that there may be shifts in the kinds of stories that are appropriate for different social groups to tell. In his long-term research among the Kwaio of the Solomon Islands, Roger Keesing (1985) at first found men ready to talk about their lives, whereas women "were fragmented and brief, distancing themselves from serious autobiography with reciprocal jests" (p. 29). On return visits, he found that men's efforts to codify cultural rules and conventions or *kastom* as a form of post-colonial resistance to outside influences had also inspired women to think of culture as an objectifiable "thing" and to lay claim to their own accounts of *kastom* in which women's importance was given its due. When Kwaio women finally spoke out, they did so in counterpoint to the men, who had previously been working with Keesing to codify *kastom*. Also, senior women recounted their lives "*as moral texts,* as exemplifications of the trials, responsibilities, virtues and tragedies of A Woman's Life" (p. 33). Speaking out, for Kwaio women, was a bid to power. While acknowledging the wider historical shifts that made women perceive their life stories as valuable texts to transact, Keesing also mentions the importance of what he terms "the politics of the elicitation situation" (p. 37)—that is, the particular interpersonal circumstances of the interview. That he was joined by a female field-worker during the time that he was finally able to record women's stories was also a key factor in his coaxing Kwaio women who had previously been silent about their lives to become animated speaking subjects.

Anthropologists have typically addressed the self-revelatory content of one life story at a time. However, moving beyond one life story to compare several related life stories brings expected narrative forms and their transgressions into clearer focus. Oscar Lewis (1961) pioneered this method of juxtaposing life stories in his work with a poor Mexican family, where each family member recounted his or her own stories, revealing multifaceted, cross-cutting, and even diverging perspectives on the same episodes. Other researchers have also used this method to show how positioned perspectives and gendered conventions pervade the shaping of life stories (see Mintz [1960] 1974; Viramma, Racine, and Racine 1997).

For folklorists, there is an implicit understanding that any retelling is a version rather than *the* story. To track the wider lives of entire stories and their constituent parts beyond particular iterations, folklorists have developed such tools as tale-type indexes and motif indexes. At the same time, attention to performance has revealed how stories emerge within the parameters of particular contexts rather than as perfect forms that float above social life. The same attention to the surfacing of versions in performance can be applied to life histories. So, for example, Laurel Kendall (1988) was able to record multiple versions of the stories that Yongsu's Mother, a Korean shaman, dramatically retold to Kendall, neighbors, and clients to make varied points about gender, about the power of gods, about dangers of ritual lapses, and so on.

We would like to emphasize how valuable it is for researchers to elicit several versions of folktales and life stories—from the same persons through time and from different individuals—so that they can see how the uniqueness of particular tellings emerges within larger patterns. Collecting multiple versions of folk narratives and life stories, and talking to different storytellers, is vital to researchers' understanding of how narrative traditions are creatively reworked by particular tellers for particular social ends. Also, situating the performance of different versions within social interactions reveals the role of storytelling in the exercise of power, authority, and identity.

◆ Interviews about Stories

Getting a story during an interview still leaves unfinished the intellectual work of making sense of the story. Many researchers have found that there are great rewards in engaging the subjects of their research in the interpretive process, through asking for their opinions on meaning and through dialogues exposing the interpretive biases of both the storytellers and the scholars.

For folklore scholarship, Alan Dundes (1966) has coined the term *oral literary criticism* to characterize the move beyond eliciting texts to also comprehending indigenous meanings. In Dundes's classic formulation, oral literary criticism involves the collection of (a) metafolklore, that is, folklore about folklore (for example, folktales about folktales) that gives a sense of how a genre is locally conceived; (b) asides and explanations during folklore performances; (c) systematic exegeses of texts by storytellers and their audiences; and (d) analysts' attempts to comprehend possibly unconscious symbols by also looking at other texts in which the same symbols are used (p. 507). In an article affirming the theoretical and methodological value of this method, Narayan (1995) also adds the elicitation of generalized testimonies about a genre of folklore, supplementing talk about particular texts. Thus if an interviewee finds it too revealing to explain *why* he or she tells a particular story, the interviewer can elicit valuable insights by asking about why people more generally tell stories, and what kinds of meanings certain sorts of stories might carry.

Narayan sought to put this method to work through a collaboration with Urmila Devi Sood, or "Urmilaji," the wise woman we met earlier. After hearing Urmilaji's tales, Narayan transcribed them, thought about them, and came back to talk more

about texts in particular and what meanings they held, and about storytelling in general. Sometimes her questions mystified Urmilaji, and at other times Urmilaji expounded implicit meanings in the tales, self-evident to most Kangra people but perplexing to Narayan. Speaking with Urmilaji about her stories, Narayan also came to understand how stories can be associated with particular prior tellers, keeping their wisdom and influence alive. Urmilaji, for example, loved many of these tales because they had been gifts, lovingly imparted, by her father and ancient aunt-in-law.

In addition to interviewing storytellers, it is also valuable for researchers to interview a range of people about what particular stories mean to them. Kay Stone (1985), for example, interviewed Americans of all ages about their memories of and reactions to popular fairy tales, in particular the story of Cinderella. She found that the males tended not to remember fairy tales, whereas the females worked out their self-images partly in dialogue with fairy-tale characters. Girls and women sometimes chafed at the messages in fairy tales, and some also reworked the stories to carry alternate endings. So, for example, a 9-year-old girl who preferred the character of Jack in "Jack and the Beanstalk" to Cinderella suggested that perhaps Cinderella could recover her slipper from the prince, and then "maybe she doesn't marry him, but she gets a lot of money anyway, and she gets a job" (p. 144).

Talking to people about stories gives researchers a chance to learn how the stories work interpersonally and psychologically. Keith Basso (1996) has explored how, among the Western Apache, historical tales bearing moral points are associated with various sites in the landscape. A place called "Trail Goes Down between Two Hills" for example, is associated with a story about lascivious Old Man Owl and how he is tricked by two beautiful girls; one might tell this story to comment on how someone's behavior involves uncurbed appetites and so is laughable and offensive (pp. 113-

20). By telling a story instead of speaking directly, an individual can imply criticism rather than state it directly. The moral points carried within stories become embodied within the geographic landscape, reminding people of occasions when places have been pointed out to them. As Nick Thompson, a spirited elderly Apache, explained to Basso, stories "go to work on your mind and make you think about your life" (p. 58). Using the metaphor of hunting to characterize how stories are aimed at appropriate quarry, Thompson went on to describe how, when a person acts inappropriately, someone goes hunting for that person:

> So someone stalks you and tells a story about what happened long ago. It doesn't matter if other people are around—you're going to know that he's aiming that story at you. All of a sudden it *hits* you! It's like an arrow, they say. Sometimes it just bounces off—it's too soft and you don't think about anything. But when it's strong it goes in deep and starts working on your mind right away. No one says anything to you, only that story is all, but now you know that people have been watching you and talking about you. They don't like how you've been acting. So you have to think about your life. (Pp. 58-59)

The messages, then, are reinforced by place: "You're going to see the place where it happened, maybe every day if it's nearby. . . . If you don't see it, you're going to hear its name and see it in your mind" (p. 59). Even when the original storyteller dies, the place will continue to stalk the person, reminding him or her how to live right. In this conception of storytelling, then, a good story pierces deep and transforms a person from inside even while its effects are continually reinforced by the outer landscape.

In some societies, much of the power of stories lies in the ways they are internalized and embodied—"living myth," as Young

(1983) memorably puts it. Thus an interviewer's inviting someone to stand aside so that he or she can extract explicit meaning may have no cultural frame of reference and, indeed, may be annoying. As Elsie Mather, a Yup'ik teacher, forcefully wrote to Phyllis Morrow (1995) when the question of explication came up in the course of their collaboration in documenting Yup'ik oral traditions:

> Why do people want to reduce traditional stories to information, to some function? Isn't it enough that we hear and read them? They cause us to wonder about things, and sometimes they touch us briefly along the way, or we connect the information or idea into something we are doing at the moment. This is what the old people say a lot. They tell us to listen even when we don't understand, that later on we will make some meaning or that something that we had listened to before will touch us in some way. Understanding and knowing occur over one's lifetime. . . .
>
> Why would I want to spoil the repetition and telling of stories with questions? Why would I want to know what they mean? (P. 33)

Like Nick Thompson, Morrow reminds us how stories live in ongoing reverberations through lived practices, not just in analytic reflection. Asking people for meaning isolated from particular contexts of retelling or remembering is to fix meaning in inappropriate ways. As Margaret Mills (1991) found in her research in Afghanistan, storytellers may actually thrive on the ambiguity of storytelling and the intertextual relations among stories, as this allows them to make sly commentaries on the sociopolitical world beyond the stories.

The analytic stance that breaks up stories may be perceived as dangerous for other reasons, too. In a dramatic example of the dangers of a researcher's blithely asking about stories without being cognizant of their social role or power, Barre Toelken (1996) has traced different moments of "enlightenment" in his long-term research on Navajo Coyote tales. With growing understanding of these Coyote tales, he was told that the tales were not just entertainment for winter months, but were also used in Navajo healing ceremonies. As Toelken was discussing the use of these tales with an elderly Navajo singer one night, the singer asked him, "Are you ready to lose someone in your family?" Baffled, Toelken asked him to explain. That is the cost of taking up witchcraft, the singer told him. Without being aware of it, Toelken had gained a reputation among the Navajo as someone with an interest in witchcraft because of the sorts of questions he had asked, and this had potentially malevolent repercussions for the Navajo people around him. As Toelken (1996) writes:

> For just as the tales themselves in their narration are normally used to create a harmonious world in which to live, and just as elliptical references to the tales can be used within rituals to clarify and enhance the healing processes, so the tales can be dismembered and used outside the proper ritual arena by witches to promote disharmony and to thwart the healing processes. In discussing parts and motifs separately, by dealing with them as interesting ideas which might lead me to discoveries of my own, I had been doing something like taking all the powerful medicines to be found in all the doctors' offices in the land and dumping them by the bucket-load out of a low-flying chopper over downtown Los Angeles. (P. 11)

For researchers, then, asking for help with interpretations is like walking a razor's edge: On one hand, in asking, researchers run the danger of making severe cultural faux pas, as Toelken did; on the other hand, in not asking, they risk attributing their own interpretive frames to their subjects. The same dangers hold for both folk narratives and personal narratives, although with personal narratives people may be even more sensitive to interpretations that researchers make without consulting them.

A powerful example of the conflict that can arise when informants do not share the interpretations with their interviewers is described in an essay by Katherine Borland (1991). Borland interviewed her grandmother, Beatrice Hanson, about events that had taken place in 1944 when Beatrice attended a horse race and bet against the wishes of her father. Borland then wrote a student essay in which she interpreted her grandmother's actions as enacting a female struggle for autonomy and, thus, as being feminist. Her grandmother, however, after reading the essay, wrote back a 14-page letter in which she pointedly objected to being theorized in her feminist granddaughter's framework and asked questions that all scholars would do well to heed:

> So your interpretation of the story as a female struggle for autonomy within a hostile male environment is entirely YOUR interpretation. You've read into the story what you wished to—what pleases YOU. That it was never—by any wildest stretch of the imagination—the concern of the originator of the story makes such an interpretation a definite and complete distortion, and in this respect I question its authenticity. The story is no longer MY story at all. The skeleton remains, but it has become your story. Right? How far is it permissible to go in the name of folklore [or scholarship generally] and still be honest in respect to the original narrative? (P. 70)

This disagreement resulted in a dialogue in which both grandmother and granddaughter explained the assumptions they were working from and the different associations they brought to the term *feminist*. In the process of this conflict and the ensuing discussion, each woman stretched to understand the other's position, and each was educated in the process.

Indeed, feminist work on life stories has been at the forefront of the exploration of issues of possible reciprocity amid the hierarchical imbalances of interviews and their outcomes (see Personal Narratives Group 1989; Gluck and Patai 1991). Sociologist Ann Oakley (1981), for example, long ago advocated replacing a distanced interviewing technique that seeks to deflect questions aimed at the interviewer with a "different role, that could be termed 'no intimacy without reciprocity,'" especially for in-depth interviewing through time. As she writes: "This involves being sensitive not only to those questions that are asked (by either party) but to those that are not asked. The interviewee's definition of the interview is important" (p. 49). Elaine Lawless (1991) has worked out a system of "reciprocal ethnography" that she used in eliciting the life stories of Pentecostal women ministers; even as she sought to interpret their personal narratives, she allowed the women to critique and reflect on her ethnographic practices. Such an openness to the perspectives of the people interviewed can radically reframe the scholarly project, enhancing accountability to the contradictions and inequalities of the real world.

◆ *Reflecting on Interviews*

We have found that researchers can learn much not just from looking to the work of others, but from looking back at their own interview practices, whether this involves listening again to tapes or studying transcripts. Most immediately, such a review can help a researcher to frame questions about stories already recorded, and so more self-consciously engage interviewees in an unfolding interpretive process. More generally, encountering one's own shortcomings can be very instructive for future practice. For example, interviewers may

discover moments where they have asked questions that elicited yes or no responses instead of stories, moments where they have interrupted, or moments where they have radically misunderstood what someone was trying to say and taken an interview off on a new tangent. Bruce Jackson (1987) summarizes what many interviewers likely feel as they transcribe their own tapes: "The most important thing I learned was that I talked too much" (p. 81).

We now turn to a segment from an interview conducted by Narayan, who will reflect critically on her own practices. This interview was conducted in the fall of 1995, with a second-generation South Asian American called Zeynab (Z). At the time, Narayan (KN) was interviewing partly to comprehend second-generation South Asian American experience as an anthropologist and partly to construct a character for a novel she was writing. In her questions, she was striving to enter experience from within. In this segment, Zeynab has been talking about growing up in Southern California, and how her father's brother and his wife had come to live with the family, creating conflict and even urging Zeynab's father to divorce. Narayan's commentary appears in italics.

Z: And my mother didn't have anyone to talk to about these things.

KN: So she would talk to you? *[This query is based on Zeynab's having earlier told me that she was very close to her mother.]*

Z: Yeah. I still remember. I didn't understand exactly what was going on at the time. All I remember was my mother in the kitchen. Like I'll be doing the dishes and she'll be cleaning the floor and she'll be crying. And it wasn't ever that she told me, she never said that my sister-in-law was saying this and that, it was like, "I'm very alone, I have no one to talk to, I miss home." She did not have any intention of turning my father against his brother. So she just kept quiet. She took all of that in.

KN: When she said "home," what images came into your mind? *[Here my own agenda of understanding how second-generation South Asian Americans construct "home" is breaking in, redirecting the narrative flow. Ideally, I would have waited until a break in the larger narrative of growing up to ask this question.]*

Z: I guess for me, I had very strong images of when I was there as a child. Because my Nana [maternal grandfather] was still alive at that time.

KN: How old were you? Cause you were born here . . . *[Again, looking back, I am breaking in to ask for specification and possibly redirecting the story. I should have just kept my mouth shut, making affirmative sounds, then later asked her about her visits back to Pakistan.]*

Z: I was born in Los Angeles and maybe after a year or two we went back, and then every maybe year or two we would go back. My mother would take us. Some of my earliest memories are from there. My fondest memories too. We used to go to my Nana's house. It was a very nice house. One of the women who worked in the house, her husband was breeding pigeons on the roof. So we used to go up on the roof. Some of my NICEST memories are from that time. So . . .

KN: What did you see from the roof? *[In retrospect, I wish I could clap my hand over my mouth. With my desire to imaginatively participate in her experience, and my own strong visual sense, I am interrupting Zeynab from her own story. Zeynab, however, found her way back to what she was trying to say].*

Zeynab responded, "I think it's more the air I remember. The color of the sky. You know, seeing the other rooftops from the distance." In her own construction of the story, what she saw from the roof was less key than her going up there to play with

pigeons, and then returning to playing games with cousins, or going out to be treated to ice cream by her uncles. With time, Narayan hopes to have become more attentive to allowing stories to take shape without her intervention, learning to keep questions in her head until the teller has finished speaking. Narayan is also puzzling over whether her practice of turning off the tape recorder when an interviewee asks her questions (that is, when she tells stories about her own South Asian American experience) is appropriate or misleading. On the one hand, she is not interested in recording her own stories; on the other hand, might the inclusion of her own storytelling input in interview situations lessen the hierarchical imbalance?

Yet, as Narayan looks back at this exchange with Zeynab, she sees that there is something grand and lovely about the spaciousness she evoked with her hasty question about the views from that rooftop. Perhaps one of the most important lessons interviewers can learn from the mortifying process of looking back at their own interviews is to forgive themselves, make the best of what they have done, and look ahead to the next interview. In querying their own interview practices, researchers would do well to recall the poet Rainer Maria Rilke's (1984:34) stricture to "live the questions" rather than look for fixed and certain answers.

◆ Conclusions

The interest in "getting stories" has an institutional backdrop and a place within broader fields of everyday inquiry. As we stated at the opening of this chapter, it is not just scholars who want to obtain stories; police officers, medical and psychiatric diagnosticians, journalists, refugee agents, shamans, social workers, state and corporate bureaucrats, courts, and human rights workers want stories too. Interview narratives have been put to use not just by anthropologists and folklorists, but also by colonizers seeking to comprehend "the native mind," by nationalists wanting to mobilize support around an imagined "spirit of the people," and by those promoting regional and state articulations of identity.

The distinction between "personal" and "folk" narrative, we have argued, is often blurred in practice, and so cross-fertilizing methodologies and theories usually associated with one body of stories or the other may be sources of creative insight. We have emphasized the need for researchers to follow other people's own conceptions of stories, as speech genres and as interpersonal, politically charged transactions with lives outside an interview context. Paying attention to the kinds of people who are storytellers, the kinds of stories appropriate to tell within social locations, transformations in the kinds of stories told, and the shifting multiplicity of versions enhances researchers' appreciation for the specificity of stories that emerge within interviews.

We have underscored the value for researchers of talking about stories with both storytellers and listeners, in addition to gathering stories in interviews. Researchers' sensitivity to indigenous conceptions of the meanings and psychological impacts of stories can bring the researchers' own interpretive biases to light, where they can be transformed in constructive dialogues. Sometimes, cultural sensitivity may require that interviewers hold back on analytic questions that carve up stories into constituent elements, cutting them away from the ongoing flow of lived experience.

Finally, we have noted the fruits that researchers may glean by critically examining their own interview tapes or transcripts, learning to ask and to listen with greater skill. Often, being a good interviewer for stories involves not just asking the right questions, but sympathetically listening and holding back questions so the person being interviewed can shape stories in his or her own way. Equally, being a good interviewer may involve responding to questions from an interviewee, and so entering into a reciprocal exchange.

Telling and listening to stories is at the heart of social and cultural life. Much of what we understand as personhood, identity, intimacy, secrecy, experience, belief, history, and common sense turns on the exchange of stories between people. In receiving stories, we are often receiving gifts of self; it is incumbent on us as researchers to handle these gifts with respect as we pass them onward in our scholarly productions.

■ *References*

Abu-Lughod, L. 1993. *Writing Women's Worlds: Bedouin Stories*. Berkeley: University of California Press.

Atkinson, R. 1998. *The Life Story Interview*. Thousand Oaks, CA: Sage.

Azadovskii, M. 1974. *A Siberian Tale Teller*. Translated by J. Dow. Austin: University of Texas Press.

Basso, K. 1996. *Wisdom Sits in Places: Landscape and Language among the Western Apache*. Albuquerque: University of New Mexico Press.

Bauman, R. and C. L. Briggs. 1992. "Genre, Intertextuality and Social Power." *Journal of Linguistic Anthropology* 2:131-72.

Behar, R. 1993. *Translated Woman: Crossing the Border with Esperanza's Story*. Boston: Beacon.

Ben-Amos, D. [1969] 1976. "Analytical Categories and Ethnic Genres." Pp. 215-42 in *Folklore Genres*, edited by D. Ben-Amos. Austin: University of Texas Press.

Boas, F. 1916. *Tsimshian Mythology* (31st Annual Report of the Bureau of American Ethnology). Washington, DC: Smithsonian Institution.

Borland, K. 1991. " 'That's Not What I Said': Interpretive Conflict in Oral Narrative Research." Pp. 63-76 in *Women's Words: The Feminist Practice of Oral History*, edited by S. B. Gluck and D. Patai. New York: Routledge.

Briggs, C. L. 1986. *Learning How to Ask: A Sociolinguistic Appraisal of the Role of the Interview in Social Science Research*. Cambridge: Cambridge University Press.

Cain, C. 1991. "Personal Stories, Identity Acquisition and Self-Understanding in Alcoholics Anonymous." *Ethos* 19:210-53.

Cruikshank, J. with A. Sidney, K. Smith, and A. Ned. 1990. *Life Lived Like a Story: Life Stories of Three Yukon Native Elders*. Lincoln: University of Nebraska Press.

Dégh, L. 1969. *Folktales and Society: Story Telling in a Hungarian Peasant Community*. Translated by E. M. Schossberger. Bloomington: Indiana University Press.

Dundes, A. 1966. "Metafolklore and Oral Literary Criticism." *Monist* 60:505-16.

Dwyer, K. 1982. *Moroccan Dialogues: Anthropology in Question*. Baltimore: Johns Hopkins University Press.

George, K. M. 1978. " 'I Still Got It': The Conversion Narrative of John C. Sherfey." M.A. thesis, University of North Carolina, Chapel Hill.

———. 1996. *Showing Signs of Violence: The Cultural Politics of a Twentieth-Century Headhunting Ritual*. Berkeley: University of California Press.

Gluck, S. B. and D. Patai, eds. 1991. *Women's Words: The Feminist Practice of Oral History*. New York: Routledge.

Grima, B. 1991. "Suffering in Women's Performance of *Paxto*." Pp. 78-101 in *Gender, Genre and Power in South Asian Expressive Traditions*, edited by A. Appadurai, F. J. Korom, and M. Mills. Philadelphia: University of Pennsylvania Press.

Gubrium, J. F. and J. A. Holstein, eds. 2001. *Institutional Selves: Troubled Identities in a Postmodern World*. New York: Oxford University Press.

Harding, S. 1987. "Convicted by the Holy Spirit: The Rhetoric of Fundamental Baptist Conversion." *American Ethnologist* 14:167-81.

Holstein, J. A. and J. F. Gubrium. 1995. *The Active Interview*. Thousand Oaks, CA: Sage.

———. 2000. *The Self We Live By: Narrative Identity in a Postmodern World*. New York: Oxford University Press.

Ives, E. D. 1995. *The Tape Recorded Interview: A Manual for Fieldworkers in Folklore and Oral History*. 2d ed. Knoxville: University of Tennessee Press.

Jackson, B. 1987. *Fieldwork*. Urbana: University of Illinois Press.

———. 1996. "The Perfect Informant." Pp. 206-26 in *The Word Observed: Reflections on the Fieldwork Process*, edited by B. Jackson and E. D. Ives. Bloomington: Indiana University Press.

Keesing, R. 1985. "Kwaio Women Speak." *American Anthropologist* 87:27-39.

Kendall, L. 1988. *The Life and Hard Times of a Korean Shaman: Of Tales and the Telling of Tales*. Honolulu: University of Hawaii Press.

Langness, L. L. and G. Frank. 1981. *Lives: An Anthropological Approach to Biography*. Novato, CA: Chandler & Sharp.

Lawless, E. 1991. "Women's Life Stories and Reciprocal Ethnography as Feminist and Emergent." *Journal of Folklore Research* 29:35-60.

Lepowsky, M. 1994. *Fruit of the Motherland: Gender in an Egalitarian Society*. New York: Columbia University Press.

Lewis, O. 1961. *The Children of Sánchez: Autobiography of a Mexican Family*. New York: Random House.

Mills, M. 1991. *Rhetorics and Politics in Afghan Traditional Storytelling*. Philadelphia: University of Pennsylvania Press.

Mintz, S. [1960] 1974. *Worker in the Cane*. New York: Norton.

Morrow, P. 1995. "On Shaky Ground." Pp. 27-51 in *When Our Words Return: Writing, Hearing and Remembering Oral Traditions of Alaska and the Yukon*. Logan: Utah State University Press.

Myerhoff, B. 1978. *Number Our Days*. New York: Simon & Schuster.

Narayan, K. 1989. *Storytellers, Saints and Scoundrels: Folk Narrative in Hindu Religious Teaching*. Philadelphia: University of Pennsylvania Press.

———. 1995. "The Practice of Oral Literary Criticism: Women's Songs in Kangra, India." *Journal of American Folklore* 108:243-64.

———. 1997. *Mondays on the Dark Night of the Moon: Himalayan Foothill Folktales* (assembled in collaboration with U. D. Sood). New York: Oxford University Press.

———. n.d. "Unspeakable Lives: Silences in the Life Stories of Women in Kangra, Northwest India." Unpublished manuscript.

Oakley, A. 1981. "Interviewing Women: A Contradiction in Terms?" Pp. 30-61 in *Doing Feminist Research*, edited by H. Roberts. London: Routledge & Kegan Paul.

Peacock, J. L. and D. C. Holland. 1993. "The Narrated Self: Life Stories in Process." *Ethos* 21:367-83.

Personal Narratives Group, ed. 1989. *Interpreting Women's Lives: Feminist Theory and Personal Narratives.* Bloomington: Indiana University Press.

Rilke, R. M. 1984. *Letters to a Young Poet.* Translated by S. Mitchell. New York: Random House.

Rosaldo, R. 1976. "The Story of Tukbaw: 'They Listen as He Orates.' " Pp. 121-51 in *The Biographical Process,* edited by F. Reynolds and D. Capps. The Hague: Mouton.

———. 1986. "Ilongot Hunting as Story and Experience." Pp. 97-138 in *The Anthropology of Experience,* edited by V. W. Turner and E. M. Bruner. Urbana: University of Illinois Press.

Shostak, M. 1981. *Nisa: The Life and Words of a !Kung Woman.* Cambridge, MA: Harvard University Press.

Spradley, J. P. 1979. *The Ethnographic Interview.* New York: Holt, Rinehart & Winston.

Steedly, M. M. 1993. *Hanging without a Rope: Narrative Experience in Colonial and Postcolonial Karoland.* Princeton, NJ: Princeton University Press.

Stone, K. 1985. "The Misuses of Enchantment: Controversies on the Significance of Fairy Tales." Pp. 125-45 in *Women's Folklore, Women's Culture,* edited by R. A. Jordan and S. J. Kalcik. Philadelphia: University of Pennsylvania Press.

Taggart, J. M. 1990. *Enchanted Maidens: Gender Relations in Spanish Folktales of Courtship and Marriage.* Princeton, NJ: Princeton University Press.

Titon, J. T. 1988. *Powerhouse for God: Speech, Chant, and Song in an Appalachian Baptist Church.* Austin: University of Texas Press.

Titon, J. T. and K. M. George. 1977. "Dressed in the Armor of God." *Alcheringa: Ethnopoetics* 3(2):10-31.

———. 1978. "Testimonies." *Alcheringa: Ethnopoetics* 4(1):69-83.

Toelken, B. 1996. "From Entertainment to Realization in Navajo Fieldwork." Pp. 1-17 in *The Word Observed: Reflections on the Fieldwork Process,* edited by B. Jackson and E. D. Ives. Bloomington: Indiana University Press.

Tsing, A. 1993. *In the Realm of the Diamond Queen: Marginality in an Out-of-the-Way Place.* Princeton, NJ: Princeton University Press.

Viramma, J. Racine, and J.-L. Racine. 1997. *Viramma: Life of an Untouchable.* London: Verso.

von Sydow, C. 1948. *Selected Papers in Folklore.* Copenhagen: Rosenhilde & Bagger.

Young, M. 1983. *Magicians of Manumanua: Living Myth in Kalauna.* Berkeley: University of California Press.

8

THE CINEMATIC SOCIETY AND THE REFLEXIVE INTERVIEW

◆ Norman K. Denzin

We inhabit a secondhand world, one already mediated by cinema, television, and other apparatuses of the postmodern society. We have no direct access to this world; we experience and study only its representations. A reflexive sociology studies society as a dramaturgical production. The reflexive interview is a central component of this interpretive project.

In this chapter I examine the nexus of the cinematic society and the interview society. I show how postmodern society has become an interview society, how our very subjectivity "comes to us in the form of stories elicited through interviewing" (Holstein and Gubrium 2000:129; see also Atkinson and Silverman 1997). The interview, whether conducted by social researchers, mass-media reporters, television journalists, therapists, or counselors, is

now a ubiquitous method of self-construction (Holstein and Gubrium 2000). I will discuss the concept of the active, dialogic interview, anchoring this complex formation in the postmodern, cinematic society (Holstein and Gubrium 1995; Gubrium and Holstein 1997; Jackson 1998; Denzin 1995a, 1995b, 1997; Scheurich 1995). The reflexive interview is simultaneously a site for conversation, a discursive method, and a communicative format that produces knowledge about the self and its place in the cinematic society—the society that knows itself through the reflective gaze of the cinematic apparatus. A cinematic sociology requires a concept of the reflexive interview.

A two-part question organizes my argument: First, how does the postmodern, cinematic world mediate the ways in which we represent ourselves to ourselves? And

LIVERPOOL JOHN MOORES UNIVERSITY
LEARNING SERVICES

◆ 141

second, what is the place of the interview-interviewer relationship in this production process? I begin by outlining the central features of the postmodern, cinematic-interview society. I then show how the interview and the interviewer, as a voyeur, are basic features of this society. I thicken this argument by demonstrating how popular media representations shape and define situated cultural identities. I show how these representations become anchor points for the postmodern self; that is, how they occupy a central place in the background of our cultural consciousness. They mediate structures of meaning in the cinematic-interview society. A circular model of interpretation is thus created. Interviews, interviewers, and storytellers are defined in terms of these dominant cultural images and understandings. Thus does the cinematic society structure the interview society, and vice versa. I conclude with a series of epistemological observations on the significance of the relation between the cinematic society and the reflexive interview (see also Mishler 1986; Heyl 2001; Burawoy 1998; Bourdieu 1996).

◆ The Postmodern, Cinematic Society

Members of the postmodern society know themselves through the reflected images and narratives of cinema and television. On this, Altheide (1995) observes, "Culture is not only mediated through mass media . . . culture in both form and content is constituted and embodied by the mass media" (p. 59). The postmodern landscape is distinguished, as Simon Gottschalk (2000) argues, by "its constant saturation by multiple electronic screens which simulate emotions, interactions, events, desires. . . . From TV screens to computer terminals, from surveillance cameras to cell phones, we increasingly experience everyday life, reality

. . . via technologies of spectacle, simulation and 'telepresence' " (p. 23).

Consider the following exchange between ESPN sports journalist Sal Paolantonio and Kurt Warner, quarterback of the St. Louis Rams, named Most Valuable Player in the 2000 Super Bowl:

Sal: There's a minute and 54 seconds left in the game. The Titans have just tied the score. Now look, let me show you your 73-yard winning pass to Isaac Bruce. Kurt, what were you thinking when Isaac caught that pass?

Kurt: [Looks up at replay] We'd called the same play earlier and Isaac was open. So we thought it would work. It was a go route. We thought we could get a big one right off the bat. I just thought it was meant to be, it was meant to work.

Sal: This has been a terrific year for you. Five years ago you were sacking groceries in the IGA. Two years ago you were playing arena football in Cedar Rapids, Iowa. This is better than a Hollywood script. Tell me how you feel about what has happened to you this year.

Kurt: I don't think of it as a Hollywood story. It's my life. I take it one day at a time.

Sal: It has not been easy, has it?

Kurt: I was getting to the point of thinking how much longer am I going to have before people say he is too old to give him an opportunity. It has been tough for us until this last year. Even when I was playing arena football we did all right, but a lot of tough decisions . . . When I first started dating my wife, she was on food stamps, and I was in between jobs. That is why I ended up stocking shelves; I had to do something at nights so I could work out and keep my chances in football. A lot of things like that have helped keep things in perspective, even though we are not making a million dollars, we are very fortunate to be where we are at, in this position, and don't look beyond that, don't take anything for granted.

Sal: Thanks Kurt. Is there anything else you want to say?

Kurt: I'm truly blessed. If I can be a source of hope to anybody, I'm happy to be a part of it. The good Lord has blessed me. I am on a mission. He has called me to do this. I can only share my testimony with others. Thank you Jesus. (*SportsCenter,* ESPN, January 31, 2000; see also Vecsey 2000)

Kurt's self-narrative is grafted onto the replay of the winning touchdown pass. Indeed, this Super Bowl victory symbolizes the larger-than-life triumph that he has experienced over the course of the preceding five years. Sal elicits this self-story by asking Kurt how he feels about his award-winning year, comparing it to a Hollywood script. Kurt complies by giving him a socially acceptable answer; indeed, Sal's questions establish Kurt's right to give this extended account of his life and what it means (see also Holstein and Gubrium 2000:129). The viewer vicariously shares in this experience.[1]

The ingredients of the postmodern self are modeled in the media. The postmodern self has become a sign of itself, a double dramaturgical reflection anchored in media representations on one side and everyday life on the other. These cultural identities are filtered through the individual's personal troubles and emotional experiences in interactions with everyday life. These existential troubles connect back to the dominant cultural themes of the postmodern era. The electronic media and the new information technologies turn everyday life into a theatrical spectacle where the dramas that surround the decisive performances of existential crises are enacted. This creates a new existential "videocy," a language of crisis coded in electronic, media terms.

The media structure these crises and their meanings. A 38-year-old male alcoholic is standing outside the door to a room where Alcoholics Anonymous (A.A.) meetings are held. He asks:

> How do I get into one of those A.A. meetings? What do I say? I seen them in the movies. That Michael Keaton in *Clean and Sober.* He went to one of them. He just stood up and said he was an alcoholic. Do I have to do that? I ain't even sure I am one, but I drank a fifth of Black Jack last night and I started up agin this mornin'. I'm scared. (Quoted in Denzin 1995b:260)

This is a postmodern story waiting to be heard, already partially told through the figure of Michael Keaton, himself an actor, playing a fictional character (Daryl Poynter) who goes to a fictional A.A. meeting in a Hollywood film. Texts within texts, movies, everyday life, a man down on his luck, A.A., a door into a room where meetings are held, anxiety, fear. The everyday existential world connects to the cinematic apparatus, and our drunk on the street hopes to begin a story that will have a happy ending, like Michael Keaton's.

◆ *The Birth of Cinematic Surveillance*

In the space of the period from 1900 to 1930, cinema became an integral part of American society. Going to the movies became a weekly pastime for millions of Americans. Motion pictures became a national institution. Hollywood stars became personal idols, fan clubs were formed, and movie theaters, with their lighted marquees, were a prominent part of virtually every American community.

The cinematic, surveillance society soon became a disciplinary structure filled with subjects (voyeurs) who obsessively looked and gazed at one another, as they became, at the same time, obsessive listeners, eavesdroppers, persons whose voices and telephone lines could be tapped, voices that could be dubbed, new versions of the spoken and seen self. A new social type was created; the voyeur, or Peeping Tom, who would, in various guises (ethnographer, social scientist, detective, psychoanalyst, crime reporter, investigative journalist, innocent bystander, sexual pervert), elevate the concepts of looking and listening to new levels.

With the advent of color and sound in films in the mid-1920s, there was a drive toward cinematic realism. This impulse to create a level of realism that mapped everyday life complemented the rise of naturalistic realism in the American novel and the emergence of hard-nosed journalistic reporting by major American newspapers and radio networks (Denzin 1997). During the same period, an ethnographic, psychoanalytic, and life history approach was taking hold in the social sciences and in society at large. Like journalists, sociologists, market researchers, and survey researchers were learning how to use the interview to gather and report on the facts of social life (Fontana and Frey 1994, 2000; Denzin 1997).

Robert E. Park (1950), a founder of the Chicago school of ethnographic research (Vidich and Lyman 1994), clarifies the relationships among journalism, social science, and the use of the interview:

> After leaving college, I got a job as a reporter. . . . I wrote about all sorts of things. . . .
>
> My interest in the newspaper had grown out of the discovery that a reporter who had the facts was a more effective reformer than an editorial writer. . . .
>
> According to my earliest conception of a sociologist he was to be a kind of super-reporter. . . . He was to report a little more accurately, and in a little more detail. (Pp. v, vii-ix)

And so although sociologists and journalists both used interviews, the duties and practices of the two occupational groups were separated, organizing surveillance in distinct ways.

THE INTERVIEW SOCIETY

The interview society emerges historically as a consequence, in part, of the central place that newspapers and cinema (and television) came (and continue) to occupy in daily life. Holstein and Gubrium (1995) invite us to

> think of how much we learn about contemporary life by way of interviews. Larry King introduces us to presidents and power brokers. Barbara Walters plumbs the emotional depths of stars and celebrities. Oprah . . . and Geraldo invite the ordinary, tortured and bizarre to "spill their guts" to millions of home viewers. (P. 1)

The media, human services personnel, market researchers, and social scientists "increasingly get their information via interviews" (Holstein and Gubrium 1995:1). The interview society has turned the confessional mode of discourse into a public form of entertainment (Atkinson and Silverman 1997; Holstein and Gubrium 2000). The world of private troubles, the site of the authentic, or real, self, has become a public commodity.

THE INTERVIEW GOES TO HOLLYWOOD

It remained for Hollywood to authorize the interview as a primary method of gathering information about social issues, selves, and the meanings of personal experience. Soon Hollywood was telling stories about newspaper reporters (*The Front Page*, 1931), detectives and private eyes (*The Maltese Falcon*, 1931, 1941), psychoanalysts and psychiatrists (*Spellbound,* 1945), spies and secret agents (*Saboteur,* 1942), and market researchers (*Desk Set,* 1957). More recently, the movies have offered spoofs of sociologists (*The Milagro Beanfield War,* 1988) and anthropologists (*Krippendorf's Tribe,* 1998).

Each of these film genres glamorized the interview as a form of interaction and as a strategy and technique for getting persons to talk about themselves and others (see Holstein and Gubrium 1995). Journalists, detectives, and social scientists were presented as experts in the use of this conversational form. Hollywood led us to expect that such experts will use this form when interacting with members of society. Furthermore, it led us to expect that persons, if properly asked, will reveal their inner selves to such experts.

And thus the key assumptions of the interview society were soon secured. The media and Hollywood cinema helped solidify the following cluster of beliefs: Only skilled interviewers and therapists (and sometimes the person) have access to the deep, authentic self of the person; sociologists, journalists, and psychoanalysts know how to ask questions that will produce disclosures, often discrediting, about the hidden self; members of the interview society have certain experiences that are more authentic than others, and these experiences are keys to the hidden self (these are the experiences that have left deep marks and scars on the person); adept interviewers can uncover these experiences and their meanings to the person; nonetheless, persons also have access to their own experiences, and this increases the value of first-person narratives, which are the site of personal meaning.

When probing for the inner self, or when seeking information from an individual, interviewers are expected to use some method to record what is said in the interview. In the film *True Crime* (1999), Clint Eastwood plays Steve Everett, a burned-out, alcoholic reporter who becomes convinced that Frank Beachum, a black man due to be executed within 24 hours, is innocent. Eastwood tracks down Mr. Porterhouse, the man whose testimony led to Beachum's conviction. Everett and Porterhouse meet in a café and the following exchange unfolds:

Everett: Let me get this straight, you didn't really see the murder?

Porterhouse: I never said I did.

Everett: What did you see?

Porterhouse: I can't tell you how many times I've been over this. I went into Pokeums to use the phone. My car had overheated. Beachum jumped up from behind the counter. He was covered with blood and had a gun in his hand. He was bending over, stealing her necklace. He got one good look at me and then he ran out the store. My concern was for the girl. So I immediately dialed 911. I figured why should I run after a killer, when the police should do their job.

Everett: And they sure did it, didn't they?

Porterhouse: Aren't you gonna take some notes, or somethin'? Or use a tape recorder? Usually when I'm talkin' to a reporter they wanta keep some sort of record of what I've been sayin'.

Everett: I have a photographic memory [points to head]. I have a notebook right here [pulls a notebook and pen out of his jacket pocket].

Everett refuses to write anything in his notebook, and Porterhouse challenges him: "I did some checking on you. You're the guy who led the crusade to get the rapist released. That lying what's his name? Had all your facts straight on that one too, didn't you?"

Everett next interviews Beachum in his prison cell. Beachum's wife, Bonnie, is there too. (The reporter who had originally been assigned to the case was killed in a car accident.)

Beachum: I guess you wanta hear how it feels to be in here.

Everett: Yeah, it's a human interest piece.

Beachum: I feel isolated. I feel fear, pain, fear of prison, fear of being separated from my loved ones. All those fears rolled up into one.

[Everett takes notebook out of pocket.]

Beachum: I want to tell everyone that I believe in Jesus Christ, our Lord and Savior.

[Everett scribbles on page of notebook: BLV, JC.]

Beachum: I came into my faith late in life. Did a lot of bad things. . . . I believe that the crooked road remains straight, that's what the Bible says.

[Everett scribbles on page of notebook: LORD, SAV, CARO, STRAIT.]

Beachum: Is there any more that you want?

Everett: You don't know me. I'm just a guy out there with a screw loose. Frankly I don't give a rat's ass about Jesus Christ. I don't even care what's right or wrong. But my nose tells me something stinks, and I gotta have my faith in it, just like you have your faith in Jesus. . . . I know there's truth out there somewhere. . . . I believe you.

Bonnie Beachum: Where were you?

Everett: It wasn't my story.

Beachum clearly expected Everett to ask him how he felt about being on death row. Beachum expected to tell a reporter a deeply personal story about what this ex-

perience means to his inner, authentic self. Indeed, Everett's presence in the prison elicits such a story from Beachum. To paraphrase Holstein and Gubrium (2000:129), the prison interview with a journalist is now a natural part of the death row identity landscape. But Everett, through his note taking, mocks this assumption. He has no desire to record the inner meaning of this experience for Beachum. This is unlike the desire illustrated in the excerpt from the *SportsCenter* interview above, in which Sal Paolantonio sought and got from Kurt Warner a self-validating, self-congratulatory story about hard work and success in American life.

THE INTERVIEW MACHINE AS AN EPISTEMOLOGICAL APPARATUS

The interview society uses the machinery of the interview to methodically produce situated versions of the self. This machinery works in a systematic and orderly fashion. It structures the talk that occurs in the interview situation. There is an orderly mechanism "for designating who will speak next" (Holstein and Gubrium 2000:125). Using the question-answer format, this mechanism regulates the flow of conversation. Talk occurs in question-answer pairs, for the asking of a question requires an answer. Turn taking structures this give-and-take. The rule of single speakership obtains: One persons speaks at a time. Interviews, in this sense, are orderly, dramaturgical accomplishments. They draw on local understandings and are constrained by those understandings. They are narrative productions; they have beginnings, middles, and endings.

The methodology of asking questions is central to the operation of this machine. Different epistemologies and ideologies shape this methodological practice. Four epistemological formats can be identified: the objectively neutral format, the entertainment and investigative format, the collaborative or active interview format, and the reflexive, dialogic interview format.[2] In each format, the asking of a question is an incitement to speak, an invitation to tell a story; in this sense the interview elicits narratives of the self (Holstein and Gubrium 2000). The place of the interviewer in this process varies dramatically. In the *objectively neutral format*, the interviewer, using a structured or semistructured interview schedule, attempts to gather information without influencing the story that is being told. Holstein and Gubrium (2000) correctly observe that the demands of ongoing interaction make the " 'ideal' interview a practical impossibility, because the interview itself always remains accountable to the normative expectancies of competent conversation as well as to the demand for a good story to satisfy the needs of the researcher" (p. 131).

In the *entertainment and investigative format*, the interviewer often acts as a partisan, seeking to elicit a story that will sell as an entertainment commodity or can be marketed as a new piece of information about a story that is in the process of being told. In this format, the interviewer asks leading, aggressive questions as well as friendly questions, questions that allow the subject to embellish on a previous story or to give more detail on the meanings of an important experience. Paolantonio's interview with Warner employs the entertainment format. This is a friendly interview that shows both Warner and Paolantonio in a good light. Steve Everett's interview with Mr. Porterhouse in *True Crime* illustrates the investigative version of this format. Everett is aggressive and hostile; he seeks to discredit Porterhouse as a witness.

In the *collaborative or active format*, interviewer and respondent tell a story together (see Holstein and Gubrium 1995: 76-77). In this format a conversation occurs. Indeed, the identities of interviewer and respondent disappear. Each becomes a storyteller, or the two collaborate in telling a conjoint story. The *SportsCenter* interview excerpt above also illustrates this format, as together Sal and Kurt tell a story

about the meaning of this victory for Kurt's life.

In the *reflexive interview format*, two speakers enter into a dialogic relationship with one another. In this relationship, a tiny drama is played out. Each person becomes a party to the utterances of the other. Together, the two speakers create a small dialogic world of unique meaning and experience. In this interaction, each speaker struggles to understand the thought of the other, reading and paying attention to such matters as intonation, facial gestures, and word selection (see Bakhtin 1986:92-93).

Consider the following excerpt from the 1982 film *Chan Is Missing*, directed by Wayne Wang. Set in contemporary San Francisco, the film mocks popular culture representations of stereotypical Asian American identities. It also mocks social science and those scholars who point to language as an answer to cultural differences. The following Lily Tomlin-like monologue is central to this position. In the monologue, racial and ethnic identities are constructed. This construction is directly connected to the use of the objective interview format. The speaker is a female Asian American attorney. She is attempting to find Mr. Chan, who had an automobile accident just days before he disappeared. She is speaking to Jo, a middle-aged Chinese American cab driver, and Jo's young "Americanized" nephew, Steve. They are at Chester's Cafe. The young attorney is dressed in a black masculine-style suit, with a white shirt and dark tie.

> You see I'm doing a paper on the legal implications of cross-cultural misunderstandings. [nods head] Mr. Chan's case is a perfect example of what I want to expose. The policeman and Mr. Chan have completely different culturally related assumptions about what kind of communication [shot of Steve, then Jo] each one was using. The policeman, in an English-speaking mode, asks a direct factual question—"Did you stop at the stop sign?" He expected

a yes or a no answer. Mr. Chan, however, rather than giving him a yes or a no answer, began to go into his past driving record—how good it was, the number of years he had been in the United States, all the people that he knew—trying to relate different events, objects, or situations to what was happening then to the action at hand. Now this is very typical. . . . The Chinese try to relate points, events, or objects that they feel are pertinent to the situation, which may not to anyone else seem directly relevant at the time. . . . This policeman became rather impatient, restated the question, "Did you or did you not stop at the stop sign?" in a rather hostile tone, which in turn flustered Mr. Chan, which caused him to hesitate answering the question, which further enraged the policeman, so that he asked the question again, "You didn't stop at the stop sign, did you?" in a negative tone, to which Mr. Chan automatically answered, "No." Now to any native speaker of English, "No" would mean, "No I didn't stop at the stop sign." However to Mr. Chan, "No I didn't stop at the stop sign" was not "No I didn't stop at the sign" [Jo shakes head, looks away]. It was "No, I didn't not stop at the stop sign." In other words, "Yes I did stop at the stop sign." Do you see what I'm saying? [Camera pans room]

Then, in a voice-over, Jo comments, "Chan Hung wouldn't run away because of the car accident. I'm feeling something might have happened to him" (see Denzin 1995a:105).

Here the speaker, the young attorney, attempts to dialogically enter into and interpret the meanings that were circulating in Mr. Chan's interview with the policeman. In so doing, she criticizes the concept of cross-cultural communication, showing through her conversation that meanings are always dialogic and contextual.

This text from Wang's film is an example of how the reflexive, dialogic interviewer deconstructs the uses and abuses of the interview—uses that are associated with the objectively neutral and entertainment/investigative formats. This text suggests that interpretations based on the surface meanings of an utterance sequence are likely to be superficial. To paraphrase Annie Dillard (1982:46), serious students of society take pains to distinguish their work from such interpretive practices.

At another level, reflexively oriented scholars, such as Mikhail Bakhtin, contend that there is no essential self or private, real self behind the public self. They argue that there are only different selves, different performances, different ways of being a gendered person in a social situation. These performances are based on different interpretive practices. These practices give the self and the person a sense of grounding, or narrative coherence (Gubrium and Holstein 1998). There is no inner or deep self that is accessed by the interview or narrative method. There are only different interpretive (and performative) versions of who the person is.

Steve Everett embodies one version of the reflexive interviewer. He has no interest in the inner self of the person he is interviewing, no interest in right or wrong. He only seeks the truth, the truth that says an injustice may have been done. Wang's Asian American attorney is another version of this interviewer; she understands that the self is a verbal and narrative construction.

THE INTERVIEW AND THE DRAMATURGICAL SOCIETY

The text from the Kurt Warner interview presented above suggests that the metaphor of the dramaturgical society (Lyman 1990), or "life as theater" (Brissett and Edgley 1990; Goffman 1959:254-55), is no longer a metaphor. It has become interactional reality. Life and art have become mirror images of one another. Reality, as it is visually experienced, is a staged, social production.

Jonathan Raban (1981) provides an example of how life and television coincide. In a TV ad "beamed by the local station in Decorah, an Iowa farmer spoke stiffly to the camera in testimony to the bags of fertilizer that were heaped in front of him" (p. 123). Here the personal testimony of the farmer, a hands-on expert, authorizes the authenticity and value of the product. This message is carried live, staged in the frame of the TV commercial; a real farmer says this product works. The farmer's awkwardness comes, perhaps, from the fact that he must look at himself doing this endorsement, knowing that if he sees himself looking this way, others will as well.

The reflected, everyday self and its gendered presentations are attached to the cinematic/televisual self. Herbert Blumer (1933) provides an example. An interview respondent connects her gendered self to the Hollywood screen:

> *Female, 19, white, college freshman.*— When I discovered I should have this coquettish and coy look which all girls may have, I tried to do it in my room. And surprises! I could imitate Pola Negri's cool or fierce look. Vilma Banky's sweet and coquettish attitude. I learned the very way of taking my gentlemen friends to and from the door with that wistful smile, until it has become a part of me. (P. 34)

Real, everyday experiences are judged against their staged, cinematic, video counterparts. The fans of Hollywood stars dress like the stars, make love like the stars, and dream the dreams of the stars. Blumer provides an example:

> *Female, 24, white, college senior.*— During my high-school period I particularly liked pictures in which the setting was a millionaire's estate or some such elaborate place. After seeing a picture of this type, I would imagine myself living such a life of ease as the society girl I had seen. My day-dreams

would be concerned with lavish wardrobes, beautiful homes, servants, imported automobiles, yachts, and countless suitors. (P. 64)

With this dramaturgical turn, the technology of the media "disengages subjects from their own expressions. . . . Individuals become observers of their own acts. . . . Actions come to be negotiated in terms of a media aesthetic, both actor and spectator live a reality arbitrated by the assumptions of media technicians" (Eason 1984:60). David Altheide and Robert Snow (1991) provide an example from the Richard Nixon presidency. In a memo to H. R. Haldeman dated December 1, 1969, Nixon wrote:

> We need a part-or full-time TV man on our staff for the purpose of seeing that my TV appearances are handled on a professional basis. When I think of the millions of dollars that go into one lousy 30-second television spot advertising deodorant, it seems to me unbelievable that we don't do a better job of seeing that Presidential appearances [on TV] always have the very best professional advice. (quoted in Altheide and Snow 1991:105; see also Oudes 1989:46)

And because of the same media aesthetic, Kurt Warner has learned how to talk the form of sports talk that Ron Shelton mocks in his 1988 film *Bull Durham*. So, too, does Frank Beachum expect Steve Everett to record his moral story.

The main carriers of the popular in the postmodern society have become the very media that are defining the content and meaning of the popular; that is, popular culture is now a matter of cinema and the related media, including television, the press, and popular literature. A paradox is created, for the everyday is now defined by the cinematic and the televisual. The two can no longer be separated. A press conference at the 1988 Democratic National Convention is reported thus:

> A dozen reporters stood outside CBS's area, and as was so often the case at the convention, one began interviewing another. A third commented wryly on the interview: "Reporter interviews reporter about press conference." (Weiss 1988:33-34; also quoted in Altheide and Snow 1991:93)

Reporters are reporting on reporters interviewing reporters.

◆ Studying the Interview in Cinematic Society

The cinematic apparatuses of contemporary culture stand in a twofold relationship to critical inquiry. First, the cultural logics of the postvideo, cinematic culture define the lived experiences that a critical studies project takes as its subject matter. How these texts structure, and give meaning to the everyday must be analyzed. At the same time, critical ethnographies of the video-cinematic text must be constructed, showing how these texts map and give narrative meaning to the crucial cultural identities that circulate in the postmodern society.

Consider race, the racial self, and Hollywood cinema. Ana Lopez (1991) reminds us that "Hollywood does not represent ethnics and minorities; it creates them and provides an audience with an experience of them" (pp. 404-5). Consider her argument in terms of the following scene from Spike Lee's highly controversial 1989 film *Do the Right Thing*. Near the film's climax, as the heat rises on the street, members of each racial group in the neighborhood hurl vicious racial slurs at one another:

Mookie: [to Sal, who is Italian, and Sal's sons, Vito and Pino] Dago, wop, guinea, garlic breath, pizza slingin' spaghetti bender, Vic Damone, Perry Como, Pavarotti.

Pino: [to Mookie and the other blacks] Gold chain wearin' fried chicken and biscuit eatin' monkey, ape, baboon, fast runnin', high jumpin', spear chuckin', basketball dunkin' ditso spade, take you fuckin' pizza and go back to Africa.

Puerto Rican man: [to the Korean grocer] Little slanty eyed, me-no speakie American, own every fruit and vegetable stand in New York, bull shit, Reverend Sun Young Moon, Summer 88 Olympic kick-ass boxer, sonofabitch.

White policeman: You Goya bean eatin' 15 in the car, 30 in the apartment, pointy red shoes wearin' Puerto Ricans, cocksuckers.

Korean grocer: I got good price for you, how am I doing? Chocolate egg cream drinking, bagel lox, Jew asshole.

Sweet Dick Willie: [To the Korean grocer] Korean motherfucker . . . you didn't do a goddamn thing except sit on your monkey ass here on this corner and do nothin. (See Denzin 1991:129-30)

Lee wants his audience to believe that his speakers are trapped within the walls and streets of the multiracial ghetto that is the Bedford-Stuyvesant area of New York. Their voices reproduce current (and traditional) cultural, racial, and sexual stereotypes about blacks (spade, monkey), Koreans (slanty eyed), Puerto Ricans (pointy red shoes, cocksuckers), Jews (bagel lox), and Italians (dago, wop). The effects of these in-your-face insults are exaggerated through wide-angled, close-up shots. Each speaker's face literally fills the screen as the racial slurs are hurled.[3]

Lee's film presents itself as a realist, ethnographic text. It asks the viewer to believe that it is giving an objectively factual, authentic, and realistic account of the lived experiences of race and ethnicity. The film performs race and ethnicity, and does so in ways that support the belief that objective reality has been captured. The film "realistically" reinscribes familiar (and new) cultural stereotypes, for example, young gang members embodying hip-hop or rap culture. Lee's text functions like a documentary film.

THE CINEMATIC SOCIETY AND THE DOCUMENTARY INTERVIEW

It is this documentary impulse and its reliance on the objectively neutral interview format that I now examine through an analysis of Trinh T. Minh-ha's 1989 film *Surname Viet Given Name Nam*. This is a film about Vietnamese women, whose names change or remain constant depending on whether they marry foreigners or other Vietnamese. In this film, Trinh has Vietnamese women speak from five different subject positions, representing lineage, gender status, age status, leadership position, and historical period (see Trinh 1992). This creates a complex picture of Vietnamese culture.

The film is multitextual, layered with pensive images of women in various situations. Historical moments overlap with age periods (childhood, youth, adulthood, old age), rituals and ceremonies (weddings, funerals, war, the market, dance), and daily household work (cooking) while interviewees talk to offscreen interviewers. There are two voice-overs in English, and a third voice sings sayings, proverbs, and poetry in Vietnamese (with translations into English appearing as texts on the screen). There are also interviews with Vietnamese subtitled in English and interviews in English synchronized with the onscreen images (Trinh 1992). The interviews are reenacted in the film by Vietnamese actresses, who are then interviewed at the end of the film about their experiences of being performers in the film.

The film allows the practice of doing reflexive interviews to enter into the construction of the text itself, thus the true and the false, the real and the staged intermingle; indeed, the early sections unfold like a traditional, realist documentary film (Trinh 1992). The viewer does not know that the women onscreen are actresses reenacting interviews. Nor does the viewer know that the interviews were conducted in the United States, not Vietnam (this becomes apparent only near the end of the film).

In using these interpretive strategies, Trinh creates a space for the critical appraisal of the politics of representation that structure the use of interviews in the documentary film. In undoing the objectively neutral interview as a method for gathering information about reality, Trinh takes up the question of truth (see Trinh 1992). Whose truth is she presenting—that given in the onscreen interview situation or that of the women-as-actresses who are interviewed at the end of the film?

Trinh begins by deconstructing the classic interview-based documentary film that enters the native's world and brings news from that world to the world of the Western observer. In its use of the traditional, nondialogic interview method, documentary film, like Spike Lee's *Do the Right Thing*, starts with the so-called real world and the subject's place in that world. It uses an aesthetic of objectivity and a technological apparatus that produces truthful statements (images) about the world (Trinh 1991). Trinh (1991:39) argues that the following elements are central to this apparatus:

◆ The relentless pursuit of naturalism, which requires a connection between the moving image and the spoken word

◆ Authenticity—the use of people who appear to be real and locating these people in "real" situations

◆ The filmmaker/interviewer presented as an observer, not as a person who creates what is seen, heard, and read

◆ The capture only of events unaffected by the recording eye

◆ The capture of objective reality

◆ The dramatization of truth

◆ Actual facts presented in a credible way, with people telling them

Along with these elements, the film-interview text must convince spectators that they should have confidence in the truth of what they see. These aesthetic strategies define the documentary interview style, allowing the filmmaker-as-interviewer to create a text that gives the viewer the illusion of having "unmediated access to reality" (Trinh 1991:40). Thus naturalized, the objective, documentary interview style has become part of the larger cinematic apparatus in American culture, including a pervasive presence in TV commercials and news (Trinh 1991:40).

Trinh brings a reflexive reading to these features of the documentary film, citing her own texts as examples of dialogic documentaries that are sensitive to the flow of fact and fiction, to meanings as political constructions (see Trinh 1991). Such texts reflexively understand that reality is never neutral or objective, that it is always socially constructed. Filmmaking and documentary interviewing thus become methods of "framing" reality.

Self-reflexivity does not translate into personal style or a preoccupation with method. Rather, it centers on the reflexive interval that defines representation, "the place in which the play within the textual frame is a play on this very frame, hence on the borderlines of the textual and the extra-textual" (Trinh 1991:48). The film becomes a site for multiple experiences.

A responsible, reflexive, dialogic interview text embodies the following characteristics (Trinh 1991:188):

◆ It announces its own politics and evidences a political consciousness.

◆ It interrogates the realities it represents.

◆ It invokes the teller's story in the history that is told.

◆ It makes the audience responsible for interpretation.

◆ It resists the temptation to become an object of consumption.

◆ It resists all dichotomies (male/female and so on).

◆ It foregrounds difference, not conflict.

◆ It uses multiple voices, emphasizing language as silence, the grain of the voice, tone, inflection, pauses, silences, repetitions.

◆ It presents silence as a form of resistance.

Trinh creates the space for a version of the cinematic apparatus and the interview machine that challenges mainstream film. She also challenges traditional ethnography and its use of objective and investigative interview formats.

Reflexive texts question the very notion of a stable, unbiased gaze. They focus on the pensive image, on silences, on representations that "unsettle the male apparatus of the gaze" (Trinh 1991:115). This look makes the interviewer's gaze visible. It destabilizes any sense of verisimilitude that can be brought to this visual world. In so doing, it also disrupts the spectator's gaze, itself a creation of the unnoticed camera, the camera that invokes the image of a perfect, natural world, a world with verisimilitude. In using these interpretive strategies, Trinh creates the space for the viewer (and listener) to appraise critically the politics of representation that structure the documentary text.

CULTIVATING REFLEXIVITY

Learning from Trinh, I want to cultivate a method of patient listening, a reflexive method of looking, hearing, and asking that is dialogic and respectful. This method will take account of my place as a co-constructor of meaning in this dialogic relationship. As an active listener (Bourdieu 1996), I will treat dialogue as a process of discovery. I will attempt to function as an empowering collaborator. I will use the reflexive interview as a tool of intervention (Burawoy 1998). I will use it as a method for uncovering structures of oppression in the life worlds of the persons I am interviewing. As a reflexive participant, I will critically promote the agendas of radical democratic practice. In so doing, I hope to cultivate a method of hearing and writing that has some kinship with the kinds of issues Gloria Naylor (1998) discusses in the following passage:

> Someone who didn't know how to ask wouldn't know how to listen. And he coulda listened to them the way you been listening to us right now. Think about it: ain't nobody really talking to you. . . . Really listen this time; the only voice is your own. But you done just heard about the legend of Saphira Wade. . . . You done heard it in the way we know it, sitting on our porches and shelling June peas . . . taking apart the engine of a car—you done heard it without a single living soul really saying a word. (P. 1842)

But this is also a sociology that understands, here at the end, that when we screen our dreams and our crises through the canvases and lenses that the cinematic, electronic society makes available to us, we risk becoming storied versions of somebody else's versions of who we should be.

■ *Notes*

1. The underlying logic of the sports interview is mocked in the following dialogue from Ron Shelton's 1988 film *Bull Durham*. Kevin Costner, who plays an aging catcher named Crash Davis, says to his protégé, played by Tim Robbins, "Now you are going to the Big Show. You have to learn how to talk to interviewers. When they ask you how it feels to be pitching in Yankee Stadium, you say, 'I just thank the good Lord for all his gifts. I owe it all to him. I just take it one game, one pitch at a time.' "

2. These interview formats blur with the three types of relationships between interviewer and interviewee that Mishler (1986) identifies: informant and reporter, collaborators, and advocates.

3. Although prejudice crosses color lines in this film, racial intolerance is connected to the psychology of the speaker (e.g., Vito). It is "rendered as the *how* of personal bigotry" (Guerrero 1993:154). The economic and political features of institutional racism are not taken up. That is, in Lee's film, "the *why* of racism is left unexplored" (Guerrero 1993:154).

■ *References*

Atkinson, P. and D. Silverman. 1997. "Kundera's *Immortality:* The Interview Society and the Invention of Self." *Qualitative Inquiry* 3:304-25.

Altheide, D. L. 1995. *An Ecology of Communication.* New York: Aldine de Gruyter.

Altheide, D. L. and R. P. Snow. 1991. *Media Worlds in the Postjournalism Era.* New York: Aldine de Gruyter.

Bakhtin, M. M. 1986. *Speech Genres and Other Late Essays.* Austin: University of Texas Press.

Blumer, H. 1933. *Movies and Conduct.* New York: Macmillan.

Bourdieu, P. 1996. "Understanding." *Theory, Culture & Society* 13:17-37.

Brissett, D. and C. Edgley, eds. 1990. *Life as Theater: A Dramaturgical Sourcebook.* 2d ed. New York: Aldine de Gruyter.

Burawoy, M. 1998. "The Extended Case Method." *Sociological Theory* 16:4-33.

Denzin, N. K. 1991. *Images of Postmodern Society: Social Theory and Contemporary Cinema*. London: Sage.

———. 1995a. *The Cinematic Society: The Voyeur's Gaze*. Thousand Oaks, CA: Sage.

———. 1995b. "Information Technologies, Communicative Acts, and the Audience: Couch's Legacy to Communication Research." *Symbolic Interaction* 18:247-68.

———. 1997. *Interpretive Ethnography: Ethnographic Practices for the 21st Century*. Thousand Oaks, CA: Sage.

Dillard, A. 1982. *Living by Fiction*. New York: Harper & Row.

Eason, D. 1984. "The New Journalism and the Image-World: Two Modes of Organizing Experience." *Critical Studies in Mass Communication* 1:51-65.

Fontana, A. and J. H. Frey. 1994. "Interviewing: The Art of Science." Pp. 361-76 in *Handbook of Qualitative Research*, edited by N. K. Denzin and Y. S. Lincoln. Thousand Oaks, CA: Sage.

———. 2000. "The Interview: From Structured Questions to Negotiated Text." Pp. 645-72 in *Handbook of Qualitative Research*, 2d ed., edited by N. K. Denzin and Y. S. Lincoln. Thousand Oaks, CA: Sage.

Goffman, E. 1959. *The Presentation of Self in Everyday Life*. Garden City, NY: Doubleday.

Gottschalk, S. 2000. "Escape from Insanity: 'Mental Disorder' in the Postmodern Moment." Pp. 18-48 in *Pathology and the Postmodern: Mental Illness as Discourse and Experience*, edited by D. Fee. London: Sage.

Gubrium, J. F. and J. A. Holstein. 1997. *The New Language of Qualitative Method*. New York: Oxford University Press.

———. 1998. "Narrative Practice and the Coherence of Personal Stories." *Sociological Quarterly* 39:163-87.

Guerrero, E. 1993. *Framing Blackness: The African American Image in Film*. Philadelphia: Temple University Press.

Heyl, B. S. 2001. "Ethnographic Interviewing." In *Handbook of Ethnography*, edited by P. A. Atkinson, A. Coffey, S. Delamonte, J. Lofland, and L. H. Lofland. London: Sage.

Holstein, J. A. and J. F. Gubrium. 1995. *The Active Interview*. Thousand Oaks, CA: Sage.

———. 2000. *The Self We Live By: Narrative Identity in a Postmodern World*. New York: Oxford University Press.

Jackson, M. 1998. *Minimia Ethnographica*. Chicago: University of Chicago Press.

Lopez, A. M. 1991. "Are All Latins from Manhattan? Hollywood, Ethnography, and Cultural Colonialism." Pp. 404-24 in *Unspeakable Images: Ethnicity and the American Cinema*, edited by L. D. Friedman. Urbana: University of Illinois Press.

Lyman, S. M. 1990. *Civilization: Contents, Discontents, Malcontents and Other Essays in Social Theory*. Fayetteville: University of Arkansas Press.

Mishler, E. G. 1986. *Research Interviewing: Context and Narrative*. Cambridge, MA: Harvard University Press.

Naylor, G. 1998. "Excerpt from *Mamma Day*." Pp. 1838-42 in *Call and Response: The Riverside Anthology of the African American Literary Tradition*, edited by P. L. Hill. Boston: Houghton Mifflin.

Oudes, B. 1989. *From the President: President Nixon's Secret Files*. New York: Harper & Row.

Park, R. E. 1950. "An Autobiographical Note." Pp. v-ix in R. E. Park, *Race and Culture: Essays in the Sociology of Contemporary Man*. New York: Free Press.

Raban, J. 1981. *Old Glory: A Voyage down the Mississippi*. New York: Random House.

Scheurich, J. J. 1995. "A Postmodernist Critique of Research Interviewing." *International Journal of Qualitative Studies in Education* 8:239-52.

Trinh T. M. 1989. *Surname Viet Given Name Nam* (film). Women Make Movies, Museum of Modern Art, Cinenova, Idera, Image Forum.

———. 1991. *When the Moon Waxes Red: Representation, Gender and Cultural Politics*. New York: Routledge.

———. 1992. *Framer Framed.* New York: Routledge.

Vecsey, G. 2000. "Kurt Warner Gives Hope to Others." *New York Times,* February 1, p. C29.

Vidich, A. J. and S. M. Lyman. 1994. "Qualitative Methods: Their History in Sociology and Anthropology." Pp. 23-59 in *Handbook of Qualitative Research,* edited by N. K. Denzin and Y. S. Lincoln. Thousand Oaks, CA: Sage.

Weiss, P. 1988. "Party Time in Atlanta." *Columbia Journalism Review,* September/October, pp. 27-34.

9

THEIR STORY/MY STORY/OUR STORY

Including the Researcher's Experience in Interview Research

◆ Carolyn Ellis
Leigh Berger

I cull books on interviewing from my bookcases and arrange them alphabetically on an empty shelf, the product of the last few days of cleaning my office. Even the floor, my favorite storage area, is empty of the usual stacks of manuscripts and books. I feel free, excited to begin the chapter I'm writing with Leigh on including the researcher's experience in interview research. The task shouldn't be too difficult. The chapter is a continuation of what I've spent the last 15 years doing, which is using autoethnographic stories—stories written in an autobiographical genre about the relationship of self, other, and culture—in so-

cial science research. Since researchers now commonly discuss their own experience in their research, this project seems timely. I smile contentedly as I think about the growing recognition and acceptance of autoethnography among interpretive ethnographers.

As I muse about autoethnography, I hear Leigh's car pull in to the driveway. I herd our four barking dogs into the bedroom, then open the front door. Once Leigh is seated in my office and has admired how tidy and organized it is, I let the dogs out of the bedroom. Without pausing, they fly up the stairs. By the time I get to my office,

AUTHORS' NOTE: We thank Arthur P. Bochner, Jim Holstein, Jay Gubrium, and two anonymous reviewers for their helpful reading and editing of the manuscript for this chapter.

three of them surround Leigh, sniffing her clothes, while the fourth sits on her lap, licking her face. Leigh greets them warmly. They quickly settle down and claim their usual sleeping spots in my office.

Leigh sits beside me as I type notes from our conversation into the computer. "Okay, now let's think about what we have to do here," I start. "The paper isn't due for six months, so we have plenty of time."

"Oh, yes, plenty," Leigh agrees. "What exactly is our goal?"

"The idea is to look at the inclusion of the researcher's experience in interview research," I respond. "Not so much how we do it, but the different forms it can take and how this inclusion deepens and enriches what we know about our subjects of research. Maybe we'll try to move from lesser to greater degrees of involvement of the researcher and provide exemplars of the variety."

"So you mean a typology then?" Leigh inquires, laughing because I usually argue for stories and against typologies. "So what would we include?"

I too chuckle at the irony and continue, "I thought we'd select an excerpt from my piece with Lisa and Christine [Ellis, Kiesinger, and Tillmann-Healy 1997] on interactive interviewing where we talk about bulimia. And one from my chapter with Art [Ellis and Bochner 1992] on co-constructed narratives, where we discuss our decision to have an abortion early in our relationship."

"They both show the researcher as full participant," Leigh says thoughtfully, breaking through the emotions that arise as I think about including a selection from the abortion story. It's hard emotionally for me to confront that piece, but I want to include it because it provides an instructive exemplar of co-constructed narratives. "What will we do for exemplars that show inclusion to a lesser degree?" Leigh continues.

"That's where you come in," I respond. "Remember that interview you did with Karen, your informant at the Messianic Judaism congregation? The one where you

reflect on what the interview makes you think about in terms of your own spiritual beliefs? How about an excerpt from that interview story?"

"I thought you didn't like the Karen I presented there," Leigh says.

"I don't. It always seemed to me that you needed to write in more of your reflections on spirituality as you wrote that story. More reflection would have deepened readers' understanding of Karen's beliefs and made her a more complex character. This is your chance to add more reflection, although the focus should remain on Karen."

"So we'll have three types then—interactive interviews, co-constructed narratives, and reflexive dyadic interviews?" Leigh asks, returning the focus to the paper rather than thinking more deeply about the difficulties of revealing her thoughts about her own spirituality, especially to an academic audience.

"No, there are four. Your interview with Karen parallels the interactive interview I did with Lisa and Christine. They're both interactive and emergent in that we're concerned with the stories created and evolving in each interview context. But while the three authors act as researchers and participants alike in the bulimia study, you as researcher stay focused on the experience of your participant, Karen."

"Okay, I see where you're going. And what's the parallel case to co-constructed narrative?"

"In our co-constructed narrative about abortion, Art and I focused exclusively on our story. We wrote our experiences separately and then came together to co-construct them into a collective story we could agree on. The parallel case would be one in which a researcher carries out the same process with another couple, staying focused on them but adding her reflections. I know you've wanted to interview a family member of someone who converted to Messianic Judaism. I'd like you to do a co-constructed interview with the convert and family member, if you're willing."

"I'd love to," Leigh says hesitantly. "But after thinking about it, I'm not sure it's a good idea to interview family members of Messianic Jews. Families seem to have so much animosity toward those who convert. I don't want to cause my participants any problems."

"But I have planned to interview the rabbi of the Messianic congregation and his wife about their roles in marriage," she continues, more enthusiastically. "I could conduct this as a co-constructed interview and include questions about how their families reacted to their conversion."

"That would work," I respond.

"Though I'm not sure the couple would be willing to write anything," Leigh cautions.

"You could interview them separately and tape record their individual stories and then work with them to co-construct their collective story."

"I can do that," Leigh responds. "I'll set up the interview. What needs to be done now?"

"Before turning to the cases, let's work on the literature review to show how some of the trends in the literature have guided us to where we are. This will set the stage for the reader."

◆ Literature Review

Many researchers, particularly feminists, have debunked the myth of value-free scientific inquiry (Cook and Fonow 1986; Reinharz 1992; Roberts 1981), calling for researchers to acknowledge their personal, political, and professional interests. Instead of insisting on a rigid separation of researcher and respondent, they have construed the interview as an active relationship occurring in a context permeated by issues of power, emotionality, and interpersonal process (Holstein and Gubrium 1995).

Interviews now are commonly understood as collaborative, communicative events that evolve their own norms and rules (Briggs 1986; Kvale 1996). As a result, researchers who use interviews should not focus solely on the outcomes—the words spoken by interviewees—but should examine the collaborative activities of interviewees from which these outcomes are produced (Chase and Bell 1994; Futrell and Willard 1994; Hertz 1995; Jorgenson 1995; Langellier and Hall 1989; Miller 1996; Mishler 1986; Suchman and Jordan 1992).

The literature is replete with examples of writers who draw attention to the relational aspects of the interview and the interactional construction of meaning in the interview context (Holstein and Gubrium 1995; Langellier and Hall 1989; Oakley 1981). This interaction is situated in the context of an ongoing relationship where the personal and social identities of both interviewers and interviewees are important factors (Collins 1986; DeVault 1990; Riessman 1987), and the relationship continually changes as each responds to the other (Jorgenson 1991, 1995). Thus interpretive scholars note the "double subjectivity" (Lewis and Meredith 1988) that abounds in interviewing: how each participant's attitudes, feelings, and thoughts affect and are affected by the emerging reciprocity between the participants.

Moving away from the orthodox model of distance and separation, interactive interviewers often encourage self-disclosure and emotionality on the part of the researcher. Researcher involvement can help subjects feel more comfortable sharing information and close the hierarchical gap between researchers and respondents that traditional interviewing encourages (Bergen 1993; Cook and Fonow 1986; Douglas 1985; Hertz 1995; Oakley 1981), thus promoting dialogue rather than interrogation (Bristow and Esper 1988). In this interactive context, respondents become narrators who improvise stories in response to the questions, probes, and personal stories of the interviewers (Bruner 1986; Chase and Bell 1994; Holstein and Gubrium 1995; Mishler 1986; Myerhoff 1992; Riessman 1993).

The interactive interviewing context requires an interviewer who listens empathically (Mies 1983; Stanley and Wise 1983), identifies with participants, and shows respect for participants' emotionality (Mies 1983). Unlike traditional research, where feelings and private realms of experience often are avoided, interactive interviews assume that emotions and personal meanings are legitimate topics of research (Anderson et al. 1987). As a result, interactive interviewers explore sensitive topics that are intimate, may be personally discrediting, and normally are shrouded in secrecy (Renzetti and Lee 1993). When doing so, they pay close attention to ethical issues of privacy and confidentiality as they try to listen "around" and "beyond" the words (DeVault 1990), exploring the unsaid as much as the said (Ochberg 1996).

Research on sensitive and emotional topics has raised questions about the boundary between research interviewing and psychotherapy (Lieblich 1996; Miller 1996; see also Gale 1992; Maione and Chenail 1999). Writers ponder how a researcher should respond if a subject asks for help (Lieblich 1996; Miller 1996), and they question the morality of withholding information and assistance (Cook and Fonow 1986; Oakley 1981; Reinharz 1992; Webb 1984). Some researchers have voiced concern about the emotional harm that can be done to participants with whom they develop personal relationships (Stacey 1988) and about the emotional load such relationships can place on researchers who are not trained as psychotherapists (Brannen 1988; Edwards 1993). On the other hand, some writers emphasize the positive therapeutic benefits that can accrue to respondents and interviewers who participate in interactive interviews (Bloom 1996; Gale 1992; Hutchinson, Wilson, and Wilson

1994; Langellier and Hall 1989; Romanoff 2001; Rosenwald 1996).

Increasingly, research monographs are concerned with subjects' responses to what is written about them (see Agronick and Helson 1996; Apter 1996; Chase 1996; Josselson 1996). After spending time as an interviewee, Colleen Larson (1997) laments that she did not feel she was able to tell in the interview setting the complex and authentic stories she needed and wanted to tell (see also Tillmann-Healy and Kiesinger 2000). Along with other researchers, especially those doing participatory and action research (e.g., Stringer 1996), Larson (1997) suggests a more collaborative and longitudinal approach that gives interviewees opportunities to reflect on, elaborate, and build on the stories they have told before, as well as to respond to and change what gets reported (see also Belenky et al. 1981-82; Duelli Klein 1983; Tripp 1983). Many interactive researchers have heeded the call for research that gives something useful back to respondents and their communities, rather than research that is pointed exclusively toward restricted academic audiences (Bochner and Ellis 1996; Finch 1984; Oakley 1981). Consequently, interviewers must now face their ethical responsibility to their respondents on both personal and policy levels (Bergen 1993).

Interactive interviews offer opportunities for self-conscious reflection by researchers as well as respondents. Some interviewers now discuss how they feel during interviews (Bar-On 1996; Berger 1997b; Kiesinger 1998; Markham 1998; Miller 1996) and how they use their feelings, experiences, and self-analysis to understand and interpret the experiences of others (DeVault 1999; Douglas 1985; Ellis 1998; Griffith and Smith 1987). Barbara Rothman (1986), for example, writes poignantly about the pain she suffered as she took on the feelings of women who had undergone amniocentesis. By immersing herself in the women's emotional worlds, she felt able to understand and to write about their experiences in a more powerful and empathic way than she could have by keeping herself emotionally distanced. Other researchers discuss how they gained insight into themselves and were changed in the process of interviewing others (Miller 1996). For example, Janet Yerby and Bill Gourd (1994) show how their interviews with members of a nontraditional family had a therapeutic effect on their own marital relationship. Kristin Langellier and Deanna Hall (1989), moreover, report that their research on mother-daughter storytelling strengthened their relationships with their own mothers.

Some writers now advocate that researchers interview peers with whom they have already established relationships (Platt 1981; Segura 1989) and that researchers make use of the everyday situations in which they are involved (Stanley and Wise 1983). Qualitative researchers have co-constructed narratives with family members and friends (Austin 1996; Berger 1997b; Bochner and Ellis 1992; Ellis and Bochner 1992; Fox 1996; Kiesinger 1992; Yerby and Gourd 1994). They have studied themselves reflexively in the process of observing, communicating with, and writing about others (Abu-Lughod 1995; Adler and Adler 1997; Angrosino 1998; Behar 1995; Blee 1998; Crapanzano 1980; Dumont 1978; Ellingson 1998; Goodall 1991, 1999; Jones 1998; Karp 1996; Kondo 1990; Lagerwey 1998; Lather and Smithies 1997; Linden 1993; Markham 1998; Myerhoff 1978; Mykhalovskiy 1997; Ponticelli 1996; Rabinow 1977; Richardson 1992, 1997; Rosaldo 1989; Tillmann-Healy 1996; Zola 1982b). They have conducted interactive interviews about emotional and personal topics (Ellis et al. 1997; Kiesinger 1998; Macleod 1999). And they have introspectively written about their own experiences and their own families as the focus of research (Behar 1996; Berger 1997a, 1997b, 1998; Bochner 1997; Clough 1999; Coyle 1998; Denzin 1999; Eisenberg 1998; Ellis 1993, 1995, 1996; Ellis and Bochner 1996, 2000; Jago 1996;

Kolker 1996; Kulick and Willson 1995; Krieger 1991, 1996; Lewin and Leap 1996; Murphy 1987; Pacanowsky 1988; Paget 1993; Payne 1996; Perry 1996; Quinney 1996; Richardson 1997, 1998; Robillard 1997, 1999; Ronai 1992, 1995; Ross and Geist 1997; Shostak 1996; Tillmann-Healy 1996; Trujillo 1998; Williams 1991; Zola 1982a).

Following the trajectory suggested here, interviewing then changes in function as well as form (J. A. Holstein and J. F. Gubrium, personal communication). The interviewing process becomes less a conduit of information from informants to researchers that represents how things are, and more a sea swell of meaning making in which researchers connect their own experiences to those of others and provide stories that open up conversations about how we live and cope.

◆ Types of Collaborative Interviewing

The stories interviewers write about themselves range from descriptions of the researcher's positioning and experience with the subject at hand to reflections on the research process and the researcher's feelings about the subject being explored, to including the researcher as a central character in the story, to making the personal experience of the researcher the focus of the study. In this section, we organize these variations into several categories, which we call reflexive dyadic interviews, interactive interviews, mediated co-constructed narratives, and unmediated co-constructed narratives. We present an exemplar for each of these categories to illustrate how the different types of interviews unfold. After this discussion, we return to our introductory narrative and conclude with a co-constructed story that reflects on the methodological issues involved in the writing of this chapter and on how including the researcher's self in interviews deepens and enriches our understanding of our own research interests.

REFLEXIVE DYADIC INTERVIEWING: ACTS OF FAITH

Reflexive dyadic interviews follow the typical protocol of the interviewer asking questions and the interviewee answering them, but the interviewer typically shares personal experience with the topic at hand or reflects on the communicative process of the interview. In this case, the researcher's disclosures are more than tactics to encourage the respondent to open up; rather, the researcher often feels a reciprocal desire to disclose, given the intimacy of the details being shared by the interviewee. The interview is conducted more as a conversation between two equals than as a distinctly hierarchical, question-and-answer exchange, and the interviewer tries to tune in to the interactively produced meanings and emotional dynamics within the interview itself (Gubrium and Holstein 1997). When telling the story of the research, the interviewers might reflect deeply on the personal experience that brought them to the topic, what they learned about and from themselves and their emotional responses in the course of the interview, and/or how they used knowledge of the self or the topic at hand to understand what the interviewee was saying. Thus the final product includes the cognitive and emotional reflections of the researcher, which add context and layers to the story being told about participants, such as in the exemplar discussed below.

* * *

Since January 1998, I (Leigh) have been conducting ethnographic fieldwork for my dissertation at Dalet Shalom Messianic Jewish Congregation. Messianic Jews believe that they can retain their cultural and ethnic ties to Judaism while recognizing Jesus (whom they refer to by the Hebrew name "Yeshua") as the Messiah. My disser-

tation research traces my own spiritual journey throughout the ethnographic process, showing how my stories and feelings about religion interact with the stories told by my participants.

The congregation's secretary, Karen, immediately became my main "informant," guiding me through the world of Messianic Judaism. Although I brought some questions to my first interview with Karen, I let the conversation evolve as naturally as possible. Karen spoke at length about her spiritual experiences over the course of her life and also asked me several questions about my own experiences, such as how often I had thought about Jesus and what my religious experiences were like as I was growing up. As we became more comfortable with each other, I began volunteering information, for example, pointing out similarities between our relationships with our grandparents. Although our taped interviews focused mainly on Karen, what she expressed during the interviews undoubtedly was dependent on "the particularities of the subject/researcher relationship" (Angrosino 1989:315-16). For example, my identity as a Jewish woman gave us several points of connection. Several times, Karen said, "Well, you understand what it's like to be Jewish," or "There are all these Jewish cultural things, but I know I don't have to explain all that to you."

An added dimension to our research relationship was that Karen wanted me to accept Yeshua as the Messiah. I felt uncomfortable about her desire for me to convert, while I simultaneously felt that my resistance disappointed her. These relational and emotional dynamics shaped our interview process. Kathleen Blee (1998) explains that the interaction between interviewer and respondent is intensely complex, shaped by positive and negative emotions, and that "just as researchers may try to invoke rapport to facilitate data collection in interviewing situations, so too respondents may attempt to create emotional dynamics to serve their strategic interests" (p. 395).

Karen's stories led me to reflect on my own experiences with and feelings about religion and spirituality. At times, I related to the story Karen told, able because of our similarities to appreciate her attachment to Jewish ritual. Other times, it was difficult for me to understand her transformation from a fairly liberal, secular Jew to an evangelical Messianic Jewish believer. I reflect on these many complexities within the story that follows.

I sip my herbal tea and place the cup back down on the small Formica café table. Karen and I have been in the Barnes and Noble coffee shop for about 15 minutes. "So, how did you find Dalet Shalom?" I ask her.

Karen adjusts her glasses and smiles, "A woman I know heard about it. I was telling her that I had been thinking a lot about Yeshua, but that I also knew I loved being Jewish. I could never change from being Jewish because that is so much a part of who I am. After this woman told me about it, I found the phone number in the phone book and called. I remember the rabbi spoke to me for about an hour. He was so warm and understanding! He told me to come to services on Saturday to see how I felt." She laughs at the memory. "I remember that I arrived late and the place was packed! I couldn't find a seat. Finally, I noticed there was one right up front—right under the rabbi's nose! So there I am, right up front, and . . ." Her eyes fill with tears in the pause before she continues, "I can't even name one of the songs I heard that day. I can't even tell you what the sermon was about. All I know is I was filled with emotion, and I couldn't stop crying. Finally, the rabbi asked if there was anyone who wanted to come know Yeshua, so I raised my hand. I was still crying, and as I moved to go up to the rabbi, I saw a male figure next to me wearing white. I felt this sense of comfort, as if I could just rest my head on his shoulder."

She picks up a napkin to wipe her eyes. "I felt the presence of his arm around me, and I knew it was Yeshua, welcoming me."

"Wow," I respond. I wonder what I would have done if I had ever felt a spiritual presence during a religious service. I wonder if I will ever experience during fieldwork the kind of visions of which Dalet Shalom congregants often speak.

"So were services at Dalet Shalom very different from what you were used to growing up?" I continue, seeking a point of contact.

She nods, "Yes. At home we basically celebrated Passover and Hanukkah."

I smile in recognition. "Yes, me too. At least in my parents' house. I mostly learned about religion from my grandparents because they were more observant. They kept kosher and my grandfather walked to synagogue."

Her eyes light up with familiarity. "Yes! Exactly! We have pictures of my grandfather saying the morning service prayers."

"So would you say your perspective on life has changed a lot since your conversion?"

"Oh, definitely! I can't even express how much happier I am, Leigh. One day you'll get to feel that too. I know that Yeshua is calling to you. Just don't be afraid of what the Lord has to offer you. Just ask Him what He wants. Have you had questions—questions you've wanted to ask God?"

I contemplate what she is asking me, feeling awkward about having to answer questions about my own beliefs. I know I shouldn't feel this uncomfortable. After all, she's been open to answering my questions. I decide that I owe her an honest response. "Yes, I suppose I have. Sometimes I wonder why certain things happen, like why my sister is deaf and diabetic, or why my father is mentally ill. And I wonder about why good things happen too, like what causes things to go extremely well."

She is quiet for a moment. "So, what do you think about Dalet Shalom?"

"Oh, there are many things I like about Dalet Shalom. I like the dancing and the praise and worship. I think the people are warm and inviting." I remain silent about the things that I do not feel comfortable

with or agree with, such as their fundamental belief in the Bible, and their stance against homosexuality and abortion.

"Where do you think the Lord is taking you?" Karen pushes some strands of hair behind one ear.

"I don't know. That's not really a question I ever ask," I confess.

"Do you think about Yeshua a lot?"

I smile because doing this research has caused me to think of Yeshua almost daily. "Of course. But thinking about Yeshua has always been scary for me." The image of Jesus I held in my mind prior to my excursions into the Messianic world was one of dangerous attraction. Salvation extends its hands of allure and promise, a sense of safety blanketed with acceptance. I have always been afraid of Jesus, a fact I hesitate to admit. After all, how can I fear the epitome of peace and kindness? But for me, Jesus was too complicated to face. I didn't know what to do with the concept of Him, and of salvation. I was fascinated by the ease with which some people seemed to believe—really believe—in their religion. Not only fascinated, but envious. Why couldn't it be that easy for me? Why was I constantly questioning, debating, doubting?

"Intellectualizing it makes it harder. I think that is where the fear comes from. But I've also seen a big change in you since you've been coming to services."

Surprised by this observation, I inquire, "What change?"

"You seem more peaceful. I think the Lord is trying to talk to you." She watches as some people order pastries and coffee. "I just can't imagine how I lived my life without Yeshua in it. I just . . . I am a completely different person now. I look at these people, and ask myself how they all do it." As she says this, I wonder if her real question is how I do it. "How do they live their lives without Him? Not having that belief . . ." Her voice breaks and tears slip from her eyes. "The thought of it just makes me so sad."

Witnessing her deep emotional reaction, I think about my own emotional discomfort when the conversation turned to me and my beliefs. Am I being dishonest by not telling her the things that trouble me? I know that I cannot convert to Messianic Judaism, so am I unfairly deceiving her by not directly telling her this?

In listening to and writing Karen's stories about faith and conversion, I come to understand more fully the complicated array of emotions that accompanies religious belief. By revealing her stories, Karen presents me with an opportunity to witness her religious experiences and try them on for size. When Karen begins to ask me questions about my beliefs, she opens a window into how she sees me and allows me to reflect upon how it feels to be an interviewee. This leaves me better able to understand Karen's emotions as a participant in my research. Rather than Karen's merely reporting information to me, the researcher, our emotions are produced in an unfolding conversation (Holstein and Gubrium 1995). Here, readers can connect to the story either through my perceptions or through Karen's, interpreting our experiences for themselves.

As a researcher, I do not dismiss Karen's beliefs as mere social constructions, but allow that she actually experienced something spiritually transcendent during her conversion. Although I am unable to relate fully to Karen's religious beliefs, I remain open to her descriptions and gain new insights into my own beliefs by questioning my faith and comparing it to her spiritual beliefs. Her descriptions of visions, in fact, cause me to reflect on whether or not I may someday experience something similar.

Although qualitative researchers often focus on how positive and empathic feelings shape their interactions in the field, my not being able to identify completely with Karen illuminates how negative or differing emotions can shape ethnographic relationships as well (Blee 1998). Both participant and researcher negotiate the emotional dynamics of any situation, positive or negative. Narrative's openness to multiple perspectives can successfully communicate the difficulties and dilemmas of studying those with whom we do not connect as well as those we do.

INTERACTIVE INTERVIEWS: EXPERIENCING BULIMIA

Sometimes interviewers desire to position themselves in a more self-consciously collaborative way than occurs in reflexive one-on-one interviews. The prototype of this approach is the interactive interview, which usually takes place in a collaborative, small group setting (Ellis et al. 1997). The goal of an interactive interview is for all those participating, usually two to four people, including the primary researcher, to act both as researchers and as research participants. Each is given space to share his or her story in the context of the developing relationships among all participants. Interactive interviewing works especially well when all participants also are trained as researchers (see, e.g., Ellis et al. 1997; Tillmann-Healy and Kiesinger 2000). Even if that is not the case, however, participants can be given an important role in determining the research process and its content, as well as in interpreting the meanings of the interviews (see, e.g., Macleod 1999). Likewise, the feelings, insights, and stories that the primary researcher brings to the interactive session are as important as those of other participants; the understandings that emerge among all parties during interaction—what they learn *together*—are as compelling as the stories each brings to the session. Ideally, all participants should have some history together or be willing to work to develop a strong affiliation. It is helpful for the researcher as well as coparticipants to have personal experience with the topic under investigation; if that is not the case, the researcher should be willing to take on the role and lived experience of other participants in this regard. This strategy is particularly useful when the researcher is examining personal and/or emotional topics that require reciprocity and the building of trust, such as eating disorders, as in the case elaborated below.

* * *

The article "Interactive Interviewing: Talking about Emotional Experience" (Ellis et al. 1997) describes a project about the embodiment and meanings of bulimia. The research was conducted by three researchers: Lisa, at the time a Ph.D. candidate; Christine, a recent Ph.D.; and Carolyn, a professor. Lisa and Christine have had direct personal experience with bulimia; I (Carolyn) have not. But we all share concerns about food and bodies that arise from women's immersion in cultural contradictions of thinness of bodies and abundance of food and commodities. Also, we share a desire to work within a methodological and theoretical orientation that privileges emotional and concrete details of everyday life and that critically interrogates traditional social science interviewing practices.

In this project, we were interested in learning more about bulimia and how we might methodologically access important bodily, emotional, and interactive details of the experience. Our final paper consisted of four stories, two written from transcripts of dyadic interviews between Christine and Lisa (Kiesinger 1995; Tillmann-Healy 1996), one from the numerous interactive sessions in which all three of us participated, and the last from a dinner at a restaurant written as a narrative ethnography. These accounts tell the story of the development of our interactive interviewing project, with each story adding another textured layer to the approach.

The excerpts below come from the story I wrote about our group discussions. I reflect from the position of a participant who did not engage in the bulimic behaviors we sought to understand. As an "outsider," I show how I consider the problems and risks in this kind of interview situation, how I attempt to get inside a world I know little about, and how Christine and Lisa move me to consider my own relationship to my body and food and to see the similarities between their world and mine.

Initially I do not understand that I am fashioning my story as well (Parry 1991). I hesitantly add my thoughts about food— how I too love to eat and am a "sugar junky," how I try to remember to pause after one helping to wait for fullness cues. I also speak of our differences—how my generation enjoyed adventure and being out of control, while theirs seems to want to have it all—adventure and control, fullness and thinness. . . .

They say that going out to dinner is their favorite activity. I admit it is one of mine too. They say they obsess about food. I deny that I do, but then think about how much food enters my consciousness on any given day. As Christine and Lisa say, working on this project makes me think more about food and my body. Is it healthy to concentrate so much on these details? "There's too much to accomplish to become consumed by these issues," I think. For me, perhaps, but not for young women like Christine and Lisa whose lives are intertwined so intricately with the subject. I wonder how our research can help us to refashion personal and cultural scripts about women's bodies.

Sometimes I think I understand their world so well, it frightens me. I imagine being them and purging, and then admiring my thin body. Then I recoil, knowing I won't engage in such an unhealthy activity. At age 45, health is more important than appearance. What about when I was 20? What if someone had suggested purging to me then? Were the diet pills I occasionally took so different?

I understand the desire to be physically attractive. In my sophomore year in college I lost 47 pounds by eating 500 calories a day. I wore contact lenses, even when I had to take Excedrin each time I inserted the lenses into my watery, itchy, red eyes. What really separates me from Lisa and Chris-

tine? Twenty years? Growing up in an earlier decade where those in my cohort rebelled against gender stereotypes and were less inclined to take on cultural labels? Coming of age in a decade where the thrill of "getting away with something" involved drugs and sex, not bingeing and purging? We all have our temptations.

Being thin is less important to me now than ever. Is that because other issues have my attention now, and I have a career I enjoy and a mate who loves and accepts me? Or is it only because a "beautiful" body is less attainable now? I remember a scene that I've never told anyone about. At a conference a few years ago, I wore a bathing suit to the hotel pool and ran into Christine and her sister; their perfection moved me to wrap my body in a towel.

All these thoughts abound as I try to enter their worlds, become their bodies with their concerns. I neither can nor want to distance myself from this intimate, interactive situation. I try to normalize what they do, to take away some of the stigma of shit and vomit. That doesn't mean I support their self-destructive behaviors; it means I am willing to consider that they are not so different from the rest of us. All women are affected by cultural messages of abundance and thinness.

Prior to this study, I had some contact with women who were bulimic. Although I voiced concerns about the role that cultural expectations played in their behavior, I saw them as "other," as strange, different from me. The more they told me about themselves, in some ways the more other they became. It was only when I put myself in an interview situation with them and we talked in depth about our relationship to food that I started to see the similarities between them and me. It is only since then that I can admit how much food and the desire to be physically attractive have affected my life. As we share stories, we create deeper understandings in interaction with each other. I am no longer healthy and they sick; I am not their professor and they my students. We are three women together trying to understand an intimate part of our lives. We have taken different routes, but even those become more understandable as we trace our histories, think about the messages and values of the different eras in which we grew up, and discuss where we are in our lives now. By seeing myself as a subject as well as a researcher, I am able to move from the distanced observer to the feeling participant and learn things I could not learn before, both about them and about me.

Eating dinner together also provides another occasion for learning about eating disorders. The short excerpt below shows the co-construction from our three independent accounts of our collective story of eating together.

When Carolyn sits down across from her, Christine instantly is aware that they have never eaten together. Because she tends to synchronize her eating pattern with others, she panics. Will Carolyn eat quickly or slowly? Does she talk while eating? Is she a sharer? Will Carolyn, a seasoned ethnographer, be watching her every move?

Lisa's stomach growls continuously as they sit talking without picking up their menus. Why don't they order? When finally the waitress stops to ask if they want an appetizer, Carolyn looks questioningly at Lisa and Christine. Lisa can almost taste the salty-greasy choices—oozing processed-cheese nachos, fried mozzarella sticks, and hot chicken wings. But she's not feeling particularly "bad," and she knows Christine almost never eats appetizers. They shake their heads "no" simultaneously. Carolyn had considered ordering some for the table, but after their response, she thinks that she really shouldn't have them either.

Carolyn takes one of the menus tucked behind the salt and pepper shakers. Immediately Christine and Lisa reach for menus as well. It seems they have been waiting for Carolyn to make the first move. Right away, Carolyn knows what she wants. But Christine and Lisa grasp their menus tightly, immersed, reading line by line. For what seems like minutes to Carolyn, they say nothing.

Carolyn continues holding her menu in front of her face so they don't feel rushed. She'd like to know what they're thinking. Minutes go by.

This excerpt portrays the impact of bulimia on how we thought, felt, and related as we ate a meal. These stories reveal our concerns about sharing food, our rules for eating with others, the inner dialogues that occupy us during dinner, our obsession with the food in front of us, our concerns about how we were being perceived by others, and the similarities and differences in the eating experiences of women who do and do not have bulimia.

MEDIATED AND UNMEDIATED CO-CONSTRUCTED NARRATIVES

Researchers also may share their stories through co-constructed narratives, or tales jointly constructed by relational partners about epiphanies in their lives (see Bochner and Ellis 1996; Ellis and Bochner 1996). This approach may be *mediated,* meaning a researcher may monitor the conversation of two relational partners, or *unmediated,* meaning a researcher might study his or her own relationship with a partner or two researchers might study their relationship with each other. In either case, these stories show dyads engaged in the specific, concrete, and unique details of daily living. They cope with the untidy ambiguities, ambivalences, and contradictions of relationship life and try to make sense of their local situations. This type of research focuses on the interactional sequences by which interpretations of lived experiences are constructed, coordinated, and solidified into stories. The local narratives that are jointly produced thus display couples in the process of "doing" their relationships as they try to turn fragmented, vague, or disjointed events into intelligible, coherent accounts.

MEDIATED CO-CONSTRUCTED NARRATIVES: ONE FLESH

Mediated co-constructed narrative research is similar to conjoint marital therapy (Satir 1983), where couples participate together in therapy after providing their different perspectives on the same events. It also is related to interpersonal process recall (Elliott 1986; Gale 1992), where an interviewer asks two participants to watch a tape of their therapy session and rate and comment on meaningful moments. In mediated co-constructed narratives, a researcher serves as coordinator and moderator as a couple engages in a joint construction of an epiphany in their relationship. The researcher asks them to reflect on the event and to write, talk into a tape recorder, or be interviewed separately about the experience. Then, in the presence of the researcher, the participants hold a discussion about the event. Sometimes the participants are asked to exchange transcripts or stories written independently and read each other's constructions before the discussion, although this may not always be feasible. Nevertheless, the goal is to produce or co-construct a version of the event that takes into account each individual's perspective.

The researcher stays in the role of researcher as he or she take notes on (and/or tapes) the interaction. The researcher then writes the participants' story from the materials they provide as well as from his or her own observation of and participation in their co-construction. While writing their story, the researcher reflects on how he or she, as the researcher, views the participants and analyzes their conversational style and their negotiation of the co-construction of their separate stories. The researcher might describe events leading up to the interview, the physical and emotional environment of the interview, and his or her role in the interview (for example, what the researcher asked the participants, how he or she responded to them, and how the researcher possibly influenced the conversation). The account of the interview process becomes part of the story told. The researcher also might include his or her views on and experience with the topic at hand and discussion of how his or her views and feelings have developed and changed as a result of observation of and interaction with the participants. Including the researcher's experience helps readers understand more about the researcher's interest in the topic and provides background for how he or she interprets what is going on. Although the researcher becomes a character in the story, his or her identity remains one of researcher rather than researcher-participant as in interactive interviewing. As shown below, the focus stays on the experience of the other research participants rather than on the interviewer.

* * *

As my (Leigh's) dissertation research continued, I wanted to interview a couple about the role of Messianic belief in married life. Every congregant I asked referred me to Rabbi Aaron Levinson and his wife, Rebecca. I was repeatedly told that they "really live up to biblical guidelines for marriage." Both Aaron and Rebecca had Messianic conversion experiences in the early 1970s. Aaron became very involved at the organizational level of the Messianic movement and opened Dalet Shalom in 1980. A few years later, he and Rebecca met and married. When I approached Aaron and Rebecca, they were happy to be interviewed, and I set up an appointment with them in June 1999.

Originally, I conducted two-hour taped interviews separately with Aaron and Rebecca about their marriage and Messianic expectations for marriage roles. I then conducted a follow-up joint interview once the initial interviews were transcribed. Ideally, I would have preferred that Aaron and Rebecca had had a chance to read and comment on one another's transcripts, but because of their schedules, we were not able to arrange for this. In addition, once I read the original transcripts, I realized that Aaron and Rebecca agreed with one another about every topic we had discussed. Asking them to comment on each other's individual stories most likely would not have produced stories any different from the ones they had already told me. I thought that I might be able to show the collaborative nature of their relationship by writing a story of our interview that included details about how they interacted.

In writing a story based on our follow-up joint interview session, I used what I already knew about Aaron and Rebecca, shaping their mannerisms and voices. I recalled the way Aaron had cried when he described first meeting Rebecca. I remembered Rebecca's blush at detailing their first telephone conversation, and how nervous she had been. Many times while volunteering in the Dalet Shalom office, I witnessed Aaron's romantic gestures toward Rebecca, such as unexpectedly buying her flowers. All of these elements filtered my understanding of their relationship prior to our interviews.

In this excerpt, I interview Aaron and Rebecca together, reflecting on their interaction with one another and the emotions present in the interview. In addition, I show how Rebecca's reflections on her family's reaction to her conversion cause me to reflect on my own family relationships. Unlike Karen, Aaron and Rebecca do not ask me questions about my own experiences; they remain focused on the questions I have for them.

I shuffle my transcripts and smile at Rabbi Aaron Levinson and his wife, Rebecca. "Well, I have the transcripts from the last interview here." I pat the papers beneath my hand. A few weeks earlier, I had interviewed Aaron about the role of men in Messianic theology, following that with a separate interview with Rebecca about women's roles. "And I must say that even though I interviewed you separately, there is no disagreement between the two of you."

They both smile, and Aaron takes Rebecca's hand in his own. "We're always together. We have to be, as it says in the Bible, one flesh." I notice the intimacy and genuine caring for one another that their gestures communicate.

"Well, I did have some questions about some things we didn't get to cover in our previous interviews."

"Yes?" Aaron runs his hand over his white beard and adjusts his glasses. The sparkling brown eyes behind them inquisitively meet my own.

"How do you advise congregants about handling nonbelieving family members?" In the Messianic world, non-Messianic followers (especially Jewish ones) are referred to as "nonbelievers."

"Well, I'll let Rebecca handle that. She's dealt a lot with that issue." Aaron willingly gives the floor to Rebecca, showing a trust and respect for her experience with this topic. This give-and-take, primarily orchestrated by Aaron, seems characteristic of much of their communication with one another.

Pushing some of her curly brown hair behind her shoulders, Rebecca takes the floor without missing a beat. "How do you handle nonbelieving family members? First of all, you do so with love because love really does conquer all. I'll give you an example. I have a family member who lives in Israel, and who is an observant and religious Jew—not Messianic. When he addresses less observant family members, he pounds ideas into them: 'You have to do this, you have to do that.' The more he does that, the more the rest of the family resists worshiping the Lord. They see him as forcing beliefs on them. Now when Aaron and I go visit my family in Israel, we love them. We don't force any ideas on them, and because of that, they're more willing to be open to our ideas."

She pauses, contemplating her next words, and I wonder if she is considering whether or not to say anything else. I wait, allowing the silence to encourage further information. "I will say that when I first came to know the Messiah, I was very anxious about how this would be received in my family. I had all these questions about how to deal with my loyalty to my family, our rabbi, my friends . . ." Her voice trails off, and I perceive that her eyes are focused somewhere on the past. Her gold bracelets quietly clink together as she adjusts her hair once again, and her expression is sad as she finds her voice. "My family sat shivah [a Jewish mourning practice for the dead] when I came to accept the Messiah. I was no longer a part of the family, and we didn't speak for a long time." Aaron reaches out to touch her shoulder, offering emotional support. She touches his hand and smiles, reassuring him that she is okay.

Sitting in my seat, I feel my chest tighten, and I wonder at the power of a newfound faith that allowed her to face this pain in exchange for her belief. I try to imagine my own family cutting me off for choosing an alternative belief system. If that were the fate that awaited me, how many of my choices in life would be different? Biting my lip, I think about how much my grandparents were opposed to family members' dating and marrying anyone outside of the Jewish faith. If they were still alive, would I be in a long-term relationship with a Christian man? I wonder if I would have crossed that line anyway, and what the results would have been. Although I cannot imagine my grandparents completely cutting me off, I cannot say for sure. I ponder whether anticipation of their deep disappointment might have been enough to dissuade me from dating men outside of Judaism.

I realize Rebecca has continued to talk, and I snap back to attention. "Eventually, someone in the Jewish community spoke to my parents. To this day, I have no idea what this person said to them, but whatever it was, I know she is resting in peace with the Lord because my family decided to ask me for forgiveness, and I was accepted back into the family again." She says this quickly, as if to brush aside the emotions this story makes her recall. "But I never ever push any of my beliefs on them. All I do is act with love, and

show them through my loving actions and attitude how strong my dedication to the Lord is. And although at this time they do not know the Messiah as we know the Messiah, they see that Aaron and I are very observant. Their acceptance comes through our love and through us letting the fruit of our belief show." She turns to Aaron for confirmation, and he smiles and nods at her words.

I hesitate, wanting to probe further into this experience. Rebecca has tied things up a little too nicely, and I know that her feelings regarding her family's sudden "forgiveness" were probably not as simple as she describes. Certainly, she must have felt some residual anger for their rejection. Did she really "forgive and forget" that easily? But I don't want to force her into areas she may not be emotionally ready or willing to enter. I decide to let it go for now. Maybe there will be a better time or place for such questions later.

In the scene above, I am open with readers about my own thoughts and feelings during my conversation with Aaron and Rebecca. Letting readers know what I think and how I emotionally react to Aaron and Rebecca brings them into the interview context with me, allowing them to watch as the interview progresses and to imagine how they might respond in a similar situation. Some readers may draw conclusions that are different from mine, or may interpret Aaron's and Rebecca's words and actions in a different light.

Throughout our interview, Aaron and Rebecca enact marriage roles through actions rather than words. Although they hold more traditional views about marriage than I do, I am able to see and understand how and why these roles work for them. Their silent exchanges reinforce Messianic views on how spouses should interact: The man is considered the head of the household and the person who, after discussions with the wife, has the final say on all decisions. For example, even though Rebecca holds the floor when answering my question about non-Messianic family members, she does so only after Aaron has directed her to do so. Rebecca seeks Aaron's confirmation and support of what she says through nonverbal behaviors such as exchanging glances and touching. Aaron reassures her through actions such as nodding and placing a hand on her shoulder. Allowing their interaction to evolve more naturally reveals how Aaron and Rebecca's co-construction is beneath the surface of their words, in a conversational dance so skillfully performed that their give-and-take appears almost flawless.

UNMEDIATED: CO-CONSTRUCTED NARRATIVES: DECIDING ABOUT ABORTION

In unmediated co-constructed narratives, the focus turns directly to the self, as researchers examine their own relationships rather than the relationships of others. In such narratives, researchers use the same procedures as described above, except there is no outside researcher mediating the interview process. The two researchers, or a researcher and partner, write their stories separately, exchange them with each other, read them, and then discuss them. Then they attempt to co-construct a collective version. They might present the result in the form of a script, a short story, or an essay; or they might analyze or even perform their narrative for an audience. Other participants in the event might be asked to add their voices as well. Although the result is a collective interpretation, individual voices might be kept separate, as the exemplar below demonstrates.

* * *

"Telling and Performing Personal Stories: The Constraints of Choice in Abortion" (Ellis and Bochner 1992; see also Bochner and Ellis 1992) tells the story of a decision my partner, Art, and I (Carolyn)

had to make upon discovering only 10 weeks into our relationship that I was pregnant. After much agonizing, I had an abortion. This experience had a profound impact on our relationship and our personal lives. For the next two months, we were numb, self-protective, and unable to express our thoughts and feelings about the abortion. When we finally broke through our resistance, we realized how much the experience had affected us and how deeply we had ventured into our private and submerged registers of emotion.

With a self-consciously therapeutic motive, we decided to write a story about our experience to try to understand what had happened at a deep emotional level. We wanted to reveal ourselves to ourselves as we revealed ourselves to others. Hoping to provide companionship to others who may have been similarly bruised by the ambivalence and contradictions associated with the constraint of making such a choice, we attempted to share the complex emotions that were part of this experience so that readers might experience our experience—actually feel it—and consider how they might feel or have felt in similar situations. We tried to write in an open, revealing way that would connect us to readers, especially those who had themselves suffered the complexities of abortion. We hoped to tell enough in our story so that readers might, as Jaber Gubrium and James Holstein (1997) point out, connect our emotions to the cultures in which they arise.

In telling our story, we first independently constructed a detailed chronology of the emotions, events, decisions, and coping strategies that had taken place. After completing our individual accounts, we read each other's versions and began to co-construct a single story of what had happened. We took notes on our discussions and asked others with whom we had consulted during the decision making about the abortion to contribute to the narrative, thus producing a multivocal text.

We wrote our final story as a script that presented, in sequence, critical scenes in which we expressed our self-reflections, feelings, and analysis of the main events— the discovery and shock of the pregnancy, pre- and postdecision interactions, and the abortion procedure described side by side in both the female and male voices. Later, we performed this narrative at a professional social science conference, a step that became a vital part of our attempt to cope with and bring closure to this experience. The excerpt below details the abortion procedure in two voices, Ted's as Art's voice and Alice's as Carolyn's voice.

Alice: *The suction machine is turned on. I tighten my grip on Ted's wrists, he tightens his. I feel excruciating pain. I moan and scream. Everything speeds up. The nurse yells, "Deep breaths. Deep breaths." I try to, but the screams get in the way. Ted's face is now right next to mine. I hear his voice, sense his encouragement. I don't know what Ted is saying, but I'm glad he's here. There is confusion. I hear the suctioning noise, and then they're pulling out my whole uterus. I bear down, my nails sink into Ted's wrists. Then I am in the pain, going round and round like in a tangled sheet. I feel it being sucked out of my vagina. My god I can't stand the pain. I hear gut-wrenching screams. Then the doctor's voice, "Five more seconds, just five more seconds, that's all." I am comforted and know that I can stand anything for five seconds. I feel I am with friends. The nurse continues yelling, "Breathe. Breathe." And I try as hard as I can to breathe as I imagine one should when having a baby. Ted is encouraging, gripping. Then I feel another cutting as the doctor does a D&C to make sure nothing was missed. The pain takes over my full consciousness.*

Ted: *Suddenly I hear the rumble of the suction machine and I feel a vibration pass through Alice's body as the machine extracts the last remnants of the fetus. I see the blood and am repulsed by the horror of this crude technological achievement. I want to look away, but I can't. I am face-*

to-face with the terror of creation and destruction. Alice has a firm hold on my hands. I cannot turn away. She cannot escape the physical pain; I cannot feel it. I cannot evade the horror of what I see in front of me; she cannot witness it. My ears are ringing from the frenzied sound created by the simultaneous talking and screaming and rumbling that is engulfing the room. The action is fast and furious. Alice's ferocious cries submerge the sound of the machine. "Hold on, baby," I say. I clutch her hands as tight as I can. Her breathing intensifies, growing louder and louder. "Oh, god," she screams. "Oh, my god." Ironically, her cries and screams echo the sounds of orgasmic pleasure she released the afternoon this fetus was created.

Alice: *Then Quiet. The machine is turned off. "That's all," the doctor says. A nurse puts a pad between my legs and I have visions of blood gushing from my angry uterus. Ted's grip eases. I relax, but the leftover pain continues to reverberate through my body.*

Ted: *Then, abruptly, with no forewarning, the machine is turned off. Alice lies still, out of breath, quiet. The doctor's assistant whisks away the tray of remains covered by a bloody towel.*

In the literature on abortion, details of the emotional and communicative processes of the experience are obscure, leaving readers without a sense of the complexity, confusion, and vacillation often associated with the lived experience of abortion. The emotional trauma seems bleached of its most profound and stirring meanings. Most of the literature bypasses interpersonal and emotional conflicts in favor of political ideology or moral indignation. Because Art and I are both authors and subjects in our story, we have the freedom to explore emotional trauma as we experienced it separately and together. Although our own relationship may be vulnerable, we are not limited by concerns of doing emotional harm to other research participants or our fears about losing control of our words and experiences to another researcher. Thus we are able in our story to explore emotional complexities from both the female and male perspectives and to consider such graphic differences as those between Art's experience of grief and my experience of unworthiness or the meaning of my repeated use of the term *baby* juxtaposed against Art's references to *fetus*. These descriptive revelations lead us to contemplate further the significance of frames: grief versus self-contempt, physical pain juxtaposed against emotional pain, and the experience-near female voice compared to the more distanced male voice. Writing and discussing this story helps us to unify the past (the pregnancy and abortion) with an anticipated and hopeful future—to bring closure to this experience as one we might live with together.

◆ In the Middle of Flexibility and Confusion: Two or Three Things We Know for Sure (Allison 1995)

Books and papers cover my desk and surround my chair. Humming from the computer and printer fills the room. Staring at the screen, I feel walled in; the only way out is to finish this chapter. I pick up the stack of pages in front of me. The ragged edges, unevenly stapled paragraphs, and half sheets refute the order I try to impose by tapping all four sides of the stack on the desk. I read through the draft Leigh and I have written of "Their Story/My Story." It's already November 17th, I remind myself as I squint at the small date on my watch. I look again, just in case I've misread it. Jay Gubrium periodically reminds us of the December 1st deadline, and I don't want to be late. Besides, I need to move to all the other unfinished commitments I have taken on. I sigh. This chapter isn't coming together as we'd hoped.

Leigh and I have constructed a typology of kinds of interview studies that include the researcher's experience and have used four exemplars from our own studies to demonstrate. The chapter works well enough in theory, but I'm not sure it's working in practice. Our interview exemplars don't quite match the ideal types we have described. And the continuum from lesser to greater involvement of the researcher—well, that hasn't worked either. What do we do now? It's too late to conduct other interviews or select other studies as exemplars.

I should have chosen my excerpts more carefully; Leigh and I should have worked more closely while she was doing her interviews for this chapter, I admonish myself. Now I have to rewrite my description of the types so that our exemplars are really exemplars. Or I will have to choose other excerpts, and Leigh will have to rewrite her interview stories to fit our types.

Choosing the former, I frantically start to edit our text. I glance again at my watch as I type. Leigh will be here in 30 minutes, and this is the only day this week I can work on our chapter. Next week is filled with dissertation defenses, proposal hearings, conference planning, and other deadlines. I type faster.

Suddenly a ray of light makes its way through a crack in the wall and a smile breaks over my face. I stop editing and start to type what I am thinking: In doing this chapter, Leigh and I are engaged in writing what we have called in the text an unmediated co-constructed narrative. She brings her (interview) stories and I bring mine, and we work to put them together in a co-constructed story we both agree on. We have written about how difficult these projects are to accomplish, how they never quite work out as you think they will, how it is important to leave room for improvisation, and how difficult it is for researchers to include their stories without taking over the stories of others. We agree that in our interview studies we're trying to reflect life as lived, not simply follow traditional social science procedures. But until now, we had forgotten to take our own advice in writing this chapter. Given our goals and flexible procedures, should it be a surprise that we are having trouble fitting our work into neat categories and traditional social science sections? Should it be a surprise that I feel compelled to include here our reflexive story of writing this chapter?

As I type this paragraph, Leigh pulls in to my driveway. I open the front door only a crack, so the dogs can't run out. Leigh squeezes through the narrow opening I provide and greets me and the barking dogs. "Quite a doorbell," she says, laughing.

I start to offer apologies for the noise, but instead just shrug, "I know. What can I say?"

As I fix glasses of tea, all four dogs take turns sniffing the smells of Leigh's dog hidden on her clothes. Our Australian shepherd Sunya, wide-eyed and poised in anticipation, drops a ball in front of Leigh, enticing her to play. Ande, our Jack Russell, jumps into her arms when she reaches down to pet Likker and Traf, the two rat terriers. As we move to my office, the dogs run in behind us. They knock the piles of books and papers across the floor, eliminating any possibility of organization, before they jump on Leigh and vie for attention. When I yell at them to be quiet, then squirt them with water from a bottle I keep in my office, they scamper playfully into the hallway, still barking. Apologizing to Leigh for the mess, I quickly close the office door. "There's no room," I yell as they whine and scratch on the wooden door.

I tell Leigh that our interview types and the excerpts we have chosen aren't quite fitting together. She seems disheartened and offers to rewrite her excerpts or to write other stories from her interviews. "Maybe it's okay that they aren't working," I offer. She looks at me quizzically, perhaps thinking that the herbal tea we're drinking has gone to my head. "Well, just think how you did your interviews," I say. "That summer we both were traveling. You also were writing your dissertation proposal and I was working on a book. We didn't have much time to talk about how you'd do the interviews with your participants to fill in our last two 'cells.'"

Smiling at my use of the term cells, she replies, "I knew we were using your articles on co-constructed narratives and interactive interviews as two of our cases. So I reread those and then just let my interviews evolve."

"I know," I reply, "and often that's the best way to do it. Anyway, I didn't want to be too rigid about how you did them. I wasn't in the interview context with you, so there was much I didn't know. You also were using the interviews to gather data for your dissertation, not just this chapter."

"And my participants had their own constraints and agendas," Leigh says.

"As all participants do," I reply and we nod in agreement. "As we do in the writing of this chapter. Think how long it's taken us to find time to get together. That's the nature of research. Why should I have expected this to work exactly as planned? Why did I expect this situation to be any different?"

"So what's not working?" Leigh asks.

"Your dyadic interview. It doesn't really show you reflecting during the interview, like we say happens. Instead, you tell Karen's story and then you tell yours."

"Well, I was trying to show how Karen's story led me to reflect while I transcribed and wrote the interview. As Laurel Richardson [1994] says, writing served as a process of inquiry . . ."

"Just as in this piece we're writing now," I interrupt, "and it's all an evolving process."

Leigh nods and continues, "I also reflected during the interview process. But I was unsure of which reflective moment to focus on for the chapter. What else?"

I am impressed, as always, by her lack of defensiveness. Reminding myself that she is my student and this is the first time we have worked together as coauthors, I choose my words carefully. "Your interview participants in the co-constructed mediated narrative didn't read each others' individual transcripts before you met for a joint interview.

I've always thought of that as an important part of the process."

"I asked them to, but when they said they didn't have time to read the transcripts before I came back for a second interview, well, I pushed a little, but I also didn't want to negatively impact my relationship with them because . . . well mainly because I care what they think. . . ."

"And it's not your style to be pushy . . . ," I interrupt, thinking about her reticence to push Rebecca on the emotions surrounding her family's sudden forgiveness of her conversion.

"No, it isn't," Leigh laughs. "Besides, Rabbi Aaron and Rebecca are authority figures in the temple. I needed them for my dissertation research. It didn't seem appropriate to push." (Similar to your relationship to me, I think.) "With Karen, it was different. We're peers and the interaction was on a different level."

I think about how different Leigh's interviews were from mine. Although both of us knew our respondents, my participants were close friends, long-term students, and loved ones. Leigh's interviews involved relationships made in the process of fieldwork that probably would not continue after her dissertation was done. My situation provided more latitude and, at the same time, less than hers did. In some ways, my participants and I could ask for more from each other and reveal more in the process because we knew each other so well. But because our lives were so intertwined, we also had a lot to lose if the interviews didn't go well. No matter the circumstances, though, my style was to push more than Leigh. I am reminded that we all have to find a comfortable interactive style in interviews that emphasizes relationship and communication.

"There didn't seem to be much to co-construct anyway," Leigh continues, breaking into my thoughts. "In the individual interviews, both of them said almost the same things and portrayed the same images in their stories about gender roles and religion. It was clear they had talked this over a lot."

"Even in the joint conversation," Leigh continues, "when I probed, they basically agreed. I took notice of the nonverbals, such as hand-holding and how they looked at each other, and they do seem to have a good relationship. But rather than both of them answering, each took over certain questions. That seemed to be where the agreement took place—they agreed on who should speak on which question. You can see how focused I am on dynamics in the interview."

"That explains, then, why your narrative doesn't have much of a co-constructed feeling," I say. "It's not so much they co-constructed a story as that they took turns telling individual stories . . ."

"Which, of course, is a form of co-construction," Leigh interjects.

I nod, pleased at her insight, and continue. "I think you might have gotten different stories had you asked them to discuss an epiphany that was yet unresolved, which may be necessary for this kind of interview to work best. What they gave you didn't center on a crisis or turning point that had not yet been processed, which is the idea."

As I talk, I think about my own unmediated co-constructed story with Art about abortion. "When Art and I wrote our stories, it was about an unresolved epiphany in our relationship. I couldn't wait to read his transcript and show him mine. The co-construction process we went through was very important. I wonder, then, why I chose an excerpt to present here that kept the two individual stories side by side instead of one that showed the co-construction process."

"There's also a problem with the portion I chose to demonstrate interactive interviews," I add, thinking that pointing out the problems in my cases will make Leigh feel more comfortable about the problems in hers. "It's all me and doesn't show Christine, Lisa, and me in interaction, and that's the whole point of interactive interviews— that what happens in the interaction is as important as the stories each brings to the interview. Maybe I should show a different

excerpt from both of these pieces or add a second."

"And I could always rewrite my story about Karen," Leigh offers, "to show how I reflected during the interview. But with Rebecca and Aaron . . . well how could I know ahead of time that they might not provide a good example of co-constructed narrative . . ." Her voice trails off. "I guess I should have concentrated more on an unresolved event, as you said, or pushed more in the interviews about their families' responses to their conversion." We stare at each other for a while. Then we simultaneously look at our watches, as though the gun is ready to go off to signify time to run toward the finish line.

"Well, we still have to be careful that we are trying to be truthful about what happened in the interviews, and not intruding too much into their stories," I respond. "At what point are we taking too much control over the stories that get told? Are we manipulating the 'data' to fit the categories and in doing so privileging our categories over the stories and the interview contexts? I'm concerned about that. I don't think I want to second guess the excerpts I initially chose from my published pieces, although I think I'll add an excerpt from my interaction with Christine and Lisa at dinner."

"Good idea," says Leigh. "I don't know how I could rewrite the story of Rebecca and Aaron to fit more with the way you describe co-construction in your article with Art."

"You can't. It's important for readers to see that this process doesn't always go the way you planned. Anyway, both excerpts, yours and mine, demonstrate that co-constructed stories sometimes retain individual voices, or sometimes never had them in the first place. But the co-constructed version presented is still the agreed-upon collective story."

"Good point. I do think, though, that there are good reasons to present another portion of Karen's story to show the reflection that went on during the interview process. I have all that in my notes, so it wouldn't be that difficult."

"I agree. I like that we're concentrating more on making our story work, flexibly dealing with what happened, rather than being too concerned with methodological rules."

"What do you think about using the conversation we're having as the conclusion to our chapter?" I ask suddenly. "Or is it too much of us, the authors, intruding into the research story?"

Leigh laughs, "It is interesting that the issues we deal with in writing this chapter are the same ones we encountered in doing our interview studies in the first place."

"Well, at least now I don't have to worry about our typology and our categories bleeding into each other. Instead we can view our schema as a heuristic device to introduce readers to the variety of ways interviewers can insert themselves into their interviews and the stories they write about others."

"Glad we resolved all that," Leigh says, breathing a sigh of relief.

"Not so fast. We still have the conclusion to write," I remind her, then silently remind myself not to dominate the conversation, as Leigh sometimes seems hesitant to challenge my authority. "What do we want to leave the readers with?"

"Well, the point of all this, other than showing the ways in which researchers can add their experiences to an interview, has been to show how what we learn in and about interviews can be deepened by our participation," Leigh offers.

"I agree. As I see it, the most important thing that happens is that you get a deeper understanding both of self and of others in this process, because you're not only exploring them, you're exploring you."

"Yes, as Jack Douglas [1985] and Michael Jackson [1989] emphasize, 'Understanding ourselves is part of the process of understanding others.' "

"And vice versa."

"That's certainly true for me," Leigh acknowledges. "For example, I understood Karen's background by thinking about my own and how similar they were, and she

made me examine my own religious beliefs, especially the possibility of believing
in Jesus."

"And working with Christine and Lisa
certainly helped me to understand bulimia
on a cultural level and to reframe my own
concerns with eating. In doing this," I continue, "I was drawn to how much we can
come to understand by concentrating on
our similarities with those we study, in addition to our differences. So often we see those
we study as different from us but similar to
each other. In this research, I was forced to
consider how they and I were alike as well. I
had to try on their worlds."

Leigh chimes in, "When I first decided to
study Messianic Judaism, I was sure I would
dislike the congregants and be angry with
them for claiming to be both Jewish and be-
lievers in Jesus. Now after spending so much
time with members and exploring my own
feelings that come up in the interviews, I've
come to understand the complexity of their
beliefs and I connect to their ability to express and be in their emotions."

"So really what we're advocating here is
mutual understanding as opposed to advocating that we, as all-knowing researchers,
understand the other unidirectionally. It's
similar to what happens in our day-to-day
lives, where we try to understand others by
comparing our experiences to theirs. We ask
them, What do you think, do, what are your
relationships like? Sometimes we tell stories
about ours and wait to hear them compare
their lives to ours. The exchange becomes
more of a conversation than, as Holstein
and Gubrium [1995] describe traditional
interviews, information produced for the
interviewer."

"I hope our texts also encourage readers
to think about and feel their commonalities
with our participants and with us," I continue. "As we examine ourselves, we invite
readers to do the same, and to enter into
their own conversations."

"I think the multiple voices in the text
also play a part here."

"Yes, things are revealed and constructed
in interaction that might not be accomplished with one voice."

"Well, there's that. But I was still thinking of readers," Leigh responds. "As Laurel
Richardson and Ernest Lockridge [1998] remind us, multiple voices in co-constructed
pieces give readers multiple places to stand
and look. Some readers might relate to
Rebecca and Aaron's relationship, where
they seemingly agree on everything. Or they
might relate to me as an outside observer
trying to decipher from nonverbal cues
whether something else might be going on."

"In letting them look with you as a researcher, you provide an interview frame
for readers to enter, as you did with Rabbi
Aaron and Rebecca. This allows readers to
understand more fully what went on there
or even to come up with alternate interpretations. They also can feel with you as a researcher. Or feel with you as a character in
your story. That's what Art and I had in
mind in the abortion piece. We wanted to
present a version of both the female and
male experience of abortion, within the
context of our collective confusion, ambivalence, and feelings. These are feelings that
other respondents most likely wouldn't reveal. And even if they did, it might not be
ethical to ask them to. To be able to invite
readers to enter our emotional, physical,
and spiritual, as well as cognitive, experience—well, that's what can happen when
you include yourself as a character. It opens
up other realms of existence."

"As long as you can handle the vulnerability it entails," Leigh says quietly. "Our
own emotionality, physicality, spirituality
—these realms seem to bring with them
a great deal more vulnerability than we're
accustomed to in traditional social science."

"That's for sure," I respond. We sit silently, both contemplating the vulnerability
in the stories we tell in this chapter. Simultaneously, we shake out of our reverie.

"I think we should retitle our chapter
'Their Story/My Story/Our Story,'" I say,
typing the words as I speak them.

■ *References*

Abu-Lughod, L. 1995. "A Tale of Two Pregnancies." Pp. 339-49 in *Women Writing Culture*, edited by R. Behar and D. A. Gordon. Berkeley: University of California Press.

Adler, P. A. and P. Adler. 1997. "Parent-as-Researcher: the Politics of Researching in the Personal Life." Pp. 21-44 in *Reflexivity and Voice*, edited by R. Hertz. Thousand Oaks, CA: Sage.

Agronick, G. and R. Helson. 1996. "Who Benefits from an Examined Life? Correlates of Influence Attributed to Participation in a Longitudinal Study." Pp. 80-93 in *The Narrative Study of Lives*, Vol. 4, *Ethics and Process in the Narrative Study of Lives*, edited by R. Josselson. Thousand Oaks, CA: Sage.

Allison, D. 1995. *Two or Three Things I Know for Sure*. New York: Plume.

Anderson, K., S. Armitage, D. Jack, and J. Wittner. 1987. "Beginning Where We Are: Feminist Methodology in Oral History." *Oral History Review* 15:103-27.

Angrosino, M. V. 1989. "The Two Lives of Rebecca Levengstone: Symbolic Interaction in the Generation of the Life History." *Journal of Anthropological Research* 45:315-26.

———. 1998. *Opportunity House: Ethnographic Stories of Mental Retardation*. Walnut Creek, CA: AltaMira.

Apter, T. 1996. "Expert Witness: Who Controls the Psychologist's Narrative?" Pp. 22-44 in *The Narrative Study of Lives*, Vol. 4, *Ethics and Process in the Narrative Study of Lives*, edited by R. Josselson. Thousand Oaks, CA: Sage.

Austin, D. A. 1996. "Kaleidoscope: The Same and Different." Pp. 206-30 in *Composing Ethnography: Alternative Forms of Qualitative Writing*, edited by C. Ellis and A. P. Bochner. Walnut Creek, CA: AltaMira.

Bar-On, D. 1996. "Ethical Issues in Biographical Interviews and Analysis." Pp. 9-21 in *The Narrative Study of Lives*, Vol. 4, *Ethics and Process in the Narrative Study of Lives*, edited by R. Josselson. Thousand Oaks, CA: Sage.

Behar, R. 1995. "Writing in My Father's Name: A Diary of *Translated Woman's* First Year." Pp. 65-82 in *Women Writing Culture*, edited by R. Behar and D. A. Gordon. Berkeley: University of California Press.

———. 1996. *The Vulnerable Observer: Anthropology That Breaks Your Heart*. Boston: Beacon.

Belenky, M. F., B. M. Clinchy, N. R. Goldberger, and J. M. Tarule. 1981-82. "Listening to Women's Voices." *Newsletter, Education for Women's Development Project* (Simon's Rock of Bard College, Great Barrington, MA), no. 2.

Bergen, R. K. 1993. "Interviewing Survivors of Marital Rape: Doing Feminist Research on Sensitive Topics." Pp. 197-211 in *Researching Sensitive Topics*, edited by C. M. Renzetti and R. M. Lee. Newbury Park, CA: Sage.

Berger, L. 1997a. "Between the Candy Store and the Mall: The Spiritual Loss of a Father." *Journal of Personal and Interpersonal Loss* 2:397-409.

———. 1997b. "Sister, Sister: Siblings, Deafness, and the Representation of Signed Voice." M.A. thesis, University of South Florida, Tampa.

———. 1998. "Silent Movies: Scenes from a Life." Pp. 137-46 in *Fiction and Social Research: By Ice or Fire*, edited by A. Banks and S. P. Banks. Walnut Creek, CA: AltaMira.

Blee, K. M. 1998. "White-Knuckle Research: Emotional Dynamics in Fieldwork with Racist Activists." *Qualitative Sociology* 21:381-99.

Bloom, L. 1996. "Stories of One's Own: Nonunitary Subjectivity in Narrative Representation." *Qualitative Inquiry* 2:176-97.

Bochner, A. P. 1997. "It's About Time: Narrative and the Divided Self." *Qualitative Inquiry* 3: 418-38.

Bochner, A. P. and C. Ellis. 1992. "Personal Narrative as a Social Approach to Interpersonal Communication." *Communication Theory* 2:165-72.

———. 1996. "Talking over Ethnography." Pp. 13-45 in *Composing Ethnography: Alternative Forms of Qualitative Writing*, edited by C. Ellis and A. P. Bochner. Walnut Creek, CA: AltaMira.

Brannen, J. 1988. "The Study of Sensitive Subjects." *Sociological Review* 36:552-63.

Briggs, C. L. 1986. *Learning How to Ask: A Sociolinguistic Appraisal of the Role of the Interview in Social Science Research.* Cambridge: Cambridge University Press.

Bristow, A. R. and J. A. Esper. 1988. "A Feminist Research Ethos." In *A Feminist Ethic for Social Science Research,* edited by Nebraska Sociological Feminist Collective. New York: Edwin Mellen.

Bruner, J. 1986. *Actual Minds, Possible Worlds.* Cambridge, MA: Harvard University Press.

Chase, S. 1996. "Personal Vulnerability and Interpretive Authority in Narrative Research." Pp. 45-59 in *The Narrative Study of Lives,* Vol. 4, *Ethics and Process in the Narrative Study of Lives,* edited by R. Josselson. Thousand Oaks, CA: Sage.

Chase, S. and C. Bell. 1994. "Interpreting the Complexity of Women's Subjectivity." Pp. 63-81 in *Interactive Oral History Interviewing,* edited by E. McMahon and K. L. Rogers. Hillsdale, NJ: Lawrence Erlbaum.

Clough, P. T. 1999. "And Now Writing." Presented at the annual meeting of the Society for the Study of Symbolic Interaction, August, Chicago.

Collins, P. H. 1986. "Learning from the Outsider Within: The Sociological Significance of Black Feminist Thought." *Social Problems* 33:14-32.

Cook, J. A. and M. M. Fonow. 1986. "Knowledge and Women's Interests: Issues of Epistemology and Methodology in Feminist Sociological Research." *Sociological Inquiry* 56:2-27.

Coyle, S. 1998. "Dancing with the Chameleon." Pp. 147-63 in *Fiction and Social Research: By Ice or Fire,* edited by A. Banks and S. P. Banks. Walnut Creek, CA: AltaMira.

Crapanzano, V. 1980. *Tuhami: Portrait of a Moroccan.* Chicago: University of Chicago Press.

Denzin, N. K. 1999. "Performing Montana: Part II." Presented at the annual meeting of the Society for the Study of Symbolic Interaction, August, Chicago.

DeVault, M. L. 1990. "Talking and Listening from Women's Standpoint: Feminist Strategies for Interviewing and Analysis." *Social Problems* 37:96-116.

———. 1999. *Liberating Method: Feminism and Social Research.* Philadelphia: Temple University Press.

Douglas, J. D. 1985. *Creative Interviewing.* Beverly Hills, CA: Sage.

Duelli Klein, R. 1983. "How to Do What We Want to Do: Thoughts about Feminist Methodology." Pp. 99-121 in *Theories of Women's Studies,* edited by G. Bowles and R. Duelli Klein. New York: Routledge & Kegan Paul.

Dumont, J.-P. 1978. *The Headman and I: Ambiguity and Ambivalence in the Fieldworking Experience.* Austin: University of Texas Press.

Edwards, R. 1993. "An Education in Interviewing: Placing the Researcher and the Research." Pp. 181-96 in *Researching Sensitive Topics,* edited by C. M. Renzetti and R. M. Lee. Newbury Park, CA: Sage.

Eisenberg, E. M. 1998. "From Anxiety to Possibility: Poems 1987-1997." Pp. 195-202 in *Fiction and Social Research: By Ice or Fire,* edited by A. Banks and S. P. Banks. Walnut Creek, CA: AltaMira.

Ellingson, L. 1998. " 'Then You Know How I Feel': Empathy, Identification, and Reflexivity in Fieldwork." *Qualitative Inquiry* 4:492-514.

Elliott, R. 1986. "Interpersonal Process Recall (IPR) as a Psychotherapy Process Research Method." Pp. 503-28 in *The Psychotherapeutic Process: A Research Handbook,* edited by L. Greeneberg and W. Pinsof. New York: Guilford.

Ellis, C. 1993. " 'There Are Survivors': Telling a Story of Sudden Death." *Sociological Quarterly* 34:711-30.

———. 1995. *Final Negotiations: A Story of Love, Loss, and Chronic Illness.* Philadelphia: Temple University Press.

———. 1996. "Maternal Connections." Pp. 240-43 in *Composing Ethnography: Alternative Forms of Qualitative Writing,* edited by C. Ellis and A. P. Bochner. Walnut Creek, CA: AltaMira.

———. 1998. "Exploring Loss through Autoethnographic Inquiry: Autoethnographic Stories, Co-constructed Narratives, and Interactive Interviews." Pp. 49-61 in *Perspectives on Loss: A Sourcebook,* edited by J. H. Harvey. Philadelphia: Taylor & Francis.

Ellis, C. and A. P. Bochner. 1992. "Telling and Performing Personal Stories: The Constraints of Choice in Abortion." Pp. 79-101 in *Investigating Subjectivity: Research on Lived Experience,* edited by C. Ellis and M. G. Flaherty. Newbury Park, CA: Sage.

————, eds. 1996. *Composing Ethnography: Alternative Forms of Qualitative Writing.* Walnut Creek, CA: AltaMira.

————. 2000. "Autoethnography, Personal Narrative, Reflexivity: Researcher as Subject." Pp. 733-68 in *Handbook of Qualitative Research,* 2d ed., edited by N. K. Denzin and Y. S. Lincoln. Thousand Oaks, CA: Sage.

Ellis, C., C. E. Kiesinger, and L. M. Tillmann-Healy. 1997. "Interactive Interviewing: Talking about Emotional Experience." Pp. 119-49 in *Reflexivity and Voice,* edited by R. Hertz. Thousand Oaks, CA: Sage.

Finch, J. 1984. " 'It's Great to Have Someone to Talk To': The Ethics and Politics of Interviewing Women." Pp. 70-87 in *Social Researching: Politics, Problems, Practice,* edited by C. Bell and H. Roberts. London: Routledge & Kegan Paul.

Fox, K. 1996. "Silent Voices: A Subversive Reading of Child Sexual Abuse." Pp. 330-47 in *Composing Ethnography: Alternative Forms of Qualitative Writing,* edited by C. Ellis and A. P. Bochner. Walnut Creek, CA: AltaMira.

Futrell, A. and C. Willard. 1994. "Intersubjectivity and Interviewing." Pp. 83-105 in *Interactive Oral History Interviewing,* edited by E. McMahon and K. L. Rogers. Hillsdale, NJ: Lawrence Erlbaum.

Gale, J. 1992. "When Research Interviews Are More Therapeutic Than Therapy Interviews." *Qualitative Report* 1 [On-line]. Available Internet: http://www.nova.edu/ssss/QR/QR1-4/gale.html

Goodall, H. L., Jr. 1991. *Living in the Rock 'n' Roll Mystery: Reading Context, Self, and Others as Clues.* Carbondale: Southern Illinois University Press.

————. 1999. *Writing the New Ethnography.* Walnut Creek, CA: AltaMira.

Griffith, A. and D. Smith. 1987. "Constructing Cultural Knowledge: Mothering as Discourse." Pp. 87-103 in *Women and Education,* edited by J. Gaskell and A. T. McLaren. Calgary, Alberta: Detselig.

Gubrium, J. F. and J. A. Holstein. 1997. *The New Language of Qualitative Method.* New York: Oxford University Press.

Hertz, R. 1995. "Separate but Simultaneous Interviewing of Husbands and Wives: Making Sense of Their Stories." *Qualitative Inquiry* 1:429-51.

Holstein, J. A. and J. F. Gubrium. 1995. *The Active Interview.* Thousand Oaks, CA: Sage.

Hutchinson, S., M. Wilson, and H. S. Wilson. 1994. "Benefits of Participating in Research Interviews." *Image: Journal of Nursing Scholarship* 26:161-64.

Jackson, M. 1989. *Paths toward a Clearing: Radical Empiricism and Ethnographic Inquiry.* Bloomington: Indiana University Press.

Jago, B. 1996. "Postcards, Ghosts, and Fathers: Revising Family Stories." *Qualitative Inquiry* 2:495-516.

Jones, S. H. 1998. *Kaleidoscope Notes: Writing Women's Music and Organizational Culture.* Walnut Creek, CA: AltaMira.

Jorgenson, J. 1991. "Co-constructing the Interviewer/Co-constructing 'Family.'" Pp. 210-25 in *Research and Reflexivity,* edited by F. Steier. London: Sage.

————. 1995. "Relationalizing Rapport in Interpersonal Settings." Pp. 155-70 in *Social Approaches to Communication,* edited by W. Leeds-Hurwitz. New York: Guilford.

Josselson, R. 1996. "On Writing Other People's Lives: Self-Analytic Reflections of a Narrative Researcher." Pp. 60-71 in *The Narrative Study of Lives,* Vol. 4, *Ethics and Process in the Narrative Study of Lives,* edited by R. Josselson. Thousand Oaks, CA: Sage.

Karp, D. A. 1996. *Speaking of Sadness: Depression, Disconnection, and the Meanings of Illness.* New York: Oxford University Press.

Kiesinger, C. 1992. "Writing It Down: Sisters, Food, Eating, and Body Image." Unpublished manuscript, University of South Florida, Tampa.

————. 1995. "Anorexic and Bulimic Lives: Making Sense of Food and Eating." Ph.D. dissertation, University of South Florida, Tampa.

————. 1998. "Portrait of an Anorexic Life." Pp. 115-36 in *Fiction and Social Research: By Ice or Fire,* edited by A. Banks and S. P. Banks. Walnut Creek, CA: AltaMira.

Kolker, A. 1996. "Thrown Overboard: The Human Costs of Health Care Rationing." Pp. 133-59 in *Composing Ethnography: Alternative Forms of Qualitative Writing*, edited by C. Ellis and A. P. Bochner. Walnut Creek, CA: AltaMira.

Kondo, D. K. 1990. *Crafting Selves: Power, Gender, and Discourses of Identity in a Japanese Workplace.* Chicago: University of Chicago Press,

Krieger, S. 1991. *Social Science and the Self: Personal Essays on an Art Form.* New Brunswick, NJ: Rutgers University Press.

———. 1996. *The Family Silver: Essays on Relationships among Women.* Berkeley: University of California Press.

Kulick, D. and M. Willson, eds. 1995. *Taboo: Sex, Identity, and Erotic Subjectivity in Anthropological Fieldwork.* London: Routledge.

Kvale, S. 1996. *InterViews: An Introduction to Qualitative Research Interviewing.* Thousand Oaks, CA: Sage.

Lagerwey, M. 1998. *Reading Auschwitz.* Walnut Creek, CA: AltaMira.

Langellier, K. and D. Hall. 1989. "Interviewing Women: A Phenomenological Approach to Feminist Communication Research." Pp. 193-220 in *Doing Research on Women's Communication*, edited by K. Carter and C. Spitzack. Norwood, NJ: Ablex.

Larson, C. L. 1997. "Re-presenting the Subject: Problems in Personal Narrative Inquiry." *International Journal of Qualitative Studies in Education* 10:455-70.

Lather, P. and C. Smithies. 1997. *Troubling the Angels: Women Living with HIV/AIDS.* Boulder, CO: Westview.

Lewin, E. and W. L. Leap. 1996. *Out in the Field: Reflections of Lesbian and Gay Anthropologists.* Urbana: University of Illinois Press.

Lewis, J. and B. Meredith. 1988. *Daughters Who Care: Daughters Caring for Mothers at Home.* London: Routledge & Kegan Paul.

Lieblich, A. 1996. "Some Unforeseen Outcomes of Conducting Narrative Research with People of One's Own Culture." Pp. 151-84 in *The Narrative Study of Lives,* Vol. 4, *Ethics and Process in the Narrative Study of Lives,* edited by R. Josselson. Thousand Oaks, CA: Sage.

Linden, R. R. 1993. *Making Stories, Making Selves: Feminist Reflections on the Holocaust.* Columbus: Ohio State University Press.

Macleod, V. A. 1999. " 'Getting It Off Our Chests': Living with Breast Cancer Survival." Ph.D. dissertation. Department of Interdisciplinary Education, University of South Florida, Tampa.

Maione, P. V. and R. J. Chenail. 1999. "Qualitative Inquiry in Psychotherapy: Research on the Common Factors." Pp. 57-88 in *The Heart and Soul of Change: The Role of Common Factors in Psychotherapy*, edited by M. A. Hubble, B. L. Duncan, and S. D. Miller. Washington, DC: American Psychological Association.

Markham, A. M. 1998. *Life Online: Researching Real Experience in Virtual Space.* Walnut Creek, CA: AltaMira.

Mies, M. 1983. "Toward a Methodology for Feminist Research." Pp. 117-39 in *Theories of Women's Studies*, edited by G. Bowles and R. Duelli Klein. New York: Routledge & Kegan Paul.

Miller, M. 1996. "Ethics and Understanding through Interrelationship: I and Thou in Dialogue." Pp. 129-47 in *The Narrative Study of Lives,* Vol. 4, *Ethics and Process in the Narrative Study of Lives,* edited by R. Josselson. Thousand Oaks, CA: Sage.

Mishler, E. G. 1986. *Research Interviewing: Context and Narrative.* Cambridge, MA: Harvard University Press.

Murphy, R. F. 1987. *The Body Silent.* New York: Holt.

Myerhoff, B. 1978. *Number Our Days.* New York: Simon & Schuster.

———. 1992. *Remembered Lives: The Work of Rituals, Storytelling, and Growing Older.* Ann Arbor: University of Michigan Press.

Mykhalovskiy, E. 1997. "Reconsidering Table Talk: Critical Thoughts on the Relationship between Sociology, Autobiography and Self-Indulgence." Pp. 229-51 in *Reflexivity and Voice,* edited by R. Hertz. Thousand Oaks, CA: Sage.

Oakley, A. 1981. "Interviewing Women: A Contradiction in Terms?" Pp. 30-61 in *Doing Feminist Research,* edited by H. Roberts. London: Routledge & Kegan Paul.

Ochberg, R. L. 1996. "Interpreting Life Stories." Pp. 97-113 in *The Narrative Study of Lives,* Vol. 4, *Ethics and Process in the Narrative Study of Lives,* edited by R. Josselson. Thousand Oaks, CA: Sage.

Pacanowsky, M. 1988. "Slouching towards Chicago: Fiction as Scholarly Writing." *Quarterly Journal of Speech* 74:453-68.

Paget, M. 1993. *A Complex Sorrow: Reflections on Cancer and an Abbreviated Life.* Philadelphia: Temple University Press.

Parry, A. 1991. "A Universe of Stories." *Family Process* 30:37-54.

Payne, D. 1996. "Autobiology." Pp. 49-75 in *Composing Ethnography: Alternative Forms of Qualitative Writing,* edited by C. Ellis and A. P. Bochner. Walnut Creek, CA: AltaMira.

Perry, J. 1996. "Writing the Self: Exploring the Stigma of Hearing Impairment." *Sociological Spectrum* 16:239-61.

Platt, J. 1981. "On Interviewing One's Peers." *British Journal of Sociology* 32:75-91.

Ponticelli, C. 1996. "The Spiritual Warfare of Exodus: A Postpositivist Research Adventure." *Qualitative Inquiry* 2:198-219.

Quinney, R. 1996. "Once My Father Traveled West to California." Pp. 349-74 in *Composing Ethnography: Alternative Forms of Qualitative Writing,* edited by C. Ellis and A. P. Bochner. Walnut Creek, CA: AltaMira.

Rabinow, P. 1977. *Reflections on Fieldwork in Morocco.* Berkeley: University of California Press.

Reinharz, S. 1992. *Feminist Methods in Social Research.* New York: Oxford University Press.

Renzetti, C. M. and R. M. Lee, eds. 1993. *Researching Sensitive Topics.* Newbury Park, CA: Sage.

Richardson, L. 1992. "The Consequences of Poetic Representation: Writing the Other, Rewriting the Self." Pp. 125-37 in *Investigating Subjectivity: Research on Lived Experience,* edited by C. Ellis and M. G. Flaherty. Newbury Park, CA: Sage.

———. 1994. "Writing: A Method of Inquiry." Pp. 516-29 in *Handbook of Qualitative Research,* edited by N. K. Denzin and Y. S. Lincoln. Thousand Oaks, CA: Sage.

———. 1997. *Fields of Play: Constructing an Academic Life.* New Brunswick, NJ: Rutgers University Press.

———. 1998 "Meta-Jeopardy." *Qualitative Inquiry* 4:464-68.

Richardson, L. and E. Lockridge. 1998. "Fiction and Ethnography: A Conversation." *Qualitative Inquiry* 4:328-37.

Riessman, C. K. 1987. "When Gender Is Not Enough: Women Interviewing Women." *Gender & Society* 1:172-207.

———. 1993. *Narrative Analysis.* Newbury Park, CA: Sage.

Roberts, H., ed. 1981. *Doing Feminist Research.* London: Routledge & Kegan Paul.

Robillard, A. B. 1997. "Communication Problems in the Intensive Care Unit." Pp. 252-64 in *Reflexivity and Voice,* edited by R. Hertz. Thousand Oaks, CA: Sage.

———. 1999. *Meaning of Disability: The Lived Experience of Paralysis.* Philadelphia: Temple University Press.

Romanoff, B. D. 2001. "Reclaiming Voice: Ethnographic Inquiry and Qualitative Research in a Postmodern Age." In *Meaning Reconstruction and the Experience of Loss,* edited by R. A. Neimeyer. Washington, DC: American Psychological Association.

Ronai, C. R. 1992. "The Reflexive Self through Narrative: A Night in the Life of an Erotic Dancer/Researcher." Pp. 102-24 in *Investigating Subjectivity: Research on Lived Experience,* edited by C. Ellis and M. G. Flaherty. Newbury Park, CA: Sage.

———. 1995. "Multiple Reflections of Child Sex Abuse: An Argument for a Layered Account." *Journal of Contemporary Ethnography* 23:395-426.

Rosaldo, R. 1989. *Culture and Truth: The Remaking of Social Analysis.* Boston: Beacon.

Rosenwald, G. 1996. "Making Whole: Method and Ethics in Mainstream and Narrative Psychology." Pp. 245-74 in *The Narrative Study of Lives,* Vol. 4, *Ethics and Process in the Narrative Study of Lives,* edited by R. Josselson. Thousand Oaks, CA: Sage.

Ross, J. L. and P. Geist. 1997. "Elation and Devastation: Women's Journeys through Pregnancy and Miscarriage." Pp. 167-84 in *Courage of Conviction: Women's Words, Women's Wisdom,* edited by L. A. M. Perry and P. Geist. Mountain View, CA: Mayfield.

Rothman, B. K. 1986. "Reflections: On Hard Work." *Qualitative Sociology* 9:48-53.

Satir, V. 1983. *Conjoint Family Therapy*. 3d ed. Palo Alto, CA: Science & Behavior.

Segura, D. 1989. "Chicana and Mexican Immigrant Women at Work: The Impact of Class, Race and Gender on Occupational Mobility." *Gender & Society* 3:37-52.

Shostak, A., ed. 1996. *Private Sociology: Unsparing Reflections, Uncommon Gains*. Dix Hills, NY: General Hall.

Stacey, J. 1988. "Can There Be a Feminist Ethnography?" *Women's Studies International Forum* 11:21-27.

Stanley, L. and S. Wise. 1983. " 'Back into the Personal'; or, Our Attempt to Construct 'Feminist Research.' " Pp. 20-62 in *Theories of Women's Studies,* edited by G. Bowles and R. Duelli Klein. London: Routledge & Kegan Paul.

Stringer, E. 1996. *Action Research: A Handbook for Practitioners*. Thousand Oaks, CA: Sage.

Suchman, L. and B. Jordan. 1992. "Validity and the Collaborative Construction of Meaning in Face-to-Face Surveys." Pp. 241-67 in *Questions about Questions: Inquiries into the Cognitive Bases of Surveys,* edited by J. M. Tanur. New York: Russell Sage Foundation.

Tillmann-Healy, L. M. 1996. "A Secret Life in a Culture of Thinness: Reflections on Body, Food, and Bulimia." Pp. 77-109 in *Composing Ethnography: Alternative Forms of Qualitative Writing,* edited by C. Ellis and A. P. Bochner. Walnut Creek, CA: AltaMira.

Tillmann-Healy, L. M. and C. Kiesinger. 2000. "Mirrors: Seeing Each Other and Ourselves Through Fieldwork." Pp. 81-108 in *The Emotional Nature of Qualitative Research*, edited by K. R. Gilbert. Boca Raton, FL: CRC.

Tripp, D. 1983. "Co-authorship and Negotiation: The Interview as Act of Creation." *Interchange* 14:32-45.

Trujillo, N. 1998. "In Search of Naunny's Grave." *Text and Performance Quarterly* 18:344-68.

Webb, C. 1984. "Feminist Methodology in Nursing Research." *Journal of Advanced Nursing* 9:249-56.

Williams, P. 1991. *The Alchemy of Race and Rights: Diary of a Law Professor*. Cambridge, MA: Harvard University Press.

Yerby, J. and W. Gourd. 1994. "Our Marriage/Their Marriage: Performing Reflexive Fieldwork." Presented at the annual Couch and Stone Symposium of the Society for the Study of Symbolic Interaction, University of Illinois, Urbana-Champagne.

Zola, I. K. 1982a. *Missing Pieces: A Chronicle of Living with a Disability*. Philadelphia: Temple University Press.

——. 1982b. *Ordinary Lives: Voices of Disability*. Watertown, MA: Applewood.

Part III

POETICS
AND POWER

10

POETIC REPRESENTATION OF INTERVIEWS

◆ **Laurel Richardson**

How we write has consequences for ourselves, our disciplines, and the publics we serve. *How* we are expected to write affects *what* we can write about; the form in which we write shapes the content. Prose is the form in which social researchers are expected to represent interview material. Prose, however, is simply a literary technique, a convention, and not the sole legitimate carrier of knowledge.

For the past 15 years, I have been exploring alternative forms of presenting research texts (see Richardson 1990, 1997). My purposes have been several: to examine how knowledge claims are constituted in scientific writing, to write more engaged sociology, and to reach diverse audiences. In this chapter, after briefly addressing some poststructuralist writing issues, I discuss one alternative way of conveying interview material: by means of poetic representation. I consider both the long narrative poem and the short poem (formerly called the lyric poem). Then I offer suggestions, for beginners especially, and some examples of poetic representation. I draw heavily upon my own work because I am most familiar with its construction.

My goal in this chapter is not to compare poetic representation with other evocative or mimetic forms, but to discuss the poetic form on its own terms as it relates to the representational issues under consideration. Consequently, the reader may find that some of what I say applies to other forms for presenting research material; I don't view this as problematic or distressing. I do not contend that poetic representation is the only or even the best way to represent all social research knowledge. But I do claim (a) that for some kinds of knowledge, poetic representation may be preferable to representation in prose, and (b) that poetic representation is a viable method for seeing beyond social scientific conventions and discursive practices, and therefore should be of interest to those concerned with epistemological issues and challenges.

◆ Poststructuralist Writing Issues

My theoretical position is that of poststructuralism. The core of that position is the doubt that any discourse has a privileged place, any method or theory a universal and general claim to authoritative knowledge. Truth claims are suspected of masking and serving particular interests in local, cultural, and political struggles. Wherever truth is claimed, so is power; the claim to truth is also a claim to power. Once the veil of privileged truth is lifted, the opportunities for addressing how we think, who can legitimately think, and what we can think are legion; with this comes the possibility of alternative representations of research material.

Language is a constitutive force, creating a particular view of reality (see Foucault 1978). This is as true of writing as it is of speaking, and as true of science as it is of poetry (see Haraway 1988). Producing "things" always involves value—what to produce, what to name the productions, and what the relationship between the producers and the named things will be. Writing "things" is no exception. Writing always involves what Roland Barthes calls "the ownership of the means of enunciation" (quoted in Shapiro 1985-86:195). A disclosure of writing practices is thus always a disclosure of forms of power (Derrida 1982). No textual staging is ever innocent in that regard, including this one.

Social science writing, like all other forms of writing, is a sociohistorical construction that depends upon literary devices such as narrative, metaphor, imagery, invocations to authority, and appeals to audiences, not just for adornment, but for cognitive meaning (Lakoff and Johnson 1980). The truth value of social science writing depends upon a deep epistemic code regarding how knowledge in general is figured. Imminent in this prefiguring are metaphors so entrenched and familiar that they do their partisan work in the guise of neutrality, passing as literal (Derrida 1982).

For example, the grammatical split between subject and object goes wholly unnoticed as metaphor for the separation of "real" subjects and objects, for "objectivity" and a static world fixed in time and space. The temporal and human practices that reified the objects are rendered invisible, irrelevant. The technical mechanisms of explanation are quarantined from the human processes of interpretation. The actual linguistic practices in which the researcher/writer is engaged are hidden, but they are not eradicated.

A deep and totally unnoticed trope used by social researchers is the reporting of interview material in prose. In writing this chapter, I myself am using the prose trope and will for the next several pages. Its conventions allow me to stage my arguments in ways that are familiar to the reader, which is my goal here. The reader is not distracted by a different genre, and I am aided in my argument by the invisible power inherent in the adoption of conventional writing. Those conventions are particularly helpful for the making of abstract arguments, which I am rhetorically interested in doing before I demonstrate violations of those conventions.

In the routine work of the interviewer, the interview is tape-recorded, transcribed as prose, and then cut, pasted, edited, trimmed, smoothed, and snipped, just as if it were a literary text—which it is, albeit usually without explicit acknowledgment or recognition as such by the researcher. Underlying this process is the belief that the purpose of the text is to convey information, as though information consists of facts or themes, notions that are taken to exist independent of the context in which they are articulated, as if the story the researcher has recorded, transcribed, edited, and rewritten as snippets is the true one: a "research" story. The use of standard writing conventions, including the use of prose, conceals the handprint of the researcher who produced the written text.

According to the oral historian Dennis Tedlock (1983), however, when people talk, whether as conversants, storytellers, informants, or interviewees, their speech is closer to poetry than it is to prose. Nobody talks in prose. For example, everybody, including so-called literate and nonliterate people, adults and children, male and female, speaks using a poetic device, the pause. Indeed, in American speech, estimates are that about half of the time we are speaking, we are not; we are pausing. And some 25 percent of these pauses cannot be explained by physiological needs for breath or grammatical demands for closure, such as is required at the ends of sentences or for clauses (Tedlock 1983:198). Unlike prose, poetry writes in the pauses through the conventions of line breaks, spaces between lines and between stanzas and sections, and for sounds of silence.

"Poems exist in the realm of making (mimesis) rather than of knowing or doing; they are representations of human experience . . . not speech uttered by, or speech acts performed by individuals who happen to be poets" (Borroff 1993:1032). That is, poems are consciously constructed to evoke emotion through literary devices such as sound patterns, rhythms, imagery, and page layout. Even if the prosodic mind resists, the body responds to poetry. It is *felt*. To paraphrase Robert Frost, poetry is the shortest emotional path between two people.

These understandings also map onto semiotics (Eco 1979; Manning and Cullum-Swan 1994). Semiotics is an approach to texts, such as interview transcriptions, that emphasizes the centrality of the reader in the interpretation of texts, including the researcher-reader of the transcript. Readers find and name meanings; they clump meanings together, creating categories and codes. In this respect, texts are always subject to multiple readings; no singular reading is definitive (see Gilgun 1999).

Constructing interview material as poems does not delude the researcher, listener, or readers into thinking that the one and only true story has been written, which is a temptation attached to the prose trope, especially in a research context. Rather, the facticity of the findings as constructed is ever present. Moreover, because the poetic form plays with connotative structures and literary devices to convey meaning, poetic representations have a greater likelihood of engaging readers in reflexive analyses of their own interpretive labor, as well as the researcher's interpretive labor in relation to the speaker's interpretive labor. The construction of text is thus positioned as joint, prismatic, open, and partial.

Poetry belongs to both written and oral traditions. It can be read silently, read aloud, or performed. Unlike conventional social science writing, poetry is welcome in diverse settings and can bring theoretic understandings to life for audiences as diverse as those found in poetry bars, theaters, policy-making settings, literary conventions, street scenes, and the mass media.

Poetic representation also may be used as one of the discursive practices within other oppositional paradigms whose goals are to challenge the power relationships inscribed through traditional writing practices. Gregory Ulmer's (1989, 1994) "mystory" is one such paradigm. A mystory is writing that juxtaposes personal narrative, popular culture, and scholarly discourses. Mystories are published in academic journals, yet they dethrone academic writing. They honor a journey of discovery, a process of meaning construction, not only about the subject but about the self. Private and public knowledges are interlaced, but the reader assembles the connections. The collage created from interview studies would be intensified should one of the mystories—the respondent's or the researcher's—be a poetic representation.

Writing is never innocent. Writing always inscribes. One can write in ways that reinscribe the discourses of academia and social science as the only legitimate form of knowledge, or one can write in ways that empower those whose "ideas and beliefs are not cast in the rhetoric of science" (Danforth 1997:104-5). The inscriptions of academic discourse are not harmless—

words hurt. Academic discourse names, categorizes, and constructs others in racist, masculinist, and colonial texts. Those who speak in "nonscience" voices are marginalized (Danforth 1997:105; P. Smith 1999: 246). Poetic representation offers social researchers an opportunity to write about, or with, people in ways that honor their speech styles, words, rhythms, and syntax.

◆ The Long and the Short of It

Poststructuralism proposes that systems of knowledge are narratively constructed. Traditionally, ethnographies, oral histories, social histories, biographies, and other qualitatively oriented research are constructed with fairly straightforward, obvious, and visible plotlines. The author intends that the reader gets "the" story. "The" story is understood as taking place within, or reflecting, a particular experience or culture. Writing in-depth interviews as a long narrative poem, while transgressing representational practices, also can cohere with the narrative traditions of qualitative research and in-depth interview reporting. It, too, aims to convey "the" story, but leaves this open to interpretation. Such transgressive writings reinscribe the possibility of "the" story, even as they challenge the format through which the story is told. The narrative structure is familiar and comprehensible, but urges the reader to unsettle the truths under consideration.

I constructed a long narrative poem, "Louisa May's Story of Her Life" (1992; the poem is reproduced in whole in the appendix to this chapter). The poem, which I have presented to different audiences, is about an unwed mother. Listening to the poem, introduced as a sociology poem, altered people's ways of hearing; boundaries were broken. Poets in these audiences theorized about the social construction of nor-

mality, genre boundaries, and authorship. Women's studies audiences theorized the poetry as a method for "demasculinizing" the production of social research. Culture studies audiences perceived a welcoming place for different cultural displays of, and claims to, knowledge. Oral historians saw this poetic representation as a method for capturing the "essence" lacking in their own reporting conventions. Folklorists saw it as another, legitimate, performance method. Social workers and policy makers claimed the poem altered their stereotypical thinking about unwed mothers.

When the goal of poetic representation is to re-present significant moments in lived experience, such as something epiphanous, the short poem and especially a sequence of short poems with an implied narrative works well. More than the long narrative poem, short poems focus and concretize emotions, feelings, and moods—the most private kind of feelings—in order to recreate moments of experience. The poem "shows" another person how it is to feel something.

Each short poem represents a candid photo, an episode, or an epiphany. People organize their sense of self around and through such epiphanous moments (Denzin 1989). Lived experiences are not primarily organized around the long biographical account, the epic poem, or the life history. Rather, people tell stories about *events* in their lives and the meanings of these events change through the invocation of different narratives. Not all events are stuffed into the same narrative. A life may indeed have a plotline, but not everything lived, or everything of significance to the person, fits neatly into a lengthy unfolding story. We are not characters. The points of our lives are not morals. Our lives are not even in-depth narratives.

Of course, cultures do provide prefabricated narratives that we use to assemble the events of our lives. As cultural studies and discourse analysis demonstrate, those narratives are multiple, contradictory, changing, and differentially available to us (Richardson 1988). But as agents in our own constructions, we artfully choose among available cultural stories and apply them to our experiences. We sometimes get stuck in an especially strong metanarrative, often operate with contradictory story lines, and sometimes seek plots that transgress the culturally condoned ones. Any or all of these processes through which the self is constructed and reconstructed may be going on simultaneously. A sequence of short poems can echo this complexity—the artful openness of the process and the shifting subjectivities by which we come to know and not to know ourselves, and then to know ourselves again, differently.

My own collection of poems titled "Nine Poems: Marriage and the Family" exemplifies this process (Richardson, 1994). Unlike in "Louisa May," in "Nine Poems" a narrative is only implied. Each of the nine poems is short, each is a mini-narrative, an episode, representing an emotionally and morally charged experience. The order of the poems implies a plot, but the spaces between the poems invite greater readerly response and interpretive work than would a long narrative poem. The nine poems could be reordered, implying yet different plots. Reversing the title and subsuming "Nine Poems" under the narrative rubric "Marriage and the Family" can imply a different metanarrative, the poetic co-construction of the two concepts "marriage" and "family," and a seeming relationship between them, "marriage *and* the family." The implied narrative would change again if, alternatively, "Nine Poems" were titled "Gender," "Maturing," "Socialization," "Treason," or "Paper Airplanes."

Constructing a series of short poems reflecting the chronological or thematic concerns of an interviewee can deepen the researcher's attachment to the interviewee and help the researcher see through preconceptions and biases. A series of alternatively arranged short poems offers the researcher the possibility of exploring other unexamined assumptions of interview representation, challenging accepted repre-

sentational conventions such as the "ideal typical" portrait and snippets linked by theme (see Richardson 1997).

Poetic representation can both cohere and conflict with normative writing. It offers opportunities for alternative expressions of people's lives as well as opportunities for critical attention to knowledge claims about them.

◆ Constructing Poetic Representations

As both ethnomethodology and deconstruction have made clear, there is no way to provide a complete list of "how-tos" and "not tos" regarding any human enterprise. I certainly would not want to try to provide such a list for poetic representation, which I view as a creative, emergent, changing form. What I would like to do instead, especially for the beginner, is to share some recommendations and practices that I and others have found useful in constructing poetic representations from interviews and interview experiences.

PRELIMINARIES FOR THE BEGINNER

If you are a beginning poet, my strongest recommendation is that you take a class in poetry, attend poetry workshops and poetry readings, join a poetry circle, read contemporary poetry, and peruse extensively the books in the Poets on Poetry series published by the University of Michigan Press. Learning poetry is like learning a second language. The more you immerse yourself in it, the better you can communicate within it. Learning to write poetry will not result in your unlearning your ability to write social science prose, any more than learning any second language undoes a person's proficiency in the first one.

Most contemporary poets consider three elements: sound, sight, and ideation. *Sound* refers to alliteration, assonance, rhythms, pauses, rhymes, and off-rhymes. Poems do not have to rhyme, and poems do not have to bounce (da-dah, da-dah, da-dah). *Sight* refers to images and imagery. This normally requires concrete language, similes, and metaphors that allow the reader to imagine what the poet is saying. *Ideation* is the feeling and thought behind, beneath, before, and after the poem—what the poet is trying to express. All the various poetic techniques are harnessed to support the communication of the idea at hand parsimoniously. Remind yourself:

> A line
> break does
> not
> a poem
> make.

And revise, revise, revise. During the revision process, it helps to read the poem aloud. Listen to someone else read the poem aloud. Put the poem away for a while. And then revise some more. Write different poems about the material. Work toward a series of portraits, different angles on the same interviewee.

Do not imagine that all poetic transcriptions are publishable. Many will be drafts, never finished, perhaps because these particular poetic representations never please you or perhaps because they have served their purpose of opening your mind to alternative interpretations. Many experienced poets stash their work for years because, as they realize later, it is preparatory; the material is not ready to be closed down.

And do not imagine that your work cannot be published. Most qualitative journals at this point accept poetic representation. Nor need you imagine, if you are a student, that your adviser will not approve of your work. There are many advisers today who are open to alternative forms of representation. Usually their questions stem from

their wanting to know about the "method" of representation and whether or not you can get a job. Refer them to this chapter or to the second edition of the *Handbook of Qualitative Research* (Denzin and Lincoln 2000). Supply them with copies of the respected journals that publish poetic representations, such as *Sociological Quarterly, Symbolic Interaction, American Anthropologist, Journal of Contemporary Ethnography, Journal of Aging Studies, Qualitative Inquiry, Qualitative Research, International Journal of Qualitative Research in Education, Qualitative Studies in Psychology, Qualitative Sociology, Waikato Journal of Education,* and *Text and Performance Quarterly,* among others. The research annuals *Studies in Symbolic Interaction* and *Cultural Studies* showcase evocative writing. Publishers such as AltaMira, Routledge, University of Chicago Press, University of Michigan Press, Indiana University Press, Temple University Press, and Sage Publications regularly feature works that include poetry. Entire conferences are devoted to experimentation in social research representation, such as the recent "Redesigning Ethnography" conference held at the University of Colorado and the Year 2000 Couch-Stone Symbolic Interaction Symposium.

A final suggestion is one you should implement early in the research process. Because poems (and prose, too) are more interesting if they include metaphoric language, construct your interview schedule in such a way as to elicit images and similes. For example, you might ask the interviewee something like, "If you could be any animal, what would it be? And why?" Language is enriched when you probe images and metaphors. Corrine Glesne (1997) actually asked and probed an interviewee about what metaphor would best describe her, which led to this stanza: "I would be a flying bird. / I want to move so fast / so I can see quickly, everything. / I wish I could look at the world / with the eyes of God, / to give strength to those that need" (p. 202).

A writer of poetic representation can have different, often overlapping, intentions; he or she may start with one goal and find that another takes over. That is often the case with creative activity. It is as if the writing had a mind of its own, strange as that may sound. (I think what happens is that the censorious left brain gives up, and the more playful right brain takes over, so to speak.)

One can write poetic representations in order to (a) fulfill as best as possible both traditional research and traditional poetic criteria, (b) express the sense of the whole or the essence of the experience as constructed by the interviewer, (c) transform normative discourse and actions, (d) relieve emotional pressure, or (e) some combination of the above—or, as always, (f) for other reasons. I illustrate and discuss some poetic representations below, but I encourage the reader to explore the wealth of poetic representations and discussions of them that are now available (e.g., Austin 1996; Baff 1997; Brady 1998; Ellis and Bochner 1996; Hones 1998; Jones 1998, 1999; Poindexter 1998; L. Richardson 1995, 1996, 1997, 1999a, 1999b; M. Richardson 1998, 1999; Rinehart 1997; B. Smith 1999; Sommerville 1999; St. Pierre 1997; Travisano 1998, 1999).

LOUISA MAY'S STORY

My goal in writing the long narrative poem "Louisa May's Story of Her Life" was to meet both scientific and poetic criteria. As part of a research project on unwed mothers, I completed a five-hour interview with "Louisa May" (a pseudonym), transcribed the tape into 36 pages of prose, and then shaped the transcript into a five-page poem. Following social research protocol, I used only Louisa May's words, tone, and diction, but relied upon poetic devices such as repetition, off-rhyme, sounds, meter, and pauses to convey her narrative. The speech style is Louisa May's, the words are hers, but the poetic representation, including the ordering of the material, are my own.

Below, I present an extract from the beginning of the transcript of Louisa May's interview. I invite the reader to contrast it with its poetic representation, which appears in its entirety in the appendix. The reader will note that I have taken liberties with the placement of words, but not with Louisa May's language or her sense-making process. In constructing the poem, I have depended also upon the tape itself, which recorded Louisa May's accent, pauses, tempo, and asides; these are missing in the extract. Further, because Louisa May returns again and again to the idea of "normal life" in her interview, I use that as the central theme of the poem, featuring poetically what was of chief importance to her as she described her life to me. The extract follows, with her many pauses noted as elipses.

> Well, most important to say in . . . terms of that is that I grew up in the South— which puts a definite stamp on what you think you are and what you think . . . you're going to be.
>
> [Louisa May looks at the tape recorder] I remember my origins when I hear . . . myself on tape—that Lady Bird kind of accent—and I think, "Oh my Lord. I'm from Tennessee." I had no idea I sounded like . . . that. In any event that [being Southern] shapes it and in . . . terms of . . . aspirations. I grew up in a very poor . . . with parents . . . who were uneducated but who lived in a very normal sort of . . . middle-class neighborhood where we rented a house. So my . . . friends were not in the same situation, but no one ever . . . suggested to me that anything might happen *with* my life. So . . . when I was 12, I suppose, and with my friends— and they . . . really, ah very nice, wonderful friends, some of whom I . . . still see. I remember thinking at the time that I would . . . want a large number of children.

Because scientific protocol usually requires information about the method of data collection, as the reader of the poem in the appendix will see, I constructed it to inscribe the interactional nature of the interview. Louisa May's responses were produced in a particular kind of speech context, which is the research interview. I am the implied listener throughout the poem. When Louisa May speaks to me, referring directly or indirectly to the interview process itself, her words are italicized. In that respect, the poem registers the interview conversation's research buttress, reminding the reader that this is the recording of a particular kind of speech performance.

How one talks and what one talks about is always circumscribed by the context in which speech unfolds. Louisa May's story arises in the context of an interview; the context is written into the poem. Because an interview is a jointly constructed text arising from the intersection of two subjectivities (see Mishler 1986), framing the findings as though they are independent of the method in which they were produced (a standard claims-making procedure of interview reporting) is falsifying and misleading. Framing the by-product as "results" tells the reader how the words were "found," ignoring how they were produced.

THE "ESSENCE" OF DOÑA JUANA

Another example is drawn from Corrine Glesne's (1997) "poetic transcriptions" of interviews with Doña Juana, an 86-year-old professor of education at the University of Puerto Rico. These "transcriptions" are short poems written to meet both literary and scientific criteria with the intention of constructing an "essence." Glesne began her analysis by sorting interview material thematically, reducing data and segregating thoughts. But then, rather than progressively coding and categorizing, she reread the words she coded under a particular theme and reflected on them, trying to "understand the essence" of Doña Juana's words (p. 206).

In the process, Glesne discovered that the theme she had constructed was connected to other themes, that the orderliness of the usual analytic process needed to be superseded by a freer movement through the transcript. She searched to illuminate "the wholeness and interconnections of thoughts" (p. 206). Like a scientist showing us a table or graph, moreover, Glesne provides an example of a transcript page with selected words underlined, which then appear in a first version of a poem, and then in a second, where Glesne has drawn from other parts of the interview and taken more license with word forms. We can judge the "validity" of the resulting poem, should we care to, but we probably would not, at least not in the usual terms, because the emotional pull of the poem dominates, as illustrated by the "flying bird" stanza quoted earlier.

TESS'S TEACHING STORY

A third example comes from a remarkable dissertation based on an interview study of teachers on the cusp of retirement. In the dissertation, Judy Erskine Lawton (1997) deploys a variety of alternative representations. Her goal is to represent as truly as possible the life experiences of the teachers and to honor their advice for making the transition out of teaching less stressful.

Lawton tells tells the teaching story of "Tess"—Trudy Plummer—through narrative and lyric poetry, some culled directly from interviews and some chosen from "symbolic representations" provided by Plummer for Lawton's analysis. Plummer and Lawton at times, become co-authors.

In the interview, Tess spoke like a poet, in images, metaphors, symbols, sounds, and sights. To write her interview as other than a poetic representation, I think, would have been a violation of Tess's sensibility, Tess's way of communicating her world.

Lawton recognizes the richness of Tess's language and capitalizes on it in both the construction and the discussion of Tess's story. For example, Tess envisions "the end of her career as the shadow of an umbrella, which Lawton describes as 'a vivid image conveying a shift from sunrise to sunset, a literal and symbolic awareness of a shadow at the end of a day, and maybe as Tess expressed it in symbolic representation . . . at the end of a life'" (p. 199).

Here is more of Tess's interview, this set to poetry that almost literally "pencils in" the minutiae of her classroom life.

Pencilling It In

The Schaefer is gone.
The gold-tipped Parker's
relegated to the drawer,
its decisive black
used only on checks.

The felt-tip is abandoned
as too indelible.

For a time the blue automatic pencil
shot words off its tip.
Now its occasional care and feeding,
its hardened eraser
are too much.
He has become a pencil person.
The Number Two is all he pockets.
Its yellow (eraser worn with indecision)
can be forgotten if dropped,
tapped to splinter
snapped in anger.

Light and hesitant, its words
make less and less impression,
weaken blurrily as they
reach the bottom
of a page
or a life.   (P. 189)

In the poem, Lawton enlists Tess's interview's central images as analytic guideposts—"the treadmill," "the downhill roller coaster," and "a hill to climb." Throughout her analysis, Lawton enlists Tess's metaphors as analytical guideposts, a truly remarkable blending of literary analysis with social scientific analysis; a socio-poetics that honors the interviewee and speaks to readers poetically and analytically.

FOOD TRUCK'S STORY

In an absolutely stunning long narrative poem, Phil Smith (1999) tells us the story of Food Truck, a 65-year-old developmentally disabled man who has been living for 40 years in Langdon, a facility for the "mentally retarded." Smith does not inform the reader of how he constructed the poem; he does not state that he wants to meet scientific and aesthetic criteria. What he does tell us, however, is that his journey into conventional scientific writing convinced him that an alternative representation was necessary to prevent his further harming Food Truck. Smith wanted his representation to be a "*nam shub,*" as he calls it, a Sumerian term meaning "speech with magical force" (Stephenson 1992:211). He wanted to write a *nam shub* that would change how people thought about and acted toward persons with developmental disabilities.

In seven sections covering 11 pages, Smith takes us on a journey into Food Truck's world. In the process, we learn how Food Truck looks and moves; his routines; his words for people, things, and events that matter to him; his complex emotional life; the struggles of both Food Truck and Smith to communicate with each other; and Smith's indebtedness to Food Truck for being his teacher. The descriptive grace is apparent from the opening words of the poem—"He looks me square in the face, square as a man can whose head doesn't/ ever stop bobbing and weaving, swooping and diving"—to the conclusion, which follows:

Food Truck looks up
he says quietly
in a voice falling apart
tumbling in on itself

Grandma's not feeling good
huge old man tears
flow out from his eyes

drip down his cheek
to make a small wet mark on his shirt.
All I can ever think to do
all I can ever do

is

rub

the back
of his
neck—

One surely cannot doubt that Smith engaged in ethnographic interviewing as an emotionally present witness to and advocate for Food Truck (see Behar 1996). Because Smith has mastered the sounds, sights, and images of poetic representation, we are taken into Langdon, walk in Food Truck's steps, take on his categories and words. We do all of this without judgment. We are changed by the writing; we feel differently about the developmentally disabled, the cultural narratives have been resisted. I believe this would not have happened if Smith had reported Food Truck's world in conventional social science writing, rather than in the *nam shub* that he did write.

CLAIRE PHILIP'S "LIFELINES"

In poststructuralist representational practice, not only are the interviewees subject to analysis, but so is the interviewer. A new genre and new specialty—the sociology of subjectivity—has emerged based on "interviews of the self" (Ellis and Flaherty 1992; Ellis 1991, 1995; Richardson 1992, 1994, 1997; St. Pierre 1997). Many of these self-interviews are published in prose or bricolage and are referred to as "auto-ethnography," but some are published as poems.

A moving example of the narrative of the self as poetic representation appears in social worker Claire E. Philip's (1995)

"Lifelines," which includes her journal and her poems. For eight years, Philip kept a journal that was focused on her living with cancer. The journal served as a creative and therapeutic resource, a safe place for dialoguing with herself, a venue for writing about the ethical and interactional consequences of "self-disclosures." Whom should she let know about the diagnosis and her impending death? What would be the consequences of revelation? Of concealment? She wrote to untangle her complex emotions and to help fellow therapists deal with the comparable realities of their lives. In Philip's words, "The journal changed me as the cancer changed me, but throughout, the inner self was constant, recognizable, and reachable. . . . Creativity within the self seeks to connect and in doing so, transforms" (p. 267).

Philip transformed some of her thoughts, interactions, and experiences into poems. Many of the poems arose from interactions and "interviews" with her oncologist. Reading the poems puts the reader into Philip's experiences, evokes compassion and anger, engages and teaches in ways that a research or clinical account— or even poems written by an ethnographer about someone else—would not. Two of Philip's "doctor/patient" poems follow.

Hair

I have spent the last week
In my hospital room
Tidying up fallen hair.
Something to do, anyway.
Doctor, don't say to me
Your wig looks nice.
Rather, say something like
I'll bet you can't wait
Until your hair grows back.
You could say the wig's okay, though.
(Dated 5/89) (P. 276)

Losing Faith

I tried to tell you how my husband holds
 his head
in his hands

and doesn't know it,
his despair more apparent each week.
Our shared stress ebbs and flows
while time
 moves forward
carrying us along. Bad or good,
test results will anchor this grief,
give it brief respite
 from uncertainty.
You sought to reassure, saying there's
 no proof yet
it's not working
or it is,
 implying his and my lack of faith
is perhaps premature.
You compare this to your wife's recent
 fear
during the storm
 that the electricity would go out.
It's not the same, doctor;
My husband worries his wife will
 go out.
     (Dated 8/93) (P. 300)

Because Philip's journal has been published along with her poems, we can trace how she constructed the poems from her "field notes." Following her example, we quickly realize that poetry can be found in our own research and personal journals. Poetry's task is to represent actual experiences—episodes, epiphanies, misfortunes, pleasures; to retell those experiences in such a way that others can experience and feel them. Poems, therefore, have the possibility of doing for social research what conventional social research representation cannot. Philip's "Lifelines" gives us a lifeline into methods for transforming field notes and personal notes into poetry that moves us.

◆ Conclusion

In literary writing and ethnographies of the self, the boundary line is personal; the boundary is between the foreign territory of one person's psyche and that of another.

The Other that is the foreign territory, the *terra exotica,* is the inner experience, the inner life of the writer. Writing about the self as both subject and object distances the self from the usual codifications of ethnographic interviewing, even while the writing points out how the self depends upon social and cultural discourses to "know" itself, to position itself.

Poems have the capability of reducing the distance between the "I" and the "Other," and between the "writing-I" and "experiencing-I" of the writer. It can move us to rethink the boundaries between ourselves and our work, help us to feel how our work might be situated within the self (Krieger 1991; see also Rosenblatt, Chapter 12, this volume).

The research self is not separable from the lived self. Who we are and what we can be, what we can study, and how we can write about what we study are all tied to how a knowledge system disciplines its members and claims authority over knowledge. Needed are concrete practices through which we can construct ourselves as ethical subjects engaged in ethical research, even if that means challenging the authority of a discipline's cherished modes of representation. Poetic representation is one such practice.

Self-reflexivity brings to consciousness some of the complex political and ideological agendas hidden in the controls exercised over how interview materials are represented. Minorities entering academia—including members of nonmajority ethnic, class, racial, and postcolonial groups, gays and lesbians, the physically challenged, and returning students—are often tied to traditions, cultures, and meaning making that are in opposition to the conventions and discourses of hegemonic disciplinary practices. These students find the option of poetic representation beckoning and supportive, as they do other representations that honor the arts as a legitimate path to knowing and expressing truths about lived experiences (see Ellis and Berger, Chapter 9, this volume). Science is one lens, creative arts another. Do we not see more deeply through two lenses?

Alternative representational methods create a welcoming space in which to build a community of diverse, socially engaged researchers in which everyone profits. This new research community could, through its theory, analytic practices, and diverse membership, reach beyond academia to teach us about social injustice and methods for alleviating it. Poetic representation, I submit, is a practical and powerful, indeed transforming, method for understanding the social, altering the self, and invigorating the research community that claims knowledge of our lives.

◆ *Appendix*

Louisa May's Story of Her Life

i

The most important thing
to say is that
I grew up in the South.
Being Southern shapes
aspirations shapes
what you think you are
and what you think you're going to be.

> (*When I hear myself, my Ladybird*
> kind of accent on tape. I think, "Oh Lord.
> You're from Tennessee.")

No one ever suggested to me
that anything
might happen *with* my life.

I grew up poor in a rented house
in a very normal sort of way
on a very normal sort of street
with some very nice middle-class friends
> (*Some still to this day*)
and so I thought I'd have a lot of children.

I lived outside.

Unhappy home. Stable family, till it fell apart.
The first divorce in Milfrount County.

So, that's how that was worked out.

ii

Well, one thing that happens
growing up in the South
is that you leave.   I
always knew I would
I would leave.

> (I don't know what to say . . .
> I don't know what's germane.)

My high school sweetheart and I married,
went north to college.
> I got pregnant and miscarried,
and I lost the child.
> (*As I see it now it was a marriage*
> situation which got increasingly horrendous
> where I was under the most stress
> and strain without any sense
> of how to extricate myself.)

It was purely chance
that I got a job here,
and Robert didn't.
I was mildly happy.

After 14 years of marriage,
That was the break.

We divorced.

A normal sort of life.

iii

So, the Doctor said, "You're pregnant."
I was 41.   John and I
had a happy kind of relationship,
not a serious one.
But beside himself with fear and anger,
awful, rageful, vengeful, horrid,
Jody May's father said,
"Get an Abortion."

I told him,
"I would never marry you.

I would never marry you.
I would never.

"I am going to have this child.
I am going to.
I am.   I am.

"Just Go Away!"

But he wouldn't. He painted the nursery.
He slept on the floor. He went to therapy.
We went to LaMaze.
> (We ceased having a sexual relationship
> directly
> after I had gotten pregnant and that has
> never again
> entered the situation.)

He lives 100 miles away now.
He visits every weekend.
He sleeps on the floor.
We all vacation together.
We go camping.

I am not interested in a split-family,
her father taking her on Sundays.
I'm not interested in doing so.

So, little Jody Mae always has had a situation
which is normal.

Mother—bless her—the word "married" never
crossed her lips.
> (I do resent mother's stroke. Other moth-
ers
> have their mother.)

So, it never occurs to me really that we are
unusual in any way.

No, our life really is very normal.
I own my house.
I live on a perfectly ordinary middle-class street.

So, that's the way that was worked out.

iv

She has his name. If she wasn't going to have a
father,
I thought she should have a father, so to speak.

We both adore her.
John says Jody Mae saved his life.

Oh, I do fear that something will change—

v

(Is this helpful?)

This is the happiest time in my life.

I am an entirely different person.

With no husband in the home there is less
tension.
And I'm not talking about abnormal families
here.
Just normal circumstances.
Everyone comes home tired.

I left the South a long time ago.
I had no idea how I would do it.

So, that's the way that worked out.

> (I've talked so much my throat hurts.)

■ *References*

Austin, D. A. 1996. "Kaleidoscope: The Same and Different." Pp. 206-30 in *Composing Ethnography: Alternative Forms of Qualitative Writing*, edited by C. Ellis and A. P. Bochner. Walnut Creek, CA: AltaMira.

Baff, S. J. 1997. "Realism and Naturalism and Dead Dudes: Talking about Literature in 11th-Grade English." *Qualitative Inquiry* 3:468-90.

Behar, R. 1996. *The Vulnerable Observer: Anthropology That Breaks Your Heart*. Boston: Beacon.

Borroff, M. 1993. "Cluster on the Poetic: From Euripides to Rich." *Publications of the Modern Language Association of America* 108:1032-35.

Brady, I. 1998. "A Gift of the Journey." *Qualitative Inquiry* 4:463-64.

Danforth, S. 1997. "On What Basis Hope? Modern Progress and Postmodern Possibilities." *Mental Retardation* 35:93-106.

Denzin, N. K. 1989. *Interpretive Interactionism*. Newbury Park, CA: Sage.

Denzin, N. K. and Y. S. Lincoln, eds. 2000. *Handbook of Qualitative Research*. 2d ed. Thousand Oaks, CA: Sage.

Derrida, J. 1982. *Margins of Philosophy.* Translated by A. Bass. Chicago: University of Chicago.

Eco, U. 1979. *A Theory of Semiotics.* Bloomington: Indiana University Press.

Ellis, C. 1991. "Sociological Introspection and Emotional Experience." *Symbolic Interaction* 14:23-50.

———. 1995. *Final Negotiations: A Story of Love, Loss, and Chronic Illness.* Philadelphia: Temple University Press.

Ellis, C. and A. P. Bochner, eds. 1996. *Composing Ethnography: Alternative Forms of Qualitative Writing.* Walnut Creek, CA: AltaMira.

Ellis, C. and M. G. Flaherty, eds. 1992. *Investigating Subjectivity: Research on Lived Experience.* Newbury Park, CA: Sage.

Foucault, M. 1978. *The History of Sexuality,* Vol. 1, *An Introduction.* Translated by R. Hurley. New York: Pantheon.

Gilgun, J. F. 1999. "Fingernails Painted Red: A Feminist, Semiotic Analysis of a 'Hot' Text." *Qualitative Inquiry* 5:181-207.

Glesne, C. E. 1997. "That Rare Feeling: Re-presenting Research through Poetic Transcription." *Qualitative Inquiry* 3:202-21.

Haraway, D. J. 1988. "Situated Knowledges: The Science Question in Feminism and the Privilege of Partial Perspective." *Feminist Studies* 14:575-99.

Hones, D. F. 1998. "Known in Part: The Transformational Power of Narrative Inquiry." *Qualitative Inquiry* 4:225-48.

Jones, S. H. 1998. "Kaleidoscope Notes: Writing Women's Music and Organizational Culture." *Qualitative Inquiry* 4:148-77.

———. 1999. "Torch." *Qualitative Inquiry* 5:280-304.

Krieger, S. 1991. *Social Science and the Self: Personal Essays on an Art Form.* New Brunswick, NJ: Rutgers University Press.

Lakoff, G. and M. Johnson. 1980. *Metaphors We Live By.* Chicago: University of Chicago Press.

Lawton, J. E. 1997. "Reconceptualizing a Horizontal Career Line: A Study of Seven Experienced Urban English Teachers Approaching Career End." Ph.D. dissertation, Ohio State University.

Manning, P. K. and B. Cullum-Swan. 1994. "Narrative, Content, and Semiotic Analysis." Pp. 463-77 in *Handbook of Qualitative Research,* edited by N. K. Denzin and Y. S. Lincoln. Thousand Oaks, CA: Sage.

Mishler, E. G. 1986. *Research Interviewing: Context and Narrative.* Cambridge, MA: Harvard University Press.

Philip, C. E. 1995. "Lifelines." *Journal of Aging Studies* 9:265-322.

Poindexter, C. C. 1998. "Poetry as Data Analysis: Honoring the Words of Research Participants." *Reflections: Narratives of Professional Helping* 4(3):22-25.

Richardson, L. 1988. "The Collective Story: Postmodernism and the Writing of Sociology." *Sociological Focus* 21:199-208.

———. 1990. *Writing Strategies: Reaching Diverse Audiences.* Newbury Park, CA: Sage.

———. 1992. "The Consequences of Poetic Representation: Writing the Other, Re-writing the Self." Pp. 125-37 in *Investigating Subjectivity: Research on Lived Experience,* edited by C. Ellis and M. G. Flaherty. Newbury Park, CA: Sage.

———. 1994. "Nine Poems: Marriage and the Family." *Journal of Contemporary Ethnography* 23:3-13.

———. 1995. "Vespers." *Chicago Review* 41:129-46.

———. 1996. "Educational Birds." *Journal of Contemporary Ethnography* 25:6-15.

———. 1997. *Fields of Play: Constructing an Academic Life.* New Brunswick, NJ: Rutgers University Press.

———. 1999a. "Dead Again in Berkeley." *Qualitative Inquiry* 5:141-44.

———. 1999b. "Feathers in Our Cap." *Journal of Contemporary Ethnography* 28:660-68.

Richardson, M. 1998. "Poetics in the Field and on the Page." *Qualitative Inquiry* 4:451-62.

———. 1999. "The Anthro in Cali." *Qualitative Inquiry* 5:563-65.

Rinehart, R. 1997. "Concatenations: Three Lives . . . to Be Continued." *Cultural Studies* 11:169-90.

St. Pierre, E. A. 1997. "Nomadic Inquiry in the Smooth Spaces of the Field: A Preface." *International Journal of Qualitative Studies in Education* 10:363-83.

Shapiro, M. 1985-86. "Metaphor in the Philosophy of the Social Sciences." *Cultural Critique* 2:191-214.

Smith, B. 1999. "The Abyss: Exploring Depression through a Narrative of the Self." *Qualitative Inquiry* 5:264-79.

Smith, P. 1999. "Food Truck's Party Hat." *Qualitative Inquiry* 5:244-61.

Sommerville, M. 1999. *Body/Landscape Journals.* Melbourne: Spinifex.

Stephenson, N. 1992. *Snow Crash.* New York: Bantam.

Tedlock, D. 1983. *The Spoken Word and the Work of Interpretation.* Philadelphia: University of Pennsylvania Press.

Travisano, R. 1998. "On Becoming Italian American: An Autobiography of an Ethnic Identity." *Qualitative Inquiry* 4:540-63.

———. 1999. "Kansas City Woman." *Qualitative Inquiry* 5:262-63.

Ulmer, G. L. 1989. *Teletheory: Grammatology in the Age of Video.* New York: Routledge.

———. 1994. *Heuretics: The Logic of Invention.* Baltimore: Johns Hopkins University Press.

11

ANALYTIC STRATEGIES
FOR ORAL HISTORY INTERVIEWS

◆ Richard Cándida Smith

Two understandings of the past confront each other across the tape recorder. In the encounter between scholar and informant, oral history interviews juxtapose the oldest and newest forms of historical method. For millennia, communities created and preserved their understanding of the past through spoken accounts passed entirely by word of mouth. No less today than in the past, people create and sustain a shared imaginative life wherever they gather and converse, be it at the kitchen table, the tavern counter, the street corner, the wedding reception, or the office lunchroom. Oral history interviews tap into a continuous outpouring of words that provide matrices defining both community and individual identity.[1] Informal collective modes of knowledge permeate the background of contemporary oral history

interviews, even though academic researchers conduct interviews primarily to collect firsthand testimony that may assist them in describing historical events or the experience of social processes. In the unusual exchange that occurs specifically for an oral history interview, collectively generated popular understandings of the past enter scholarly discourse in a verbatim record accessible for scholarly analysis.[2]

In this chapter, I explore how scholars have used narrative analysis to understand more fully the historical foundations of the personal experience documented in oral history interviews. I begin with Luisa Passerini's (1987b) now classic model of interviews as drawing upon preexisting oral cultural forms that translate historical processes into symbolically mediated experiences. In the second section, I discuss how scholars have explored tensions and contradictions within narrative structures as the starting points for their analyses. In conclusion, I look at efforts to rethink the ways in which memory encodes historical processes into experience and the consequent possibilities for oral history interviews to augment historical understanding.

In common with other types of evidence, interviews contain a mix of true and false, reliable and unreliable, verifiable and unverifiable information. Details of accounts can often be incorrect. Interviews may contradict each other, and, occasionally, interviewees provide inconsistent accounts in different interview situations. Researchers need to approach oral sources with cautious skepticism. A good starting point for evaluating the veracity of oral testimony can be found in Paul Thompson's (1988:240-41) extrapolation to interviews of three basic principles fundamental to all historical research: (a) Assess each interview for internal consistency; (b) cross-check information found in interviews with as many other published, oral, and archival sources as possible; and (c) read the interview with as wide a historical and theoretical understanding of relevant subjects as possible.[3]

Narrative analysis allows for a historical interpretation of interview-based source material that is not dependent upon the ultimate veracity of the accounts provided. Even if only tacitly expressed, explanatory assumptions affect every aspect of an interview, from the organization of the story line or the plot to the presentation of personalities and events, to patterns of factual errors, omissions, and contradictions. The stories that interviewees share provide insight into the narrative and symbolic frameworks they use to explain why things turned out as they did. The first step in using interviews to reconstruct links among personal experience, collective memory, and broad historical processes is to address the role of storytelling in popular consciousness.

◆ Popular Memory and Oral Narratives: The Translation of History into Experience

In approaching interviews, whether unearthed in the course of archival research or taped specifically for one's own project, making them speak intelligibly can initially prove a frustrating challenge. Confronting the transcripts of the 67 interviews that constituted the core set of sources for the study reported in her book *Fascism in Popular Memory*, Luisa Passerini (1987b:10-16) at first felt that there was an impassable gulf separating popular expression from scientific historical understanding. The interviews were full of anecdotes, irrelevancies, inaccuracies, contradictions, silences, and self-censorship, as well as out-and-out lies. The interviews contained plenty of colorful material, but the scattered recollections offered few immediately clear insights into the period or the effects of the fascist dictatorship on the lives of working-class Italians.

Passerini addressed her problem of making her interviews speak historically by doing some reading in anthropology and folklore. The perspectives she acquired helped her to think about how people use language to synthesize their experience into memorable images that make for interesting, often dramatic conversation. She looked for recurrent motifs in her interviews, many of which had documentable roots in Italian peasant folktales and folk songs. Everyday storytelling conventions might in themselves be historical evidence of past social relations.

Although the interviews were ostensibly firsthand testimony, personal experience dissolved into deeply rooted oral cultural forms that provided a ready set of stereotypes for structuring memories and filling them with meaning (see Narayan and George, Chapter 7, this volume). The interviews, Passerini concluded, provided evidence of how communities had talked about the past and arrived at collective conclusions as to what had happened to them all. With these insights, Passerini advanced a sophisticated reconstruction of recurrent patterns within her subjects' representations. Different interviewees used the same narrative structures to recount the stories of their lives, an understanding that syntagmatic analysis could decode. The same metaphors occurred across interviews, used to emphasize conclusions about the meanings of past events. The personalities narrators ascribed to themselves and to others involved stereotyped character traits. Through analysis of these and other paradigmatic elements, Passerini (1987b:1-4, 8-11, 51-52) focused on narrative forms present in all interviews and used to express judgments and relationships (see also Passerini 1988; Portelli 1991:1-26).

Passerini no longer viewed interviews as products of narrators' immediate, personal memories. They provided no privileged access to actual historical experiences. Without external supporting evidence, one could never be certain that even deeply emotional accounts were factual firsthand reports of events the interviewee had undergone. Narrators often borrowed available mythic forms to articulate emotional truths they had formed about their pasts. For all intents and purposes, the past disappeared into a narrative structure of plot turns and symbolic motifs that embedded speakers in a particular discursive community.

THE RECORD OF A CULTURAL FORM

The cornerstone of Passerini's (1987b) textual analysis is her definition of the oral history interview as the record of a cultural form. "When someone is asked for his life-story," she writes, "his memory draws on pre-existing storylines and ways of telling stories" (p. 8). Thus *memory,* as the term is used in the title of her book, is not a psychological category but the "transmission and elaboration of stories handed down and kept alive through small-scale social networks—stories which can be adapted every so often in a variety of social interactions, including the interview" (p. 19). Three critical elements follow from this definition:

1. Interviews are windows into collective thought processes; incidents and characters, even if presented in an individualized performative style, are conventionalized and shaped by a long history of responses to previous tellings.

2. Interviews draw upon a repertoire of oral-narrative sources that affect interviewees' selection of form and imagery; these sources include conversational storytelling, jokes, church sermons, political speeches, and testimonies given at Bible study groups and political party training schools.

3. Silences and other ruptures point to aspects of experience not fully mediated by group interpretation of past events.

The ideas, images, and linguistic strategies found in oral narratives constitute what Passerini (1987b) calls the "symbolic order of everyday life" (p. 67). What she means by this concept might be illustrated by an anecdote a woman factory worker recounted to Passerini about defending, in the years after World War II, her right to wear red overalls:

> [The management] asked me, "And is it because you like red or is it because you are a Communist?" I replied: "Because I like red, because I'm a Communist, because I wear what colour I like, and because G. doesn't give me overalls and I don't want to spend money on his account. Why haven't I the right to wear what colour I like?"

To which Passerini (1987b) comments, "The girl's reply summarises rather better than we could the multiplicity of meanings that a red outfit could assume in the daily struggle and balance of forces in the factory" (p. 106).

READING FOR
SYMBOLIC ORDER

Passerini argues that reading for the symbolic order of her interviews illuminates an otherwise invisible subjective experience of the fascist period. Her aim is a broader interpretation of subjectivity as a historical rather than a natural phenomenon. She demonstrates the conventionalized nature of narratives by comparing written and oral self-representations of workers. When picking up pen to write about their lives, working-class authors typically adopt the literary conventions of the classic novel. They focus their narratives on a process of education and growth, a movement that dramatizes the hero's increasing competence in handling life's challenges. Passerini's narrators, on the other hand, showed no growth but tended toward stereotypical, timeless, "fixed" identities that closely corresponded to age, gender, and skill levels. Women, for example, particularly those born before 1900, often presented themselves as "born rebels." Men, however, described themselves as capable workers with "instinctive" or "natural" know-how, a convention that preserved traditional patriarchal and artisanal virtues when such roles no longer had any direct relationship to actual working conditions.

Such stereotypes are neither self-deceptions nor reductive but ultimately valid representations of reality. Passerini (1987b) observes that many (although not all) women who characterized themselves as "born rebels" exhibited socially and politically conservative attitudes in their testimonies. The "rebel" self-appellation, she concludes, was part of a complex reaction to the radical changes industrialization brought to women's social roles:

> The stereotypical notion of "having the devil in her" justifies and explains certain innovative choices made in moments of crisis—the decision to marry without her father's permission, the wish to work in the factory even after the birth of her son, the call for a different division of labor in the house. (P. 28)

The "rebel woman" image, deriving from Italian folklore traditions about women's supposed propensity for sweeping away conventions, is what Passerini calls a "survival." Urban working-class women reworked the tradition and changed its content to fit the emotionally ambiguous and unsettling circumstances of their lives. The power of the image derived precisely from its not being "true." The symbol helped women narrate to each other their confusions over female identity in a changing society. Modern Italy remained oppressive of women but nonetheless demanded that they abandon stable relationships promising, even if not always delivering, reciprocal responsibilities within family relationships. A self-proclaimed character trait mitigated compulsory social transformations through an assumption of responsibility that, because it was inborn rather than acquired, evaded questions of choice and decision. The symbol allowed for the transmission of an awareness of oppression and a sense of otherness from the social order within which working-class women lived. It helped them develop an openness to change, which they nonetheless often resented, as they forged new lifeways for themselves. Self-representation necessarily involves an individual's acquiescence to the role his or her character plays in supporting group interpretations of historical events and processes (Passerini 1987b:27-28).

Stereotypical self-representations typically lend themselves more readily to humorous accounts than to tragic accounts of the past. Retelling anecdotes about individuals' lives is a form of entertainment in which the community can identify and interpret factors shaping life patterns. There is room for both tears and laughter, but humor is more likely to succeed in providing a satisfactory resolution to the tensions crystallized in an anecdote. In a collective storytelling situation, response shapes the way an individual comes to tell an oft-repeated story, causing him or her to drop those elements that elicit indifference or antagonism and sharpen those that promote good company.

Passerini recorded several brutal accounts of fascist terror, but her subjects spoke of life under fascism much more frequently with humor, laughter, and even joviality. The absurd posturing and venality of the regime loomed larger in their collective memory than its viciousness. Were the interviews evidence of a more benign image of fascism than that presented by other sources? Hardly. Behind the laughter, Passerini uncovered a complex of social and psychological forces that etched a darker picture.

Passerini notes that the humor in her interviews conducted in the 1970s, as well as that found in police documents from the 1930s, most frequently took the form of self-ridicule. One could interpret this recurrent feature as a marker of shame and guilt, as even an uneasy admission of complicity when daily life required some form of cooperation with the rulers of the nation. Passerini (1987b:125) observes, however, that although any form of antifascist statement was dangerous, police authorities were more likely to be lenient if a violator of public order appeared to be a drunk, playing the fool and making statements in jest. Police records show that verbal antifascism evaded judicial proceedings if it took the form of regression to childhood language and humor.

In analyzing working-class humor, Passerini did not look for hidden political meanings. She understood humor as at once a symptom of the regimentation of life under fascism and a sign of resistance to it. In the fascist period, popular culture was a substitute for politics. A sense of self distinct from that of the oppressor could be expressed through jokes and laughter instead of through political action. When the world situation changed and the Allied invasion precipitated the collapse of Mussolini's government, laughter could suddenly turn into actual resistance, fueling an armed political warfare that previously would have been futile. The hidden side of humor suddenly became visible. Laughter and self-ridicule had all along been weapons of struggle, preserving identity against a hated regime intent on eradicating the rights of individuals to have personal opinions, to reflect on their lives, or to make judgments of any kind about the state of the nation. Humor helped express working-class self-identity, as well as a sense of pride in having endured and survived to have the last laugh.

Passerini's observations on Italian women's resistance of fascist demographic policy illustrate her use of oral sources to reveal the intersection of historical processes and personal experience in the generation of new possibilities for self-understanding. The natalist policies of the fascist regime subjected women to constant propaganda praising large families as a sign of femininity. Mothers were offered significant material inducements to bear additional children. Passerini's (1987b:155) interviews reveal that this propaganda had some continuing subjective effect: Even antifascist women praised themselves as being "fertile" and dismissed their enemies as "barren."[4] Nonetheless, birthrates continued to decline, and the number of illegal abortions, the most widespread form of birth control, continued to rise among the working classes. One-third of the women interviewed acknowledged having had abortions in those years, and Passerini assumed that other women interviewed for the project must also have had abortions but did not want to discuss this aspect of their past.

How had these women learned about birth control, given that they lived in a culture in which the practice was universally condemned? Passerini could not find evidence of underground traditions passed from mother to daughter, nor did she find evidence of working-class women's having access to or knowledge of middle-class birth control methods. Knowledge about abortion apparently spread clandestinely through social networks contained within the community and the age group most concerned about pregnancy. The choice to have an abortion was difficult and involved a radical break with community traditions. All dominant ideological institutions—the Fascist and Communist Parties and the Catholic Church—equally condemned abortion. A woman arrested for ending a pregnancy faced heavy legal penalties, with little likelihood of sympathy or support from anyone. Even 40 years later, the subject remained painful for the women who elected to share this part of their experience, although they defended their choice as an effort to make their lives better than those of their mothers or grandmothers. Passerini (1987b) concludes that, to some degree, their understanding of past behavior was influenced by feminist ideas of the 1970s retrospectively projected onto their actions in the 1930s. Still, she argues, "the fact that the meaning of actions is perceived with the wisdom of hindsight, when they had not been so clear and conscious for our subjects in the past, does not diminish the importance of their intuition in the present" (p. 181).

This aspect of Passerini's analysis suggests a model for understanding the subjective ground of ideological change. The women had recognized a need so strong that they ignored both universal ideological condemnation and heavy legal penalties. This new behavior, conflicting with preexisting community values, made the women particularly receptive to new ideas, new values, and new ideologies that might justify what self-interest had said was necessity. A tentative process of ideological shift had begun documented by a retrospective effort to justify past transgressions that subsequently could be more broadly recognized as heroic.

LINKING PERSONAL AND HISTORICAL TIME

The conceptual tools Passerini chose are particularly suitable for reading contradictions in interview texts. Silences, self-censorship, lies and exaggerations, an overabundance of insignificant episodes told in minutest detail, the reworking of the past in terms that serve present-day interests—these offer rich sources for historical insight because such narrative blemishes indicate areas of conflict: The individual and the group could not arrive at a satisfying way of narrating painful or contentious events. Symbolic turns within a text link personal and historical time. All oral history interviews, Passerini (1987a) has written, involve

> decision-making about the relationship between the self and history, be it individual history or general. . . . The problem is [to determine] what forms the idea of historical time takes at different levels of abstraction and in various philosophical or daily conceptions; and in what ways the idea of historical time is connected with historical narration and self-representation. (P. 412)

Two different but subjectively undifferentiated conceptions of time alternate in interviews. These modes of temporal experience are markedly more complex than the common observation that interviews involve a retrospective reworking of past experience into terms meaningful for the present. Interviews include a linear conception of change, and interviewees feel obligated to explain differences between the present and the past. Spiraling around efforts to understand change by narrating its causes and effects, however, is a condition of atemporality, in which a "fixed" identity locates the speaker in an eternal present.

Passerini (1987a:420) argues that this combination reflects a desire to see change in the surrounding world but not in oneself, because recognition of personal temporality involves acceptance of death. The idea of personal time is inseparable from an idea of a tragic fate. A fixed identity is a narrative strategy, an imaginative leap that allows a speaker to talk about historical change and still repress confrontation with mortality.

Symbols fuse judgment of historical events with retreats into the imaginary. Analysis of the "symbolic order of everyday life" found in interviews allows historians to separate these two aspects of consciousness. Symbolization is the process that mediates the ongoing, continuous dislocation of the self between the real and the imaginary. Symbols through such mediation constitute subjective experience as both encounter and evasion of history. Reflection on individual historical experience takes on the forms of literary expression: Through metaphor and other verbal juxtapositions, interviews create their experience as symbolic expressions. In a particularly eloquent account, a woman told Passerini how the fascists administered castor oil to political opponents to humiliate them in front of their neighbors. She linked a number of distinct anecdotes about fascist terror by leaping from feces to menstrual blood to the blood of victims of politically motivated beatings. The connections between the episodes emerged in the narrator's metonymic stringing together of images linked by the transformation of bodily discharges. Feces, menstrual blood, and blood from beatings became symbols for each other, and the ensemble illuminated for Passerini a past emotion that continued to live through a linguistic, aesthetic device. Tracing the shifts among these three symbols, she argues that shame, vulnerability, and rage still defined her interviewee's subjective experience of the fascist years. Metaphorical leaps are seldom arbitrary, even when clumsy, misguided, or fabulous. Narrative figures refer the listener (and subsequently

the analyst) to an aspect of the speaker's mental representations that most clearly express her understanding of historical reality. Displaced meaning allows speakers to redescribe—in other words, reinterpret—experiences in ways that are more emotionally satisfying to them than usages that are more literal would allow.[5]

By focusing on oral narratives as cultural objects, Passerini shows that what one might dismiss as malapropism can be a key to reading oral texts. However, if metaphoric figures used by interviewees are never arbitrary, critical readings can easily be. Passerini locates the solution to this problem in the simple but fundamental observation that the structures of oral narratives arise to communicate ideas and feelings within a group. The narrative traditions of that group necessarily limit interpretations of figurative representations to what members of that group would likely find intelligible. Individuals push the boundary of sense at the risk of becoming incomprehensible. The guarantee that narrative structure must contribute to sense combines with the performative opportunities in every speech situation to generate a field of regularities and innovations vital to understanding the play of ideas within popular memory. Every interview contains within it a guide to the plotlines and symbolic structures of the interviewee's most important communities, as well as evidence of the social tensions narratives express and often displace. Passerini applied ethnographic and folkloric study of Italian working-class and peasant cultures along with psychological theory to decode the historically specific meaning of symbol systems used to narrate the experience of fascism. Underlying her method was a semiotic approach to language acts such as storytelling. Many scholars working with life history and oral history sources have found that before they can interpret the symbolic orders converting historical events into personal experience, they first need to analyze the narrative structures interviewees use to convey that experience.

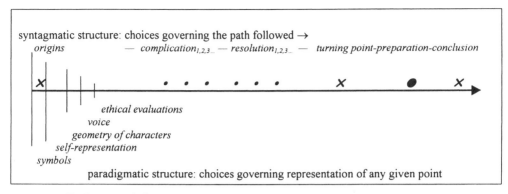

Figure 11.1. The Two Axes of Narratives

◆ *Syntagmatic and Paradigmatic Analysis: The Organization of Plot and Symbol*

Contemporary thought on narrative is structured by two contradictory ideas: Language is a set of rules that impose categories of knowledge upon speakers, but all performative acts are unique expressions that push against boundaries established by genre, content, or form of expression. Researchers undertaking analysis of the linguistic aspects of interviews begin by identifying regular verbal and narrative patterns, knowing that performance will never be precisely regular. This distinction parallels the relation of speech to language in the semiotic theories of Ferdinand de Saussure, who held that languages are best understood not as they are actually spoken but as ideal forms comprising regular value distinctions combined in predictable sets. These recurrent codings render historical forces into narrative symbols and meaningful explanatory narratives (Culler 1986; Gadet 1989; Harris 1988; Holland 1992).

Narratives have two axes. In Figure 11.1, syntagmatic structure appears as a horizontal arrow that represents the emplotted, temporal dimension of narration: how a story begins and what problem is posed, what complications mark change in the development of the problem, what the turning point is that makes the conclusion inevitable, how the story concludes, with what kind of resolution. Paradigmatic analysis focuses on recurrent images that can appear at any point in the story. It describes and explains symbolic vocabulary and the ways in which associational registers express both judgments and affective responses.

Both syntagmatic analysis and paradigmatic analysis look for coded regularities. Because these understandings expressed through regularities in the interview arise in communicative acts, repetition of storytelling motifs across interviews with different informants provides evidence of a shared construction of the past. Whether marked by individual variations or presented in a stereotyped form, narrative and symbolic structures tend to reappear in different interviews conducted in the same community. Recurrent images found in more than one interview reveal a storytelling language that provides a finite set of preferred expressive forms for the recollection of experience. Analysis of regularities across interviews can help define the boundaries of discursively defined communities—that is, of groups of people who may or may not know each other personally, but who are connected through shared languages (Joutard 1981; Joyner

1979; McMahan 1989:89-90; Tonkin 1992:97-112).

SYNTAGMATIC ANALYSIS

Syntagmatic analysis focuses on strategies of emplotment. Any story, whether a firsthand account of a specific event, a humorous anecdote, or a life history recounted across several sessions, must have a starting point, markers of transition, a turning point, and a conclusion. Emplotment involves the selection and highlighting of some events as most important. Other aspects may simply be dropped from the account altogether for the sake of narrative efficiency. Narrative form may also require the hypothetical construction of past events that may or may not have occurred but that the logic of the plotline demands. The conclusion determines that logic. Narratives are teleological, meaning that every story element flows from an effort to make the ending appear necessary and intelligible. Choices of significant details reveal "causes" that explain the inevitability of the conclusion. One may like the outcome or not, but narration enacts a process of coming to terms with the state of affairs that the narrator assumes characterize the conclusion.

One can find a clear example of syntagmatic analysis in Elliot G. Mishler's (1992) use of interviews to study career paths. Mishler categorizes an anecdote as articulating an "on-line" choice when the episode led to the narrator's taking another step toward his ultimate career goal. Even events that occur before the "turning point," the account in the story in which the narrator becomes aware of his goal, take their meaning from the conclusion. Complications and resolutions account for an accretion of factors that ultimately made the final status of the narrator inevitable. Mishler categorizes anecdotes about events that took the narrator away from his goal as "off-line" choices. The alternation of on-line and off-line choices develops dramatic

tension. Adjusting the tempo of alternation heightens or diminishes the tension by increasing or decreasing the feeling that a detour could have affected the ultimate outcome. Dramatic tension is a narrative effect, as the outcome, even if unknown to the audience, is pregiven. The sequence presents the factors that had to be addressed and the obstacles that had to be overcome for the outcome to occur. Interviews can be broken down into discrete sections, each of which is defined by its relation to the plot. Off-line choices present complications, whereas on-line choices present resolutions that allow the story to continue. The presentation of each episode underscores the "logic" of the outcome. Mishler's approach allows for analytic abstraction to replace a sequence of anecdotes with a structure of episodes, each articulating an important step in the movement to achieved identity (pp. 2-25, 28-33).

In Mishler's case study of a furniture craftsman, the outcome is satisfactory, and the story affirms the ability of the narrator to overcome his own confusions by taking a dramatic leap into a new line of work (see Table 11.1). Mishler identifies "intuition" as the causal factor the narrator uses to explain his ultimate ability to overcome a previous personal history determined more by chance events than by active decision making (see episode 7 in Table 11.1, the turning point). "Intuition" does not appear as a direct explanation in every episode, but each episode is presented in a way that supports the explanatory framework the interviewee has developed to explain his personal history. To understand a narrative is to have command of the rules governing the selection and ordering of events into a plot. The events that serve as plotting points are symbols in that they merge description with ethical evaluation. The evaluation appears to be the result of examining consequences, but it flows from the principles that narrators assume can and do provide explanation of the concluding point.

This distinctly conservative aspect of narration reconciles narrators (and their

Table 11.1   ACHIEVING A CRAFT IDENTITY: THE NARRATIVE OF AN
ARTIST-FURNITURE MAKER

Narrative Episode	Identity Narrative: Interview Excerpts
1. Origins	"My beginnings were in—uh I did a little bit of woodworking when I was a kid, mostly with wooden boats."
2. Complication$_1$	"I'm one of those people really vague about what I wanted to do. I—I entered—I got accepted to college as a chemical engineer, because I was interested in plastics at the time."
3. Resolution$_1$	"I decided I wanted to do something else. . . . I started in an undergraduate program as an architect."
4. Complication$_2$	"And ah after school I had a job for a while with a firm. ah The firm . . . collapsed. Folded. And uh I met an architect, and he and I decided to design some geodesic domes, and do that kind of thing."
5. Resolution$_2$	"And I met a third-generation craftsman in Indiana, who uh allowed me to share his shop space with—And ah that's when I really started to do woodworking. . . . But he just knew so much technically, and I learned an awful lot."
6. Complication$_3$	"I felt like I was wasting all my—my ah schooling as a landscape architect. So [we] moved [and] I started working as a landscape architect. And I did that for five and a half years."
7. Turning point	"And ah it just wasn't what I wanted to do for the rest of my life. . . . So I did a search, and uh decided to go to graduate school in furniture. . . . I made the—ah the decision to ah, go into furniture. Just in that I had an intuitive sense about woodworking, which I didn't about landscape architecture."
8. Preparation	"So three years altogether, totally investing myself in—in ah the furniture world as a craftsman. Got a—degree in crafts, .hh ah treating furniture as an art form."
9. Conclusion	"I started teaching . . . I collected more equipment and set up the shop here. . . . Started doing some shows and commission work, and that all went pretty well."

SOURCE: Adapted from Mishler (1992:29-31).

communities) to the patterns of change they have experienced. At times, however, the conclusion can be unbearable. Utopian aspiration refuses reconciliation and prompts a reconstruction of memory so that possibilities for change are accentuated. In his essays "The Death of Luigi Trastulli: Memory and the Event" and "Uchronic Dreams: Working-Class Memory and Possible Worlds," Alessandro Portelli (1991:1-26, 99-116) analyzes patterns of narrative reconfiguration he found in interviews with working-class residents of Terni, Italy. Their reconstructions of the past were factually wrong. Their accounts merged or scrambled events and at times referred to events that never occurred. In effect, their collective stories had created an alternative chronology that allowed them to maintain their own historical experience.

Portelli argues that chronological inaccuracy in the narrative helped the community maintain a sense of continuing to have a future and retaining the possibility of political resurgence during a time of retreat. Notwithstanding modernization of economic structures, the growth of educational opportunities, and a growing differentiation occurring as a result of individuals' differing personal responses to a changing society, the community maintained its political cohesion. Portelli's analysis suggests that the community's ability to maintain identity rested on a utopian, historically inaccurate, but culturally effective myth of the past. The narratives kept alive an alternative future that preserved for several decades the possibility of independent, worker-based action, even if, for the most part, members of the community were actively participating in the reconstruction of Italian society around international markets.

Disjunction between discursive and pragmatic behavior may be quite widespread and could provide insight into discrepancies in the political, economic, social, and cultural actions of social groups. The disjunction between subjective and objective factors in social relationships is an area for which oral history documents provide ideal sources of evidence. Paul Ricoeur's (1983:52-87) model of threefold mimesis may help researchers to see how individual textual configurations (mimesis$_2$) found in oral history interviews intersect with collective processes of prefiguration (mimesis$_1$) and refiguration (mimesis$_3$). *Prefiguration* refers to the metaphorical transpositions that are normally available and allowed in a community, which for these purposes we can define as a group built around regularly shared communicative acts. *Refiguration* refers to the process of reconstruction of texts into experiences of meaning. In simplified terms, prefigured time (ideology) becomes refigured time (experience) through the mediation of configured time (narrative accounts).

Prefiguration sets limits as to what will be a refigurable text—that is, one that potential audiences will accept as meaningful. Nonetheless, prefigurative conventions do not predetermine the shape of any configured text. Texts are propositions that members of a community put forward to each other. Texts must convince others that the narration accounts for what a group accepts as fact. Texts prove their aptness as explanations by providing satisfying understandings of the present and by identifying key events that others will accept as suitable evidence for the conclusion proffered (Ricoeur 1973).

As individual performances of collective prefigurations circulate with varying degrees of success, ideology becomes a fluid part of individual lives and social relations. Accepted narratives create a temporal world within which people have "experiences" that they can continue to share; that is, they have a sense of actions that remain meaningful and related logically to conclusions understood as "necessary" or, less strongly, "probable." Action may not necessarily be dependent upon narrative explanations available to a group, but stories that people exchange and accept as satisfying help establish a sense of proper, effective action, which can then be configured into new narratives. The truth of narratives rests on their ability to instigate and sustain new action. One of the values of examining how oral history interviews emplot explanatory frameworks is the degree to which they can point researchers to preferred actions as well as to likely blockages, clues that will assist with the identification and reading of other sources.

PARADIGMATIC ANALYSIS

Paradigmatic analysis complements the study of emplotment by examining recurrent symbols and other expressive motifs that are the basic constructive units of narrative flow. Oral accounts in particular tend to synthesize complex series of events into readily comprehensible and expressible images. Symbols take their place within stories as instantiations of narrative logic (Allen 1982; Ashplant 1998; McMahan 1989:100-105; Tonkin 1992:126-30). For example, in my work on interviews recorded with painters in California (Cándida Smith 1989, 1995), I found that the special quality of light and climate in the state was a recurrent symbolic motif. Interviewees used the image to articulate a special condition that shaped their work and set them apart from painters in other parts of the world. The motif appeared to the interviewees as an indubitable natural fact that explained the particularities of painting in the region. In fact, the symbol as deployed in narratives had little to do with nature but appeared typically when interviewees wanted to encapsulate their sometimes pleasant, sometimes difficult relationship to society into a ready metaphor. In one interview recorded over several sessions, the narrator described California light as clarifying and liberatory to underscore the freedom he felt when he began painting and exhibiting. Several sessions later, he described California light as blinding and stultifying as he discussed a point when his career had reached a dead end. In either case, light was not a physical phenomenon but a symbolic displacement of professional self-representation. The value that the symbol expressed depended in both cases upon its location within a narrative plotline and the conclusion it had to reinforce (Cándida Smith 1989:3-4).

Symbols often appear in patterned relationships. Women painters in post-World War II California, for example, often found as they struggled to establish their careers that critics couched favorable reviews in highly sexualized terms. Joan Brown was "everybody's darling," according to one writer, who proceeded to describe her as a talented, energetic "receptacle of attitudes" for the "germinating" ideas of her (male) teachers. In the several oral history interviews conducted with Brown over a 30-year period, she alternated two distinctive voices as she recounted her life story. One voice used humorous hyperbole to accentuate the surreality of commerce and business and those who live within that world. This inflection drew a veil across painful elements of her life by rendering them into sharp, quick, brittle images designed to shock and get a laugh. The other voice used more expansive, philosophical language to express the wonder and excitement that a once young woman felt embarking on her career. Painting was explicitly a symbol for a journey of initiation that would ultimately result in wisdom and inner peace.

Brown never recursively marked the transition between these two voices. Her vocabulary and sentence structures changed unself-consciously as she went back and forth between the two modes of her career. She was, however, quite aware of a double self-representation that enacted her response to the sexualization of herself and her art. She used archly stereotypical sexual imagery to portray herself in interaction with the absurd world of career building. She presented herself as a compulsive liar who used dress and appearance to make fools of people she encountered. This mendacious, opportunistic character appeared in her accounts as a person who drank too much, participated in parties to excess, and let herself be carried to unspecified extremes by others. Opposed to a gendered, sexualized conception of self, another voice called within the interviews, invoking the deeper reality of an initiate who survived spiritually through recurrent journeys into the alternative worlds that painting realized for her. This self-consciously degendered self-representation gave her strength to stand her ground and make difficult practical career decisions that alienated critics, curators, and gallery owners (Cándida Smith 1995:172-89).

The recurrence of paradigmatic motifs across interviews and their structural logic suggests that they are not simply individual performative expressions. They help articulate the logic of a communication by stressing the justice of a conclusion. Self-representation is a privileged symbolic feature of oral narrations because it articulates the moral position that the speaker has taken on the turning point and its consequences. Eva M. McMahan (1989), building on the theoretical work of Livia Polanyi (1985), argues that the framing of a speaker's evaluative conclusions is particularly strong in oral narratives as they establish the relationship between speaker and listeners. McMahan (1989) states that

> the teller must constantly address the implicit evaluative response of the listener: "So what?" The teller must show that the story is both topical and meaningful—that it makes a point. Generally, the interviewee as storyteller is expected to "(a) tell a topically coherent story; (b) tell a narratable story— one worth building a prolonged telling around; (c) introduce the story so that the connection with previous talk is clear; (d) tell a story that begins at the beginning, that is, one in which time moves ahead reasonably smoothly except for flashbacks that seem to serve a justifiable purpose in the telling; and, (e) evaluate states and events so that it is possible to recover the core of the story and thereby infer the point being made through telling." (Pp. 80-82; McMahan quotes Polanyi 1985:200)

In oral accounts, bracketing sections are frequently introduced so that the narrator can comment explicitly on the ethical meaning of the story, just in case listeners do not quite intuit how to feel the symbols. The narrator may elicit responses from listeners, often by asking questions. By the end of the story, as the conclusion becomes inevitable, McMahan argues, ethical evaluation begins to merge with self-representation. How listeners respond to the story determines how they respond to the storyteller, and through the account an ethical relationship has been proposed, if not established (pp. 89-92, 93-96).

Just as emplotment can lead to a re-imagination and reordering of events to strengthen the inevitability of the conclusion, paradigmatic elements may be reworked to strengthen the moral evaluation and consequently the subject position that the storyteller takes in relation to his or her listeners. Mariano Vallejo, in his testimonial collected in 1874 for Hubert Bancroft's multivolume history of California, discussed at length a meeting he claimed took place in 1846, on the eve of the American invasion of Mexico. Subsequent historians have largely dismissed Vallejo's account as legendary and in the process missed the vital political content his possible fabulation conveys. As war loomed, Californio leaders convened to discuss their options. Nominally, they were citizens of Mexico, but since a local revolution in 1836, California had been for all practical purposes autonomous of the central government. Vallejo's story condensed a series of debates that occurred within Californio society over many years into the arguments of one evening. As Rosaura Sánchez (1995) has analyzed the anecdote, the participants in the debate represented four positions. Spokesmen for a liberal, federalist, republican future opposed those who were promonarchist. Liberals were evenly divided between those who favored immediate independence and those, like Vallejo, who sought annexation to the United States. The monarchists were divided between those who wanted British annexation and those who sought French intervention. The characters presented in the anecdote articulate a geometry of political positions. Whether or not the meeting actually occurred, the characters were paradigmatic inventions that allowed the speaker to articulate his evaluation of the meeting and its ultimate consequences.

Throughout his account, Vallejo editorialized on the strengths and weaknesses of each position. He linked the arguments to several practical issues for Californio society, such as trade and property regimes, while he ignored other issues entirely, such as slavery and implications for relations with the indigenous peoples. Vallejo's anecdote, however symbolic, articulated in crystalline form the competing ideological positions of his people in 1846 while explaining the political strategies that he and others followed. He defended his support for annexation to the United States by articulating his understanding of the American Revolution of 1776 and its, to his mind, still-universal promises of freedom, equality, and due process of law. He structured his account largely to convince his listeners, primarily the Anglo-American readers who would encounter him either directly in the transcript of his interview or indirectly through Bancroft's history, of their hypocrisy. His overall testimonial builds around his protest of the theft of the Californios' property and their political marginalization. American expansion had in fact betrayed the hopes that Vallejo and others had felt 30 years earlier. He wanted to convince his listeners that the outcome might have been very different had the Californios adopted policies opposed to annexation by the United States. Vallejo's account, motivated by moral fervor and foregrounding political and ideological choices of his people, still provides an important corrective to accounts that present westward expansion as a story with only American actors (Sánchez 1995:245-48).

◆ Recuperating Experience Back into History

In the context of narrative analysis, the "data" of interviews are first and foremost the ways in which a person has reconstructed the past to negotiate an ever-fluid process of identity construction. The subjective position in narration differs from psychological consciousness in its exterior manifestation and the element of self-reflective purpose. Vallejo's interview unfolds as a conscious effort to speak through his interviewers to a broad public. Although this is not uncommon, particularly in interviews with elite figures, many interviews remain within the local, intimate historical contexts that stories shared between friends help establish. In a world of close acquaintances, anecdotes convey possibly useful impressions about what individuals

might expect in future encounters. The cues are couched in explanations that, however trivial in form, remove arbitrariness from the relationship. Fred will flame you at the least provocation because "he's always like that." Characterization in this case is more of a predication than an explanation, but it serves to warn those who must or might be exposed to Fred of what to expect (Cándida Smith 1995:xxi-xxvi; Clark, Hyde, and McMahan 1980; Frank 1979; Halbwachs 1993:38; Thompson 1988:150-65).

In reading emplotment and paradigm codes, scholars often must assign meanings and values to these images that they may not have had in their original context in order to make them speak to a broader historical context. Isabelle Bertaux-Wiame (1982:192-93), for example, analyzed interviews with migrants from the countryside into Paris and found recurrent patterns in the choices of pronouns used by the interviewees. Men typically used first-person singular forms to speak of themselves as actors making decisions and changing their lives and those of their families. Women, on the other hand, tended to avoid first-person singular forms and to speak more usually either with first-person plural forms or with the impersonal third-person pronoun *on* (one). This observation allowed Bertaux-Wiame to develop a rich psychological argument about gendered conceptions of power and historical action prevalent among the French working class at a particular historical conjuncture. She readily acknowledges that her categories would seem irrelevant and foreign to the narrators whose accounts stimulated her insight. Many historians might likewise question the validity of her interpretation. Gendered selection of pronouns became meaningful because Bertaux-Wiame turned to feminist theory for assistance in reading "data" that would otherwise be ignored. Interpersonal relations symbolized through the selection of pronouns would likely not register as relevant to the study of larger transpersonal social forces without a theoretical perspective that reread intimate interactions as dialectically constituted with political and economic structures.

The distinction between psychological consciousness and narrative self is foundational to the examination of regularities, whether syntagmatic or paradigmatic, within interviews. The narrative self takes shape in the unfolding stories within which it is deployed as one of several codes. Changes in self-representation do not provide evidence in and of themselves about how people "felt." Such studies trace instead how understandings of the self have grown from and altered in relation to other social and cultural phenomena *also* represented within a narrative.

Symbolic contradictions within narrative texts indicate areas of conflict about how to represent and understand the past. The storyteller and his or her group could not arrive at a satisfying way of narrating painful or contentious events, so they deflected issues into a variety of evasive symbolic strategies. Isolation of contradictory, confused, and evasive elements within a narrative has served historical analysis by highlighting areas of concern that communities have not been able to resolve narratively. Analysis presents a field of symbolic measures that in and of themselves are subject to multiple interpretations, but these areas of contention themselves reveal places for further historical contextualization and exploration. Careful analysis of the subject positions contained within these symbols in particular can elucidate a pattern of self-imagining that includes perceptions of the dangers that "others" pose (Passerini 1987a).

Conflicts between identity and subjectivity may be a recurrent paradigmatic feature in interviews. The challenge of reconciling differences between the subject position assigned a person due to his or her social classification with a more complex, varied sense of relationships may reveal itself at the paradigmatic level through such measures as Joan Brown's double self-representation. The challenge may also appear in performative tensions that undercut a narrator's ability to articulate either a clear ethical evaluation or a clear self-representation.

Feminist scholars in particular have worked with contradictions in self-representation to identify the translation of gendered power structures into historically situated experience of gender relations. Women's accounts of their lives negotiate, as Joan Brown's does with great elegance, the discrepancy between the self-image they have developed in the course of their everyday activities and the images of themselves that they receive from men. Kathryn Anderson and Dana C. Jack (1991) argue that women's oral history interviews usually have two channels working simultaneously across the episodes narrated. On the one hand, many women may tell their stories using dominant, masculinist emplotment and paradigmatic codes. They enunciate through the selection of complications, resolutions, turning point, and conclusion, as well as through the symbols used, concepts and values that affirm male supremacy, and the appropriateness of women's reduced social position. Within the performance, however, there may be a muted story that expresses painful disappointments and resentments as a set of ironies that suggest the purely fictional character of dominant values. Anderson and Jack advise that interviewers and analysts should focus on difficult choices that women have had to make in their lives, much as Passerini did when probing for information on birth control and abortion. They also advise paying careful attention to expressions of pain and subjects that address the margins of acceptable behavior, particularly feelings and behaviors that the interviewees themselves identify as "unwomanly." Stereotypes about women invoked in the interview provide the analyst with an opportunity to see efforts to reconcile derogatory images with an interviewee's positive self-images. In these areas, narrative structures will be less likely to effect a comfortable ethical evaluation that reconciles the interviewee and her listeners to the inevitability of the conclusion. Anecdotes and images that women use to address their weakness in a situation often lead to a layering of codes conveying the storyteller's intellectual and emotional conflict. In these situations, logic collapses and the storyteller abruptly tacks on a conclusion to a story that was headed in another direction. A pat ending realigns her account with dominant values in her community but does so in a way that signals an experience of tensions (see also Borland 1991; Passerini 1987b:138-49).

Catherine Kohler Riessman (1992), in her work on women's accounts of abusive marriages, has observed critical differences in how women relate stories of victimization and stories of resistance. At the beginning of the 1980s, stories about marital rape were difficult to narrate, in part because the term itself did not yet have currency. Neither laws nor social custom recognized a wife's right to refuse sexual relations with her husband. As a political movement developed to demand legal change, new narrative structures emerged that helped women transform brutal facts in their lives into communicable experience. In seeking security and the right to divorce, abused women learned to speak to each other, to counselors, and to lawmakers. A shared language allowed for crisp, articulate stories in which the pain endured was coded typically in inflections of speech patterns, such as the introduction of unusually long pauses. Stories of resistance typically became less articulate when self-defense was angry or violent. Not even the women involved were sure that their efforts to protect themselves from further abuse were ethical. Riessman (1992) observes that the language structures surrounding abusive marriages provide "for women's depressed emotions but not for their rage" (p. 246). Consequently, narration of anger is more episodic and confused, as if the storyteller herself had to struggle to understand her emotions and

actions, which are ostensibly out of character for a "good" woman. A political movement had succeeded by establishing one emplotment code, which then blocked positive reception of alternative narratives arriving at conclusions less consonant with the nobility of victimhood.

Emplotment structures as well as symbolic motifs established in one discourse are then available for use in other situations. Work on narrative plotlines, and the subject positions they entail, allows for analysis of individual narrating style. William R. Earnest (1992) has examined the relation of workplace narratives to typical patterns for the interviewee's life story. In an interview with an employee in an automobile factory, Earnest noticed a syntagmatic pattern that recurred across several sessions. A grievance about work conditions in the factory welled up with considerable bitterness, but then the issues in dispute found resolution through a pattern of "self-effacement, criticism of other workers, sympathy for management rationales, and then final absolution of management" of any responsibility for the problem (pp. 257-58). When the questioning turned to family background and personal life, Earnest heard the same syntagmatic pattern applied to the interviewee's relationship with his father. Whenever anger at paternal neglect flared up, the interviewee's story line displaced his rage into criticism of others in the family. Family stories paralleled workplace stories by concluding with the interviewee's acceptance of his father's rationales and affirmation of father-son identity. The interviewee was unconscious of this storytelling pattern. When told of it, he was surprised and doubtful, but he accepted the validity of the conclusion when shown the evidence. Confronting his experience as a narrative effect jolted him into reexamining his memories and his organization of his recollections into discrete episodes directing him to preordained conclusions. The interviewee was thrown out of experience into a historical reconsideration of how he had come to form his social relationships.

His self-reexamination began with his examination of the points in his narratives where he felt the most tension. The movement toward reevaluating the codes he used to create meaning arose, according to George Rosenwald's (1992) analysis of this case, from a conflict between identity and subjectivity that the interview process brought to the surface. Rosenwald contends that the culture-specific narrative rules ensuring intelligibility also govern identity. In opposition to the relatively stable and stabilizing patterns of self that arise as one talks in ways that are comprehensible to others, Rosenwald poses the force of subjectivity, which he defines as the "restlessness of desire" (p. 265). Recursive recognition of the rules of narration can allow normally repressed imagination of other ways of being to enter into the storytelling process.

The introduction of such self-reflection into oral history interviews is not common—at least not as a conscious aim of the interviewer and the narrator. Portelli (1997), however, in his recent work on genre in oral history, suggests that the encounter of historian and interviewee, each with such different strategies for understanding the past, must inevitably generate cognitive tension. One way interviewers have coped with this has been by effacing themselves and allowing narrators to tell their stories with a minimum of response or guidance. That strategy imposes highly artificial requirements upon dialogic exchanges. No matter how silent interviewers strive to be, they are not invisible, and the interview situation, although drawing upon narrative repertoires that interviewees have developed, has little in common with everyday conversation.

"What is spoken in a typical oral history interview has usually never been told *in that form* before," Portelli (1997:4) argues. Even if interviewees rely upon twice-told tales to answer questions posed to them, they have usually never previously strung their stories together in a single, extended account. Narrators are also aware, like Mariano Vallejo, that they speak through their interviewers to a larger audience. Portelli notes that this leap into an imagined public realm often involves a marked change in diction. Interviewees begin to speak in a formally correct style. Even more important, Portelli adds, "the novelty of the situation and the effort at diction accentuate a feature of all oral discourse—that of being a 'text' in the making, which includes its own drafts, preparatory materials, and discarded materials" (p. 5). The task that the narrator faces is new and not reducible to the rules of everyday conversation, even if words and anecdotes spring largely or exclusively from that source.

What distinguishes oral history from folklore, Portelli (1997) claims, is the move away from "storytelling," from the sharing of familiar accounts with workmates, friends, and family that help bind them together into communities. Narrators discover a genre of discourse that Portelli calls "history-telling" (p. 6). Flowing out of researchers' theoretical and analytic assumptions, interview questions challenge narrators to transform their personal anecdotes. The process provokes narrators to reflect consciously upon the larger historical and social meanings of what has happened to them as individuals.

The relationship at the heart of oral history, as Portelli describes it, is a groping toward mutual understanding that is equally taxing for both parties to the interview. Interviewers must work to understand the connections that narrators are providing as they consider additional lines of questioning that will build upon rather than cut short the dialogue. Historians' questions ask narrators to apply their experiences to frameworks that they may never have thought with before, but that they need to intuit if they are to respond with helpful and relevant information. An attempt to reconstruct memory so that it can speak to history proceeds within this dialectic, which if it breaks down leads to an interview lacking in either texture or information. Successful oral history interviews take on a special verbal quality that Portelli calls "thick dialogue," and the recorded conversation ceases to be a rehearsal of comfortable and conventional formulas and becomes a deeper probing of what happened and why.

Oral history has been part of a broader deontological trend in the social sciences. Collaboration between historian and narrator has helped generate greater understanding that personal experience has historical impact and is not simply an aftereffect of social process. The possibility of communication, and not simply translation, across quite different modes of representing the past rests in an understanding of the symbolic structures that narrators use to posit themselves as subjects who know the objects of their worlds—past, present, and future—in specific, practical, and community-based ways. A focus on the practical underpinnings of meaning systems reintegrates ethics, politics, and knowledge.

Memory and history confront each other across the tape recorder. Separately, both struggle with syntagmatic and paradigmatic codes that structure comprehension of what the present situation means. From their collaboration occasionally emerges a richer, more nuanced understanding of the past, the power of which lies in its having transcended the particular languages that engulf both participants in the interview. (On the alienation of both academic and community understandings of the past through the oral history process, see Friedlander 1975:xxiii-xxvii.) The first step in analyzing oral history interviews is to recognize that they are not raw sources of information. Oral sources are themselves already analytic documents structured with complex codes and achieved meanings. An analyst can make visible neither the limitations nor the critical capaci-

ties of those meanings without delving into the text of the interview and beginning a process of dialogue with its narrator.

■ *Notes*

1. Jan Vansina's *Oral Tradition: A Study in Historical Methodology* (1965) is the classic text on oral tradition. On the relationship between oral tradition and oral history, see Elizabeth Tonkin (1992) and Isabel Hofmeyr (1992). On the selectivity of sources and the relation of oral traditions to documentary archives, see Michel-Rolph Trouillot (1995).

2. A large literature has developed on the social construction of memory. The classic sociological texts were written by Maurice Halbwachs prior to World War II. Lewis Coser has edited a selection of Halbwachs's work in a volume titled *On Collective Memory* (1993). See also the work of Alan Confino (1997), Susan Crane (1997), Noa Gedi and Yigal Elam (1996), Patrick H. Hutton (1993, 1997), Andreas Huyssens (1995), Iwona Irwin-Zarecki (1994), Jacques Le Goff (1992), Allan Megill (1989), Pierre Nora (1989), Jeffrey K. Olick and Joyce Robbins (1998), Michael Roth (1995), Michael Schudson (1995), David Thelen (1989), Frances Yates (1966), and James Young (1993).

3. For recent discussions of rules of evidence and verifiability in historical investigation after the narrative turn, see Joyce Appleby, Lynn Hunt, and Margaret Jacob (1994), Susan Stafford Friedman (1995), Lynn Hunt (1996), David Lowenthal (1989), Allan Megill (1998), and Peter Novick (1988). For classic discussions of the historical method, see Raymond Aron (1961), Lee Benson and Cushing Strout (1965), Marc Bloch (1953), Fernand Braudel (1980), R. G. Collingwood (1946), William Dray (1957), Louis Mink (1965, 1970), and Paul Veyne (1984).

4. Fascist demographic propaganda drew upon preexisting ideas and cultural expressions, which may explain to a degree the hold such ideas had on women, even those who did not act in conformity with older ideals of femininity.

5. For the classic account of displacement through narrative figures, see Aristotle's *Poetics* (1982:secs. 1451b5-6, 1458a18-23, 1457b6).

See also Roland Barthes (1982), Seymour Chatman (1975), Leon Golden (1962), and Paul Ricoeur (1977).

■ References

Allen, B. 1982. "Recreating the Past: The Narrator's Perspective in Oral History." *Oral History Review* 10:33-45.

Anderson, K. and D. C. Jack. 1991. "Learning to Listen: Interview Techniques and Analyses." Pp. 11-26 in *Women's Words: The Feminist Practice of Oral History,* edited by S. B. Gluck and D. Patai. New York: Routledge.

Appleby, J., L. Hunt, and M. Jacob. 1994. *Telling the Truth about History.* New York: Norton.

Aristotle. 1982. *Poetics.* New York: Norton.

Aron, R. 1961. *Introduction to the Philosophy of History: An Essay on the Limits of Historical Objectivity.* Boston: Beacon.

Ashplant, T. 1998. "Anecdote as Narrative Resource in Working-Class Life Stories." Pp. 99-113 in *Narrative and Genre,* edited by M. Chamberlain and P. Thompson. London: Routledge.

Barthes, R. 1982. "Introduction to the Structural Analysis of Narrative." Pp. 251-95 in R. Barthes, *A Roland Barthes Reader.* New York: Hill & Wang.

Benson, L. and C. Strout. 1965. "Causation and the American Civil War: Two Appraisals." Pp. 74-96 in *Studies in the Philosophy of History: Selected Essays from History and Theory,* edited by G. H. Nadel. New York: Harper Torchbooks.

Bertaux-Wiame, I. 1982. "The Life History Approach to the Study of Internal Migration." Pp. 186-200 in *Our Common History: The Transformation of Europe,* edited by P. Thompson. London: Pluto.

Bloch, M. 1953. *The Historian's Craft.* New York: Alfred A. Knopf.

Borland, K. 1991. " 'That's Not What I Said': Interpretive Conflict in Oral Narrative Research." Pp. 63-76 in *Women's Words: The Feminist Practice of Oral History,* edited by S. B. Gluck and D. Patai. New York: Routledge.

Braudel, F. 1980. *On History.* Chicago: University of Chicago Press.

Cándida Smith, R. 1989. "Exquisite Corpse: The Sense of the Past in Oral Histories with California Artists." *Oral History Review* 17:1-34.

———. 1995. *Utopia and Dissent: Art, Poetry, and Politics in California.* Berkeley: University of California Press.

Chatman, S. 1975. "The Structure of Narrative Transmission." Pp. 213-57 in *Style and Structure in Literature: Essays in the New Stylistics,* edited by R. Fowler. Ithaca, NY: Cornell University Press.

Clark, E. C., M. J. Hyde, and E. M. McMahan. 1980. "Communicating in the Oral History Interview: Investigating Problems of Interpreting Oral Data." *International Journal of Oral History* 1:28-40.

Collingwood, R. G. 1946. *The Idea of History.* Oxford: Oxford University Press.

Confino, A. 1997. "Collective Memory and Cultural History: Problems of Method." *American Historical Review* 102:1386-1403.

Crane, S. 1997. "Writing the Individual Back into Collective Memory." *American Historical Review* 102:1372-85.

Culler, J. D. 1986. *Ferdinand de Saussure.* Ithaca, NY: Cornell University Press.

Dray, W. 1957. *Laws and Explanations in History.* London: Oxford University Press.

Earnest, W. R. 1992. "Ideology Criticism and Life-History Research." Pp. 250-64 in *Storied Lives: The Cultural Politics of Self-Understanding,* edited by G. C. Rosenwald and R. L. Ochberg. New Haven, CT: Yale University Press.

Frank, G. 1979. "Finding a Common Denominator: A Phenomenological Critique of Life History Method." *Ethnos* 7:68-94.

Friedlander, P. 1975. *The Emergence of a UAW Local, 1936-1939: A Study in Class and Culture.* Pittsburgh, PA: University of Pittsburgh Press.

Friedman, S. S. 1995. "Making History: Reflections on Feminism, Narrative, and Desire." Pp. 11-54 in *Feminism beside Itself,* edited by D. Elam and R. Wiegman. New York: Routledge.

Gadet, F. 1989. *Saussure and Contemporary Culture.* London: Hutchison Radius.

Gedi, N. and Y. Elam. 1996. "Collective Memory: What Is It?" *History and Memory* 8:30-50.

Golden, L. 1962. "Catharsis." *Proceedings of the American Philological Association* 43:51-60.

Halbwachs, M. 1993. *On Collective Memory,* edited by L. Coser. Albany: State University of New York Press.

Harris, R. 1988. *Language, Saussure, and Wittgenstein: How to Play Games with Words.* London: Routledge.

Hofmeyr, I. 1992. " 'Nterata'/'The Wire': Fences, Boundaries, Orality, Literacy." Pp. 69-92 in *International Annual of Oral History, 1990: Subjectivity and Multiculturalism in Oral History,* edited by R. J. Grele. New York: Greenwood.

Holland, N. N. 1992. *The Critical I.* New York: Columbia University Press.

Hunt, L. 1999. "Psychoanalysis, the Self, and Historical Interpretation," presented at the symposium "History and the Limits of Interpretation," March 15-17, Rice University, Houston. Available Internet: http://www.ruf.rice.edu/~culture/papers/hunt.html

Hutton, P. H. 1993. *History as an Art of Memory.* Hanover, NH: University Press of New England.

———. 1997. "Mnemonic Schemes in the New History of Memory." *History and Theory* 36:378-91.

Huyssens, A. 1995. *Twilight Memories: Marking Time in a Culture of Amnesia.* New York:

Irwin-Zarecki, I. 1994. *Frames of Remembrance: The Dynamics of Collective Memory.* New Brunswick, NJ: Rutgers University Press.

Joutard, P. 1981. "A Regional Project: Ethnotexts." *Oral History* 9:47-51.

Joyner, C. W. 1979. "Oral History as Communicative Event: A Folkloristic Perspective." *Oral History Review* 7:47-52.

Le Goff, J. 1992. *History and Memory.* New York: Columbia University Press.

Lowenthal, D. 1989. "The Timeless Past: Some Anglo-American Historical Preconceptions." *Journal of American History* 75:1263-80.

McMahan, E. M. 1989. *Elite Oral History Discourse: A Study of Cooperation and Coherence.* Tuscaloosa: University of Alabama Press.

Megill, A. 1989. "Recounting the Past: 'Description,' Explanation, and Narrative in Historiography." *American Historical Review* 94:627-53.

———. 1998. "History, Memory, and Identity." *History and the Human Sciences* 11:37-62.

Mink, L. 1965. "The Autonomy of Historical Understanding." *History and Theory* 5:24-47.

———. 1970. "History and Fiction as Modes of Comprehension." *New Literary History* 1:556-69.

Mishler, E. G. 1992. "Work, Identity, and Narrative: An Artist-Craftsman's Story." Pp. 21-40 in *Storied Lives: The Cultural Politics of Self-Understanding,* edited by G. C. Rosenwald and R. L. Ochberg. New Haven, CT: Yale University Press.

Nora, P. 1989. "Between Memory and History: *Les Lieux de mémoire.*" *Representations* 26:7-25.

Novick, P. 1988. *That Noble Dream: The "Objectivity Question" and the American Historical Profession.* Cambridge: Cambridge University Press.

Olick, J. K. and J. Robbins. 1998. "Social Memory Studies: From 'Collective Memory' to the Historical Sociology of Mnemonic Practices." *Annual Review of Sociology* 22:105-40.

Passerini, L. 1987a. "Documento autobiografico e tempo storico." *Rivista di Storia Contemporanea* 16:412-20.

———. 1987b. *Fascism in Popular Memory: The Cultural Experience of the Turin Working Class.* Cambridge: Cambridge University Press.

———. 1988. "Conoscenza storica e fonti orali." Pp. 31-66 in L. Passerini, *Storia e soggetività: Le fonti orali, la memoria.* Florence: La Nuova Italia.

Polanyi, L. 1985. "Conversational Storytelling." Pp. 183-201 in *Handbook of Discourse Analysis,* Vol. 3, edited by T. A. van Dijk. London: Academic Press.

Portelli, A. 1991. *The Death of Luigi Trastulli and Other Stories: Form and Meaning in Oral History.* Albany: State University of New York Press.

———. 1997. *The Battle of Valle Giulia: Oral History and the Art of Dialogue*. Madison: University of Wisconsin Press.

Ricoeur, P. 1973. "The Model of the Text: Meaningful Action Considered as a Text." *New Literary History* 5:91-117.

———. 1977. *The Rule of Metaphor: Multidisciplinary Studies of the Creation of Meaning in Language*. Toronto: University of Toronto Press.

———. 1983. *Time and Narrative*, Vol. 1. Chicago: University of Chicago Press.

Riessman, C. K. 1992. "Making Sense of Marital Violence: One Woman's Narrative." Pp. 231-49 in *Storied Lives: The Cultural Politics of Self-Understanding*, edited by G. C. Rosenwald and R. L. Ochberg. New Haven, CT: Yale University Press.

Rosenwald, G. C. 1992. "Conclusion: Reflections on Narrative Self-Understanding." Pp. 265-89 in *Storied Lives: The Cultural Politics of Self-Understanding*, edited by G. C. Rosenwald and R. L. Ochberg. New Haven, CT: Yale University Press.

Roth, M. S. 1995. *The Ironist's Cage: Memory, Trauma, and the Construction of History*. New York: Columbia University Press.

Sánchez, R. 1995. *Telling Identities: The Californio Testimonios*. Minneapolis: University of Minnesota Press.

Schudson, M. 1995. *Memory Distortion: How Minds, Brains, and Societies Reconstruct the Past*. Cambridge, MA: Harvard University Press.

Thelen, D. 1989. "Memory and American History." *Journal of American History* 75:117-29.

Thompson, P. 1988. *The Voice of the Past*. Oxford: Oxford University Press.

Tonkin, E. 1992. *Narrating Our Pasts: The Social Construction of Oral History*. Cambridge: Cambridge University Press.

Trouillot, M.-R. 1995. *Silencing the Past: Power and the Production of History*. Boston: Beacon.

Vansina, J. 1965. *Oral Tradition: A Study in Historical Methodology*. London: Routledge & Kegan Paul.

Veyne, P. 1984. *Writing History: Essay on Epistemology*. Middletown, CT: Wesleyan University Press.

Yates, F. 1966. *The Art of Memory*. Chicago: University of Chicago Press.

Young, J. E. 1993. *The Texture of Memory: Holocaust Memorials and Meaning*. New Haven, CT: Yale University Press.

12

INTERVIEWING AT THE
BORDER OF FACT AND FICTION

◆ Paul C. Rosenblatt

For many social scientists there is still a distinct boundary between fact and fiction in interviewing. For them, interviewing is a matter of finding the best ways to elicit true, valid, factual answers to interview questions. However, for ever more of us, the boundary between fact and fiction has blurred (Denzin 1997). We see the boundary not as a reality that transcends time and culture, but as a social construction, like other boundaries (Rosenblatt 1994). We live in a world of postmodernist thought in which, even if we are affirmatively postmodern (Rosenau 1992) and resist an anarchy of standards and the annihilation of anything that could be called truth, we understand that social science facts and truths are at best perspectival. We hear our interview respondents relating narratives about their lives that seem to be like what we read in novels (Polkinghorne 1988:163). We have come to recognize that what we write is fiction in the sense of having been fashioned by us (Clifford 1986). It no longer is clear that the voice of the social scientist has more claim to be heard than the voice of anyone else (Kenneth Gergen, cited in Gülerce 1995). It seems no longer to make sense to evaluate what we think we know against standards of predictive utility, empirical fact, or other criteria championed by positivists (Gergen 1988).

In this chapter, I use my own experiences as researcher and hopeful writer of fiction to inform my discussion of interviewing at the boundary of fact and fiction. Most of my interviewing research has focused on families or couples dealing with difficult issues. Among these studies are book-length qualitative works on business-owning families (Rosenblatt et al. 1985), farm families dealing with an economic crisis in farming (Rosenblatt 1990), multiracial couples (Rosenblatt, Karis, and Powell 1995), and married couples dealing with the death of a child (Rosenblatt 2000). As an aspiring fiction writer, I am in the midst of work on an action-adventure novel set in a nursing home and on the cotranslation of a novel from Korean to English. I have also drafted a detective novel that focuses on a farm family dealing with a death on the farm. These efforts at writing fiction, plus my research experience, converge to provide a basis for my comments here on the boundary between fact and fiction.

◆ Blurring the Boundary between Fact and Fiction

The postmodern interviewer understands that interviewing produces a social co-construction in which interviewer and interviewee are both players (Holstein and Gubrium 1995). The postmodern interviewer also understands that the language researchers use to communicate what they think they have learned creates, highlights, limits, and obscures what some people might consider to be fact and truth (see Gubrium and Holstein 1997). The postmodern interviewing world is one of standpoint perspectives (Smith 1987) and of cultural and experiential diversity, where a shift from one perspective to another can radically alter realities. We may still be influenced by Karl Popper (e.g., 1962) and Donald T. Campbell (e.g., 1988) to doubt systematically and to challenge our provisional truths as though we have faith that challenging will lead to truths that are ever more resistant to challenge. But in our awareness of the social construction of reality, the rhetoric of writing social research reports, and the inevitable limits, biases, and subjectivity (often covert) of research, we are ever more skeptical of the status of

the provisional truths we have to offer (see Fontana, Chapter 3, this volume).

We might be so modest as to call our truths suggestions, possibilities, or perspectives, but we may still seek grants on the promise of documenting something like truth. We often are published, read, and cited by people who think we have truths to offer. And many of us who are in some ways postmodernist are still using methodological approaches that were developed in the days when social science realities were real. Perhaps we use those methodologies because they are what we have or because they legitimate our work for important constituencies.

I am not uncomfortable that my interviewing approaches and ways of working with interview material are related to modernist research approaches because I think they help me to get at something like truth, and I still want to learn something like truth. I still think it is possible to be ignorant or wrong, and I want to be less ignorant and no longer wrong. I do my interview research because I think I can get closer to whatever is "right" by hearing what people have to say. I know I could do interviews simply to learn what people say—to do research on storytelling—but I still think what I hear in interviews gives me more than mere stories.

When, for example, bereaved parents tell me about their grieving and their closest relationships after their child's death, I believe I am learning something that is real and true for them. I am not simply learning their stories. When I hear similar stories from many bereaved parents, I think I am learning something about parent grief. I don't think I am learning immutable truths, but I think I am learning something important about many bereaved parents. With Robert Weiss (1994:148-49) and others who have written about qualitative research, I do not consider the truths I learn to be unambiguous, invariant, the whole truth and nothing but the truth. But I still feel I am doing the right thing in making something out of what I hear from interviewees.

We can also view the blurring of the boundary between fact and fiction from the perspective of the writers and readers of fiction. For some of them, the boundary between fact and fiction has been blurred if not destroyed in part because it is now clear that much of fiction has strong autobiographical, experiential, and observational elements. Also, many people read works of fiction as guides to life and as sources of insight. For them, there is truth in fiction. In fact, readers may find in fiction truths that are for them more profound, persuasive, and trustworthy than those they find in social science writings.

◆ Research Interviewing in Postmodern Hindsight

With postmodern blurring of boundaries and borders, what can we make, in hindsight, of research interviewing?

INTERVIEWEES' BELIEF IN TRUTH

Every person I have ever interviewed seemed to believe in truth and to try hard to deal with the truth. They were all psychological essentialists (Gergen 1994) in that they talked as though there is a real reality to be known and told (or withheld). So even if we as interviewers are postmodernists, the social construction of our interview interactions is to some extent driven by truth and essentialism. People think I want to know the truth. The context, and to some extent the language, of our interview interaction is a language of truth and falsity, of trying to get to accurate memories and accurate reports of events, feelings, and beliefs. In fact, some people I interview will telephone or write after an interview in order to give what they consider to be a more accurate statement about something, to clarify something they said during the interview, or to add something they had forgotten.

Often an interviewee will interview me about what I think about something, what my experience has been, or what I have learned from others I have interviewed. An interviewee might, for example, ask me, "What do the parents you have talked with already say about how family members and friends treated them after the child's death?" Typically I reply with something that has a postmodern tone to it, for example: "I don't know. It's hard to say. Most parents I've talked with so far have said that they felt that after the funeral most family members and friends avoided them. But there are lots of ways of understanding that, and I don't know whether the family members and friends would say they were trying to avoid. It's difficult to generalize or to say what's true." But even if I offer my postmodern perspectives in the interviews, respondents always return to the modern language of truth and facts.

The interviews people give me are carried out in the context of their notions of reporters, detectives, medical researchers, pollsters, and others interviewees believe to seek the truth. Interviewees have the concept of the investigator searching for the truth and also believe that it is crucial to the investigator that the truth be given. I think they also believe that not giving the truth is, except in exceptional circumstances, immoral. Many people I have interviewed seem to me to feel an almost sacred obligation to provide the truth. So even if I am in a postmodern and perspectival world as I read and write social science, the people I interview offer me truth and push me to be like the reporters, detectives, and others they believe to be seekers of truth.

This naive realism influences me. Although I can frame what people say to me in terms that are quite foreign to them and quite compelling to me, I often write my social science in ways that honor their real realities. I don't want them to read what I have written and wonder where their realities went. I also don't want to abandon their realities because I think part of what I have to offer readers is what the people I interview seem to say is real and true.

ENTITLEMENT TO DECEIVE

Interviewees think that some people lie or mislead—for example, politicians and defendants in legal proceedings. I think they look down on those people and do not want to be like them. Still, I think often people feel entitled in an interview not to tell the whole truth and nothing but the truth. I think in my interviewing, the key "deceptions" or failures to tell the whole truth and nothing but the truth come from people wanting to avoid embarrassment and from the dynamics of family members being interviewed together who do not want to reveal something that might hurt, embarrass, or offend another family member.

Sometimes the "deception" comes from what is probably normal in the early part of an interview. Interviewees don't know if they can trust me; I haven't engaged them fully, they don't know how deep I want them to go, and they are using the etiquette they would use with strangers (which involves not disclosing anything that might make me think less well of them). I know there are "deceptions" early in interviews because sometimes as an interview unfolds things that were hidden earlier are brought out. For example, it may only be after an hour into an interview in which a couple has represented their marital relationship as problem-free that I discover that the wife has serious alcohol problems and her husband has often hit her.

In his advice to interviewers, based on his own experience as an interviewer and as a manager of interviewers, Weiss (1994) offers a number of suggestions for getting to what interviewees may have withheld. Perhaps the key suggestions are that the interviewer should pick up on clues the interviewee may have dropped and should use good interviewing skills to build a rapport that will lead the interviewee to disclose more as the interview progresses. From a postmodern perspective, what constitutes a clue could be said to differ from interviewer to interviewer, and sometimes the clue is that something has not been mentioned at all. And from a postmodern perspective, the building of rapport may be understood as the interviewer building, with the interviewee, a sense of how embarrassing, emotional, or otherwise possibly difficult topics can be brought up and how they will be co-constructed. The processes of building rapport and what is gained and lost through the building of rapport in various ways are, I think, matters that we postmodern interview researchers should not take for granted but should study carefully and understand well.

ELICITING POSSIBLY CONTRADICTORY TRUTHS

I allow respondents great latitude to construct our relationship and to define what is important. Good postmodern qualitative interviewing is much less controlling and directive than is the model for positivist interviewing. But still I will push people to talk about what is important to them from various viewpoints. For example, I might ask a couple how their clergyman or -woman might think about something, or how they would have thought about something 10 years ago. Or I might ask a question that I hope will move an interviewee to a different way of thinking about an event (for example, feelings based versus biomedical versus religious versus legal). So, even though I expect that interviewees will tell me what they consider to be the truth and I honor their efforts to tell that truth, I do not accept that the truth they have just given me is the truth that others share or that will be the whole truth after they reply to my next question.

When interviewees signal me in some way that they have told all they know about something, I might stop digging and go on to my next question. But on important matters, I often return to a question that seemingly has already been answered completely. I might ask the question from another angle, or with different words, or with additional permission to the interviewee to say something that could be embarrassing or otherwise difficult. Or I might ask that the question be answered from another perspective. I might frame the renewed questioning as a matter of aiding interviewee memory, so the whole truth can be given. Or I might frame it as looking for additional specifics.

RESEARCHER OPENNESS TO DIVERSE REALITIES

A continuing challenge for the interviewer is to be open-minded, to decenter from one's own realities so as to be able to move into realities that are not only different from one's own but also surprising, alien, uncomfortable, a direct challenge to one's thinking, disgusting, horrifying, anxiety-provoking, boring, or otherwise difficult. If I had lived a totally realist life, without reading fiction, seeing films, having a rich fantasy life, or having come to know a diversity of people whose different realities have challenged me, it would be more difficult to be open. What Andrea Fontana and James H. Frey (1994) call "understanding the language and culture of the respondents" can be understood as learning culture and new languages, but I also think it is about being comfortable with realities that are new to one.

Good interviewing will draw out from interviewees what they would be reluctant to tell most people. Sometimes the reluctance arises from concerns that people will think what they have to say is a fiction. Perhaps it is their experience of spirit possession. Perhaps it is an allegation (inconsistent with what everyone else in the family

believes and inconsistent with what the authorities have said) that a family death was murder, not an accident or a death by natural causes. Perhaps it is about communications they have received from the dead, about their past lives, about their experiences of prescience, or about their fantastic powers.

As I interview, I think about how I may construct the interview material I am hearing/seeing when I analyze the interview transcript and write up my research. I do not want these preliminary "takes" on the interview to swamp whatever respondents say. That is, I am still trying to write works that are empirically grounded (grounded in experiences not wholly my own). I am still open to learning that my preliminary interpretations are wrong, or wrong for particular respondents. So I try out my interpretations on the people I interview. I push as I interview for more information consistent and inconsistent with my emerging interpretations (Rosenblatt 1981) and try to elicit a great deal of concrete documentation on what seem ever more likely, as an interviewing study goes on, to be central interpretive points.

DOUBT AND THE ELICITATION OF NEW INFORMATION

Occasionally I think a respondent is not telling what she or he would consider to be the truth or the whole truth. When I think someone is hiding something, being evasive, making things up, I feel that I am on shaky ground. On the one hand, I think that I must accept that this person's claimed reality is her or his reality. On the other hand, when people seem to be outliers, are giving off verbal and nonverbal cues that I think are deceptive, are saying things that are internally inconsistent, are saying things that I doubt are their truths, I push for more.

It is my experience that when I probe in an area that seems to be one of untruth or not full truth, I sometimes learn that what I thought was fiction was fiction. For example, the person was too embarrassed to tell me at first that he drinks 6 to 12 cans of beer each day. And sometimes I learn that the fiction is, for the person, totally believable. For example, a widow believes that her deceased husband was a saint. Or, to take an example offered by Melvin Pollner and Lynn McDonald-Winkler (1985) and that I have come across in my own interviewing, parents believe that a child who is disabled and developmentally delayed at the extreme is very able.

NARRATIVES GOOD ENOUGH TO BE FICTION

As interviewees talk to me, I think about what will make for fascinating reading—for example, the vivid story, the powerful metaphor, the touchingly authentic statement of feelings, or the family battle that erupts with a *Who's Afraid of Virginia Woolf?* volcanic power. My sense of what will make good reading comes partly from my reading of fiction. I relish interview narratives that are as gripping as those in a powerful and moving work of fiction. I feel deep satisfaction on hearing an interviewee say something that I know will make a vivid, attention-grabbing, memorable quote in print. Thus my sense of what makes for good reading in fiction as well as in social research reports provides guidelines that are important to me in my interviewing.

I am not sure it is so different for the people being interviewed. I think many have a sense of what is a good story, and some delight in telling a story well. Some are obviously experienced storytellers who are telling me stories they have told on many previous occasions. However, not infrequently, individuals will say to me that they have never told their stories, or their whole stories, to anyone. They seem grateful for the opportunity to have somebody hear them out. They also seem grateful to hear the stories themselves and feel that they

learned something from hearing what it is they had to say.

Another connection between fiction and research based on interviews that generate "good" narrative is that it is much easier to carry out interview research or to write fiction in areas in which people have passionate feelings and speak eloquently and at length. You do not see much fiction or interview research dealing with topics about which people are inarticulate or have almost nothing to say. In that sense, "Would it make good fiction?" is a good question to ask of a qualitative research interview. Qualitative research can be understood as constructed out of people's stories (Paget 1983). If people in good fiction would not speak these words because there is no story there, or no story that could interest anyone, perhaps there is not much to the interview.

IMAGINING THE INTERVIEWEE; IMAGINING THE INTERVIEWER

All research begins with imagined research subjects (Holstein and Gubrium 1995; see also Gubrium and Holstein, Chapter 2, this volume). We cannot decide on an issue to study or what data to gather without imagining the research subject. In qualitative interviewing, the interview schedule and the ongoing interaction with interviewees always involves our imagination of who the interviewees are, what is going on with them, and how they will react to various things we might ask or do. The process of constructing the subject begins prior to the interview, but it is modified during the course of an interview session, so once we begin the interview the imagined subject is co-constructed. And no matter how much we believe we know an interviewee or all the interviewees in a study we have carried out, we are still imagining them. Thus, when I said earlier that interviewees believe in truth, I was asserting as true what is a construction I believe I have reached with interviewees. But my belief does not make what is in a sense fiction into fact. However much we believe in constructed selves, they are still constructed and are capable of being constructed in other ways. Similarly, at times I try to "bracket" my presuppositions about interviewees in order to be as open as possible to their constructions of themselves. But that does not mean I have left the realm of constructed, construed, and, in a sense, fictional selves.

I think my reading and writing of fiction have made me a better interviewer because I bring a broader range of hypothesized selves and experiences to an interviewee and have more openness to possible interviewee selves and experiences. I am comfortable with the idea that an interviewee is in her 15th reincarnation, that God has sent me to her, that I am interviewing a married couple who have almost not spoken to each other in six years, or that an interviewee is right in believing that a powerful spirit has stopped my tape recorder from working.

I am also aware that the interviewee will have hypotheses about what I am up to and what is behind my questions (Alasuutari 1995). From that perspective, part of what goes on in the interview is that the interviewee tests out hypotheses about me and my questions. As the interview progresses, the interviewee is likely to develop a more precise sense of who I am and what I am up to, and, if correct, may do a better job by my standards of addressing the issues I want addressed in ways that I value.

INTERVIEWING AND WHAT IS DEEP INSIDE THE INTERVIEWER

So far, I have been writing as though I know what I am doing when I carry out qualitative interviews and as though I and most respondents are rational. But I assure you that there is much going on beneath the surface for me and, I think, for the people being interviewed, a great deal that is not rational or in awareness (Scheurich 1995).

One thing that persuades me that there is a great deal beneath the surface of interviewers is my experience doing studies with multiple interviewers. No matter how much I work at having us all understand the research questions and the interview guide in the same way, no matter how much we practice interviewing, no matter how much we cointerview before we solo, interviewers are inevitably quite different in their interviews. They differ in the kind of rapport they develop with respondents, how they ask certain questions, how they interact as they listen to respondents, what they pick up on, what they accept without questioning, how and what they probe, how much they allow the interviewee to go off on what could be taken as tangents, and how long their interviews run. One could say these things are a matter of social skills or research experience, but one can also take them as beneath-the-surface stuff. I have never done the research, but I believe that the differences among interviewers in what they pick up from respondents are related to differences in what is beneath the surface in the interviewers.

I think the interviewers who do the best are people who are comfortable with under-the-surface emotional matters related to the research. For example, if one is not comfortable with death and mortality issues, one will find it hard to draw bereaved people out, hear them out, and coconstruct realities with them. (For further discussion about how some interviewers might not "click" with some interviewees, see Weiss 1994:136-41, 145-47.)

One can also take interviewer differences as connected to the inherent ambiguity in language (Scheurich 1995), which leaves interviewer and interviewee free, to some extent, to make any question or comment a projective test. I think repeatedly in an interview the respondent and the interviewer are choosing among many different possible understandings of things said. Interview transcripts map those choices and often give hints of possible alternative choices. An interviewee who is a recent widow might say, for example, "I read the newspaper every day, but I can't stand to look at the sports section." One interviewer might follow that comment up with a question about what the widow does like to read; another might ask why she can't stand the sports section. The former interviewer might learn about the widow's interest in local news and the television schedule. The latter interviewer might learn about the widow's sense that it was the sports section that her husband most liked, that it makes her feel sad to be reminded of him, and that she tries to avoid feeling sad by avoiding reminders of him. Perhaps the difference between the two interviewers would simply be a matter of what to do with the ambiguity of language, but my guess is that it might also have to do with their comfort with a widow's pain and with their own feelings connected to death.

DATA ANALYSIS AS PART OF AN INTERVIEW

Many sources on how to do qualitative interview research say that data analysis can and should begin during the interviewing phase of the research (e.g., Kvale 1996; Strauss and Corbin 1998). Part of what they mean is that one should question based on what one thinks one has learned so far in the study. From a constructionist perspective (Holstein and Gubrium 1995), that means that one should be actively planful about one's part in cocreating truths with interviewees. In a sense that means that based on what one believes one has found out so far in the research, one should try to elicit words from interviewees that refute, support, or qualify one's developing interpretation. One may develop these preliminary analyses during one's interviews, by thinking things through by means of a field diary, by listening to interview tapes, or—what works best for me— by transcribing interviews immediately and analyzing as one goes what seems to be sig-

nificant and what one wishes one had asked.

From another perspective, the process of analysis during the interview seems to me to blur the boundary between two texts—the "text" that is the verbal and nonverbal performance of the interview and the "text" that is the transcription of the interview. The interviewer's on-the-fly analysis of the former text cocreates that text, in a postmodern sense, and intrudes into the interview transcription text.

There was, however, a time in my life when I caught myself creating research findings that were more fictional than I was comfortable creating. At the time, I was a quantitative positivist researcher teaching experimental social psychology and modernist research methods. As a standard part of my research, I "debriefed" respondents. That is, after the data gathering part of the research was complete, I interviewed respondents about their experience of the research. Initially, I conducted such debriefing primarily to tell them about deceptions in the research and to be sure that they were not leaving the research setting in anger or pain. But my interviews with respondents led to them talking about how they understood my instructions to them, my experimental manipulations, and my paper-and-pencil psychological measures. I also began to interview "pilot" respondents in my sample survey studies about how they understood questions in my survey questionnaires and what their own responses meant to them. It was my qualitative interviewing at the end of experimental sessions and as part of piloting survey studies that set me on the road to being a qualitative researcher.

As I debriefed subjects in my experiments, I became aware of how arrogantly ignorant and wrong my assumptions were about the people I was researching. They often understood things differently and in more complex ways than I assumed. Similarly, with my survey questionnaires, my interviews showed that virtually all questions, even the questions I thought were most straightforward, were engaged by people in ways that made my interpreting their responses without knowledge of the complexities of their understandings a work of fiction. A simple question like "How much sleep did you have last night?" would be interpreted differently depending on what a respondent decided "sleep," "last night," and "night" meant, and depending on whether the respondent thought I really wanted to know about "last night" or about a typical night. Multiply such complexities by the number of questions in the survey, and it became clear to me that I might best become a qualitative interview researcher.

◆ Writing Fiction

I now turn to the writing experience and how a research context relates to the way findings are presented. I am especially concerned here with how fiction can inform the interpretation of interview findings.

FICTION AND THE WRITING UP OF QUALITATIVE INTERVIEW RESEARCH

When I write up qualitative interview research, there is again a blurred boundary between fiction and fact. Part of it is that when I write about my research methods, the conventions of writing about methods (Harré 1990), the rhetoric of research reporting (Gusfield 1976), and the page limits imposed by editors guarantee that I simplify in ways that could be misleading. Somebody could see such simplifying as necessary for reader sanity or see it as the essence of respectable research reporting. But in that simplifying, there is a kind of fictionalizing. By contrast, in the detective novel I have drafted about a researcher who specializes in qualitative interviewing and who has been recruited to help a farm family understand and deal with what may have been an accidental death or may have

been murder, the researcher discusses the interview craft in detail. For example, he talks about what he does when a speaker pauses or seems to change the topic of conversation, what he does with his anxiety during an interview, how he decides what to ask when he is not sure what to ask, and how he processes an interview in the hours following the interview.

Laurel Richardson (1994), in reviewing and commenting on experimental representations in qualitative research, shows how such representations grow out of postmodern irreverence, doubt, and impatience with standard reporting in qualitative research. In a sense, my detective novel is what she calls a "narrative of self," a self who provides unusual detail about the range of things to which he, as a researcher, attends. For example, in the fictional account, I talk about how people sit as they talk, what they ask me, how they smell, how their language changes as who is present changes, how their dogs are players in family experience, their use of facial tissues when they cry, how they slide by family disagreements during a family interview, the ways they can blithely and unapologetically be inconsistent, and how much they seem trapped by culture, neighbors, property ownership, and much else into thinking along certain lines and not others.

FICTION THAT TELLS WHAT HAS BEEN LEARNED IN RESEARCH

My detective novel is based on my interview studies of farm families who have lost a family member in a fatal farm accident (e.g., Rosenblatt and Karis 1993, 1993-94). Writing the novel has enabled me to give more context to the situations of the people I have interviewed and to describe characters with far greater texture than I ever could in a research publication. I can also detail the starts, stops, blind alleys, mistakes, and evolution of an investigative journey, as opposed to what I can do in research reports, which usually give only a picture of what is intended to be the end of the journey. In those ways, writing fiction enables me to be true to much that I can never report so honestly within the standard venues for publishing in the social sciences.

If I am providing readers with fictionalized accounts that seem to me to be reasonable representations of things I know about grieving families dealing with fatal accidents, how can the reader judge what I have written? Laurel Richardson and Ernest Lockridge (1998), in discussing the writing of fictional ethnography, explore several criteria. One is that the text inspires something—research, action, a change in the reader. A critic of fictional representations of research might argue that something invalid or inauthentic in the fiction could inspire, and what it inspires might be invalid or inauthentic. As a postmodernist, I squirm when a discussion turns to matters of validity and authenticity, because those terms imply certainties, criteria, and truths that I think are at best questionable.

Determining what readers derive from a text is a complex matter, because a text can be perceived and felt at many different levels and in many different ways (Ang 1985; Holland 1968). So a critic who considers something invalid in a text may miss that some people are picking up on something very different from what the critic sees in the text or sees as invalid. But even if a reader makes use of something a critic considers invalid, I see no problem with that. I think readers are fully capable of taking personally valid and authentic inspiration from texts that in some way are not valid or authentic by somebody's standards. So a critic who is concerned about what fiction might inspire would do well to focus on the reader, not the fiction. And, in fairness, the focus should also encompass readers of scholarly articles and books. I think we need studies of readers of social science and what they take from what they read. My suspicion is that we might find that readers will at times be stimulated to think

thoughts they consider new and valuable even by social science writings they, or others, consider to be flawed.

Another criterion explicated by Richardson and Lockridge (1998) for evaluating fictionalized research accounts is the "aesthetic." They include in the "aesthetic" the relationship between the reader and the writer, the integration of the writing, the sensory qualities of what is being written about (how it tastes, smells, sounds, looks, feels), the characters coming to life, and the conveying of profundity, mystery, magic, and possibility.

It seems to me that in the typical social science reporting mode, the writer is supposed to be aloof from the particulars, not supposed to be "distracted" by the details that do not speak directly to the research agenda. The writer is supposed to emphasize theory and ideas (in contrast to sensory qualities, characters coming to life, profundity, mystery, magic, and perhaps possibility). In such reporting, the aesthetic is very different from what it is for fiction. It is an aesthetic that makes the material much less accessible to most of the reading public. To the extent that I want what I have learned from carrying out my research to be accessible to a wide range of readers, fiction offers a much better venue for making the interview material and what I think of it accessible. If my fiction is written well, the characters and their experiences come alive. In my social science writing, I may be able to sneak in aesthetic qualities with interview quotes, but it is not a sustained vitality, as in fiction. My sense is that bad fiction will, by definition, fail to meet what Richardson and Lockridge consider to be aesthetic qualities, but it is much easier to meet those aesthetic qualities with fictionalized accounts than with standard research reports.

I have come to appreciate deeply social scientists who have written fiction that reflects what they have learned as scholars—for example, anthropologists such as Oliver La Farge (e.g., 1929) and Zora Neale Hurston (e.g., 1937) and womanists such as Charlotte Perkins Gilman (e.g., 1979). I no longer think of scholarly writing as something that necessarily communicates what I most want readers to know about what I have learned from my research. Also, I have been influenced by sociologists and psychologists such as Howard Becker, Kenneth Gergen, Michal McCall, and Marianne Paget, who have explored alternative means of communicating about social research (e.g., McCall et al. 1990).

As I have moved further into trying to write fiction, I have experienced most powerfully the realization that in creating fiction I have been freed to tell readers far more than I could while working within the constraints of conventional social science writing. At the same time, I worry a great deal about how to persuade myself and the reader that what I have to offer has some kind of validity and truth to it.

Writing fiction challenges me with the same concerns about validity as writing a research report. I still wonder whether what I say has validity by some standard, however imperfect, makes sense, and is understandable to the reader in ways that I intend it to be understood. I still worry about whether what I have the characters say fits what the text I write around those quotes says is going on with them.

Years of interviewing, transcribing interviews, checking transcriptions, coding transcriptions, and creating manuscripts that quote from transcriptions has given me, I think, a good sense of how people speak. Sometimes when I read fiction or watch drama or film, I marvel at the authenticity the writer has captured. But sometimes I think the writer is off base, missing something important about how people speak. You might think that my good sense of how people speak would be a benefit in my writing of fiction, and I think it is some of the time. But sometimes it is not. One way it is not is that I am lost when my fictional characters are supposed to say things that are remote from what I have heard, transcribed, and coded people saying. At that point, I am probably less equipped than most fiction writers to use

the resources of my fantasy, because I have come to rely so much on my experience with research interviews.

The other way my experience with ordinary speech is not an advantage is that I know ordinary speech is ungrammatical, redundant, often unpunctuated, sometimes incoherent, filled with "you know," "uh," "er," and restarts, and often internally inconsistent. I also know that ordinary speech has rhythm and pitch variations that are impossible to represent in an ordinary written text. Those things are very tricky to incorporate into fictional dialogue on a sustained basis (and why some scholars [e.g., Paget (1993) 1995] have tried dramatic representations to disseminate their personal and research insights). I think to make fiction readable, a writer almost has to have fictional characters most of the time speak more clearly than ordinary people do.

As an aspiring novelist who is an experienced researcher, teacher of researchers, and reviewer for social science journals, I find that my writing of fiction is complicated in that I have never totally abandoned my modernist concern about evidence, validity, and certainty. My concern weighs me down like concrete shoes on a runner. It has the potential to make my writing process tedious and labored, and to make what I write ponderous to read. On the other hand, the kind of thinking I do as a researcher makes, I think, for mystery writing that is smart. In fact, the parallels between the detective in the detective novel genre (Alasuutari 1998; Hoppenstand 1987; Sanders 1974) and the researcher in the modern social research genre are clear. Both are learned and rational, both are smart about finding clues to help solve a puzzle, both are able to see what the untrained and inexperienced person cannot see, and both have worked hard to master a craft that enables them to seek and evaluate information.

However, the modern has been engulfed in the postmodern. Like me as a researcher, the fictional researcher who is acting as a detective in the novel I have written has epistemological and ontological concerns that have become in many ways postmodern. He searches for many different kinds of evidence and he questions the evidence given him, which are respectably modern things to do. But he is postmodern in that he also questions his and other people's categories of reality, the nature of certainty, and how he affects the realities that emerge through his investigating. And he is humble and provisional about what he knows.

My concerns as a researcher also show up in how much I research the fiction I may write. In preparing to write a novel about missionaries and the Spokane Indians they tried to convert in the 1830s, I have put in many hours reading ethnohistory, 19th-century diaries and letters, anthropological accounts, and Indian accounts. Writing a novel about Indians and missionaries in the 1830s is extremely difficult for me, because I cannot find writings that I am confident present the Indian perspective in the 1830s. In a sense, the problem I have is why I do interview research—to learn things that are not already in journals, books, and other repositories of knowledge. But the Spokane Indians in the 1830s are not available to be interviewed. And as a committed empiricist I can be exquisitely uncomfortable about making up the thoughts and conversations of people about whom I know too little. I fear they will sound like me, movie Indians, 19th-century Euro-American idealizations of Indians, modern-day Indians, or nobody in particular. At this point, the novel is emplotted; I know what I want to say. But I am too much anchored in my epistemological concerns to write, because I have not found what I consider to be reasonably authentic voices and perspectives for Indian characters.

The demands for something like truth in the writing of social science can be impossibly burdensome, but in some ways they make for easier writing than the writing of fiction. As a social scientist, I only have to say what I have research grounding to say,

meeting reasonable social science truth standards. When I do not know something, I can say that, or slide away from it. Not only do I not have to make things up, I must not. When writing fiction, I must write as though I know much. If I am not sure what a character would think or do, I have to come up with something that fits, seems plausible, and is interesting. It is a luxury for the social scientist not to know. The writer of fiction in some ways has a much tougher job.

QUALITATIVE INTERVIEWING IN TRANSLATING A WORK OF FICTION

I am currently collaborating with Sungeun Yang on translating into English the Korean novel *The Most Beautiful Farewell in the World,* by Hee Gyoung Noh. Yang is a native speaker of Korean, and I have no proficiency in the language. So our translation process involves my interviewing her intensively about her translation decisions and dilemmas. Using qualitative interviewing techniques, I recurrently question her about her choices of English words or what a word or phrase in Korean means to native speakers of Korean. During our interview discussions, she teaches me an enormous amount of what is truth for herself, for Koreans as she understands and represents them, and for the novel's author. I am learning a great deal that is outside of my experience and culture and that challenges the English language to do a reasonable rendering.

For example, in Korean there is a kind of respect that is paid to things that seems to me to be outside of how respect is talked about in American English. Also, the Korean language draws finer distinctions among kinds of danger than does American English. In this situation, I think that my qualitative interviewing skills do an excellent job of identifying the many challenges in the translation project and give Sungeun Yang and me a solid base for doing the best translation possible by at least one of the many standards for evaluating translations (Wilss 1982).

However, the best translation possible by the standard we have pursued (fidelity to what seems to us to be the original meanings, although not to the exact wording) involves fictionalizing in the sense that even the best translation is a painfully imperfect representation of the text in the original language. The translation loses what cannot easily be translated if translated at all, and even much of what can be translated becomes altered in subtle ways at many places in each chapter. A translated work of fiction may be experienced as a superb book, but it is not the same book as the original. And the qualitative interviewing I have done with Yang has made the imperfections of the translation crystal clear.

One can take the changes that happen when fiction is translated as an allegory for qualitative interviewing research. Perhaps the translations we make from interviewees' original understandings and narratives to our research reports are like translated works of fiction. At best we can hope for good, interesting writing, but the reports invariably lose things that cannot be "translated" into them and alter much else away from the meanings and understandings the interviewees thought they were conveying.

FACT AND FICTION
IN THE CONSUMPTION
OF RESEARCH FINDINGS

What happens when research reports are quoted in other research reports, in textbooks, and in the mass media? I believe that research findings are often fictionalized in such situations. Many of us have had the experience of having our published research findings distorted in textbooks or in the research reports of others, perhaps even to the point of being unrecognizable or of saying the opposite of what we thought we said. Similarly, the media interviews we give about our research often, perhaps al-

ways, come out in such selective and distorted ways that it is often an embarrassment to be quoted in the media as an expert. Even speaking for oneself, using one's expertise about one's own research, in radio and television interviews is often a losing battle against the fictionalizing of that work. (For a fascinating account of such experiences, see Richardson 1987.) Many postmodernists would say that what an author intends to write has little or nothing to do with how that author's text can, will, or should be read (Rosenau 1992). But from my authorial perspective, at the level of consumption of research findings, there is not so much a blurred boundary between fact and fiction as there is a broken dam with a great torrent of something that is not fact threatening to inundate anything that might be a reasonable representation of what I want to communicate to others.

◆ Critical Views of
the Blurred Boundary

I have a postmodernist view of truth, and yet in my interview research, I never want to write fiction. I am afraid of eliciting fiction from interviewees and mistaking it for fact. I am afraid of analyzing and interpreting interview material in a way that makes the research reports I write into fiction. I hope to write truth, not *the* truth, but certainly a truth. My truths may be provisional, situation-bound, perspectival, even personal, but I work very, very hard to ground them empirically, rhetorically, and logically and to make them seem sound and persuasive to me and, I hope, to the reader.

Still, positivist critics may interpret this chapter to mean that qualitative interviewing is too subjective to be science or to be worth taking seriously. However, as the reader can gather from my discussion of my experiences doing qualitative interviewing as an adjunct to experimental social psychology and sample surveys, I think qualitative interviewing is good protection against the fictions of "objective," positivist research. From this perspective, refusing to force the world into a positivist social science template in which the researcher posits meanings and understandings for the people studied may have greater truth value than maintaining a strict fact-versus-fiction dichotomy.

I realize that critics of the perspectives I represent in this chapter may feel raging indignation about the ways the ideas represented here seem to slight scientific sociology and psychology. To understand and accept postmodern doubting is to end certainty and confidence about what is right and what is wrong. There are fascinating qualitative studies and novels to be written about any confrontation of doubt with orthodoxy, or of multiple realities with a monolithic reality. I think it is obvious why people would resist postmodern thinking. Who would want to give up certainty and a simple and unambiguous world if they had them? On the other hand, a person who brought certainty and an unambiguous view of the world to qualitative interview research would find it very hard to maintain certainty, orthodoxy, and a simple worldview. What people have to say in qualitative interviews challenges simple views of the world.

In all this, what is good interviewing and what is a good research report? If it is not unambiguous truth that we seek, what are we after? What if in my research reports (e.g., Rosenblatt 2000) I claim to analyze narratives (people's organized stories of experience), not objective, unambiguous, true, as-accurate-as-possible statements? The old questions, drawn from positivist research, about reliability and validity have a great deal of currency in the social sciences and are certainly matters that many of us, as qualitative researchers, write about. And yet the questions are not quite the right questions for disciplining qualitative interview research. We differ from positivist researchers in terms of the realities that we write about, the goals of our re-

search, and our sense of reality. If we are at the boundary between fact and fiction, we need to think of reliability and validity in a different sense; perhaps we might use the words but change the meanings. What is reliable and valid becomes based not on objective truth but on what we believe to be fact (Denzin 1997:159, n. 5) established as well as we can from some perspective.

Questions of validity can be separated into questions about the quality of the interviews, questions about the quality of the texts created to represent the interviews, and questions about the quality of claims about the realities the researcher takes the interviews to represent (see Alasuutari 1995). For each of the three, there may be different grounds for doubting absolute truth or anything like firm validity. For each there may be different things a qualitative researcher can do to persuade self and reader that the research is worth taking seriously. To the extent that the data analysis and claims about the data are made on the basis of texts that others can know (for example, through interview quotes), it may be easiest to establish something like validity for the data analysis. As Pertti Alasuutari has noted: "Although we cannot assume that we get to the truth of the phenomenon talked about in interviews, we CAN make more or less valid, that is more or less clearly empirically grounded and defendable claims and interpretations about the interview text: e.g., how it is organized, what narrative structures the interviewee used, what discourses are evident in it, etc." (personal communication, December 1999).

Beyond that, validity involves writing in an interesting way, saying things that readers can believe to be true from some perspective, and saying things that help readers to see the world in new ways. It is valid if we can establish facticity in some way that makes sense within a community of others (Denzin 1997) and if our narrative rings true enough by standards that are valued in that community. It is reliable if, going back into the same human morass, we, writers and readers, can see more or less the same things, the "facts," from the particular perspective we have been taking. And if it is not reliability and validity we are after—if using those terms does not ring true—how about using "memorable," "transforming," "entertaining," and "fascinating" as criteria?

Will writing fiction, or even imagining writing fiction, make one a better interviewer? I think anything that challenges an interviewer to think in new ways can be helpful. For me, the writing of fiction has given me a better ear for interviewer-interviewee dialogue and the dialogue among people being interviewed together. By a "better ear," I mean that I think I am more aware of the dialogue and the ways that one person does or does not connect well with what someone else said. I think I am more aware of how at some level the dialogue is a unit, not a collection of separate but more or less related statements. I also think I am more aware of what will read well when put into writing and what needs clarification or explication in order to be understood by a reader.

At another level, writing fiction has, I think, opened me to possibility. That is, something about going where fantasy happens to go has made me more willing to follow interviewees on tangents or even to push them out onto tangents. At times that seems to make me a less focused interviewer and makes for longer interviews and additional hours with the transcribing machine. Sometimes those tangents seem to me to be productive—another chapter in a social science research book, a new social research lead. Perhaps, once in a while, a tangent gets me thinking about something I might include, after considerable transformation, in a work of fiction. But sometimes those tangents seem to me more about my indulging my curiosity or an interviewee's desire to go far away from my research interest, and then what I have is a lot of specifics about something I believe I will never write up for social science readers.

◆ Conclusion

In writing about the boundary between fact and fiction, I am doing what I think is always good for a researcher to do: to question recurrently and determinedly the fundamental philosophical grounds on which research rests. There is nothing sacred about specific research methods or conventions of research reporting. They are so embedded in culture, in the sociology of the academic world, in the sociology of American society, that those methods are limited and limiting in myriad ways. Nor do I think I escape limits when I question. This chapter, for example, is still very much embedded in culture, society, and orthodoxies. But by raising the questions I raise, I am at least asking qualitative interview researchers to examine their presuppositions.

The perspective I offer here on the blurring of the boundary between fact and fiction points out that fiction may be a legitimate outcome of qualitative interviewing research. It also points out that there may be much in social research that can be said to be fictional. But I do not think the blurring of the boundary between fiction and fact means that if one is doing qualitative interview research, anything goes. Interviewing at the border of fact and fiction, one still must be a craftsperson, a consummate interviewer, a doubter, a systematic explorer, and a careful reporter in ways that are responsive to a community of researchers (even if it includes many people one could label as doubters). And yet, looking at fiction and the writing of fiction can help one to think through what one is doing and what it means.

At the end of this, I want to speak to the reader who is depressed or angered at the thought that the idealism, security, safety, and disciplined honesty of social *science* may have been lost to an anything-goes chaos. I think that we always had an anything-goes chaos, but it was dressed up to look like honest, realist science. The move into multiple realities, an awareness of the ways that researcher subjectivity operates even when using the trappings of science, the exploration of alternative modes of representing what we know, and all else that seems to contribute to the new chaos are, I think, actually more honest—more true to the social world and to human psychology and sociology—than what went on in the past.

At the same time, I think the exploration of alternative modes of representing what we know has given us a blessed freedom to feel, know, and communicate. As I experience it, there is a sense of using parts of one's mind, language, and awareness that have been taboo to use in modernist social science. And with that freedom comes a power to ask the people we interview new and interesting questions, to know them, and to inform ourselves and our readers in ways that were blocked in the past.

■ *References*

Alasuutari, P. 1995. *Researching Culture: Qualitative Method and Cultural Studies.* London: Sage.
———. 1998. *An Invitation to Social Research.* London: Sage.
Ang, I. 1985. *Watching* Dallas: *Soap Opera and the Melodramatic Imagination.* London: Methuen.
Campbell, D. T. 1988. *Methodology and Epistemology for Social Science: Selected Papers.* Chicago: University of Chicago Press.
Clifford, J. 1986. "Introduction: Partial Truths." Pp. 1-26 in *Writing Culture: The Poetics and Politics of Ethnography,* edited by J. Clifford and G. E. Marcus. Berkeley: University of California Press.
Denzin, N. K. 1997. *Interpretive Ethnography: Ethnographic Practices for the 21st Century.* Thousand Oaks, CA: Sage.
Fontana, A. and J. H. Frey. 1994. "Interviewing: The Art of Science." Pp. 361-76 in *Handbook of Qualitative Research,* edited by N. K. Denzin and Y. S. Lincoln. Thousand Oaks, CA: Sage.
Gergen, K. J. 1988. "The Concept of Progress in Psychological Theory." Pp. 1-14 in *Recent Trends in Theoretical Psychology,* edited by W. J. Baker, L. P. Mos, H. V. Rappard, and H. J. Stam. New York: Springer Verlag.
———. 1994. "Mind, Text, and Society: Self-Memory in Social Context." Pp. 78-104 in *The Remembering Self: Construction and Accuracy in the Self-Narrative,* edited by U. Neisser and R. Fivush. New York: Cambridge University Press.
Gilman, C. P. 1979. *Herland.* New York: Pantheon.
Gubrium, J. F. and J. A. Holstein. 1997. *The New Language of Qualitative Method.* New York: Oxford University Press.
Gülerce, A. 1995. "An Interview with K. J. Gergen (Part 1): Culture and Self in Postmodern Psychology: Dialogue in Trouble?" *Culture and Psychology* 1:147-59.
Gusfield, J. 1976. "The Literary Rhetoric of Science: Comedy and Pathos in Drinking Driver Research." *American Sociological Review* 41:16-34.
Harré, R. 1990. "Some Narrative Conventions of Scientific Discourse." Pp. 81-101 in *Narrative in Culture: The Uses of Storytelling in the Sciences, Philosophy, and Literature,* edited by C. Nash. London: Routledge.
Holland, N. N. 1968. *The Dynamics of Literary Response.* New York: Oxford University Press.
Holstein, J. A. and J. F. Gubrium. 1995. *The Active Interview.* Thousand Oaks, CA: Sage.
Hoppenstand, G. C. 1987. *In Search of the Paper Tiger: A Sociological Perspective of Myth, Formula and the Mystery Genre in the Entertainment Print Mass Medium.* Bowling Green, OH: Bowling Green State University Popular Press.
Hurston, Z. N. 1937. *Their Eyes Were Watching God.* Philadelphia: J. B. Lippincott.
Kvale, S. 1996. *InterViews: An Introduction to Qualitative Research Interviewing.* Thousand Oaks, CA: Sage.
La Farge, O. 1929. *Laughing Boy.* Boston: Houghton Mifflin.

McCall, M. M., H. S. Becker, P. Meshejian, and R. A. Hilbert. 1990. "Performance Science." *Social Problems* 37:117-32.

Paget, M. A. 1983. "Experience and Knowledge." *Human Studies* 6:67-90.

———. 1995. "Performing the Text." Pp. 222-44 in *Representation in Ethnography,* edited by J. Van Maanen. Thousand Oaks, CA: Sage. (Reprinted from M. A. Paget, *A Complex Sorrow: Reflections on Cancer and an Abbreviated Life.* Edited by M. L. DeVault. Philadelphia: Temple University Press, 1993.)

Polkinghorne, D. E. 1988. *Narrative Knowing and the Human Sciences.* Albany: State University of New York Press.

Pollner, M. and L. McDonald-Winkler. 1985. "The Social Construction of Unreality: A Case Study of a Family's Attribution of Competence to a Severely Retarded Child." *Family Process* 24:251-54.

Popper, K. R. 1962. *Conjectures and Refutations: The Growth of Scientific Knowledge.* New York: Basic Books.

Richardson, L. 1987. "Disseminating Research to Popular Audiences: The Book Tour." *Qualitative Sociology* 10:164-76.

———. 1994. "Writing: A Method of Inquiry." Pp. 516-29 in *Handbook of Qualitative Research,* edited by N. K. Denzin and Y. S. Lincoln. Thousand Oaks, CA: Sage.

Richardson, L. and E. Lockridge. 1998. "Fiction and Ethnography: A Conversation." *Qualitative Inquiry* 4:328-36.

Rosenau, P. M. 1992. *Post-modernism and the Social Sciences: Insights, Inroads, and Intrusions.* Princeton, NJ: Princeton University Press.

Rosenblatt, P. C. 1981. "Ethnographic Case Studies." Pp. 194-225 in *Scientific Inquiry and the Social Sciences,* edited by M. B. Brewer and B. E. Collins. San Francisco: Jossey-Bass.

———. 1990. *Farming Is in Our Blood: Farm Families in Economic Crisis.* Ames: Iowa State University Press.

———. 1994. *The Metaphors of Family Systems Theory.* New York: Guilford.

———. 2000. *Parent Grief: Narratives of Loss and Relationship.* Philadelphia: Brunner/Mazel.

Rosenblatt, P. C., L. de Mik, R. M. Anderson, and P. A. Johnson. 1985. *The Family in Business: Understanding and Dealing with the Challenges Entrepreneurial Families Face.* San Francisco: Jossey-Bass.

Rosenblatt, P. C. and T. A. Karis. 1993. "Economics and Family Bereavement Following a Fatal Farm Accident." *Journal of Rural Community Psychology* 12(2):37-51.

———. 1993-94. "Family Distancing Following a Fatal Farm Accident." *Omega* 28:183-200.

Rosenblatt, P. C., T. A. Karis, and R. D. Powell. 1995. *Multiracial Couples: Black and White Voices.* Thousand Oaks, CA: Sage.

Sanders, W. B. 1974. *The Sociologist as Detective: An Introduction to Research Methods.* New York: Praeger.

Scheurich, J. J. 1995. "Interviewing." *International Journal of Qualitative Studies in Education* 8:239-52.

Smith, D. E. 1987. *The Everyday World as Problematic: A Feminist Sociology.* Boston: Northeastern University Press.

Strauss, A. L. and J. Corbin. 1998. *Basics of Qualitative Research: Techniques and Procedures for Developing Grounded Theory.* 2d ed. Thousand Oaks, CA: Sage.

Weiss, R. S. 1994. *Learning from Strangers: The Art and Method of Qualitative Interview Studies.* New York: Free Press.

Wilss, W. 1982. *The Science of Translation: Problems and Methods.* Tübingen, Germany: Gunter Narr Verlag Tübingen.

13

INTERVIEWING, POWER/KNOWLEDGE, AND SOCIAL INEQUALITY

◆ **Charles L. Briggs**

Back in 1986, I published a book titled *Learning How to Ask: A Sociolinguistic Appraisal of the Role of the Interview in Social Science Research*. Analyzing interviews that I had conducted during more than a decade's research in New Mexico, I argued that the interview is fairly unique and rather poorly understood as a communicative event. I was particularly interested in the asymmetries of power that emerge in interview situations and how they are embodied in what I referred to as "metacommunicative norms," principles that invest interviewers with control over the referential content of what is said (by posing questions), the length and scope of answers (by deciding when to probe or ask a new question), and the way that all participants construct their positionality with respect to the interview and the information it produces. Interview data

have multiple footings, to use Erving Goffman's (1981) term, being simultaneously rooted in the dynamics of the interview, the social spheres constructed by the responses, and the academic or other domains (theoretical and empirical) that give rise to the project and to which it contributes.

I argued that differences between contrasting sets of such norms often lead to problems that range from misunderstandings to resistance and conflict between interviewers and respondents. I suggested that interviewing deploys discourse that is highly adapted to producing the precise types of information that will be recontextualized in the books, articles, reports, media productions, and the like that are envisioned as the final product. When interviews provide the nation-state and its institutions with representations of marginalized populations, the possibilities for constructing a "minority voice" that confirms the hegemonic status quo is thus acute.

My goal was not to suggest that researchers should abandon interviews, a position that would be as counterproductive as it would be unrealistic. Rather, I sought to bring into focus the discrepancy between the complex character of interview data as discursive phenomena and the way they are reified as reflections of the social phenomena depicted in questions and answers. I also attempted to demonstrate how deeply the power relations that emerge in interviews are embedded in the data they produce. Drawing on work in a number of fields, I suggested that this discursive mediation should not be viewed as a source of contamination but rather as a crucial source of insights into both interviewing processes and the social worlds they seek to document.

The present juncture provides an excellent moment to return to these questions. A great deal of work—inspired by poststructuralism; postmodernism; ethnic, cultural, and women's studies; subaltern studies; research on globalization; and other perspectives—has explored the way that discourses of difference lie at the center of producing and resisting structures of social inequality. At the same time, the social and political importance of interviews of many sorts has expanded greatly in the decade and a half since I published my study; we now live, as Paul Atkinson and David Silverman (1997) put it, in the interview society. In many countries, a populist aura attempts simultaneously to project the voice of the "average citizen" into the middle of electoral politics and to place the voices of candidates and officials as those of concerned citizens or political outsiders; this political agenda is closely tied to new communications technologies. Television and radio programs that specialize in interviews with persons who have special stories to tell, candidates, politicians, specialists, and celebrities have flourished. Political candidates use question-and-answer-based media events as central features of electoral campaigns, and polling increasingly guides who runs, what candidates say, and whom they address.

My goal in this chapter is to extend the discursive analysis of power relations in the interview that I began in *Learning How to Ask* in such a way as to connect it with approaches to discourse that emerge from these perspectives and historical developments. I hope to be able to provide some insight into why interviewing is playing such a profound role in shaping forms of knowledge and practices in contemporary society and how interviews are being used in legitimating the growing social inequality that characterizes a globalizing world. I argue that research on interviewing can deeply inform contemporary concerns with knowledge, power, and difference.

◆ Modernity, Knowledge, and Power

Zygmunt Bauman (1987) argues that modernity created pervasive asymmetries of knowledge and power and used them in recasting growing social inequality, which was being exacerbated by the emergent capitalist economy, as the product of individual differences. John Locke ([1690] 1959) played a key role in creating a new cartography of language, knowledge, and discourse that mapped social inequality. In his *Essay Concerning Human Understanding,* Locke sharply separated rational reflections on individual experience and the articulation of thought in "plain," serious speech from imprecise, shifting, ambiguous uses of words, which he associated with rhetoric, poetry, and the like. This linguistic cartography was projected onto a social one. Gentlemen, who had the leisure and training to reflect rationally on their use of language, exemplified ideal speech.

Women, the poor, laborers, merchants, cooks, lovers, and rural folk, on the other hand, spoke in the imprecise ways that Locke condemned; such persons were largely incapable of developing greater rationality and linguistic precision by virtue of their lives. Inhabitants of the Americas provided Locke with an image of the linguistic baseline, the sort of knowledge of language that humans possess before their speech is shaped by civilization. Locke's discursive model of the modern subject—autonomous, disinterested, and rational—became the model of the scientist (see Shapin 1994), the citizen (see MacPherson 1962), and the public sphere (see Habermas [1962] 1989). At the same time, another fellow of the Royal Society, John Aubrey, was interviewing the traditional people of the countryside in constructing a portrait of the customs and language that defined modernity vis-à-vis its premodern opposite (see Aubrey 1972; Bauman and Briggs in press).

The productiveness of Locke's program seems to revolve around a central contradiction. His ideology projected an overtly egalitarian tone in that it constructed language as an essential part of the makeup of all human beings. At the same time, Locke authorized a set of standardizing practices and a powerful means of assessing the rationality of each individual and instituting gatekeeping mechanisms. Locke's ideology of language and politics naturalized both the emergent social and political structures of modernity and the idea that the degree to which individuals approximate the ideal of the modern subject naturally locates them within relations of inequality.

Zygmunt Bauman (1987) goes on to argue that this knowledge-inequality connection prompted the rise of "legislators" who exercise surveillance and control over the projected transformation of their social inferiors from premodern to modern ways of knowing. Arguing that we must examine how "effects of power circulate among scientific statements, what constitutes, as it were, their internal régime of power," Michel Foucault (1980:112) has pointed to the role of legislators in medical, legal, criminological, academic, and other institutions in producing discourses that create the objects they regulate.

The power invested in interviews to construct discourses that are then legitimated as the words of others points to their effectiveness as technologies that can be used in naturalizing the role of specialists in creating systems of difference. But we can also take a larger lesson from Foucault's work. Ian Hacking (1990) suggests that the systematic collection and publication of statistics by the nation-state regarding the lives of its citizens produced a revolution in the 19th century in terms of the way in which society was conceptualized and structured, one that centered on statistical definitions of the "normal" subject and its "abnormal" counterparts. We might suggest, following Foucault, that the growing ubiquity and visibility of interviewing in the 20th century has created a widely disseminated idea that both social similarity and difference can best be explained through the use of interviews to reveal individual social and intrapsychic worlds and to compare them, thereby identifying patterns of consensus and disagreement. Interviewing is thus a "technology" that invents both notions of individual subjectivities and collective social and political patterns and then obscures the operation of this process beneath notions of objectivity and science—or, in the case of journalistic and television interviews, of insight and art.

Although Foucault draws our attention to institutions as epistemological regimes, he does little to elucidate the social dynamics that render them such powerful sites for producing discourse. Drawing on sociolinguistic research (see Hymes 1974), Pierre Bourdieu (1991) argues that forms of communicative competence constitute symbolic capital, the acquisition of which is constrained by such gatekeeping institutions as schools and professional societies (see also Erickson and Shultz 1982). Members of dominant sectors use interviews in furthering institutionalized agendas, such as the compilation of census information and the use of surveying for purposes of enhancing consumption or devising political rhetoric. Bourdieu ([1972] 1979, 1990) suggests that polling creates the illusion of a "public opinion," creating images of national conversations that serve the interests of institutions whose legitimacy derives from the relations of class-based inequality that are reproduced in the supposedly inclusive nature of this "public." Drawing on Bourdieu, we can suggest that interviews create and sustain the power relations of modern society in a variety of ways, by producing representations of social life that are deeply and invisibly informed by class relations and by providing modes of screening individuals, through employment, counseling, social service, and other interviews, for the forms of competence that will position them in relation to institutions. Dominated communities are common targets for interview projects, providing both models of difference and objects of surveillance and regulation.

Having reflected more deeply on the work of Foucault and Bourdieu during the past 15 years, I would criticize my earlier study for rooting its analysis of power too directly in interview settings themselves. Applying these writers' perspectives suggests that it is the *circulation* of discourse among a range of institutional contexts that imbues interviews with the power to shape contemporary life. Nevertheless, neither Foucault nor Bourdieu is very helpful when it comes to identifying concretely the discursive and institutional means by which this circulation takes place and how we can trace it in particular instances. Here the totalizing thrust of viewing discourse as political technology or symbolic capital can be suitably complemented by a discourse-analytic perspective that explores textual and contextual dimensions of the production, circulation, and interpretation of interviews as grounded social practice.

◆ *Heteroglossia and Recontextualization in Interviews*

Hayden White (1978) argues that the power of historical narratives derives from the way their rhetoric achieves two contradictory effects. First, historians imagine past events, thereby creating schemes of social classification and forms of agency and causation. Interview researchers similarly imagine the social worlds depicted in the content of responses, creating images of political participation, family life, work experience, and so forth. But interview materials simultaneously imagine an intrapsychic world for the interviewee, a space inhabited by opinions, memories, emotions, plans, preferences, and desires. As I argued in *Learning How to Ask,* interviews are saturated by images of the social dynamics of the interview itself, projections of the social context in which it takes place, the roles and power dynamics of interviewer and respondent, and their respective agendas. But a fourth sphere is being constructed, that of the imagined texts that will be created through the use of interview data. This realm becomes explicit in statements on consent forms regarding the textual rights that participants are granting researchers. The disclaimers that interviewees frequently insert, such as "I don't want the people who read your book to get the impression that . . . ," suggest that respondents often shape their responses in keeping with imaginings of future texts and audiences. Not only are these four realms constructed simultaneously, but interviews are punctuated by the distinct and often competing imaginations of researchers and respondents.

Second, historical rhetoric converts the arbitrary into the real, casting imaginations as reflections of what actually took place, thereby hiding the imaginary and arbitrary character of such constructions. Although a variety of strategies for converting imaginations into reality are used in the wealth of different sorts of projects that rely on interviews, erasing the third and fourth realms constructed in interviews in favor of the first two is key. In other words, some researchers highlight opinions, memories, and other reflections of the mental worlds of the respondents; others foreground the social worlds that are represented. Both of these strategies revolve around obscuring the role of constructions of the social dynamics of the interview and the way projected uses of the data are embedded in responses.

The richest rhetorical resource for the erasure of these domains consists of techniques for eliminating "distortion" and "bias"—explicit signs of the effects of the interaction and perceptions of research agendas on interview content. Suggesting that interview data (including surveys) can be obtained in such a way that their contextual grounding can be factored out (through sampling, question wording, training of interviewers, and the like) constitutes simultaneously a claim to the epistemological marginality of these realms and a prohibition on allowing any explicit evidence of their presence to appear in texts that report interview data.

Feminist interviewing has often made the position of the interviewer in relationship to the respondent a central object of description and analysis (see DeVault 1990; Harding 1987; Reinharz 1992). A great deal of attention has focused on the use of narratives that emerge in interviews as means of drawing attention to the complex processes that shape the construction of identities in interviews (see, e.g., Bruner 1990; Chase 1995; Mishler 1986, 2000; Riessman 1993). Postmodern scholars have sometimes violated this prohibition systematically and explicitly, highlighting the interaction between the participants and their visions of how the materials will be used; Ruth Behar's (1993) *Translated Woman* provides a notable example. Norman Denzin (1989) and others have brought postmodern perspectives to bear on the issue of interviewing in general, questioning the privileged authority of the interviewer or researcher and urging a decentering of subject positions.

Such notions as bias, distortion, reliability, and validity reveal a great deal about the assumptions that commonly underlie interview-based research. Elliot Mishler (1986) argues that researchers commonly see interview data as behavior that can be analyzed using stimulus-response models associated with scientific experimentation. The information obtained in this manner is seen as a set of stable "social facts" that have an objective existence independent of the linguistic and contextual settings in which they are "expressed" (see Karp and Kendall 1982). Jaber Gubrium and James Holstein (1997) suggest that this epistemological stance of naturalism, the notion that the task of researchers is to richly and accurately document the "natural" environment of the social world without disrupting it, lies at the center of much qualitative research and inspires related concerns. The reductionism of received interview practices also springs from Western ideologies of language (see Joseph and Taylor 1990; Schieffelin, Woolard, and Kroskrity 1998; Kroskrity 2000) that treat verbal interaction in Lockean fashion as a transfer of referential content from one party to another, as if participants had no interests or communicative foci that interfere with their playing the roles of interviewer and respondent (see Back and Cross 1982; Clark and Schober 1992; Dijkstra and van der Zouwen 1977, 1982: 3-4; Foddy 1993:13-14). Interviewing thus provides a valuable source of data on the ideologies of language that underlie social scientific research, particularly in that conceptions that have been banished from the realm of explicit theory are often preserved implicitly in "purely methodological" spheres.

The complexity of interviews does not emerge simply from the manner in which connections with distinct realms are imagined in the course of interviews. Rather, the process involves practices for extracting discourse from one social setting and inserting it in a range of other settings. In my work with Richard Bauman, we have argued that a vital part of the process of rendering discourse socially powerful involves gaining control over its recontextualization—rights to determine when, where, how, and by whom it will be used in other settings (Bauman and Briggs 1990; Briggs and Bauman 1992; see also Silverstein and Urban 1996). Interview discourse is maximally configured in terms of both form and content for recontextualization into the sorts of texts that the researcher anticipates creating—interviewees are granted very few rights over this process. Survey instruments and techniques for implementing them maximize the social control of interviewers by the researchers who direct the study as well of interviewees by interviewers, creating hierarchies of discursive authority that also include individuals responsible for coding data.

The recontextualization process provides another angle on the complexity of interview data. A statement that emerges in an interview is tied explicitly to the question that precedes it and generally indirectly to previous questions and responses, the broad range of texts, agendas, and contexts that shape questions and interviewing practices, and the anticipated uses of the data. Quotations or summaries taken from interviews used in publications are, of course, deeply entwined in this broad range of recontextualizations. As the work of Mikhail Bakhtin (1981) would suggest, this recontextualization process informs each word that is spoken, such that the different contexts, vocabularies, styles, subject positions, and the like are built into what is said and how it is uttered. Responses are like crossroads at which multiple paths converge, with signs pointing in all directions. The power of researchers thus lies not only in their control over what takes place in the interview itself but particularly in their ability to use that setting as a site that is geared toward creating a broad field for the circulation of discourse.

At the same time that researchers attempt to control how material will move between different sites, they seek to render all save a few dimensions of this process invisible. In order to seem "unbiased" and to be suitable for recontextualization in a range of future settings, interview materials must be systematically decontextualized in various ways, leaving only minimal road signs that point in the direction of social or intrapsychic worlds. Otherwise, data and analyses are likely to be rejected by positivistic researchers either as biased or as being too complex and contextually specific to permit abstraction and generalization. Atkinson and Silverman (1997) observe that even many critical, revisionist approaches to interviewing attempt to empower individuals to create biographical, authentic voices, thereby reifying an individual and confessional approach to discourse that is also promoted by corporate media. The indexical signs that point, as it were, to the embedding of this process in larger social and material structures are thus largely erased.

One advantage in viewing interviews not as unified political technologies but as politically situated and interested practices for producing and recontextualizing discourse is that this perspective enables us to see that respondents often attempt to resist discursive relations that are stacked against them. The literature on interviewing abounds with advice regarding "uncooperative" respondents. Scholars seldom seem to recognize that individuals who decline to participate or to answer particular questions, or who plead ignorance, "mislead" the interviewer, and the like, may be pursuing strategies designed to disrupt the recontextualization process.

I suggested in *Learning How to Ask* that the apparent failure of interviews I conducted early in my research on "Mexicanos" or Mexican Americans in New Mexico reflected precisely this type of contestation. The fact that I had a research project in hand and was asking reasonable questions of individuals who had detailed knowledge of the issues in question led me to believe that extensive answers would be forthcoming. My elderly respondents saw things differently. As the most authoritative sources of information on Mexicano cultural politics, they found it difficult to accept the idea that a young gringo should structure such discussions. Most of my initial questions were thus met with a jolting "¡Pues, quién sabe! [Well, who knows!]." By learning to respect these individuals' right to control the recontextualization of discourse about the past, I was able to gain insight not only into Mexican cultural politics but into the politics of memory and strategies of resistance to cultural and political-economic domination.

◆ Three Contradictions of Power and Knowledge in Contemporary Society

I alluded above to the way that differences in the distribution of knowledge came to be viewed as explaining social inequality in modern society. Locke clearly articulated a fundamental modernist contradiction as he simultaneously advanced the idea that common possession of capacities for language, rationality, and reflection render us all part of humanity and condemn most people to subordinate social categories on the basis of their purported failure to develop this potential. Two basic contradictions similarly seem to structure the relationship between knowledge and social inequality in late-capitalist societies, and I suggest that interviewing plays a key role in mediating them.

Lisa Lowe (1996) argues that economic and political structures place people of color in a contradictory position in the United States. On the one hand, the need to maintain a pool of cheap laborers who enjoy few legal and occupational protections prompts the racialization of populations and their placement in subordinate social categories. Immanuel Wallerstein makes a similar argument for the economic underpinnings of the construction of racial categories worldwide (see Balibar and Wallerstein 1991). Nonetheless, U.S. political ideologies are based on the imagination of a shared cultural and political community; ascriptive barriers of race, gender, and class that create hierarchies of types of citizenship thus render it difficult to conceive of U.S. society as actually reflecting this privileged political ideology, at least when these obstacles become visible. The work of critical discourse analysts suggests that similar processes are at work in European nation-states (see Blommaert 1997; Blommaert and Verschueren 1998; van Dijk 1984; Wodak 1999).

By conducting interviews among, say, African Americans, or asserting that X percentage of survey respondents are Latinos, researchers can project the sense that "minorities" are included in national conversations about politics, economics, medicine, education, or whatnot—even when significant (and currently growing) barriers limit the participation of people of color in the institutions that regulate these domains. By the same token, by classifying respondents as members of racialized groups, researchers can create a synecdochic logic that suggests that an Asian American, for example, is speaking *as* an Asian American and is representing all Asian Americans, thereby confirming a sense of people of color as one-sided subjects. These practices also project interviews as capable of including racialized, subordinated voices in a seemingly equal position within national conversations. Whereas native-born, middle-class whites just naturally seem to be part of the dialogue, people of color and working-class persons can be portrayed as needing the mediation of researchers, journalists, or other professionals to make their voices heard on public stages. Here interviewing has assumed a crucial part of the role of the legislator identified by Bauman (1987).

Second, as globalization is augmenting social inequality, both within and between countries, a number of observers have sought to characterize its effects on the participation of populations on the so-called periphery. Arjun Appadurai (1996) argues that globalization is producing new modes of inclusion, suggesting that deterritorialization and denationalization disrupt centralization of control over global flows of capital, people, goods, culture, and information. He thus suggests that the United States no longer dominates "a world system of images but is only one node of a complex transnational construction of imaginary landscapes" (p. 31). Appadurai's vision of globalization is thus one of a global egalitarianism, in that even the poor and powerless can participate actively in shaping widely distributed practices of the imagination.

Other writers view globalization as largely *exclusionary,* as exacerbating social differences based on access to capital, commodities, information, and culture. Michel-Rolph Trouillot (1991) has pinpointed a key issue here in a brief but highly suggestive passage. Insofar as a universal transition is postulated from "modern" to "postmodern" or from "national" to "deterritorialized" ideologies and social forms, what are the implications for social segments that were deemed to have failed to be incorporated into *modern* social, cultural, and economic patterns? If this supposedly universal stage of globalized, postmodern culture is tied to a questioning of the "metanarratives" and cultural premises of modernization, it would seem to exclude people who never gained access to progress and modernity. Zygmunt Bauman (1998) suggests that the production of social fragmentation, differentiation, and inequality so fundamental to globalization fixes some people in space and restricts access to the globally circulating capital and culture that others increasingly enjoy; getting localized while others get globalized "is a sign of social deprivation and degradation" (p. 2).

CNN provides a striking illustration of the power of interviewing in mediating this contradiction between the inclusive and exclusive effects of globalization. The cable television news network's broadcasts take the voices and images of East Timorese refugees or victims of Venezuelan floods and project them to audiences worldwide, creating the sense of a global conversation. Nevertheless, whereas experts, particularly those living in industrialized countries, can make broad pronouncements on global phenomena, poor victims of wars, epidemics, and disasters are called upon to speak about the most immediate and concrete dimensions of their own experience. Different segments of the same broadcast can present interviews with the president or prime minister of a rich and powerful nation-state, the CEO of a transnational corporation that has just completed a huge merger, and survivors of genocidal campaigns. The sense that the faces, songs, and stories of all people are included in these global flows is thus projected without attention being drawn to the increasingly monopolistic formations of capital and power that determine who gets to speak and when as well as what counts as a local voice.

The illusion of equality goes hand in hand with quite different constructions of historical agency as we view leaders and CEOs speaking about their roles as globalizing agents, as catalysts of changes that produce structural changes that lead to more globalized markets, transnational intervention into affairs of seemingly sovereign nation-states, and greater social inequality. Individuals constructed as localizing agents, on the other hand, are portrayed as experiencing the effects of such policies. Interviews animate the role of the legislator, who controls the production and circulation of public voices on a global basis while creating the illusion that he or she is simply a witness to conversations and events that shape history. Interviewing thus aids the large transnational corporations that own the global media in projecting images of a worldwide community of producers and consumers, and of the very different positions that they occoupy in relation to capital.

◆ Conclusion

David Harvey (1989) has argued that new technologies of transport and communication have effected a victory of time over space, producing time-space compression and continual fragmentations of time-space patterns that lead to the postmodern feeling of dislocation. The notion that global capital is undermining the power of nation-states and destroying our sense of place, identity, and authenticity has moved from scholarly discourse, where it has become increasingly criticized and qualified, into popular and corporate discourses. Such influential observers as Robert Putnam (1993) have argued that this process is undermining the foundations of democracy, which are described as resting in the face-to-face interactions that characterized civil society—as epitomized by small-town society. This postmodern nostalgia for a supposedly authentic and interactional past does not, of course, lead Putnam or the governments (including the U.S. government) that have taken up his cry to call for an end to global political intervention or corporate expansion. Rather, it creates a vast need to project what appear to be forms of face-to-face communication and decision making as forming the center of social and political processes.

Enter the interview, that archetype of dyadic communication. Whether interviews take place in interviewees' homes, on *The Oprah Winfrey Show,* or on *CNN Headline News,* or even when interlocutors are connected only by telephone lines, these encounters create vox populi that seemingly provide an interpersonal— rather than purely private or purely public and depersonalized—space for the articulation of individual perspectives. I argued in *Learning How to Ask* that this image is largely illusory, in that interviews are structured by power asymmetries and by conventions that produce discursively complex material that is geared toward the institutional ends for which it was created. I have argued here that construing the interview itself as the locus of knowledge production places audiences and analysts alike in the grip of a powerful illusion. I have suggested, rather, that the power of interviewing lies in the status of the interpersonal interaction as one site in a complex process of controlling the decontextualization and recontextualization of discourse, one that links broader scholarly, corporate, and political agendas; previously circulating messages (be they scholarly literatures or campaign slogans); forms of disciplinary authority or celebrity stature; and the creation of texts, media programs, Web sites, and the like that serve the interests of interviewers and their employers. The sense that the people have spoken through such venues is sustained by the heteroglossic nature of what is said, being shot through with the echo of the words and contexts that shaped its production and that guide its recontextualization.

We are now more thoroughly modern than ever, in the sense that the illusion of shared participation in discourse and the production of knowledge legitimates practices for creating social inequality and modes of exclusion that seem to spring naturally from differences in what individuals know and can project into the public sphere. Ironically, new technologies are reinvigorating desire for the sense that it is interpersonal interaction and self-expression that shape our identities and lives; Internet chat rooms have taken a quite visible place alongside radio and television talk shows, call-ins by listeners and viewers, electronic "town meetings," and interviews by journalists in satisfying this longing. Corporations are increasingly requiring their employees to end service encounters with the briefest of interviews: "How was everything?"

Interviews played key roles in the political technologies of the modern era, being central to the power of the state to enumerate and imagine its citizens, of physicians to medicalize their patients' ills, of psychiatrists to illuminate madness and define sanity, of lawyers and courts to construct criminals and invent crimes, and so forth. As Foucault and many others have argued, these are powers of abstraction, disembodiment, and objectification. As postmodern angst and global insecurity create resistance to master narratives and faceless, bureaucratic control, the productive power of the illusion of social interaction and self-expression that fuels both scholarly and popular senses of interviews positions them even more crucially within the technologies and social relations of a globalized world. As tools are required for inventing new forms of social inequality and the practices needed to construe them as products of passivity in the face of global forces and/or as individual failings, uses of interviewing are sure to expand.

I called in 1986 for systematic inquiry into the discursive and political underpinnings of interviews and the need to dispense with the illusion that we know what they are and what functions they serve. This call was echoed in the same year by Mishler (1986). The scholarly debates and social, political-economic, and technological transformations that have emerged since that time suggest to me that the failure to devote substantive critical attention to interviews would place scholars as passive onlookers—or willing participants—in creating new practices of imagination for producing and legitimating social inequality in the 21st century. It thus seems clearer than ever that we must establish anew that systematic inquiry into interviewing is of far more than "merely methodological" significance. Just as a political economy of the production and circulation of interview materials and their role in shaping social representations and relations can fundamentally illuminate the dynamics of the historical moment in which we live, such critical perspectives are needed to help us avoid taking on the task of providing a key discursive machinery to be used in extending and naturalizing social inequality.

■ *References*

Appadurai, A. 1996. *Modernity at Large: Cultural Dimensions of Globalization.* Minneapolis: University of Minnesota Press.

Atkinson, P. and D. Silverman. 1997. "Kundera's *Immortality:* The Interview Society and the Invention of Self." *Qualitative Inquiry* 3:304-25.

Aubrey, J. 1972. *Three Prose Works.* Edited by J. Buchanan-Brown. Carbondale: Southern Illinois University Press.

Back, K. W. and T. S. Cross. 1982. "Response Effects of Role Restricted Respondent Characteristics." Pp. 189-207 in *Response Behaviour in the Survey-Interview,* edited by W. Dijkstra and J. van der Zouwen. London: Academic Press.

Bakhtin, M. M. 1981. *The Dialogic Imagination: Four Essays.* Edited by M. Holquist; translated by C. Emerson and M. Holquist. Austin: University of Texas Press.

Balibar, E. and I. Wallerstein. 1991. *Race, Nation, Class: Ambiguous Identities.* London: Verso.

Bauman, R. and C. L. Briggs. 1990. "Poetics and Performance as Critical Perspectives on Language and Social Life." *Annual Review of Anthropology* 19:59-88.

———. in press. *Modernizing Discourse: Language Ideologies and the Politics of Inequality.* Cambridge, UK: Cambridge University Press.

Bauman, Z. 1987. *Legislators and Interpreters: On Modernity, Postmodernity, and Intellectuals.* Ithaca, NY: Cornell University Press.

———. 1998. *Globalization: The Human Consequences.* New York: Columbia University Press.

Behar, R. 1993. *Translated Woman: Crossing the Border with Esperanza's Story.* Boston: Beacon.

Blommaert, J. 1997. "The Slow Shift in Orthodoxy: (Re)formulations of 'Integration' in Belgium." *Pragmatics* 7:499-518.

Blommaert, J. and J. Verschueren. 1998. *Debating Diversity: Analysing the Discourse of Tolerance.* London: Routledge.

Bourdieu, P. [1972] 1979. "Public Opinion Does Not Exist." Pp. 124-30 in P. Bourdieu, *Communication and Class Struggle,* Vol. 1. New York: International General.

———. 1990. "Opinion Polls: A 'Science' without a Scientist." Pp. 168-74 in P. Bourdieu, *In Other Words: Essays Towards a Reflexive Sociology.* Translated by M. Adamson. Cambridge: Polity.

———. 1991. *Language and Symbolic Power.* Translated by G. Raymond and M. Adamson. Cambridge, MA: Harvard University Press.

Briggs, C. L. 1986. *Learning How to Ask: A Sociolinguistic Appraisal of the Role of the Interview in Social Science Research.* Cambridge: Cambridge University Press.

Briggs, C. L. and R. Bauman. 1992. "Genre, Intertextuality, and Social Power." *Journal of Linguistic Anthropology* 2:131-72.

Bruner, J. S. 1990. *Acts of Meaning.* Cambridge, MA: Harvard University Press.

Chase, S. E. 1995. *Ambiguous Empowerment: The Work of Narratives of Women School Superintendents.* Amherst: University of Massachusetts Press.

Clark, H. H. and M. F. Schober. 1992. "Asking Questions and Influencing Answers." Pp. 15-48 in *Questions about Questions: Inquiries into the Cognitive Bases of Surveys,* edited by J. M. Tanur. New York: Russell Sage Foundation.

Denzin, N. K. 1989. *Interpretive Interactionism.* Newbury Park, CA: Sage.

DeVault, M. L. 1990. "Talking and Listening from Women's Standpoint: Feminist Strategies for Interviewing and Analysis." *Social Problems* 37:96-116.

Dijkstra, W. and J. van der Zouwen. 1977. "Testing Auxiliary Hypotheses behind the Interview." *Annals of Systems Research* 6:49-63.

———, eds. 1982. *Response Behaviour in the Survey-Interview.* London: Academic Press.

Erickson, F. and J. Shultz. 1982. *The Counselor as Gatekeeper: Social Interaction in Interviews.* New York: Academic Press.

Foddy, W. 1993. *Constructing Questions for Interviews and Questionnaires: Theory and Practice in Social Research.* Cambridge: Cambridge University Press.

Foucault, M. 1980. *Power/Knowledge: Selected Interviews and Other Writings, 1972-1977.* Edited by C. Gordon; translated by L. Marshall, J. Mepham, and K. Soper. New York: Pantheon.

Goffman, E. 1981. *Forms of Talk.* Philadelphia: University of Pennsylvania Press.

Gubrium, J. F. and J. A. Holstein. 1997. *The New Language of Qualitative Method.* New York: Oxford University Press.

Habermas, J. [1962] 1989. *The Structural Transformation of the Public Sphere: An Inquiry into a Category of Bourgeois Society.* Translated by T. Burger. Cambridge: MIT Press.

Hacking, I. 1990. *The Taming of Chance.* Cambridge: Cambridge University Press.

Harding, S., ed. 1987. *Feminism and Methodology: Social Science Issues.* Bloomington: Indiana University Press.

Harvey, D. 1989. *The Condition of Postmodernity.* Cambridge, MA: Blackwell.

Hymes, D. 1974. *Foundations in Sociolinguistics: An Ethnographic Perspective.* Philadelphia: University of Pennsylvania Press.

Joseph, J. E. and T. J. Taylor, eds. 1990. *Ideologies of Language.* London: Routledge.

Karp, I. and M. B. Kendall. 1982. "Reflexivity in Fieldwork." Pp. 249-73 in *Explaining Social Behavior: Consciousness, Human Action, and Social Structure,* edited by P. F. Secord. Beverly Hills, CA: Sage.

Kroskrity, P. V., ed. 2000. *Regimes of Language: Ideologies, Polities, and Identities.* Santa Fe, NM: School of American Research Press.

Locke, J. [1690] 1959. *An Essay Concerning Human Understanding,* 2 vols. New York: Dover.

Lowe, L. 1996. *Immigrant Acts: On Asian American Cultural Politics.* Durham, NC: Duke University Press.

MacPherson, C. B. 1962. *The Political Theory of Possessive Individualism: Hobbes to Locke.* Oxford: Oxford University Press.

Mishler, E. G. 1986. *Research Interviewing: Context and Narrative.* Cambridge, MA: Harvard University Press.

———. 2000. *Storylines: Craftartists' Narratives of Identity.* Cambridge, MA: Harvard University Press.

Putnam, R. D. 2000. *Bowling Alone: The Collapse and Revival of American Community.* New York: Simon & Schuster.

Reinharz, S. 1992. *Feminist Methods in Social Research.* New York: Oxford University Press.

Riessman, C. K. 1993. *Narrative Analysis.* Newbury Park, CA: Sage.

Schieffelin, B. B., K. A. Woolard, and P. V. Kroskrity, eds. 1998. *Language Ideologies: Practice and Theory.* New York: Oxford University Press.

Shapin, S. 1994. *A Social History of Truth: Civility and Science in Seventeenth-Century England.* Chicago: University of Chicago Press.

Silverstein, M. and G. Urban, eds. 1996. *Natural Histories of Discourse.* Chicago: University of Chicago Press.

Trouillot, M.-R. 1991. "Anthropology and the Savage Slot: The Poetics and Politics of Otherness." Pp. 17-44 in *Recapturing Anthropology: Working in the Present,* edited by R. G. Fox. Santa Fe, NM: School of American Research Press.

van Dijk, T. A. 1984. *Prejudice in Discourse: An Analysis of Ethnic Prejudice in Cognition and Conversation.* Amsterdam: J. Benjamins.

White, H. 1978. *Tropics of Discourse: Essays in Cultural Criticism.* Baltimore: Johns Hopkins University Press.

Wodak, R. 1999. "Discourse and Racism: European Perspectives." *Annual Review of Anthropology* 28:175-99.

AUTHOR INDEX

Abu-Lughod, L., 46, 125, 161
Adler, P., 61, 161
Adler, P. A., 61, 161
Agronick, G., 160
Alanko, T., 100
Alasuutari, P., 23, 68, 231, 235, 238
Allen, B., 213
Allison, D., 173
Altheide, D. L., 142, 149, 150
Anders, E., 82
Anderson, E., 7
Anderson, K., 58, 160, 217-218
Anderson, R. M., 225-226
Ang, I., 234
Angrosino, M. V., 161, 162
Anselm, R., 6
Aoki, K., 92
Appadurai, A., 250
Appleby, J., 220
Apter, T., 160
Arbinger, P., 82
Aristotle, 220
Armitage, S., 160
Aron, R., 220
Ashplant, T., 213
Atkinson, J. M., 117
Atkinson, P., 7, 12, 13, 14, 29, 37, 51, 113, 115, 117, 141, 144, 244, 248
Atkinson, R., 124
Aubrey, J., 245
Austin, D. A., 161, 193

Aycock, A., 92
Azadovskii, M., 126

Babbie, E., 57
Bachmann, D., 86
Back, K. W., 247
Baff, S. J., 193
Bakhtin, M. M., 147, 148, 248
Balibar, E., 249
Balint, M., 36
Bannert, M., 82
Bar-On, D., 160
Barthes, R., 220
Basso, K., 132-133
Baudrillard, J., 6-7, 9, 51, 59
Bauman, R., 127, 131, 245, 248
Bauman, Z., 244, 245, 249, 250
Baym, N., 82, 92, 94
Becker, H. S., 109-114, 118, 120, 121, 235
Behar, R., 46, 58, 125, 161, 196, 247
Belenky, M. F., 160
Bell, C., 160
Ben-Amos, D., 127
Bennett, C., 83, 94, 95, 97
Benney, M., 22-23
Benson, L., 220
Benveniste, E., 13
Bergen, R. K., 159, 160
Berger, L., 160, 161
Berger, P. L., 68-69

Bertaux-Wiame, I., 216-217
Best, J., 61
Best, S., 4, 8, 51
Black, A., 89
Blair, J., 86, 88, 89
Blee, K. M., 161, 162, 164
Bloch, M., 220
Blommaert, J., 249
Bloom, L., 160
Blumer, H., 53, 68-69, 149
Boas, F., 124
Bochner, A. P., 38, 158, 160, 161, 167, 171, 193
Boden, D., 56, 117
Borland, K., 134, 218
Borroff, M., 189
Bourdieu, P., 142, 153, 245-246
Brady, I., 193
Brannen, J., 160
Braudel, F., 220
Brewer, J. P., 97
Briggs, C. L., 28, 67, 68, 124, 127, 128, 131, 159, 245, 248
Brissett, D., 148
Bristow, A. R., 159
Bruckman, A., 82
Bruner, J., 160, 247
Buchignani, N., 92
Buckholdt, D. R., 78
Burawoy, M., 142, 153
Burkhalter, B., 82

Cain, C., 125-126
Campbell, D. T., 226
Cándida Smith, R., 213-214, 216
Cannell, C. F., 34
Carrithers, M., 26
Case, D., 92
Chase, S., 160, 247
Chatman, S., 220
Chenail, R. J., 160
Christie, B., 92
Cicourel, A. V., 35, 41, 53, 55, 68
Clark, E. C., 216
Clark, H. H., 247
Clifford, J., 12-13, 38, 225
Clinchy, B. M., 160
Clough, P. T., 61, 161

Cobb, W. J., 67, 69
Coffey, A., 120
Cohen, J., 86
Collingwood, R. G., 220
Collins, M. P., 92, 94
Collins, P. H., 57, 159
Collins, S., 26
Colman, R., 88
Comley, P., 86, 88, 89
Confino, A., 220
Converse, J. M., 41, 71-72
Cook, J. A., 159, 160
Coomber, R., 84, 85, 89
Corbin, J., 232
Correll, S., 82
Counts, P., 87
Couper, M. P., 86, 88, 89
Coyle, S., 161
Crane, S., 220
Crapanzano, V., 54, 59, 161
Creswell, J. W., 86-87
Cross, T. S., 247
Cruikshank, J., 126-127
Culler, J. D., 210
Cullum-Swan, B., 189
Cutler, R. H., 94

Danforth, L., 10
Danforth, S., 189-190
Davis, B. H., 97
Daws, L., 82
Dawson, L., 61
Dean, J. P., 116
Dégh, L., 46, 126
de Mik, L., 225-226
Denzin, N. K., 6, 7, 55, 56, 58, 60, 114-115, 141, 143, 144, 148, 150, 161, 190, 192, 225, 238, 247
Derrida, J., 52, 188
Deutscher, E., 116
DeVault, M., 69, 75, 79, 159, 160, 247
Dickens, D. R., 51, 52
Dijkstra, W., 247
Dillard, A., 148
Dillman, D. A., 59, 86, 89
Dingwall, R., 56, 57
Douglas, J., 12, 53-54, 71, 72-73, 159, 160, 176

Dray, W., 220
Dreyfus, H. L., 24, 25, 59
Dubrovsky, V. J., 92
Duelli Klein, R., 160
Dumont, J. P., 161
Dundes, A., 132
Dunne, G., 83, 93, 94
Dwyer, K., 54, 129

Earnest, W. R., 218-219
Eason, D., 149
Eckerman, E., 82, 98
Eco, U., 189
Edgley, C., 148
Edmondson, R., 13
Edwards, R., 160
Eisenberg, E. M., 161
Elam, Y., 220
Elfrink, J., 86
Ellingson, L., 161
Elliott, R., 167
Ellis, C., 16, 38, 60, 158, 160, 161, 165, 167,
    171, 193, 196
Erickson, F., 246
Erikson, K. T., 38
Esper, J. A., 159

Fahy, N., 82, 96
Featherstone, M., 8
Feldman, J. J., 67, 69
Fielding, N. G., 86-87
Filstead, W. J., 109, 110
Finch, J., 160
Fine, G. A., 110
Firth, R., 10
Fischer, M. M. J., 54
Fishbein, M., 41
Flaherty, M. G., 16, 38, 196
Floyd, K., 92
Foddy, W., 247
Fonow, M. M., 159, 160
Fontana, A., 51, 52, 59, 61, 62, 91, 144, 229
Forcht, K., 87
Foucault, M., 24-26, 43, 188, 245
Fowler, F. J., 69
Fox, K., 161
Frank, G., 124, 216

Frey, J. H., 59, 91, 144, 229
Friedlander, P., 220
Friedman, J., 8
Friedman, S. S., 220
Futrell, A., 159

Gadet, F., 210
Gaiser, T., 95
Gale, J., 160, 167
Galegher, J., 96
Garfinkel, H., 41, 45, 55, 56, 57, 68-69, 73-
    74, 78
Garland, D., 26
Garton, L., 82
Gates, W., 83
Gedi, N., 220
Geer, B., 109-114, 118, 120, 121
Geertz, C., 10-11, 24, 54, 60
Geist, P., 161
George, K. M., 125, 130
Gergen, K. J., 9, 225, 227
Giese, M., 92
Gilbert, N., 116
Gilgun, J. F., 189
Gilman, C. P., 234
Gjestland, L., 86
Glesne, C. E., 192, 194
Gluck, S. B., 58, 135
Goffman, E., 43, 117, 148, 243
Goldberger, N. R., 160
Golden, L., 220
Goodall, H. L., Jr., 161
Gorden, R. L., 67
Gottschalk, S., 142
Gourd, W., 161
Griffith, A., 160
Grima, B., 123, 124-125
Gubrium, J. F., 3, 15, 16, 29, 32, 33, 34, 38,
    39, 43, 44, 54, 56-57, 61, 68, 70, 74,
    75, 77, 78, 79, 113, 115, 124, 125,
    141, 143, 144, 145, 146, 147, 148,
    160, 162, 164, 171, 177, 226, 230,
    232, 247
Guerrero, E., 153
Gülerce, A., 225
Gumperz, J. J., 35
Gusfield, J., 233

Habermas, J., 245
Hacking, I., 245
Hahn, K. L., 82
Halbwachs, M., 216, 220
Hall, D., 159, 160, 161
Hammersley, M., 115, 117
Hantrais, L., 82
Haraway, D. J., 188
Harding, S., 69, 125, 247
Harré, R., 233
Harris, R., 210
Hart, C. W., 67, 69
Harvey, D., 251
Harvey, L., 62
Haythornthwaite, C., 82
Helson, R., 160
Heritage, J., 68-69, 117
Herring, S. C., 82
Hertz, R., 57, 58, 159
Hewson, C., 92
Heyl, B. S., 142
Higgens, P. C., 15
Hilbert, R. A., 235
Hochschild, A. R., 117
Hodkinson, P., 82, 84-85
Hofmeyr, I., 220
Holland, D. C., 125
Holland, N. N., 210, 234
Holstein, J. A., 3, 16, 29, 32, 34, 39, 43, 44, 54,56-57, 61, 68, 70, 74, 75, 78, 79, 113, 115, 124, 125, 141, 143, 144, 145, 146, 147, 148, 160, 162, 164, 171, 177, 226, 230, 232, 247
Hones, D. F., 193
Hong, W. C., 84
Hoppenstand, G. C., 235
Horn, S., 93, 98
Houtkoop-Steenstra, H., 56
Hoy, M. G., 86
Huff, C., 84
Hughes, E. C., 22, 43, 111, 112, 113, 114
Hunt, L., 220
Hurston, Z. N., 234
Hutchinson, S., 160
Hutton, P. H., 220
Huyssens, A., 220
Hyde, M. J., 216
Hyman, H. H., 67, 69
Hymes, D., 35, 245-246

Irwin-Zarecki, I., 220
Ives, E. D., 124

Jack, D. C., 58, 160, 217-218
Jackson, B., 125, 126, 135
Jackson, M., 141, 176
Jacob, M., 220
Jago, B., 161
James, W., 23
Jefferson, G., 35, 78
Johnson, J. M., 15
Johnson, M., 188
Johnson, P. A., 225-226
Jones, S. H., 161, 193
Jordan, B., 159
Jorgenson, J., 159
Joseph, J. E., 247
Josselson, R., 160
Jourtard, P., 210-211
Joyner, C. W., 210-211

Kahn, R. L., 34
Karis, T. A., 226, 233
Karp, D. A., 161
Karp, I., 247
Katzman, S., 88
Keesing, R., 131
Kehoe, C. M., 82, 84, 89, 100
Kellner, D., 4, 7, 8, 51
Kendall, L., 131
Kendall, M. B., 247
Kennedy, A., 84
Kent, R., 23
Kiesinger, C. E., 158, 160, 161, 165
Kiesler, S., 92, 96
Kirk, J., 71
Kojo, M., 100
Kolker, A., 161
Kollock, P., 91
Kondo, D. K., 161
Kramarae, C., 87
Kramer, J., 87
Krieger, S., 14, 54, 161, 197
Kroskrity, P. V., 247
Krueger, R. A., 98
Kulick, D., 161
Kvale, S., 159, 232

La Farge, O., 234
Lagerwey, M., 161
Lakoff, G., 188
Langellier, K., 159, 160, 161
Langness, L. L., 124
Larson, C. L., 160
Lash, S., 8
Lather, P., 161
Latour, B., 8
Laurent, D., 92
Lawless, E., 135
Lawton, J. E., 194-195
Lea, M., 82, 92
Leap, W. L., 161
Lee, R. M., 84, 86-87, 159, 160
Le Goff, J., 220
Lepenies, W., 12
Lepowsky, M., 127
Lewin, E., 161
Lewis, J., 159
Lewis, O., 131
Lidz, T., 26
Lieblich, A., 160
Liebow, E., 7, 13
Liljeberg, M., 100
Lincoln, Y. S., 192
Linden, R. R., 161
Lindesmith, A., 6
Loader, B. D., 83
Locke, J., 244-245
Lockridge, E., 14, 177, 234
Lofland, J., 62, 110
Lopez, A. M., 150
Lowe, L., 249
Lowenthal, D., 220
Luckmann, T., 68-69
Lukes, S., 26
Lupton, D., 82, 96
Lyman, S. M., 148
Lyotard, J. F., 5-6, 8-9, 51, 52

Maccoby, E. E., 34, 69
Maccoby, N., 34, 69
Macleod, V. A., 161, 165
MacPherson, C. B., 245
Madge, C., 82, 85, 89, 94, 96
Madge, J., 69-70
Maione, P. V., 160
Malinowski, B., 62

Mangione, T. W., 69
Mann, C., 82-83, 85, 87, 89, 90, 93, 94, 95, 97, 98, 99, 100
Manning, P. K., 189
Manning, P. L., 68
Marcus, G. E., 9-10, 12-13, 14, 38, 54
Markham, A. M., 59, 160, 161
Matheson, K., 82
May, T., 90
Maynard, D. W., 56
McCall, G. J., 110
McCall, M. M., 235
McDonald-Winkler, L., 230
McGinnis, T., 60
McGuire, T., 92
McLaughlin, M. L., 82
McMahan, E. M., 210-211, 213, 214-215, 216
Megill, A., 220
Mehta, R., 86
Meredith, B., 159
Meshejian, P., 235
Mienczakowski, J., 61
Mies, M., 160
Miller, J., 26
Miller, M., 159, 161
Miller, M. L., 71
Mills, C. W., 118
Mills, M., 133
Mink, L., 220
Mintz, S., 131
Mishler, E. G., 34-36, 37-38, 41, 68, 142, 153, 160, 194, 211-212, 247, 252
Moore, M., 94
Morgan, D. L., 97
Morgan, S., 61
Morrow, P., 133
Mulkay, M., 116
Murphy, J., 59-60, 61
Murphy, K. L., 92, 94
Murphy, R. F., 161
Myerhoff, B., 129-130, 160, 161
Myers, D., 87
Mykhalovskiy, E., 161

Narayan, K., 46, 125, 126, 132
Naylor, G., 153
Ned, A., 126-127
Nora, P., 220

Novick, P., 220

Oakley, A., 58, 135, 159, 160
Oberschall, A., 23-24
O'Brien, J., 61
Ochberg, R. L., 160
O'Connor, H., 82, 85, 89, 94, 96
Olick, J. K., 220
Osborne, K., 82
Oudes, B., 149
Owens, C., 57

Pacanowsky, M., 161
Paget, M. A., 14, 161, 230, 235
Park, R. E., 144
Parker, L., 84
Parks, M., 92
Parry, A., 166
Passerini, L., 203, 204-209, 217, 218
Patai, D., 58, 135
Patrick, A. S., 89
Pawlich, D., 9
Payne, D., 161
Peacock, J. L., 125
Perry, D., 83
Perry, J., 161
Pfohl, S., 61
Philip, C. E., 196-197
Pitkow, J. E., 82, 84, 89, 100
Platt, J., 161
Plummer, K., 118
Poindexter, C. C., 193
Polanyi, L., 214-215
Polkinghorne, D. E., 225
Pollner, M., 56, 68-69, 230
Ponticelli, C., 161
Pool, I. de S., 32, 73
Popper, K. R., 226
Portelli, A., 205, 212-213, 219-220
Poster, M., 8
Postman, N., 59
Powell, R. D., 226
Propp, V. I., 79
Prus, R., 61
Putnam, R. D., 251

Quinney, R., 161

Raatikainen, K., 100
Raban, J., 149
Rabinow, P., 24, 25, 62, 161
Racine, J., 131
Racine, L., 131
Raymond, E., 91
Reed-Danahay, D. E., 38
Reid, R., 82
Reinharz, S., 58, 69, 159, 160, 247
Renzetti, C. M., 159, 160
Rice, R. E., 92
Richardson, L., 14-16, 60-61, 161, 174, 177, 187, 190, 191, 193, 196, 198-199, 233, 234, 237
Richardson, M., 193
Ricoeur, P., 213, 220
Riemer, I., 60
Riesman, D., 22-23
Riessman, C. K., 160, 218, 247
Rilke, R. M., 136
Rinehart, R., 193
Robbins, J., 220
Roberts, H., 159
Robillard, A. B., 161
Rogers, C. R., 70
Romanoff, B. D., 160
Ronai, C. R., 161
Rosaldo, R., 124, 125, 130, 161
Rose, N., 26
Rosenau, P. M., 4-5, 8, 9, 225, 237
Rosenblatt, P. C., 225-226, 229, 233, 238
Rosenwald, G., 160, 219
Ross, J. L., 161
Roth, M. S., 220
Rothman, B. K., 160
Rubin, H. J., 38
Rubin, I. S., 38
Ryan, M., 9
Ryen, A., 82, 94, 95

Sacks, H., 35, 78
Sala, L., 92
Salmon, G., 82
Sánchez, R., 215-216
Sanders, C., 61
Sanders, W. B., 235
Sarup, M., 57
Satir, V., 168
Schaefer, D. R., 59, 86, 89

Schaeffer, N. C., 56
Schatzman, L., 110
Schegloff, E. A., 35, 78
Scheurich, J. J., 141, 231
Schieffelin, B. B., 247
Schmidt, R., 61
Schneider, J., 10, 14
Schober, M. F., 247
Schudson, M., 220
Schuman, H., 41, 71-72
Schutz, A., 55, 75
Searle, J., 59
Segura, D., 161
Seidman, I., 55-56, 58, 62, 87
Seidman, S., 8
Selvin, H. C., 23
Sen, M., 82
Senior, C., 83
Sethna, B. N., 92
Seymour, W., 82, 96
Shalin, D. N., 9, 61
Shapin, S., 245
Shapiro, M., 188
Shaw, D., 82
Sheehan, K. B., 86
Shelton, A., 54
Shields, R., 82
Short, J., 92
Shostak, A., 161
Shostak, M., 126
Shultz, J., 246
Sidney, A., 126-127
Siegel, J., 92
Silverman, D., 7, 28, 29, 36, 37, 51, 52, 67,
    68, 79, 82, 94, 95, 113, 115, 116, 117,
    141, 144, 244, 248
Silverstein, M., 248
Simmons, J. L., 110
Sivadas, E., 86
Smith, B., 193
Smith, C., 82
Smith, C. B., 84, 86, 87, 88, 89-90, 100-101
Smith, D., 160
Smith, D. E., 58, 69, 236
Smith, K., 126-127
Smith, M., 83, 91
Smith, P., 190, 195-196
Smithies, C., 161
Smith-Stoner, M. J., 82, 93
Snow, R. P., 149, 150

Sommerville, M., 193
Sood, U. D., 46
Spears, R., 92
Spender, D., 82
Spradley, J. P., 124
Sproull, L., 96
St. Pierre, E. A., 193, 196
Stacey, J., 160
Stanley, L., 160, 161
Staples, W. G., 68
Steedly, M. M., 130
Stember, C. H., 67, 69
Stephenson, N., 195
Stewart, F., 82-83, 85, 87, 89, 90, 93, 94, 95,
    97, 98, 99, 100
Stone, K., 132
Stones, A., 83
Strauss, A. L., 110, 111, 112, 113, 114, 232
Strauss, L., 6
Stringer, E., 160
Strout, C., 220
Suchman, L., 159
Sweet, C., 82, 95, 97-98

Taggart, J. M., 126
Tarule, J. M., 160
Taylor, T. J., 247
Tedlock, D., 188-189
Terkel, S., 30, 69
Tesch, R., 86-87
Thelen, D., 220
Thomas, D. S., 87
Thompson, P., 204, 216
Tillmann-Healy, L. M., 158, 160, 161, 165
Ting, C. B., 84
Titon, J. T., 125
Toelken, B., 133-134
Tonkin, E., 210-211, 213, 220
Travisano, R., 193
Trinh, T. M., 151-152
Triplett, T., 86, 88, 89
Tripp, D., 160
Trouillot, M. R., 220, 250
Trow, M., 111
Trujillo, N., 161
Tse, A. C. B., 84
Tse, K. C., 84
Tsing, A., 130
Turkle, S., 82

Ulmer, G. L., 189
Urban, G., 248

van der Zouwen, J., 56, 247
van Dijk, T. A., 249
Van Maanen, J., 9, 11-12, 15, 54, 60
Vansina, J., 220
Vaz, K. M., 57
Vazzana, G., 86
Verschueren, J., 249
Veyne, P., 220
Viramma, J., 131
Vogel, c., 92
von Sydow, C., 129
Voysey, M., 116

Wagner, D. G., 8
Wallace, P., 101
Wallerstein, I., 249
Walther, J. B., 82, 92, 94
Warren, C. A. B., 57
Webb, C., 160
Weber, T. A., 82, 93
Weiss, R. S., 26-27, 226, 228, 231
Wellman, B., 82
Weston, K., 57-58
Whalen, T. E., 89
White, H., 246
Whyte, W. F., 7, 11, 116

Willard, C., 159
Williams, E., 92
Williams, P., 161
Willson, M., 161
Wilson, H. S., 160
Wilson, M., 160
Wilss, W., 236
Winter, D., 84
Wise, S., 160, 161
Witmer, D., 88
Wittgenstein, L., 6
Wittner, J., 160
Wodak, R., 249
Woolard, K. A., 247
Woolgar, S., 8, 9, 14

Yates, F., 220
Yee, K. P., 84
Yerby, J., 161
Yi, K. W., 84
Yin, C. H., 84
Young, J. E., 220
Young, M., 127, 133

Zhou, K., 82, 98
Zimmerman, D. H., 56, 117

Zola, I. K., 161

SUBJECT INDEX

Accounts:
    interview society, 45, 46, 47
    participant observation, 116, 118-119, 120
    postmodern trends, 56, 57
"A Child Is Being Killed" (Clough), 61
Active interviewer subject:
    active interviewing, 68, 72, 75, 77-78
    feminist research, 58
    interview society, 32-34, 35
    phenomenology, 32-34, 35, 55, 56
Active interviewing:
    active interviewer subject, 68, 72, 75, 77-78
    active respondent subject, 68, 70-71, 72, 73, 74-76, 77
    agency, 70
    analytic implications, 78-79
    artful narratives, 73-74, 75, 78
    authenticity, 70, 71, 72, 77, 78
    categorization, 69-70
    cinematic society, 141, 146-147
    collaboration, 68, 71, 72, 73, 76-78, 79
    constructivism, 68-69, 70-71, 72, 77-78
    conversational interviewing, 67-68, 71-72, 75, 78-79
    conversation analysis (CA), 79
    creative interviewing, 72-73
    discourse analysis, 78, 79
    dramaturgical perspective, 75, 79
    elicitation process, 69-70
    emotionality, 69, 71, 72, 73, 74, 75, 76

epistemology, 70, 72
ethnomethodology, 68-69
everyday life, 73, 78
experiential truth, 68, 70-71
facilitator role, 71-72
family discourse, 78
feminist research, 69
flexible interviewing, 69-70
formative interviews, 69-70
guidelines, 67-68, 72-73
identity formation, 74-75, 76-77
individual experiences, 68, 69, 70-71, 72, 73-79
informal interviews, 70
interactive interviews, 67, 68, 72, 73-75, 78, 79
interpersonal process, 73-74
interpretations, 71, 72, 73-74, 75, 77, 78
interview context, 71-72, 75, 76-78
interviewer control, 71-72
interviewer role, 68, 71-73, 75-79
interviewer self-disclosure, 72-73
interview society, 67, 78
knowledge assembly, 68, 70, 79
knowledge production, 68, 70
knowledge transmission, 68, 70, 73
life history, 67, 70
linguistic research, 69
mass interviews, 69-70
meaning construction, 68-71, 72, 73-74, 75, 77-79

media, 67
minimalism, 75
mining analogy, 69
mutual disclosure, 72-73
narrative activation, 71-73, 75-78
naturalism, 78
neutrality, 70, 72, 75
objectivity, 70-71
oral history, 67
passive respondent subject, 70, 71, 72, 73, 75
personal narratives, 67, 68, 71-72, 73-79
postmodernism, 68, 69
postmodern sensibilities, 16
postmodern trends, 56
poststructuralism, 68, 69
public opinion, 73
quantitative research, 67-68
rationality, 71, 72, 73, 74
reciprocity, 72
reference frameworks, 75
reflexivity, 74
research approach, 73-78
research bias, 67-68, 69, 70, 78
research reliability, 67, 71
research reports, 79
research validity, 67, 70, 71
resource activation, 75-78
respondent practitioners, 73
respondent role, 68, 70-71, 72, 73, 74-79
respondent subjects, 74-75
rigorous methods, 78
social worlds, 67, 78
standardized survey interviews, 67-68, 71-72, 75, 78
subjectivity, 69, 72, 79
subjectivity alternatives, 75, 77
subject position shifts, 75-78
vessels of answers, 70, 71-72
vs. traditional interviewing, 67-68, 69-73, 75, 78
Active respondent subject:
active interviewing, 68, 70-71, 72, 73, 74-76, 77
interview society, 32-34, 35, 45, 46-47
phenomenology, 55, 56
Aesthetics, 234
Afghanistan, 133
African Americans, 57
Agency:

active interviewing, 70
interview society, 24, 25-26, 27, 30, 31, 43-44
participant observation, 116
poetic representation, 190-191
postmodern sensibilities, 7
postmodern trends, 53, 55, 56
social inequality, 246, 250-251
Alcoholics Anonymous (AA), 39, 125-126, 143
Anthropology:
personal/folk narratives, 124-125, 126-127, 131
postmodern sensibilities, 10-11, 12-14
postmodern trends, 54
A Place on the Corner (Anderson), 10
Artful narratives:
active interviewing, 73-74, 75, 78
interview society, 45-47
poetic representation, 190-191
"Art of Leaving, The" (McGinnis), 60
Asymmetrical model, 21-22, 34, 37, 46-47
social inequality, 243, 244-246, 249-251
Asynchronous communication, 81-82, 90-91, 101n.9
Australia, 61
Authenticity:
active interviewing, 70, 71, 72, 77, 78
cinematic society, 144, 145, 146, 149, 150-151
fact/fiction border, 230, 234, 236
interview society, 29, 31, 36, 37, 38
participant observation, 117, 119
postmodern sensibilities, 7, 9
Authority:
cinematic society, 149
fact/fiction border, 237
interview society, 22, 29
personal/folk narratives, 124, 127, 129, 131-132
poetic representation, 188
postmodern sensibilities, 5, 8, 9, 10, 11, 13, 14
postmodern trends, 54
social inequality, 247, 248, 249
Autoethnography:
poetic representation, 196-197
postmodern trends, 60
researcher experience, 157

Boys in White (Becher et al.), 113, 114
Bull Durham, 149

Categorization:
    active interviewing, 69-70
    interview society, 26, 36
    personal/folk narratives, 127
    poetic representation, 189-190
Chan Is Missing, 147-148
Cinematic society:
    authenticity, 144, 145, 146, 149, 150-151
    authority, 149
    cinematic surveillance, 143-150
    collaborative-active interview format, 141, 146-147, 153
    confessional mode, 144
    constructivism, 141, 147-148
    conversational interviewing, 141, 145, 146, 147, 148
    critical inquiry, 150-153
    cultural identities, 143, 144-146, 150-151
    cultural mediation, 141-143
    death row interview, 145-146, 147, 148, 149
    democratization, 153
    documentary interview, 151-152
    dramaturgical perspective, 141, 143, 146, 148-150
    elicitation process, 146-148
    emotionality, 143
    entertainment-investigative format, 144-147, 152
    epistemology, 146-148, 153n.2
    ethnography, 144, 150-152
    everyday life, 142, 143, 144, 149-150
    experiential truth, 151, 152
    gang culture, 150-151
    historical development, 143-146
    individual experiences, 143, 144-145, 146, 149, 150-151, 152
    interactive interviews, 145, 146-147, 148-149
    interpretations, 141, 148, 151-152
    interview society, 141, 144-146
    journalist/sociologist relationship, 144, 145
    knowledge production, 141-142
    life history, 144
    meaning construction, 144, 145, 152-153
    multiple voices, 152

naturalism, 144, 151, 152
    objective-neutral format, 146-148, 150-152
    personal narratives, 141, 142-143, 144-148
    political context, 149-150, 151, 152, 153
    popular culture, 149-150
    postmodernism, 141-143, 149-150
    postmodern sensibilities, 6, 7
    psychoanalytic approach, 144
    race/ethnicity, 147-148, 150-152, 153n.3
    realism, 144, 150-151
    reference frameworks, 152
    reflexive-dialogic interview, 141-142, 146-148, 149, 151, 152-153
    research overview, 141-142
    self-reflexivity, 152
    self-representations, 141-142, 143-145, 146, 147, 148, 149, 150-151, 153
    sports interview, 142-143, 146, 147, 149, 153n.1
    subjectivity, 141
    substance abuse, 143
    traditional interviewing, 147, 151-152
    videocy, 143
    Vietnamese culture, 151-152
    voice, 143-144, 152
    voyeurism, 143-144
Clean and Sober, 143
CNN Headline News, 250, 251
Co-constructed narratives:
    mediated, 158, 167-171, 174-175
    researcher experience, 158-159, 167-177
    unmediated, 158, 167, 171-173, 175
Co-constructive process:
    fact/fiction border, 228, 230-231, 232
    interview society, 33-35
Collaboration:
    active interviewing, 68, 71, 72, 73, 76-78, 79
    cinematic society, 141, 146-147, 153
    interview society, 29, 37-38, 39-40, 41-42, 44, 45-47
    oral history analysis, 220
    participant observation, 119
    poetic representation, 194
    postmodern trends, 55-56, 57, 58, 61-62
    researcher experience, 161-173
Confessional mode:
    cinematic society, 144

interview society, 28, 29
postmodern sensibilities, 11-12, 15-16
Constructivism:
    active interviewing, 68-69, 70-71, 72, 77-78
    cinematic society, 141, 147-148
    fact/fiction border, 225, 226, 227, 228, 230-231, 232
    interview society, 31-33
    poetic representation, 188, 189-191, 194
    postmodern sensibilities, 5, 9, 10, 12-14, 16
    postmodern trends, 53, 54, 56-57, 58
Conversational interviewing:
    active interviewing, 67-68, 71-72, 75, 78-79
    cinematic society, 141, 145, 146, 147, 148
    interview society, 23, 34-35, 38, 41
Conversation analysis (CA):
    active interviewing, 79
    interview society, 34-35
    participant observation, 117
Conversations at Random (Converse/Schuman), 71
Creative interviewing:
    active interviewing, 72-73
    postmodern sensibilities, 12
    postmodern trends, 53-54
Creative Interviewing (Douglas), 53-54, 71, 72-73
Critical theory, 6, 8, 12
Culture:
    cinematic society, 141-143, 144-146, 149-152
    interview society, 23, 29, 46, 47
    oral history analysis, 205-206
    personal/folk narratives, 124-127, 131, 133
    poetic representation, 188, 190-191, 196
    popular culture, 149-150
    postmodern sensibilities, 3, 11-14, 16

Death Rituals of Rural Greece, The
    (Danforth), 10-11
Democratic National Convention (1988), 149-150
Democratization:
    cinematic society, 153
    interview society, 22-27, 28, 42
    social inequality, 251
Desk Set, 144-145
Dialogic approach:
    cinematic society, 141-142, 146-148, 149, 151, 152-153
    postmodern trends, 54
Discipline and Punish (Foucault), 24-26
Discourse analysis:
    active interviewing, 78, 79
    poetic representation, 190-191
Discourse of Medicine: Dialectics of Medical
    Interviews, The (Mishler), 35-37
Disneyland, 51
Do the Right Thing, 150-151
Dramaturgical perspective:
    active interviewing, 75, 79
    cinematic society, 141, 143, 146, 148-150
    postmodern trends, 56

Eastwood, Clint, 145-146, 148
Emoticons, 92-93
Emotionality:
    active interviewing, 69, 71, 72, 73, 74, 75, 76
    cinematic society, 143
    fact/fiction border, 231-232
    interview society, 29, 30-31, 32-33, 45
    poetic representation, 189, 190, 191, 195-196
    postmodern trends, 53-54, 55, 58
Empiricism:
    postmodern sensibilities, 4-8, 9-12, 14
    reflexive, 6, 9-11
Empowerment:
    interview society, 34-39, 41-43, 44, 46-47
    poetic representation, 189
Epiphanies, 55, 60, 190
Epistemology:
    active interviewing, 70, 72
    cinematic society, 146-148, 153n.2
    fact/fiction border, 235-236
    poetic representation, 187, 188
    postmodern trends, 54
ESPN, 142-143, 146, 147
Essentialism, 227
Ethics:
    Internet interviewing, 59, 87, 100n.4
    interviewer self-disclosure, 196-197
    oral history analysis, 217-218

postmodern trends, 58, 59
Ethnography:
    cinematic society, 144, 150-152
    fact/fiction border, 234
    poetic representation, 190, 196-197
    postmodern sensibilities, 9-14
    postmodern trends, 54, 60
    See also Autoethnography
Ethnomethodology:
    active interviewing, 68-69
    poetic representation, 191
    postmodern sensibilities, 5
    postmodern trends, 56-57
Everyday life:
    active interviewing, 73, 78
    cinematic society, 142, 143, 144, 149-150
    interview society, 24, 28-29, 32, 39, 43-44, 47
    postmodern trends, 51, 52, 56, 57, 59, 60
Experiential truth:
    cinematic society, 151, 152
    fact/fiction border, 225, 226-231, 232, 233-234, 235, 236, 238-239
    interview society, 25, 29, 31, 37
    participant observation, 116, 117, 119
    poetic representation, 188
    postmodern sensibilities, 5, 7, 9, 14

Facilitator role:
    active interviewing, 71-72
    Internet interviewing, 97-99
    interview society, 31-32
Fact/fiction border:
    aesthetics, 234
    alternative research representations, 240
    analytic implications, 229, 232-233, 234-235
    authenticity, 230, 234, 236
    authority, 237
    blurred boundary, 225, 226-227, 239
    blurred boundary critique, 237-239
    co-constructive process, 228, 230-231, 232
    constructivism, 225, 226, 227, 228, 230-231, 232
    emotionality, 231-232
    epistemology, 235-236
    essentialism, 227
    ethnography, 234

experiential truth, 225, 226-231, 232, 233-234, 235, 236, 238-239
family research, 225-226, 230, 233-234
feminist research, 234
fiction-informed interpretations, 226, 232-237
good narrative, 230
imagined subjects, 230-231
interactive interviews, 230-231
interpretations, 226, 229, 232-237, 238
interviewer control, 228
interviewer diversity, 231-232
interviewer rapport, 228, 231-232
interviewer skills, 228, 231-232, 236
interview society, 38-39
knowledge transmission, 233-236
language, 226, 227, 231-232, 236-237
media, 237
modernism, 226, 232, 235-236
multiple versions, 238
objectivity, 237-238
personal narratives, 225, 230, 233, 237, 238-239
pilot surveys, 232
positivism, 225, 228, 232, 237-238
postmodern hindsight, 227-233
postmodernism, 225, 226, 227-233, 234, 235-236, 237, 238
preliminary analyses, 232
qualitative research, 225-226, 228, 230, 231, 232-233, 236-237, 238, 239
quantitative research, 232
rationality, 231
realism, 227-228
reflexivity, 234-235
reluctant respondents, 229
research bias, 226
research conclusions, 239-240
research consumption, 237
researcher doubt, 229-230
researcher openness, 229
research overview, 225-226
research reliability, 238-239
research reports, 233-237
research validity, 234, 235, 238-239
respondent debriefings, 232-233
respondent deception, 228, 229-230, 232
respondent truth belief, 227-228
self-representations, 230-231
speech styles, 235

stand-point perspective, 226
subjectivity, 226, 237
transcriptions, 229, 232
translations, 236-237
truth contradictions, 228-229, 237-239
voice, 225, 236
Family discourse, 78
Family research, 225-226, 230, 233-234
Fascism in Popular Memory (Passerini), 348
Feedback, 46
Feminist research:
    active interviewer subject, 58
    active interviewing, 69
    fact/fiction border, 234
    oral history analysis, 208, 216-218
    personal/folk narratives, 134-135
    poetic representation, 190
    postmodern sensibilities, 15
    postmodern trends, 57-58
    researcher experience, 159
    social inequality, 244, 247
Flexible interviewing:
    active interviewing, 69-70
    personal/folk narratives, 128
    researcher experience, 174, 176
Folklore:
    metafolklore, 132
    oral history analysis, 204, 209, 219
    poetic representation, 190
    See also Personal/folk narratives
"Food Truck's Party Hat" (Smith), 195-196
Formative interviews, 69-70
France, 216-217
Front Page, The, 144-145

Gays/lesbians, 57-58
Georgia Tech University, 84, 100n.3
Globalization impact, 47, 244, 250-252
Group interviews:
    Internet interviewing, 90-91, 97-99
    interviewer control, 98-99
    interview society, 28, 45
    moderators, 97-99
    rapport, 97-98
    relational skills, 97-99
    software, 90-91

Haldeman, H. R., 149

Handbook of Qualitative Research (Denzin/Lincoln), 192
Hee Gyoung Noh, 236-237
Hyperreality:
    postmodern sensibilities, 6-8
    postmodern trends, 51, 59

Identity formation:
    active interviewing, 74-75, 76-77
    fixed identity, 206, 208-209
    Internet interviewing, 59
    interview society, 43-44, 45
    oral history analysis, 203, 206, 208-209, 211-213, 216, 218-219
    personal/folk narratives, 131-132
    postmodern trends, 57, 59
    social inequality, 247, 251
In-depth interviews:
    Internet interviewing, 59, 61
    interview society, 28, 29, 45, 46
    personal/folk narratives, 135
    poetic representation, 190
    postmodern trends, 54
India, 43, 46, 47, 125, 126, 128-129, 132, 135-136
Individual experiences:
    active interviewing, 68, 69, 70-71, 72, 73-79
    cinematic society, 143, 144-145, 146, 149, 150-151, 152
    interview society, 22-23, 24-27, 29, 30-31, 32-34, 35-37, 38-39, 44-45, 47
    participant observation, 118-119
    poetic representation, 190-191, 194-195
    postmodern sensibilities, 4-8, 9, 11-12, 14-16
    postmodern trends, 56-57, 60
    See also Experiential truth
Institutional context:
    interview society, 24, 28, 29, 30, 43-45
    personal/folk narratives, 125-126
    social inequality, 243-244, 245-246, 251
Institutional review board (IRB), 87, 100n.4
Interactive interviews:
    active interviewing, 67, 68, 72, 73-75, 78, 79
    cinematic society, 145, 146-147, 148-149

fact/fiction border, 230-231
interview society, 32, 34-35, 41-42, 44
poetic representation, 194
postmodern trends, 53-54, 56
researcher experience, 158, 165-167, 174, 175-176
Internet interviewing:
  advantages, 83-87
  asynchronous communication, 81-82, 90-91, 101n.9
  bulletin board system (BBS), 82, 84
  chat rooms, 82, 84, 85, 90
  communication gaps, 95-96, 97
  computer-mediated communication (CMC), 81-83, 84-85, 86, 88, 91-100
  conferences, 82, 84, 85, 90-91, 101n.9
  confidentiality, 87, 100n.4
  cost-efficiency, 85-86
  CoSy, 90
  cyberspace divide, 83
  digital data challenges, 86-87
  disadvantages, 83-87
  ECHO, 82, 98, 100n.1
  e-mail surveys, 82, 83-85, 86, 88-89, 90, 91, 93, 94, 95-97
  emoticons, 92-93
  ethics, 59
  ETHNO, 59-60
  Ethnograph, 59-60
  FirstClass Conferencing, 90, 101n.9
  friendships, 92-93, 94-95
  group control, 98-99
  group-interview relational skills, 97-99
  group interview software, 90-91
  group moderators, 97-99
  group rapport, 97-98
  Hotline Client, 90
  HyperText Markup Language (HTML), 88-89, 101n.6
  identity formation, 59
  in-depth interviews, 59, 61
  individual interview software, 90
  interactive skills, 95-97
  Internet relay chat (IRC), 82, 90
  interviewer control, 82, 88-89, 98-99
  legal implications, 87, 100n.4
  listening skills, 95-96
  Lotus-Notes, 90-91
  MU* environments, 82, 100n.1
  news groups, 82, 84

nonstandardized-interview rapport, 91-99
nonstandardized-interview relational skills, 90-99
nonstandardized-interview software, 90-91
political context, 84
public communication, 82
qualitative research, 84, 86-87, 91, 92, 93, 97
QualPro, 59-60
quantitative research, 86-87
reassurance skills, 95
recruitment, 83-85
research conclusions, 99-100
research overview, 81
research review, 82-83
respondent control, 82
respondent incentives, 85
sampling, 83-85
security, 87
self conceptualizations, 59
self-interviews, 86
semi-private communication, 82
shared research agendas, 93-94
shareware, 90
standardized-interview technical skills, 87-90
subjectivity, 59
survey-creation software, 88, 89, 100n.5, 101n.7
synchronous communication, 82
technologically-created rapport, 92-93
text-based communication, 81-82, 88
time requirements, 85-86
trust-based rapport, 94-95
Usenet, 82
verbal skills, 96-97
vs. face-to-face interviews, 83, 85-86, 87, 91-95, 98-99
Web-page-based surveys, 83, 84, 85, 89-90, 101n.8
WELL, 82, 100n.1
Interpersonal process:
  active interviewing, 73-74
  interview society, 23, 40-41
  postmodern trends, 55-56
Interpretations:
  active interviewing, 71, 72, 73-74, 75, 77, 78
  cinematic society, 141, 148, 151-152
  fact/fiction border, 226, 229, 232-237, 238

interview society, 33
participant observation, 112-114
personal/folk narratives, 124, 132-135
poetic representation, 190
postmodern sensibilities, 15
postmodern trends, 54, 55
Interviewer control:
    active interviewing, 71-72
    fact/fiction border, 228
    Internet interviewing, 82, 88-89, 98-99
    interview society, 1, 32, 34, 36, 37, 42-43
    postmodern trends, 54
    social inequality, 243, 248-249, 251
Interviewer skills:
    fact/fiction border, 228, 231-232, 236
    Internet interviewing, 87-99
Interviewing as Qualitative Research
        (Seidman), 55-56
Interview society:
    accountability, 45, 47
    accounts, 45, 46, 47
    agency, 24, 25-26, 27, 30, 31, 43-44
    artful narratives, 45-47
    asymmetrical model, 21-22, 34, 37, 46-47
    authenticity, 29, 31, 36, 37, 38
    authority, 22, 29
    categorization, 26, 36
    celebrity interviews, 27
    co-constructive process, 33-35
    coding process, 38, 41
    collaboration, 29, 37-38, 39-40, 41-42, 44,
        45-47
    confessional mode, 28, 29
    constructivism, 31-33
    contemporary life mediation, 27-29
    conversational interviewing, 23, 34-35, 38,
        41
    conversation analysis (CA), 34-35
    criminality, 22, 24-26
    criminal torture, 24-26
    cultural process, 23, 29
    cultural production, 46, 47
    discursive environments, 43-45
    emotionality, 29, 30-31, 32-33, 45
    empowerment, 34-39, 41-43, 44, 46-47
    empowerment discourse, 37-39
    everyday life, 24, 28-29, 32, 39, 43-44, 47
    experiential truth, 25, 29, 31, 37
    facilitator role, 31-32
    fact/fiction border, 38-39

feedback, 46
folk narratives, 46
globalization impact, 47
governmentality, 26
group interviews, 28, 45
historical development, 22-26
identity formation, 43-44, 45
in-depth interviews, 28, 29, 45, 46
individual autonomy, 25-26
individual discourse, 24-26
individual experiences, 22-23, 24-27, 29,
        30-31, 32-34, 35-37, 38-39, 44-45, 47
institutional context, 24, 28, 29, 30, 43-45
interactive interviews, 32, 34-35, 41-42,
        44
Internet interviewing, 27, 28, 47
interpersonal process, 23, 40-41
interpretations, 33
interviewer control, 1, 32, 34, 36, 37, 42-
        43
interviewer role, 21-22, 23, 30, 31-36, 37-
        38, 40-41, 45-47
interviewer self-disclosure, 45-46
interviewing industry, 28
interview participants, 37
interview theme, 29
knowledge assembly, 22
knowledge discourse, 25
knowledge production, 31, 32, 33
life story, 45
linguistic analysis, 34-36
meaning construction, 32-34, 37, 42, 46
media, 27, 28, 44, 47, 67
medical interviews, 35-37, 44, 45, 47
mining analogy, 30, 31
modernism, 22-24, 25-26, 27
modern temper, 22-24, 25-26, 27
morality, 43-45
narrative ownership, 35-37, 39-45
neutrality, 31-32, 33
objectivity, 26, 31
open-ended inquiry, 29, 35, 41
opinion democratization, 22-27, 28, 42
oral history, 45
panopticon, 24, 26
personal narratives, 28, 35-37, 38, 39-47
phenomenology, 29
poetics, 38
political context, 25, 26, 27, 28, 34, 36,
        38, 46-47

positivism, 41

postmodernism, 46

postmodern sensibilities, 7, 16, 46

power dynamics, 25, 37-38, 42, 46-47

private language, 42, 44

public opinion, 22-27, 28, 30, 32, 42, 47

qualitative research, 26

rationality, 37

reciprocity, 45

reference frameworks, 31, 35, 37, 38, 42-43

reflexivity, 23, 26, 29, 40-41, 42, 46

requirements for, 28-29

research bias, 30, 31, 32-33

research transformation, 36

research validity, 30, 31

respondent-centered research, 36

respondent interests, 36, 42

respondent practitioners, 32

respondent role, 21-22, 23, 30-31, 32-38, 40, 45-47

respondents vs. informants, 23-24

rhetorical process, 37

role formalization, 22

romantic impulse, 29, 37

scientific context, 26

self conceptualizations, 23, 24, 26, 28, 43-45

self-reflexivity, 26

self-representations, 47

self-scrutiny, 25-26

self technologies, 24, 26

social inequality, 244

social relations, 22-23

social worlds, 26, 31

speech activities, 34-36, 37, 38, 39, 40, 42, 44, 45

standardized survey interviews, 22, 28, 29, 34-35, 37, 41, 45, 46-47

stranger knowledge, 22, 23, 26-27, 28

subjectivity, 24-25, 28-29

subjectivity alternatives, 24

subject positions, 39-41

subjects, 21, 27, 29, 30-34

surveillance technology, 24, 26

symmetrical model, 46

technology impact, 24, 26, 28, 29, 47

transcriptions, 35

voice, 22, 26, 27, 29, 34, 35-36, 39-45, 46-47

World War II, 22, 24

Keaton, Michael, 143

King, Larry, 27, 144

Knowledge:

active interviewing, 68, 70, 73, 79

asymmetrical, 244-246, 249-251

cinematic society, 141-142

fact/fiction border, 233-236

interview society, 22, 23, 25, 26-27, 28, 31, 32, 33

postmodern trends, 54, 55, 56

shared, 55

social inequality, 244-246, 247, 249-251

stranger, 22, 23, 26-27, 28

See also Text-based knowledge

Krippendorf's Tribe, 145

Lake, Ricki, 27

Language:

active interviewing, 69

fact/fiction border, 226, 227, 231-232, 235, 236-237

interview society, 34-36, 37, 38, 39, 40, 42, 44, 45

linguistic analysis, 34-36

linguistic norms, 124

linguistic research, 69, 244-246, 247, 249

personal/folk narratives, 124

poetic representation, 188-190, 192, 193-195

postmodern sensibilities, 3, 5-7, 9, 12, 13

social inequality, 244-246, 247, 249

speech activities, 34-36, 37, 38, 39, 40, 42, 44, 45

speech styles, 188-190, 192, 193-195, 235

Learning from Strangers (Weiss), 26-27

Learning How to Ask: A Sociolinguistic Appraisal of the Role of the Interview in Social Science Research (Briggs), 243, 244, 246, 248-249, 251

Lee, Spike, 150-151

Life history:

active interviewing, 67, 70

cinematic society, 144

oral history analysis, 209

personal/folk narratives, 125, 126-127, 131

"Lifelines" (Philip), 196-197
Life story:
    interview society, 45
    oral history analysis, 205, 218-219
    personal/folk narratives, 123, 124-126,
        131-132, 135
    poetic representation, 190, 191, 193-194,
        198-199
    postmodern sensibilities, 14-15
Long Slow Burn (Weston), 58
"Louisa May's Story of Her Life" (Richard-
        son), 190, 191, 193-194, 198-199

*Magicians of Manumanua: Living Myth in
        Kalauna* (Young), 127
Maltese Falcon, The, 144-145
Managed Heart, The (Hochschild), 117
Mass interviews, 69-70
Meaning construction:
    active interviewing, 68-71, 72, 73-74, 75,
        77-79
    cinematic society, 144, 145, 152-153
    interview society, 32-34, 37, 42, 46
    personal/folk narratives, 132-135
    poetic representation, 189, 190
    postmodern trends, 55
Media:
    active interviewing, 67
    fact/fiction border, 237
    interview society, 27, 28, 44, 47, 67
    postmodern sensibilities, 6-7, 8, 12
    postmodern trends, 51
    social inequality, 244, 250-251
    See also Cinematic society
Memory:
    collective, 203, 204-205, 212-213
    defined, 205
    oral history analysis, 203, 204-209, 212-
        213, 220
    participant observation, 118, 119
    personal/folk narratives, 129-130
    popular, 204-209, 220
Metacommunicative norms, 243, 250
Metafolklore, 132
Metanarratives, 5-6, 7, 191
Metaphors, 188, 192, 195
Metatheories, 51
Milagro Beanfield War, The, 145
Minh-ha, Trinh T., 151-152

Modernism:
    fact/fiction border, 226, 232, 235-236
    oral history analysis, 212-213
    postmodern relation, 51, 52, 54
    social inequality, 244-246, 249, 250, 251-
        252
Morality:
    interview society, 43-45
    participant observation, 116
    personal/folk narratives, 131, 132-133
    poetic representation, 190, 191
    postmodern sensibilities, 16
Moroccan Dialogues (Dwyer), 54
Most Beautiful Farewell in the World, The
        (Hee Gyoung Noh), 236-237
Myths, 124, 126-127, 130, 133

Narcotics Anonymous (NA), 39, 42, 45
Native Americans:
    fact/fiction border, 236
    personal/folk narratives, 130, 132-133,
        134
Naturalism:
    active interviewing, 78
    cinematic society, 144, 151, 152
    participant observation, 117, 119
    postmodern sensibilities, 6, 7, 10, 11
    social inequality, 247, 251-252
Neutrality:
    active interviewing, 70, 72, 75
    cinematic society, 146-148, 150-152
    interview society, 31-32, 33
    poetic representation, 188
New Guinea, 127
New Mexico, 243-244, 246, 248-249, 251
"Nine Poems: Marriage and the Family"
        (Richardson), 191
Nixon, Richard, 149

Objectivity:
    active interviewing, 70-71
    cinematic society, 146-148, 150-152
    fact/fiction border, 237-238
    interview society, 26, 31
    participant observation, 119
    poetic representation, 188
    postmodern sensibilities, 4, 5, 9, 11, 12, 14
    social inequality, 245, 252

Open-ended inquiry, 29, 35, 41
Openness, 229
Oral history:
    active interviewing, 67
    interview society, 45
    poetic representation, 188-189, 190
    postmodern sensibilities, 13
Oral history analysis:
    abortion, 207-208, 217-218
    artistic painters, 213-214
    birth control, 207-208, 217-218
    California history, 215-216
    career paths, 211-212
    collaboration, 220
    collective memory, 203, 204-205, 212-213
    conflict, 208-209, 217-218
    contradictions, 203-204, 212-213, 217-218
    cultural form record, 205-206
    emplotment structure, 205, 209-216, 218-219
    ethics, 217-218
    fascism, 204-209, 220n.4
    feminist research, 208, 216-218
    fixed identity, 206, 208-209
    folklore, 204, 209, 219
    French migrants, 216-217
    historical contextualization, 216-220
    identity formation, 203, 206, 208-209, 211-213, 216, 218-219
    imagination, 203
    interview principles, 205
    intuition, 211
    life history, 209
    life story, 205, 218-219
    marital rape, 218
    memory defined, 205
    modernism, 212-213
    paradigmatic analysis, 210-211, 213-220
    political context, 207, 209, 212-213, 215-216, 218
    popular memory, 204-209, 220
    power dynamics, 215-218
    prefiguration, 213
    pronoun selection, 216-217
    refiguration, 213
    reflexivity, 209, 216, 218-219
    research overview, 203-204
    self-reflexivity, 216, 218-219

    self-representations, 204-205, 206-209, 214-215, 216-218
    semiotics, 209
    sexualization, 214
    stereotypical self-representations, 204-205, 206-207, 217-218
    subjectivity, 206-209, 213, 215-216, 217, 219
    symbolic orders, 205-209
    symbolic structure, 205, 209-216
    symbolic turning points, 205, 208, 210, 211, 214-215, 217
    syntagmatic analysis, 210-213, 216-220
    temporal experience, 208-209
    working class, 204-209, 212-213, 216-217, 218-219
Oral literary criticism, 132-133
Ownership, 35-37, 39-45

Pakistan, 123-125
Paolantonio, Sal, 142-143, 146, 147
Participant observation vs. interviewing:
    account enactments, 116, 118-119, 120
    action interviewing, 118
    agency, 116
    artificial enactment, 119, 120
    authenticity, 117, 119
    biographical work, 120
    collaboration, 119
    conversation analysis (CA), 117
    data distortion, 112-113, 116, 118, 119
    event data completeness, 112-114
    event enactments, 111-112, 118-119, 120
    event interpretations, 112-114
    experiential truth, 116, 117, 119
    gold standard, 111-112
    holistic approach, 112
    individual experiences, 118-119
    memory, 118, 119
    morality, 116
    naturalism, 117, 119
    objectivity, 119
    personal narratives, 116, 118, 119
    postmodernism, 113
    qualitative research, 109, 110, 120
    reflexivity, 115-116, 120
    research bias, 119-120
    research conclusions, 109-110120-121
    researcher position, 119-120

research overview, 109-110
research review, 109, 110-114
social action, 116-120
social worlds, 112, 113, 115, 119
symmetrical model, 117, 119-120
textual representation, 116
triangulation methodology, 114-116, 119
Passive interviewer subject, 31-32
Passive respondent subject:
    active interviewing, 70, 71, 72, 73, 75
    interviewer detachment, 54
    interview society, 21, 30-31, 36-37
"Pencilling It In" (Lawton), 194-195
Personal/folk narratives:
    active vs. passive bearers, 129
    Afghanistan, 133
    anecdotes, 125
    anthropology, 124-125, 126-127, 131
    authority, 124, 127, 129, 131-132
    autobiographies, 123, 124
    categorization, 127
    conflict, 134-135
    cultural norms, 131
    cultural representations, 124-127, 133
    cultural work, 127
    distinction between, 124-127
    elicitation process, 123-124, 127-132
    fairy tales, 132
    feminist research, 134-135
    flexible interviewing, 128
    folk narrative collectivism, 124, 125-126
    identity formation, 131-132
    in-depth interviews, 135
    India, 43, 46, 47, 125, 126, 128-129, 132, 135-136
    institutional context, 125-126
    interpretations, 124, 132-135
    interview context, 127-128, 131
    interview defined, 128
    interview society, 46
    Jews, 129-130
    life history, 125, 126-127, 131
    life story, 123, 124-126, 131-132, 135
    linguistic norms, 124
    meaning construction, 132-135
    memory, 129-130
    metafolklore, 132
    morality, 131, 132-133
    multiple versions, 131-132
    myths, 124, 126-127, 130, 133

Native Americans, 130, 132-133, 134
New Guinea, 127
noninterview context, 127-128
oral literary criticism, 132-133
Pakistan, 123-125
personal content, 126-127
personal journeys, 130-131
personal narrative idiosyncrasy, 124
personhood, 124-125
Philippines, 125, 130-131
political context, 127, 128, 131, 133
postcolonialism, 131
power dynamics, 127, 131-132, 133-134, 136
reciprocity, 135
reflexivity, 123-124, 127, 133, 135-136
research conclusions, 136-137
research overview, 124
retellings, 126, 128, 131
rituals, 129, 130-131, 134
social location, 130
social worlds, 127
Solomon Islands, 131
spirituality, 125, 126, 134
story social life, 124, 127
storyteller skill, 128
subject positions, 124, 131
taboos, 130
Personal narratives:
    active interviewing, 67, 68, 71-72, 73-79
    cinematic society, 141, 142-143, 144-148
    fact/fiction border, 225, 230, 233, 237, 238-239
    interview society, 28, 35-37, 38, 39-47
    ownership, 35-37, 39-45
    participant observation, 116, 118, 119
    poetic representation, 188, 190-191, 194-195, 196-197
    postmodern sensibilities, 5-6, 10-16
    postmodern trends, 56-57, 60
    social inequality, 246, 247, 250, 252
    See also Artful narratives
Philippines, 125, 130-131
Poetic representation:
    agency, 190-191
    alternative research representations, 187, 188, 194, 195, 198
    artful narratives, 190-191
    authority, 188
    autoethnography, 196-197

beginner preliminaries, 191-193
cancer patient, 196-197
career reflections, 194-195
categorization, 189-190
collaboration, 194
conferences, 192
constructivism, 188, 189-191, 194
cultural context, 188, 190-191, 196
developmentally disabled, 195-196
discourse analysis, 190-191
emotionality, 189, 190, 191, 195-196
empowerment, 189
epic poem, 190
epiphanies, 190
epistemology, 187, 188
ethnography, 190, 196-197
ethnomethodology, 191
examples, 193-197
experiential truth, 188
feminist research, 190
folklore, 190
ideation, 191-193
in-depth interviews, 190
individual experiences, 190-191, 194-195
interactive interviews, 194
interpretations, 190
interviewer self-disclosure, 196-197
interview society, 38
journals, 196-197
knowledge, 188, 189, 191
life story, 190, 191, 193-194, 198-199
long-narrative poem, 187, 190-191, 193-194, 195-196, 198-199
meaning construction, 189, 190
metanarratives, 191
metaphors, 188, 192, 195
morality, 190, 191
mystory, 189
neutrality, 188
objectives, 187, 192-193
objectivity, 188
oral history, 188-189, 190
personal narratives, 188, 190-191, 194-195, 196-197
poetic transcriptions, 194
political context, 188
postmodern sensibilities, 3, 11, 12-13, 14-16
postmodern trends, 60-61
poststructuralism, 188-190, 196

power dynamics, 188, 189
publications, 192
publishers, 191, 192
qualitative research, 190, 192
recommendations for, 191-197
reference frameworks, 194
reflexivity, 189, 190
research bias, 191
research conclusions, 197-198
research overview, 187
research transformation, 198
research validity, 194
scientific context, 189-190, 195
self conceptualizations, 190-191, 197
self-interviews, 196-197
self-reflexivity, 197-198
semiotics, 189
short-lyric poem, 187, 190-191, 194-195
sight, 191-193
sociohistorical construction, 188
sound, 191-193
speech styles, 188-190, 192, 193-195
subjectivity, 188, 191, 194, 196
subjectivity sociology, 196-197
subject position shifts, 191, 194
symbolic representations, 194-195
tape-recordings, 188, 193
transcriptions, 188, 189
vs. conventional writing, 187, 188, 189, 190, 191, 195, 196, 197
Political context:
    cinematic society, 149-150, 151, 152, 153
    Internet interviewing, 84
    interview society, 25, 26, 27, 28, 34, 36, 38, 46-47
    oral history analysis, 207, 209, 212-213, 215-216, 218
    personal/folk narratives, 127, 128, 131, 133
    poetic representation, 188
    postmodern sensibilities, 12-13, 16
    postmodern trends, 55, 58
    social inequality, 244, 245, 246, 249-252
Popular culture, 149-150
Popular memory, 204-209, 220
Positivism:
    fact/fiction border, 225, 228, 232, 237-238
    interview society, 41
    postmodern sensibilities, 8, 14, 15
Postcolonialism, 131

Postmodern Condition, The (Lyotard), 5-6
Postmodernism:
    active interviewing, 16, 68, 69
    cinematic society, 141-143, 149-150
    fact/fiction border, 225, 226, 227-233,
        234, 235-236, 237, 238
    interview society, 7, 16, 46, 51
    participant observation, 11-12, 113
    social inequality, 244, 247, 250, 251,
        252
Postmodern sensibilities:
    active interviewing, 16
    affinities, 5
    affirmations, 4, 8, 9, 16
    agency, 7
    anthropology, 10-11, 12-14
    authenticity, 7, 9
    authority, 5, 8, 9, 10, 11, 13, 14
    cinematic society, 6, 7
    confessional mode, 11-12, 15-16
    constructivism, 5, 9, 10, 12-14, 16
    creative interviewing, 12
    critical theory, 6, 8, 12
    cultural representations, 3, 11-14, 16
    empiricism, 4-8, 9-12, 14
    ethnographic distancing, 11-14
    ethnography, 9-14
    ethnomethodology, 5
    exemplary extracts, 13
    experiential truth, 5, 7, 9, 14
    expressions of, 5-8
    feminist research, 15
    hermeneutics, 6
    hyperreality, 6-8
    incredulity, 5-6
    individual experiences, 4-8, 9, 11-12,
        14-16
    Internet interviewing, 16
    interpretations, 15
    interview society, 7, 16
    knowledge, 3, 5-6, 8, 9-16
    language, 3, 5-7, 9, 12, 13
    life story, 14-15
    master narratives, 5-6
    media, 6-7, 8, 12
    metanarratives, 5-6, 7
    morality, 16
    multiple voices, 14
    naturalism, 6, 7, 10, 11
    nihilism, 8, 12, 14

    objectives of, 4-5, 8-9
    objectivity, 4, 5, 9, 11, 12, 14
    oral history, 13
    participant observation, 11-12
    personal narratives, 5-6, 10-16
    poetics, 3, 11, 12-13, 14-16
    political context, 12-13, 16
    positivism, 8, 14, 15
    power dynamics, 3, 11, 12, 16
    qualitative research, 5, 9, 13, 14
    reflexive empiricism, 6, 9-11
    reflexivity, 3, 6, 9-11, 12, 16
    relativism, 8, 9, 14
    representation confrontation, 8-14
    representation crisis, 4-5, 9, 14, 16
    representation response, 14-16
    research transformation, 3-4, 6, 8, 9, 11,
        12, 14-16
    rhetoric appreciation, 7, 9, 11-14
    self conceptualizations, 5, 6, 7, 16
    skepticism, 4, 8, 9, 10, 14
    social science manifestations, 4-5, 8, 9, 10,
        11-12, 14-16
    social theory, 5
    social worlds, 7, 10-14
    standardized vs. inventive representation,
        3-4, 6, 8, 9, 11, 12, 14-16
    structuralism, 6
    subjectivity, 5
    subjects, 6, 7, 13, 15, 16
    symbolic interactionism, 5, 6, 15
    text-based knowledge, 6, 8, 9-16
    theoretical totalization, 4-6, 8
    transcriptions, 14-15, 16
    vs. modernism, 7, 9
Postmodern trends:
    accounts, 56, 57
    active interviewing, 56
    agency, 53, 55, 56
    anthropology, 54
    authority, 54
    autoethnography, 60
    collaboration, 55-56, 57, 58, 61-62
    constructivism, 53, 54, 56-57, 58
    creative interviewing, 53-54
    dialogic approach, 54
    dramaturgical perspective, 56
    emotionality, 53-54, 55, 58
    epiphanies, 55, 60
    epistemology, 54

ethics, 58, 59
ethnography, 54, 60
ethnomethodology, 56-57
everyday life, 51, 52, 56, 57, 59, 60
feminist research, 57-58
gays/lesbians, 57-58
hyperreality, 51, 59
identity formation, 57, 59
in-depth interviews, 54
individual experiences, 56-57, 60
interactive interviews, 53-54, 56
Internet interviewing, 58-60
interpersonal process, 55-56
interpretations, 54, 55
interviewer control, 54
interviewer detachment, 53-54, 55, 57
interviewer gender impact, 58
interviewer role, 55, 56, 57, 58, 60
interviewer self-disclosure, 58
interview society, 51
knowledge production, 56
meaning construction, 55
media, 51
metatheories, 51
modernism relation, 51, 52, 54
personal narratives, 56-57, 60
phenomenology, 55-57
plays/performances, 61
poetic representation, 60-61
political context, 55, 58
polyphony, 54, 61
postmodern-informed interviewing, 52,
    53-55, 60, 62n.1
postmodernism conceptualization, 51,
    52
postmodernism influence, 52-53
postmodern sensibilities, 52-53, 55
qualitative research, 53, 54, 59-60
quantitative research, 53
race/ethnicity, 57
rationality, 53
reciprocity, 55-56
reflexivity, 58
representational practices, 60-61
research conclusions, 61-62
research overview, 51-52
research reports, 60, 61
research transformation, 53-55
research validity, 54
respondent deception, 53-54

respondent role, 54, 55, 56, 57, 60
romantic impulse, 54
scientific context, 53, 59-60
self-interviews, 60
sexuality, 57-58
shared knowledge, 55
social worlds, 53, 54, 55
subject position shifts, 57-58, 62n.2
symbolic interactionism, 53-54
text-based knowledge, 54
transcriptions, 54
voice, 54-55
vs. traditional interviewing, 53, 55, 56, 57,
    58-59, 60
Poststructuralism:
    active interviewing, 68, 69
    poetic representation, 188-190, 196
    social inequality, 244
Power dynamics:
    asymmetrical, 243, 244-246, 249-251
    interview society, 25, 37-38, 42, 46-47
    oral history analysis, 215-218
    personal/folk narratives, 127, 131-132,
        133-134, 136
    poetic representation, 188, 189
    postmodern sensibilities, 3, 11, 12, 16
    social inequality, 243-246, 248, 249-251
Public opinion:
    active interviewing, 73
    interview society, 22-27, 28, 30, 32, 42,
        47
    social inequality, 245-246, 247, 250

Qualitative research:
    fact/fiction border, 225-226, 228, 230,
        231, 232-233, 236-237, 238, 239
    Internet interviewing, 84, 86-87, 91, 92,
        93, 97
    interview society, 26
    participant observation, 109, 110, 120
    poetic representation, 190, 192
    postmodern sensibilities, 5, 9, 13, 14
    postmodern trends, 53, 54, 59-60
    social inequality, 247
Quantitative research:
    active interviewing, 67-68
    fact/fiction border, 232
    Internet interviewing, 86-87
    postmodern trends, 53

Race/ethnicity:
    cinematic society, 147-148, 150-152,
       153n.3
    postmodern trends, 57
    social inequality, 249-250
    See also specific race
Rapport:
    fact/fiction border, 228, 231-232
    Internet interviewing, 91-99
Rationality:
    active interviewing, 71, 72, 73, 74
    fact/fiction border, 231
    interview society, 37
    postmodern trends, 53
    social inequality, 244-245
Realism:
    cinematic society, 144, 150-151
    fact/fiction border, 227-228
Real TV, 51
Reciprocity:
    active interviewing, 72
    interview society, 45
    personal/folk narratives, 135
    postmodern trends, 55-56
Reflexivity:
    active interviewing, 74
    cinematic society, 141-142, 146-148, 149,
       151, 152-153
    fact/fiction border, 234-235
    interview society, 23, 26, 29, 40-41, 42, 46
    oral history analysis, 209, 216, 218-219
    participant observation, 115-116, 120
    personal/folk narratives, 123-124, 127,
       133, 135-136
    poetic representation, 189, 190
    postmodern sensibilities, 3, 6, 9-11, 12, 16
    postmodern trends, 58
    researcher experience, 157-159, 162-165,
       166, 167, 169-170, 173-177
    social inequality, 244, 246, 247
    See also Self-reflexivity
Relativism, 8, 9, 14
Report writing. *See* Research reports
Research bias:
    active interviewing, 67-68, 69, 70, 78
    fact/fiction border, 226
    interview society, 30, 31, 32-33
    participant observation, 119-120
    poetic representation, 191
    social inequality, 247, 248

Researcher experience:
    abortion, 158, 171-173, 175, 177
    autoethnography, 157
    bulimia, 158, 165-167, 176, 177
    co-constructed narratives, 158-159, 167-
       177
    collaboration, 161-173
    feminist research, 159
    flexible interviewing, 174, 176
    interactive interviews, 158, 165-167, 174,
       175-176
    Judaism, 158-159, 162-164, 168-171, 176,
       177
    literature review, 159-161
    marriage, 168-171, 174-175, 177
    mediated co-constructed narratives, 158,
       167-171, 174-175
    reflexive dyadic interviews, 158-159, 162-
       165, 174
    reflexivity, 157-159, 162-165, 166, 167,
       169-170, 173-177
    research conclusions, 173-177
    unmediated co-constructed narratives, 158,
       167, 171-173, 175
Research reliability:
    active interviewing, 67, 71
    fact/fiction border, 238-239
Research reports:
    active interviewing, 79
    fact/fiction border, 233-237
    postmodern trends, 60, 61
    See also Text-based knowledge
Research validity:
    active interviewing, 67, 70, 71
    fact/fiction border, 234, 235, 238-239
    interview society, 30, 31
    poetic representation, 194
    postmodern trends, 54
Respondent interests, 36, 42
Respondent practitioners, 32, 73
Rituals, 10-11, 129, 130-131, 134
Rivera, Geraldo, 27, 144

Saboteur, 144-145
Scientific context:
    interview society, 26
    poetic representation, 189-190, 195
    postmodern trends, 53, 59-60
Selected Writings (Poster), 8

Self conceptualizations:
    Internet interviewing, 59
    interview society, 23, 24, 26, 28, 43-45
    poetic representation, 190-191, 197
    postmodern sensibilities, 5, 6, 7, 16
    See also Identity formation
Self-disclosure:
    active interviewing, 72-73
    ethics, 196-197
    interview society, 45-46
    poetic representation, 196-197
    postmodern trends, 58
Self-interviews:
    Internet interviewing, 86
    poetic representation, 196-197
    postmodern trends, 60
Self-reflexivity:
    cinematic society, 152
    interview society, 26
    oral history analysis, 216, 218-219
    poetic representation, 197-198
Self-representations:
    cinematic society, 141-142, 143-145, 146,
        147, 148, 149, 150-151, 153
    fact/fiction border, 230-231
    interview society, 47
    oral history analysis, 204-205, 206-209,
        214-215, 216-218
Semiotics:
    oral history analysis, 209
    poetic representation, 189
Sexuality:
    oral history analysis, 214
    postmodern trends, 57-58
Shelton, Ron, 149
Social inequality:
    agency, 246, 250-251
    asymmetrical knowledge, 244-246, 249-
        251
    asymmetrical power, 243, 244-246, 249-
        251
    authority, 247, 248, 249
    civil society, 251
    conflict, 243, 246, 248-251
    contemporary capitalism, 249-251
    corporations, 250-252
    democratization, 251
    economic context, 249, 252
    feminist research, 244, 247
    globalization impact, 244, 250-252
    heteroglossia, 246-249
    identity formation, 247, 251
    institutional context, 243-244, 245-246,
        251
    interviewer control, 243, 248-249, 251
    interview society, 244
    linguistic research, 244-246, 247, 249
    media, 244, 250-251
    metacommunicative norms, 243, 250
    modernism, 244-246, 249, 250, 251-252
    naturalism, 247, 251-252
    New Mexico, 243-244, 246, 248-249, 251
    objectivity, 245, 252
    personal narratives, 246, 247, 250, 252
    political context, 244, 245, 246, 249-252
    postmodernism, 244, 247, 250, 251, 252
    poststructuralism, 244
    power dynamics, 243-246, 248, 249-251
    public opinion, 245-246, 247, 250
    qualitative research, 247
    race/ethnicity, 249-250
    rationality, 244-245
    recontextualization, 246-249, 251
    reductionism, 247
    reflexivity, 244, 246, 247
    research bias, 247, 248
    research conclusions, 251-252
    social class, 243-244, 245, 246, 249
    social worlds, 244, 245, 246-247
    subject positions, 243, 245, 247
    technological transformations, 244, 245,
        246, 248, 251-252
    text-based knowledge, 246, 247, 251
Social location, 130
Social theory, 5
Social worlds:
    active interviewing, 67, 78
    interview society, 26, 31
    participant observation, 112, 113, 115,
        119
    personal/folk narratives, 127
    postmodern sensibilities, 7, 10-14
    postmodern trends, 53, 54, 55
    social inequality, 244, 245, 246-247
Society for the Study of Symbolic Interaction,
    61
Solomon Islands, 131
Speech. *See* Language
Spellbound, 144-145
Spirituality, 125, 126, 134

Springer, Jerry, 27, 51

Standardized survey interviews:
    active interviewing, 67-68, 71-72, 75, 78
    interview society, 22, 28, 29, 34-35, 37,
        41, 45, 46-47

Street Corner Society (Whyte), 10, 11

Structuralism, 6

Subjectivity:
    active interviewing, 69, 72, 75, 77, 79
    alternatives, 24, 34, 37, 39-40, 75, 77
    cinematic society, 141
    fact/fiction border, 226, 237
    Internet interviewing, 59
    interview society, 24-25, 28-29, 30, 32-34,
        36-37, 39-45
    oral history analysis, 206-209, 213, 215-
        216, 217, 219
    poetic representation, 188, 191, 194, 196-
        197
    postmodern sensibilities, 5
    voice, 41-42, 44-45, 47

Subject positions:
    interview society, 33-34, 36-37, 39-41
    multiplicity of, 33-34, 41, 44
    personal/folk narratives, 124, 131
    social inequality, 243, 245, 247
    voice, 39-41

Subject position shifts:
    active interviewing, 75-78
    poetic representation, 191, 194
    postmodern trends, 57-58, 62n.2

Subjects:
    fact/fiction border, 230-231
    interview society, 21, 27, 29, 30-37
    postmodern sensibilities, 6, 7, 13, 15, 16
    topic sensitivity, 31
    vessels of answers, 30-31, 32, 33, 36-37,
        40, 54, 70, 71-72
    See also Active interviewer subject; Active
        respondent subject; Passive interviewer
        subject; Passive respondent subject

Sungeun Yang, 236-237

Surname Viet Given Name Nam, 151-152

Symbolic interactionism:
    postmodern sensibilities, 5, 6, 15
    postmodern trends, 53-54

Symbolic Interactionism (Blumer), 53

Synchronous communication, 82

Taboos, 130

Tales of the Field (Van Maanen), 11

Tally's Corner (Liebow), 10, 13

Tape-recordings, 188, 193

Technological transformations:
    interview society, 24, 26, 28, 29, 47
    social inequality, 244, 245, 246, 248, 251-
        252
    See also Internet interviewing

Text-based knowledge:
    Internet interviewing, 81-82, 88
    postmodern sensibilities, 6, 8, 9-16
    postmodern trends, 54
    social inequality, 246, 247, 251
    See also Poetic representation

Transcriptions:
    fact/fiction border, 229, 232
    interview society, 35
    poetic representation, 188, 189
    poetic transcriptions, 194
    postmodern sensibilities, 14-15, 16
    postmodern trends, 54

Translated Woman (Behar), 247

Translations, 236-237

Triangulation methodology, 114-116, 119

True Crime, 145-146, 147

Truth. *See* Experiential truth

Tuhami: Portrait of a Moroccan (Crapanzano),
    54

University of Kansas, 112

University of Michigan, 191

University of Puerto Rico, 194

Vietnamese culture, 151-152

Vietnam War, 126

Voice:
    cinematic society, 143-144, 152
    fact/fiction border, 225, 236
    interview society, 22, 26, 27, 29, 34, 35-
        36, 39-45, 46-47
    postmodern sensibilities, 14
    postmodern trends, 54-55
    subjectivity, 41-42, 44-45, 47
    subject positions, 39-41

Walters, Barbara, 27, 144

Wang, Wayne, 147-148
Warner, Kurt, 142-143, 146, 147, 148
We, the Tikopia (Firth), 10-11
Who's Afraid of Virginia Woolf?, 230

Winfrey, Oprah, 27, 144, 251
Working (Terkel), 30, 69

Young People and Health Risk, 98, 99

ABOUT THE EDITORS

Jaber F. Gubrium is Chair and Professor of Sociology at the University of Missouri, Columbia. His research focuses on the descriptive organization of personal identity, family, the life course, aging, and adaptations to illness. He is the editor of the *Journal of Aging Studies* and author or editor of more than 20 books, including *Living and Dying at Murray Manor, Caretakers, Describing Care, Oldtimers and Alzheimer's, Out of Control,* and *Speaking of Life.*

James A. Holstein is Professor of Sociology in the Department of Social and Cultural Sciences at Marquette University. He has studied diverse people-processing and social control settings, including courts, schools, and mental health agencies. He is the author or editor of numerous books, including *Court-Ordered Insanity, Dispute Domains and Welfare Claims, Reconsidering Social Constructionism,* and *Social Problems in Everyday Life.* He is also editor of the journal *Social Problems.*

As collaborators for more than a decade, Gubrium and Holstein have developed their distinctive constructionist approach to everyday life in a variety of texts, including *What Is Family? Constructing the Life Course, Aging and Everyday Life, The Active Interview,* and *The New Language of Qualitative Method.* They continue to explore the theoretical and methodological implications of interpretive practice as it unfolds at the intersection of narrative, culture, and social interaction. Their most recent works—companion volumes *The Self We Live By: Narrative Identity in a Postmodern World* and *Institutional Selves: Troubled Identities in a Postmodern World*—consider the impact on self-construction of a postmodern world of increasingly diverse institutional identities. They also have edited the *Handbook of Interview Research* and *Inside Interviewing.*

ABOUT THE CONTRIBUTORS

Paul Atkinson is Professor of Sociology at Cardiff University in Wales. He is currently directing two research projects on the social consequences of new genetic technologies and is completing an ethnographic study of an international opera company. His publications include the second edition of *Ethnography: Principles in Practice* (with Martyn Hammersley; 1995), *Sociological Readings and Re-readings* (1996), *Making Sense of Qualitative Data* (with Amanda Coffey; 1996), *Supervising the PhD* (with Sara Delamont and Odette Parry; 1997), and *The Doctoral Experience* (with Sara Delamont and Odette Parry; 2000). He is coeditor of the *Handbook of Ethnography* (2001) and of the journal *Qualitative Research*.

Leigh Berger received her M.A. in sociology and is pursuing her Ph.D. in the Department of Communication at the University of South Florida in Tampa. Her dissertation research is a narrative ethnography of a Messianic Jewish congregation that explores how its spirituality is experienced and also illuminates the personal journey of the ethnographer. She hopes her writing invites the reader to observe ethnographic encounters, to participate in them, and to come away with a better understanding of both their social worlds and themselves.

Charles L. Briggs is Professor and Chair of the Department of Ethnic Studies at the University of California, San Diego. He has been awarded fellowships by the Andrew W. Mellon Foundation, the National Endowment for the Humanities, the John Simon Guggenheim Memorial Foundation, the Woodrow Wilson International Center for Scholars, and the Center for Advanced Studies in the Behavioral Sciences. His books include *Learning How to Ask: A Sociolinguistic Appraisal of the Role of the Interview in Social Science Research*, *The Wood Carvers of Córdova, New Mexico: Social Dimensions of an Artistic "Revival,"* *Competence in Performance: The Creativity of Tradition in Mexicano Verbal Art*, *The Lost Gold Mine of Juan Mondragón* (with Julián Josué Vigil), and *Stories in Times of Cholera: The Transnational Circulation of Bacteria and Racial Stigmata in a Venezuelan Epidemic* (forthcoming).

Richard Cándida Smith is Professor of History at the University of California at Berkeley. He is the author of *Utopia and Dissent: Art, Poetry, and Politics in California* (1995) and *Mallarmé's Children: Symbolism and the Renewal of Experience* (1999). He is currently working on a biography of the painter Jay DeFeo.

Amanda Coffey lectures in sociology and research methods at Cardiff University in Wales. Her research interests focus on young people and citizenship, gender and education, and ethnographic representations. Her publications include *The Ethnographic Self* (1999), *Feminism and the Classroom Teacher* (with Sara Delamont; 2000), and *Education and Social Change* (2001). She is coeditor of the *Handbook of Ethnography* (2001).

Norman K. Denzin is Distinguished Professor of Communications, College of Communications Scholar, and Research Professor of Communications, Sociology and Humanities, at the University of Illinois, Urbana-Champaign. He is the author of numerous books, including *Interpretive Ethnography: Ethnographic Practices for the 21st Century, The Cinematic Society: The Voyeur's Gaze, Images of Postmodern Society, The Research Act: A Theoretical Introduction to Sociological Methods, Interpretive Interactionism, Hollywood Shot by Shot, The Recovering Alcoholic,* and *The Alcoholic Self,* which won the Charles Cooley Award from the Society for the Study of Symbolic Interaction in 1988. In 1997 he was awarded the George Herbert Award from the Society for the *Study of Symbolic Interaction.* He is the coeditor of the *Handbook of Qualitative Research* (with Yvonna S. Lincoln; second edition, 2000). He is also editor of the *Sociological Quarterly,* coeditor of *Qualitative Inquiry,* and editor of the book series *Cultural Studies: A Research Annual and Studies in Symbolic Interaction.*

Carolyn Ellis is Professor of Communication and Sociology and Co-Director of the Institute for Interpretive Human Studies at the University of South Florida. She is the author of *Final Negotiations: A Story of Love, Loss, and Chronic Illness* and *Fisher Folk: Two Communities on Chesapeake Bay.* She is coeditor of *Composing Ethnography, Investigating Subjectivity, Social Perspectives on Emotion* (Volume 3), and the book series *Ethnographic Alternatives.* Her current research focuses on illness narratives, autoethnography, and emotional sociology.

Andrea Fontana is Professor of Sociology at the University of Nevada, Las Vegas. He received his Ph.D. from the University of California, San Diego, in 1976. He has published articles on aging, leisure, theory, and postmodernism. He is the author of *The Last Frontier: the Social Meaning of Growing Old,* coauthor of *Social Problems and Sociologies of Everyday Life,* and coeditor of *The Existential Self in Society* and *Postmodernism and Social Inquiry.* He is a former president of the Society for the Study of Symbolic Interaction and a former editor of the journal *Symbolic Interaction.* His latest published essays are a deconstruction of the work of the painter Hieronymus Bosch, a performance/play about Farinelli the castrato, and an ethnographic narrative about land speed records at the Bonneville Salt Flats.

Kenneth M. George is Professor of Anthropology at the University of Wisconsin–Madison and specializes in the cultural politics of religion, art, and violence in Indonesia. He is the author of *Showing Signs of Violence* (1996), which was awarded the 1998 Harry J. Benda Prize by the Association for Asian Studies. His current research centers on contemporary Islamic art in Southeast Asia and the Indonesian artist A. D. Pirous. His recent articles include "Signature Work: Bandung, 1994" (in *Ethnos*) and "Some Things That Have Happened to 'The Sun after September 1965': Politics and the Interpretation of an Indonesian Painting" (in *Comparative Studies in Society and History*).

Chris Mann is employed by the University of Cambridge to conduct several innovative research studies that focus on equal opportunities issues in higher education. She is based in the Faculty of Social and Political Sciences and is a member of the Centre for Family Research. She is coauthor, with Fiona Stewart, of *Internet Communication and Qualitative Research: A Handbook for Researching Online* (2000).

Kirin Narayan is Professor of Anthropology and of the Languages and Cultures of Asia at the University of Wisconsin–Madison. Much of her work has addressed the place of stories in people's lives, whether in the form of folktales, oral histories, ballads, ethnographic narratives, or fiction. She is the author of *Storytellers, Saints, and Scoundrels: Folk Narrative in Hindu Religious Teaching* (1989), which won the 1990 Victor Turner Prize for Ethnographic Writing and was cowinner of the Elsie Clews Parsons Prize for *Folklore.* Working in collaboration with Urmila Devi Sood, a village woman in Northwest India, she is also author of *Mondays on the Dark Night of the Moon: Himalayan Foothill Folktales* (1997). She has published a novel, *Love Stars and All That* (1994), and has recently completed a second novel, *Becoming a Foreigner,* that builds from her fieldwork in the Himalayan foothills and interviews among second-generation South Asian Americans.

Laurel Richardson is Professor Emerita of Sociology and Visiting Professor of Cultural Studies at The Ohio State University. Her recent book *Fields of Play: Constructing an Academic Life* was honored with the Society for the Study of Symbolic Interaction's Charles Horton Cooley Award. She continues to be interested in the applications of poststructural theory, exploring the boundaries of how claims to knowledge are constructed and communicated.

Paul C. Rosenblatt is Morse Alumni Distinguished Teaching Professor of Family Social Science at the University of Minnesota. His book-length works based on intensive interviewing include *Parent Grief: Narratives of Loss and Relationship, Multiracial Couples: Black and White Voices, Farming Is in Our Blood: Farm Families in Economic Crisis,* and *The Family in Business.* His current interview and writing projects using intensive interviewing deal with couples in which one partner is Chinese and the other Euro-American, with grief in African American families, with shame in Korean families, and with the circumstances in which bereaved parents use the present tense in talking about a child who has died.

Fiona Stewart is Chief Knowledge Officer at Brands Online Ltd, an Australian on-line research company, and Director of Realworld Research & Communications. Her interests are currently focused upon the use of WAP technologies for consumer polling and on-line market research. She is coauthor, with Chris Mann, of *Internet Communication and Qualitative Research: A Handbook for Researching Online* (2000).